MEMORYLANDS

Memorylands is an original and fascinating investigation of the nature of heritage, memory and understandings of the past in Europe today. It looks at how Europe has become a 'memoryland' – littered with material reminders of the past, such as museums, heritage sites and memorials; and at how this 'memory phenomenon' is related to the changing nature of identities – especially European, national and cosmopolitan. In doing so, it provides new insights into how memory and the past are being performed and reconfigured in Europe – and with what effects.

Drawing especially, though not exclusively, on cases, concepts and arguments from social and cultural anthropology, *Memorylands* argues for a deeper and more nuanced understanding of the cultural assumptions involved in relating to the past. It theorizes the various ways in which materializations of identity work and relates these to different forms of identification within Europe. The book also addresses questions of methodology, including discussion of historical, ethnographic, interdisciplinary and innovative methods. Through a wide range of case-studies from across Europe, Sharon Macdonald argues that Europe is home to a much greater range of ways of making the past present than is usually realized – and a greater range of forms of historical consciousness. At the same time, however, she seeks to highlight what she calls 'the European memory complex' – a repertoire of prevalent patterns in forms of recollection and 'past presencing'.

The examples in *Memorylands* are drawn from both the margins and metropolitan centres, from the relatively small-scale and local, the national and the avant-garde. The book looks at pasts that are potentially identity-disrupting – or 'difficult' – as well as those that affirm identities or offer possibilities for transcending national identities or articulating more cosmopolitan futures. Topics covered include authenticity, temporalities, embodiment, commodification, nostalgia and *Ostalgie,* the musealization of everyday and folk-life, Holocaust commemoration and tourism, narratives of war, the heritage of Islam, transnationalism, and the future of the past.

Memorylands is engagingly written and accessible to general readers as well as offering a new synthesis for advanced researchers in memory and heritage studies. It is essential reading for those interested in identities, memory, material culture, Europe, tourism and heritage.

Sharon Macdonald is Anniversary Professor of Cultural Anthropology at the University of York, UK and Visiting Professor in the Institute of European Ethnology, Humboldt University, Berlin. Her authored books include *Difficult Heritage* (Routledge, 2008) and *Reimagining Culture,* and, as editor, *The Politics of Display* (Routledge, 1997) and *The Companion to Museum Studies* (Choice Outstanding Academic Title, 2007).

MEMORYLANDS

Heritage and identity in Europe today

Sharon Macdonald

Routledge
Taylor & Francis Group

LONDON AND NEW YORK

First published 2013
by Routledge
2 Park Square, Milton Park, Abingdon, Oxon OX14 4RN

Simultaneously published in the USA and Canada
by Routledge
711 Third Avenue, New York, NY 10017

Routledge is an imprint of the Taylor & Francis Group, an informa business

British Library Cataloguing in Publication Data
A catalogue record for this book is available from the British Library

Library of Congress Cataloging in Publication Data
A catalog record for this book has been requested

ISBN: 978-0-415-45333-2 (hbk)
ISBN: 978-0-415-45334-9 (pbk)
ISBN: 978-0-203-55333-6 (ebk)

Typeset in Bembo
by HWA Text and Data Management, London

Printed and bound in Great Britain by
TJ International Ltd, Padstow, Cornwall

For Tara
Once upon a time…

CONTENTS

FIGURES

ACKNOWLEDGEMENTS

This book has taken longer than intended due to a surfeit of memory – and forgetting. It has been a journey through a memoryland of my own research and that of others. En route, I kept remembering other things that I wanted to add – and at the same time I recalled that there were other changes and additions that I had once intended to make but had now forgotten just what they were. Materialised memories on scraps of paper or Word files – and physical acts such as scratching my head – sometimes helped. But I am nevertheless left keenly aware that the finished book is a product of forgetting as well as recollection.

Because of this book's own long and multi-sited history – in several research projects and numerous papers given in various versions – there are many who have helped along the way, more than I can list here. Those who were thanked in earlier texts on which this book draws must count those thanks as extending to this one too. The following, however, need to be named here as they have variously and generously provided comments and further references – as friends, colleagues and referees who revealed their identities – on the proposals for this book and the new and revised text: Simone Abram, Tara Beaney, Thomas Beaney, Victoria Kendzia Bishop, Mads Daugbjerg, Steffi de Jong, Gordon Fyfe, Anselma Gallinat, Sarah Green, Peter György, Steve Hoelscher, Angela Janelli, Stef Jansen, Siân Jones, Petra Tjitske Kalshoven, Erica Lehrer, Peggy Levitt, Jan Lorenz, Nilesh Mistry, Jennie Morgan, Jane Nadel-Klein, David Lowenthal, Jörn Rüsen, Markus Tauschek, Claske Vos, Hannah Wadle, and Gisela Welz. In addition, the following, as well as some of the former, have also helped me with specific queries, references and images: Kerstin Barndt, Isabelle Benôit, Jeanette Edwards, Alexa Färber, Jackie Feldman, Paola Filippucci, Alyssa Grossman, Anat Hecht, Michael Herzfeld, Andrew Irving, Neringa Klumbyte, Ulrich Kockel, Donald Mac Donald, Jonathan Macdonald, Peter McIsaac, Chris Rumford,

Janet Simmonds, Dan Stone, Thomas Thiemeyer and John Widdowson. Harriet Beaney found me some great quotes and gave encouragement and tea when my energy flagged. The Department of Social Anthropology at Manchester University, where I worked during the writing of this book, and the Institute of European Ethnology at the Humboldt University, Berlin, where I hold a visiting professorship, provided a wonderful mix of stimulating colleagues, whose work and intellectual engagement indelibly shape what follows. At Routledge, Amy Davis-Poynter has kept up the vital work of reminding me of deadlines – and extending them to cope with my inability to stop tampering. It is Mike Beaney, though, who has most journeyed European memorylands with me, reminding me to keep going, reading my text, challenging my interpretations, and telling me what to remember – and forget.

Although *Memorylands* was originally conceived as more or less a collection of earlier articles, it has not ended up that way. Some chapters do draw on some of my previously published writing, but just as recollecting involves reshaping, reconceiving and making new connections, rather than just reproducing, so, too, any original material has been extensively chopped up, rewritten and supplemented with new additions or different interpretations. Many chapters include research of my own that I have not previously published. The following is a list of articles that have been plumbed – in a few cases fairly substantially and in others for shorter passages. I thank all those involved in the original pieces – as editors, reviewers and other interlocutors – for their help at that stage in this continuing journey; and the publishers or other copyright holders for permission to draw from them here.

'A people's story? Heritage, identity and authenticity' in C. Rojek and J. Urry (eds) *Touring Cultures. Transformations of Travel and Theory*, London/New York: Routledge, 1997, pp. 155–75.
'Nationale, postnationale, transkulturelle Identitäten und das Museum', in R. Beier (ed.) *Geschichtskultur in der Zweiten Moderne*, 2000, Frankfurt and New York: Campus, pp.123–48.
'Historical consciousness "from below": anthropological reflections', in S. Macdonald (ed.) *European Historical Consciousness*, 2000, Hamburg: Körber Stiftung, pp.86–102.
'Trafficking in history: multitemporal practices', *Anthropological Journal on European Cultures*, 2002, 11, pp. 93–116.
'On "old things": the fetishization of past everyday life', in N. Rapport (ed.) *British Subjects. An Anthropology of Britain*, Oxford and New York: Berg, 2002, pp. 89–106.
'Commemorating the Holocaust: the ethics of national identity in the twenty-first century', in *The Politics of Heritage: The Legacies of Race,* edited by J. Littler and R. Naidoo, 2005, London: Routledge, pp. 49–68.
'Past presencing', in Ulrich Kockel, Mairead Nic Craith and Jonas Frykman (eds) *Blackwell Companion to the Anthropology of Europe,* Oxford: Wiley-Blackwell, 2012.

PROLOGUE

The cover image shows the new monument to the 1956 Hungarian Revolution shortly after its unveiling in Budapest in October 2006. Composed of durable steel bars and on a monumental scale, memorialisation is also performed here through the ephemerality and delicacy of flowers laid by members of the public. One of numerous new memorials to diverse pasts that have come to populate Europe during the late twentieth and early twenty-first centuries, the monument is redolent of many themes and ambivalences in Europe's memorylands.

Fifty years after the event, the monument commemorates Hungary's short-lived revolt against Soviet control, and calls for remembrance of lives lost by participants who were hanged for their role in the uprising. Initiated by Hungary's governing Socialist party, the monument is ostensibly a statement of national unity in shared mourning for those whose lives were lost or blighted by the Communist regime. It can also be seen as a proclamation of Hungary's national independence. Yet it was fiercely opposed by some groups within the nation, including some 1956 organisations, comprised partly of those who fought the Communists and survived (sometimes suffering years of imprisonment). Their general mistrust of the government was coupled with dissatisfaction with the abstraction of the monument. The steel pillars from which it is made, they argued, did not so much resemble human figures (as the artists – the i-Ypszilon Group – claimed) as gallows. As such, it was a reminder of abjection rather than heroism or solidarity. Following their protests, the government finally awarded these organisations funds to create a different 1956 memorial of their own. This, by contrast, is an uplifting allegorical design of human figures in forwards and upwards momentum.

The design of the national memorial is also ambiguous in other ways, as Péter György points out. The monument is comprised of numerous steel

FIGURE 0.1 The national 1956 memorial, showing the pillar design. Photograph courtesy of Péter György and Mária Neményi

FIGURE 0.2 Alternative 1956 monument: Buda memorial, sculpted by Róbert Csikzentmihály. Photograph courtesy of Péter György and Mária Neményi

pillars, shaped into a wedge, spread out and rusted at one end and coming together into a tightly packed and shiny surfaced wall at the other. As he writes: 'The architectural metaphor is almost alarmingly clear: the abstract pieces in fact stand for the ever denser crowd of demonstrators' (2008: 134). Where the pillars are spread out, it is possible for visitors to walk amongst them, so allowing them to become part of the crowd. Yet, curiously, as they move further in it becomes impossible to proceed, so creating an experience of being *ejected* by the memorial and forced to walk around it (2008: 134). The visitor, then, is tempted into history, into being part of the collective, and then expelled and turned into an onlooker rather than participant. Or perhaps – reflecting upon her blurred reflection and that of those around her in the shiny wall of the monument – she becomes a participant in a new form of memory practice, gazing not just onto the past but onto her own act of commemoration.

Then there is the question of place. The location of the monument – in Felvonulási Square – is undoubtedly historically resonant. It was here that a statue of Stalin, on an enormous pedestal, was toppled in the uprising on 23 October 1956, leaving only his boots still standing. (In an interesting translocation, a replica of those boots is now displayed in that curious meta-monument to the end of Socialism, the Budapest Statue Park of Communist Sculpture.) In addition, the Square also housed a statue of Lenin and a giant cross. Yet, György argues, there is no longer any trace of these, so rendering them 'inaccessible to all those who only have a vague notion of the events or not even that' (2008: 130). Rather than acting *with* what he calls 'the spirit of place' to enhance traces that could act as spurs to recollection, the monument takes an abstract and predominantly 'literary narrative' form that fails to engage with its own location and activate public memory in a more emplaced and meaningful fashion.

Yet, despite these 'failures', this new, abstract monument has become a site for that widespread, popular – traditional but also increasing – memorial practice of laying flowers. As we see in the cover image, these more fleeting and small-scale forms of remembrance are abundant. They are instances of numerous, and diverse, commemorative practices and contemporary marking of the past that also populate Europe's memorylands.

1

THE EUROPEAN MEMORY COMPLEX

Introduction

> The imperative of our epoch is ... to keep everything, to preserve every indicator of memory.
>
> Pierre Nora[1]

Memory has become a major preoccupation – in Europe and beyond – in the twentieth century and into the twenty-first. Long memories have been implicated in justifications for conflicts and calls for apologies for past wrongs. Alongside widespread public agonising over 'cultural amnesia' – fears that we are losing our foothold in the past, that 'eye-witnesses' of key events are disappearing, and that inter-generational memory transition is on the wane – there has been a corresponding efflorescence of public (and much private) memory work. Europe has become a memoryland – obsessed with the disappearance of collective memory and its preservation. Europe's land- and city-scapes have filled up with the products of collective memory work – heritage sites, memorials, museums, plaques and art installations designed to remind us of histories that might otherwise be lost. More and more people live or work in or visit sites of memory; and increasing numbers are engaged in quests to save or recuperate fading or near-forgotten pasts. Local history societies, re-enactment groups and volunteer-run heritage projects flourish. Books of reminiscences and sepia photos of localities and community cram the shelves of libraries and bookstores. So too, do books about our fixation with remembering and the past.

This book is, inevitably, an addition to the memory mountain; or, more specifically, to that part of it concerned with trying to understand the memory preoccupation itself. Its particular contribution is anthropological, and more specifically still it provides a perspective from anthropological research on

Europe. Central to an anthropological perspective is the attempt to understand assumptions made by people when they organise their worlds in the ways that they do. What is taken for granted when people feel compelled to act in certain ways? What assumptions inform senses of what is important? How are feelings bound up with particular as well as with more shared experiences? Are there alternative ways of seeing, doing and feeling – perhaps to be found among peoples in other parts of the world or in the less examined parts of Europe itself – that can unsettle our assumption that things must be done or felt in the ways that are more widespread or habitual?

This book was written out of a conviction that anthropological research on Europe contains much that can probe and unsettle ways in which memory, and especially the ongoing memory and heritage boom, are typically addressed and theorised. In part this stemmed from realising that my own research on a variety of topics in various parts of Europe threw up unexpected similarities or convergences. Investigating these further was another spur to write this book. So too was a degree of frustration that although there is so much excellent ethnographic research done on Europe, studies are less often brought together and synthesised than they might be – and I include my own here. As such, anthropological research often contributes less to wider debates than it could – or, in my view, should. In part, this is probably due to anthropologists' emphasis on the importance of context and the local, and insistence on recognising complexity, which makes us more wary of the kinds of generalisations that other disciplines are more ready to make. While this is in itself admirable, it can sometimes mean that ethnographers do not realise some of the broader implications of their work or what it shares with that of others. It also makes it hard for those from other disciplines to relate ethnographic research to their own; and this is compounded by the fact that ethnographic texts often require more careful and time-consuming reading. How to recognise the complexities and specificities that ethnographic research typically highlights and at the same time to identify broader patterns is the challenge. This book is the result of daring to take up this gauntlet.

In doing so, then, it attempts to meet two aspirations that might be seen as contradictory or at least as in tension – but that I regard as crucial to our improved understanding of Europe as a memoryland – or set of memorylands. The indeterminacy of the singular or plural here is indicative of what is at issue. On the one hand, my aim in this book is to identify patterns in ways of approaching and experiencing the past that are widely shared across Europe. My argument is that there is a distinctive – though not exclusive or all-encompassing – complex of ways of doing and experiencing the past within Europe. This is not some kind of static template – a cultural blueprint or the like. Rather, it is a repertoire of (sometimes contradictory) tendencies and developments. The European memoryland, I contend, is characterised more by certain changes underway, and also by particular tensions and ambivalences, than by enduring memorial forms. This is not to say that there are no relatively longstanding patterns within

Europe – there are. But they are not necessarily the most significant in the lives of European peoples. Rather than give them analytical priority just on account of their ancestry and age, my concern is to explore how they play out in relation to other parts of the memory complex.

On the other hand, I seek to show that there are also significant variations within Europe. This diversity is not only of the kind that is so often used as part of depictions of European plurality. In other words, it is not just about the 'multicultural colour' or 'local flavours' provided by, say, heritage foodstuffs or different forms that memorial practices might take. It also concerns less evident but potentially ramifying matters such as whether significance is attached to collective remembering at all, whether longer or shorter time periods are activated in local commemorative life or how personal and collective memories are brought together. This diversity is why the plural 'memorylands' is appropriate. Some of this diversity exists at fairly micro, localised – perhaps village or street – levels; but in other cases it carves up Europe along lines relating to particular histories, such as certain patterns of nostalgia in post-Socialist countries or attempts to devise 'transcultural heritage' in cities which have experienced post-colonial immigration – though even here there are more localised variations.

Recognising diversity is important for a number of reasons, not least for allowing the empirical to inform analytical understanding. Variations can act as a foil to help to highlight more common practices and assumptions, and can irritate our theorising to lead it in new, less predictable, directions. Alternatives may be brought to light when they come into conflict with majority patterns or when misunderstandings rooted in difference ensue; and, as such, recognising them – and finding better means of doing so – can also provide a basis for improved understanding of conflicts and misunderstandings. Moreover, awareness of 'cultural alternatives' can not only unsettle assumptions but can also open up new possibilities by highlighting other routes – other ways of doing memory, heritage and identity – that we might choose to take.

The memory phenomenon

The more specific focus of this book is what has variously been called 'memory fever', 'memory mania', an 'obsession with memory', 'the memory craze', a 'remembrance epidemic', 'commemorative fever', 'the memory crisis', 'the memory industry', 'the memory boom', and a time of 'archive fever' and 'commemorative excess'.[2] Aspects of it have also been characterised as a 'heritage industry', 'heritage craze' or 'heritage crusade'.[3] These terms have been coined to characterise an increase in public attention to the past, especially its commemoration and preservation. While prefigured earlier in various ways, this increase is usually dated as gathering pace from the 1970s and escalating further towards the end of the twentieth century and into the twenty-first.[4] It includes phenomena such as those sketched in the first paragraph of this book above, and others including the creation of new civic rituals to commemorate (sometimes long-) past events, arguments over which histories should be aired in the public sphere and how, popular genealogy, the creation of heritage products, such as traditional foods and the broadcasting of numerous different television programmes about the past ranging from series about archaeology, with names such as *Time Team,* to historical dramas.

One notable dimension of this historical turn is that place distinctiveness increasingly seems to be marked by public reference to the past, and – sometimes and seemingly more often – to multiple pasts. Places are publicly imbued with time-depth through reference to historical narratives, and their historical content legitimated through institutions such as exhibitions, local history books and memorial plaques. This might be described as 'historical theming' – representing places through sets of public memories in order to configure what are assumed will be identifiably individuated 'lands'. Ironically, rather than differentiating, this theming risks creating an apparent sameness of place – a set of familiar contours shaping a continuous land even as we cross boundaries – through its promulgation of similar strategies or techniques of historical marking. 'Memoryland' might easily be the name of a theme-park, or section of one; and 'place marketing' and 'image-management' are certainly involved in producing historicised village-, town- and cityscapes across Europe. But this is not the whole story and we need to probe further in order to understand why this form of thematisation occurs at all, and in order to perceive the various motives for both pursuing and challenging it. We also need to probe further if we are to perceive differences within the various ways of performing history and memory, as well as to hear the numerous voices that can be involved, and thus acknowledge the need to speak of 'memorylands' in the plural.

Many of the terms that have been coined to characterise the increased public attention to the past draw on the language of pathology ('mania', 'epidemic', 'fever', obsession', 'craze') or employ other terms that carry negative connotations ('crusade', 'industry'). This is expressive of an anxious perspective that many commentators adopt; and it is further entrenched through dualisms that pit the apparently disturbing developments against what is regarded as an organic or authentic relationship with the past – sometimes described as 'tradition', or 'social memory' – which, furthermore, is widely believed to be under threat. Here, I seek neither to straightforwardly accept nor dismiss this perspective. It is, in my view, itself thoroughly and constitutively part of that which it seeks to describe. In other words, the concern expressed about the 'memory mania' and its correlated preoccupation with questions of authenticity and loss are part of the ways in which the past is 'done' in Europe today. My choice of the term 'memory phenomenon' (cf. Kansteiner 2002: 183), then, is intended as less affectively loaded and also as a means of encompassing not only the expansion of public preoccupation with the past but also popular and academic debates and concerns about it.

The memory complex

If the memory phenomenon is the notable increase in attention to the past – and attention to that attention – that has been underway since the second half of the twentieth century, the memory complex is the wider whole of which it is part. Although I use the term memory complex, it should be seen as shorthand for something like 'the memory-heritage-identity complex' for these are all tightly interwoven. In choosing to use the term 'complex' I have been influenced by its meanings in a number of disciplines, as well as its etymology and allusion to complexity theory. Its general meaning is of an entity 'consisting of parts united or combined' (Oxford Etymological Dictionary). Its etymology also carries connotations that are apposite for my use here. Derived from the Latin *complexus,* past participle of *complectere,* meaning 'encompass, embrace, comprehend, comprise', it is also 'sometimes analysed as … woven' (Concise Oxford English Dictionary). A complex, in the sense that I want to develop it here, comprises different elements, woven more or less loosely together. It also has a propulsion towards further encompassment partly through offering what becomes an increasingly taken-for-granted form of comprehending and experiencing.

The ways in which the term 'complex' is used in various disciplines can help, by analogy, to explain this further. A chemical complex is a substance that is 'formed by a combination of compounds' (COED); 'the formation of complexes', says the Encyclopaedia Britannica, 'has a strong effect on the behaviour of solutions'.[5] In Mathematics, complex numbers are made up of real and imaginary parts, the latter being used to help solve mathematical problems that cannot be solved with real numbers alone; and in Linguistics a complex sentence is one including subordinate clauses. What I want to draw out from these is the idea of the complex as consisting of non-exhaustive patterned combinations and relationships; and of complexes themselves gaining autonomous meanings, effects and possibilities for 'going on'.

I do not, however, want to adopt the popular psychological connotation of a 'complex' as being a pathological psychic-emotional condition, though in Carl Jung's introduction of the term into psychology, he did not regard a complex as necessarily negative (Jung 1971/1921). His understanding of a complex as a meshing of parts and tendencies that add up to some pattern to which we might put a name, and that we can identify with particular effects, does capture the sense of complex that I am striving for here. In addition, Jung's emphasis on the mix of the cognitive, affective and physical, and his argument about the relevance of history and myth, resonates with what I regard as necessary to include in an understanding of the memory complex, though I do not position my perspective within, or draw on other aspects of, his wider theorising.

Assemblage and complexity

My use of the notion of 'complex' is similar to that of 'assemblage' as it has come to be used in recent years in some social and cultural theorising.[6] Both designate some kind of 'entity' made up of constituent inter-related parts that then has effects (assemblage theory often refers to 'potentials' or 'capacities') of its own. As with assemblage, I also want to stress that a complex is not an abstraction, though it may contain abstractions. Rather, it is made up, variously, of constituent practices, affects and materialisations. The memory complex can be seen, therefore, as an assemblage of practices, affects and physical things, which includes such parts as memorial services, nostalgia and historical artefacts. Moreover, assemblage theory insists that we be wary of taking particular objects or categories for granted and that to do this we should investigate specific instances – so, for example, we should examine particular shops and markets rather than simply 'the market', or particular museums and heritage sites rather than 'heritage' as a generalised category. By doing so, we can recognise the potential variety of forms that a wider term might designate. In addition, we can apprehend the particular mix of human and non-human, conceptual and physical, elements that are involved in constituting a particular assemblage/complex; and we can also identify the processes that contribute to, say, making certain notions or ways of doing things durable or making them capable of extending beyond their locality of origin.

This characterisation fits the approach of this book well, in that it gathers its material from specific instances and gives attention to a wide range of elements, including the materialisation of memory in heritage. Little of the research that I report here, however, has been conceived explicitly within an assemblage perspective. The studies on which I draw are nevertheless often amenable to consideration in relation to assemblage ideas because, as Bruno Latour, one of the architects of an assemblage approach, acknowledges, anthropological research is frequently conducted with just such an emphasis on looking at what actually goes on and interrogating what is taken-for-granted, and thus refrains as far as possible from imputing 'external' (or he says, 'magical') categories (2005: 68). Indeed, this is why much anthropological theorising proceeds by questioning existing theoretical positions by unsettling their assumptions through in-depth ethnographic examples. This methodological prudence of assemblage and much anthropological theorising extends also to its imputations of agency and causality. Again, there is an emphasis on empirical investigation coupled with a rejection of assumptions of linear causality or singular agents: instead, the stress is on the complex and particular coming together of a mix of agents (human and non-human), and on unpredictable – though not unpatterned and random – effects.

The point that complexity should not be seen as random or chaotic is important and is one reason for the fact that assemblage theory and complexity theory (which is referenced to many of the same authors and shares many of the same ideas)[7] have produced an extensive vocabulary of terms to try to identify and characterise processes and patterns. The natural sciences have provided particular inspiration here, complexity and assemblage theorising variously employing terms such as 'feedback', 'circulation', 'density', 'principles of association', 'attractors', 'emergent properties' and the like. While these can be thought-provoking and illuminating in specific analyses – and I employ some below – I do not seek to use them in any extensive way here. This is primarily because the production of these more general characterisations and distinctions is not my ambition. Rather, I am interested in exploring the specific constellation of the memory phenomenon in Europe and the memory complex of which it is part. This requires, in my view, attention also to meso-level theorising, which can often illuminate particular formations and processes better than can a jump straight to broad ontological claims. In addition, my analysis gives more emphasis to human meaning-making, linguistic connotations and the like than is typically given the case in assemblage theory, though it does not necessarily rule these out.[8] In the chapters that follow, then, I only occasionally draw directly on the language of assemblage. This includes using the term 'assemblage' for specific constellations within the peculiar agglomeration of elements concerned with memory that is the overall focus of my investigation, and that I dub the memory complex. Nevertheless, there are other ways in which much of the research discussed here resonates with assemblage theory, including an emphasis on materiality, as discussed further below.

Methodology

Although I give particular attention to research carried out by anthropologists, I put this into dialogue with theorising from many disciplines and I do not exclude empirical work carried out within other disciplinary approaches where it bears upon the discussion at hand. This is especially so in Chapter 3, which is concerned with method and includes discussion of the relationship between anthropological and historical research. Personally, I am inclined towards methodological pluralism and believe that bringing together research conducted within different disciplinary approaches can be analytically powerful, though it needs careful coordination and attention to methodological issues. Here, however, I particularly want to show what anthropological approaches can contribute to European memory debates and so for the most part my case studies are of research conducted by anthropologists of Europe. Doing so will, I hope, also be of value for future multi-disciplinary research.

My use of the term 'anthropology' needs some clarification here as not all of those who I discuss as 'anthropologists' would necessarily use this term themselves. Across Europe, as well as beyond it, there is some inconsistency in the ways in which 'anthropology' and related terms, such as 'ethnology' and 'ethnography', are used. Here, I do not include biological or physical anthropology; rather, my compass is what in the British tradition is usually called social anthropology and in North America is referred to as cultural anthropology. Although non-European societies were the main focus of these disciplines historically, this is no longer so. This is also the case in many but not all continental European traditions, in which there is often a distinction made between 'anthropology' as referring to work outside Europe and ethnology to refer to that undertaken within, or sometimes more specifically still, the home nation-state. In Germany, for example, a distinction is institutionalised between *Völkerkunde,* focusing on peoples outside Europe, and *Volkskunde,* looking at those within. Today the names have sometimes changed, with *Sozial Anthropologie* sometimes being used in place of *Völkerkunde,* and *Ethnologie,* or sometimes more specifically, 'European Ethnology' (*Europäische Ethnologie*), on research within Europe, though there is increasing overlap, represented in a greater use of the term 'cultural anthropology'.[9] As in many other continental European countries, German ethnology had and often still has a strong overlap with folklore, sometimes being indistinguishable from it. In using the term 'anthropology', then, I do so in catholic fashion, to include what might elsewhere be called 'ethnology' or equivalents in various languages. This does not mean, however, that I cover all of the various forms of 'anthropology' being conducted within Europe, and for the most part I do not include the more folkloric work. Rather, I make my arguments through selected examples of research that, while it may go under various labels, mostly adopts approaches consonant with those I outline in the rest of this section.

The research included here puts an emphasis on qualitative methods conducted within a *Verstehen* approach that aims to grasp participants' perspectives and experiences – an approach that goes beyond recording of voices and cultural collecting, typical of folklore as classically conceived.[10] It generally involves a commitment to considering social and cultural phenomena as 'total' or 'totalities' in a sense used by one of the founders of French ethnology, Marcel Mauss (1872–1950).[11] Although there is debate about his use of this term, one of the main ways in which he used it was to emphasise how what might initially appear as different aspects of social life or human experience might be interrelated. So, a social phenomenon – such as the gift or sacrifice – might cut across categories such as the economy or religion, and thus could not be properly understood if their analysis was restricted to these. Ethnology was valuable in his view precisely because it allowed for attention to the concrete and complexity that he saw as lacking in the reductionism and abstraction of the new discipline of sociology being propounded by Durkheim, his uncle (Hart 2007). Significantly, his view of the importance of 'totality' in this sense was informed by his study of diverse cultures, predominantly non-European, which also made him aware of the limitations of analysis that restricted itself to Western categories, as well as of the challenge to dominant assumptions that such studies could provide. Although Mauss' own research was conducted second-hand, through examining studies undertaken by others, other anthropologists have developed methods that allow for an ethnological grasping of 'totality' and potentially also for challenging of analytical categories.

These methods are usually called ethnographic and typically involve some kind of in-depth and fairly small-scale study, often over a lengthy time period.[12] Although participant-observation is sometimes regarded as synonymous with ethnography, anthropologists may employ a wide range of specific methods, such as oral histories, semi-structured interviews, spatial mapping, photography, film-making and other visual and sensory methodologies, as well as textual analysis, and sometimes also surveys (e.g. of households). Rather than the application of a particular methodological toolkit, what characterises the anthropological approach is a commitment to trying to see and experience life-worlds from the point of view of those who live them and within the context of which they are part. This goes beyond simply recording 'native voices' but entails a rigorous commitment to trying to grasp the patterns of relations of which utterances, practices, feelings and so forth, are part; and what they may be linked with. This frequently involves or leads to reflexivity about categories of analysis and forms of knowledge production – including the role of scholarship itself.

The emphasis on the small-scale deserves note here too. This allows for attention to detail that can potentially disrupt more generalising accounts. In addition, it may also open up the opportunity to hear 'quiet voices' or see perspectives or recognise feelings that are easily overlooked, either because they are held by people with little access to forms of expression that reach a wide public or because the forms that the expression takes are not usually recognised by the academy. A smaller scale of research also allows for direct interaction by the researcher, an approach in which their person and own history may become part of the study, as we will see in some examples below. Furthermore, a smaller scale can make it easier to see the connections between aspects of life or the multi-dimensionality of practices in a way consonant with Mauss' notion of totality. This does not mean, however, that research need only look at 'small' topics or for connections between what has been directly examined within the specific empirical study. Here, the notion of 'totality' potentially causes problems if it is understood as indicating a bounded self-integrated system, as Durkheim theorised in his functional understanding of 'society'. While many anthropological studies up until about the 1960s, and in some cases since, have been undertaken in a functionalist framework, which in European anthropological research often meant that the village was taken as the functioning unit and 'natural' object of study, since then researchers have increasingly rejected this model and sought ways of exploring connections across and beyond boundaries, and finding ways to bring insights from their micro-perspectives to 'speak out'.[13] To do so they have often developed new approaches, as we will see in later chapters, while still retaining a commitment to concrete study of specific worlds, events or phenomena. As Regina Bendix argues in a discussion of the distinctive perspective offered by cultural anthropology on the 'big' topic of 'global heritage', for example, 'only such micro approaches, in fact, can properly reveal the local specificity of a global heritage regime' (2009: 255). Only such approaches can show what notions such as 'global heritage regime' might mean and how they might work in practice. The global is, after all, inevitably imagined and realised in particular, local, worlds – 'worlds' which might equally be UNESCO meetings or remote villages.[14]

The problem with memory

Although I have so far cast the topic of this book in terms of memory – memorylands, the memory phenomenon and the memory complex – I want in this section to add some reservations, warnings and clarifications about its use. I then provide a brief introduction to some of the many classifications of types of memory and remembering that scholars have employed, and also look at some other possible ways of framing the analysis. A major problem with memory as a category of analysis is its very ubiquity and capaciousness,[15] which is itself part of the memory phenomenon that this book explores. The fact that 'memory' can refer to a mental function or faculty (the act of remembering or ability to do so), and also to content (what is remembered) renders it widely applicable. This partly accounts for why it is used in numerous disciplines and areas of popular culture, ranging from concerns over false-memory syndrome to the technical capacity of digital storage, from neurological studies of everyday mnemonic capabilities to social investigation of collective remembering. While this book mainly addresses the last of these, it is important to note that these different concerns are not disconnected but may feed into, shape and sustain one another. Loss of cultural memory, for example, may be likened to Alzheimer's; forms of organising digital storage may be configured through cultural forms such as the filing cabinet (documents, files). The analogy between individual or personal recollection and social or cultural is pervasive and informs understanding of both – and, as such, needs itself to be given analytical attention.

Making such analogies is not itself new, individual memory almost always being conceptualised through cultural forms. In medieval Europe, for example, memory was often conceptualised as parchment, and, thus, as a medium capable of bearing imprints of experience or as a hive of bees or forest or – when properly trained – a library, thesaurus or storage room.[16] Prevalent metaphors may change – today computers are more likely analogies than parchment – and this plays into how memory is understood, undertaken and even researched.[17] Some analogies, for example, more readily support attempts to train the memory, or they regard it as springing surprises as cobwebs are swept from its dark recesses or as environmental stimuli spark involuntary firing of neural connections. Not only does the cultural provide metaphors for individual memory, however, there is also, according to Pierre Nora, 'an exact chronological coincidence' between a 'preoccupation with the individual psychology of remembering' and the rise of concern about the loss of social memory (1989: 15). He dates this to the end of the nineteenth century, and associates it especially with 'the disintegration of the rural world' (1989: 15). What we see with the vanishing of the pre-modern, he writes, is that 'memory appeared … at the core of psychological personality, with Freud; at the heart of literary autobiography, with Proust' (1989: 15). 'We owe to Freud and to Proust', he adds, 'those two intimate and yet universal sites of memory, the primal scene and the celebrated *petite madeleine*' (1989: 15). Since then, he argues, preoccupation with memory has only increased, escalating in the twentieth-century modern proliferation of what he calls *lieux de memoire* – 'sites of memory' – and further still in what he sees as a late twentieth-century postmodern acceleration. The traffic between theories of individual and of collective remembering has likewise burgeoned, with psychological ideas designed to understand individual memory increasingly being applied to collective or social memory.

Individual and collective

Psychological and psychoanalytic concepts devised for individual memory that have been used in relation to collective or social memory, include 'trauma', 'the unconscious', 'repression', 'flash-bulb memories', 'semantic memory' and 'episodic remembering'. In popular accounts this use is generally seamless, with little apparent consideration of whether such terms might be appropriate, and this is sometimes the case too in academic work, though there is also careful and illuminating use (as we will see in subsequent chapters). The potential problem, however, is that the social and individual become conflated and it is assumed that collectives work in the same way that individual psychology is theorised as doing, e.g. that nations have an unconscious and that they may suffer psychological trauma from the effects of repressing memories.[18] Used loosely, such notions naturalise processes and leave exploration of what might actually be going on untouched. Furthermore, the individualised psychological model treats 'memory [as] a distinct phenomenon that can be studied in relative isolation from other mental functions' (Wertsch 2009: 122). Memory thus becomes understood as involving various relatively autonomous known processes rather than through its specific workings and possible connections of a Maussian 'total' kind.

As Michael Lambek argues, this also takes for granted a model of autonomous individuals as vessels of memory. Drawing on Mauss' notion of *personnage* – a role-related and intersubjectively constituted notion of personhood – and his ethnographic research on spirit possession in Madagascar to highlight alternatives to this model, he argues that in 'Western discourse' memory has been made a 'romanticized object' (2003: 210). By the latter – a term that he borrows from Hannah Arendt – he means a form of naturalisation, that turns a supposed quality ('Jewishness' is her example) into a 'thing', then taken for granted as, variously, explanation, property of subjects and object of investigation. This then, in turn, supports the assumption of autonomous individuals. As he notes, similar processes occur at collective level, the elision between individual and collective memory reinforcing an individuation of collectives through attribution of shared memory. In discussions of personal identity, memory is almost always a key theme, often being regarded as a kind of glue, holding identity together over time. As such, memory – as a body of recollection – can itself become an indicator of identity. This is a notion that works powerfully in the social domain and informs the centrality of memory and heritage debates in the politics of recognition and identity. Implicated here too is the conceptualisation of memory as a possession – as something that we 'have' rather than 'do' (Lambek 1996); and this is reflected in the persistence of metaphors of memory as a treasure house, museum or archive. This in turn helps substantiate the notion of identities as individuated and 'possessive', a model that political theorist C.B. MacPherson (1962) argues had become an assumption amongst seventeenth-century English liberals and is 'not abandoned yet' (1962: 4). He describes this 'possessive individualism' as entailing a 'conception of the individual as essentially the proprietor of his own person or capacities … as an owner of himself' (1962: 3). This was notably and influentially articulated by John Locke, in his 'forensic' conception of 'the person', in which primacy was given to memory – 'consciousness of the past' – as an indicator of personal identity.[19] This same conception infuses that of the nation-state, which flowered within Western Europe in the eighteenth century and has spread across much of the world since.[20] Nations are thus conceptualised as possessive individuals, with heritage acting as the materialised rendition of their memory as property. In a self-supporting reverse move, 'having' – possessing – a distinctive heritage, memory and culture helps to instantiate and substantiate the nation (or other collective) 'as a living individual' (Handler 1988: 41). These cultural assumptions are interrelated and mutually reinforcing parts in Europe's memory complex.[21]

None of this means avoiding examining the relationship between individual and collective remembering. It is, rather, a call for attention to the movement and implications of models and terms, including those used in analysis. In order to avoid some of the problems with 'memory', Jay Winter and Emmanuel Sivan (1999; see also Winter 2009) suggest employing the term 'remembrance' as a means of putting emphasis onto *processes* and *practices* of remembering and to avoid reifying 'memory' as an object. Framing research as 'remembrance', they contend, allows for investigation of the articulation of individual and collective remembering, rather than assuming a 'collective' memory that is necessarily shared by individuals. Anthropological approaches are especially well suited to accomplishing this, they argue, as they give attention to the differential roles and agency of different participants as well as to cultural forms (e.g. rituals or monuments) of remembrance.

Theirs is a thoughtful proposition that works well for the explicit forms of commemoration with which they are concerned. It does not, however, capture the full range of practices and processes that are involved in the memory phenomenon and memory complex. While these all entail reference to the past in some form, they are not necessarily forms of remembrance in the sense of either commemorating or actively remembering a particular past. Indeed, some engagements with 'the past' may entail very little 'remembering' or even memory content at all. This is one reason why I have suggested 'past presencing' as a possibly preferable alternative means of framing investigation (Macdonald 2012). Not only does this allow for consideration of a broader range of phenomena, without assuming either intentional recollection, or pre-given processes or known actors, it also avoids some of the problematic distinctions of which memory is part – especially that between history and memory. I return to it below, after consideration of various other distinctions and terms. I should note, however, that despite the shortcomings of 'memory', I continue to use it in this book because the phenomenon with which I am concerned is usually framed in this way, as is so much relevant debate.

Memory and history

In popular and also academic discourse, especially that of historians, memory is often defined through a distinction with history.[22] Like 'memory', the English word 'history' is ambiguous, referring both to the past – what happened – as well as to accounts of that past and study of it. This ambiguity supports a popular vision of historical scholarship as an objective enterprise of establishing the facts of what happened; and also of the past as a body of factual evidence. Memory, when opposed to this vision of history, is regarded as subjective and fallible, based on individual recollections rather than proper evidence verified through expert institutional practices and persons. While this opposition is prevalent in Europe today, it is increasingly – as part of the memory phenomenon – accompanied, and sometimes supplanted, by a reversed evaluation. This sees established history become suspect as the product of elites, who are said to mystify their interests under the misleading banner of value-free facts. Memory, meanwhile, is elevated to a status of greater 'honesty', and seen as relatively unmediated and transparent in its very subjectivity.[23]

Pierre Nora's classic work, which operates at one level as an insightful discussion of the memory phenomenon, has also been a significant player in a reversed evaluation – and moralisation – of history and memory. He writes, for example, of

> the difference between real memory – social and unviolated … and history, which is how our hopelessly forgetful modern societies, propelled by change, organize the past … Memory is life… History, on the other hand, is the reconstruction, always problematic and incomplete, of what is no longer.
>
> (1989: 8)

Memory here is romanticised as an organic part of life, and therefore 'real', and history vilified as a sterile and doomed attempt to capture a past that has been lost. This is part of a relentless discourse that seeks to identify and even rescue authentic forms of life, and that is more usefully seen as part of the memory phenomenon that he discusses rather than analysis of it.

Drawing and maintaining a clear-cut distinction between history and memory can cause as many analytical problems as it solves, as many commentators have

What kinds of things do you, as a writer, need to identify to your readers?

pointed out.[24] In particular, it tends to direct attention to questions of veracity – which provides the truer account of the past? While this is a legitimate question, it cannot be answered in general terms and requires clarification of what is meant by 'truth' (e.g. recounted with personal integrity, accuracy with relation to other known facts).[25] Moreover, in research practice, the line between history and memory may be blurred. For example, an historical account might draw on individual reminiscences, and remembered events may find ample substantiation in other contemporary sources – or even be recalled with reference to them (e.g. discussion of individual experience of war following a television documentary or getting out the official album of the Queen's coronation during individual reminiscence). The more important issue is the specific contexts, motives and frameworks of production of the various accounts and their forms of veracity. Also significant from an anthropological perspective – as we will see in later chapters – is how the terms themselves are variously defined and deployed in their use, and the evaluations that they are given.

Memory terminologies and alternatives

Because of the looseness of terms such as 'memory' and 'history', there has been a proliferation of related terms created either to better frame the field of study or to make distinctions between kinds of processes or practices. It is not my intention to discuss this in detail but I offer a brief commentary here on some of the terms most commonly in use, and others that I regard as particularly helpful. Others are introduced as they arise in specific discussions later in the book.

Collective, social, cultural … memory

The terms 'collective memory' and 'social memory' are used to differentiate from personal or individual memory and to refer instead to memories that are held by social groups and/or forms of remembering that are held in some kind of common. They are usually referenced to French sociologist Maurice Halbwachs (1877–1945), whose work in this field was posthumously published as *La Mémoire Collective* (1950).[26] His concern was to emphasise the importance of social groups in creating frameworks for remembering – for example, the role of the family in transmitting memory – and also the significance of shared memory for creating senses of collective solidarity. Halbwachs has been criticised for taking for granted the existence of stable social entities as the producers of memory, and for overstating the determining role of the collective memory so produced for individual remembering.[27] Most of those using the terms subsequently, however, do not adopt Halbwachs' position wholesale; and much productive work has been undertaken under these rubrics on questions such as how creating shared memories might be part of creating social entities (e.g. the nation), rather than the other way around, or investigating the various positions that individuals might adopt in relation to collective commemoration.

In my own use here I likewise use 'social memory' and 'collective memory' to refer to accounts or representations of the past that make some kind of claim to being shared rather than assuming that 'collective' means necessarily held by all. Another attractive alternative, however, is James E. Young's 'collected memory' (1993), employed in his study of memorials in order to theorise these as sites around which diverse memories may accumulate. Rather than directing attention to what is shared by participants in memory practices, a collected memory approach leaves open the question of whether those engaging in a practice necessarily attribute it with the same meanings.

'Social memory' and 'cultural memory' are sometimes deployed inter-changeably. It is useful for analysis, however, to use 'cultural memory' more specifically to indicate memory whose primary form of transmission is through cultural media, such as texts, film and television, and museums and exhibitions, rather than through direct person-to-person transmission. Although the dividing line may blur here too – visiting a museum, for example, is also a social practice involving person-to-person contact – it is helpful in that it directs analytical concern to questions of how memory is mediated and the implications of this for matters such as its durability over time or capacity to 'travel' across space. Materialised into cultural forms, the resources for cultural memory may remain even when direct transmission of social memory – or what Jan Assmann (2008) calls 'communicative memory' – no longer occurs. In some research the term 'social memory' is reserved for this direct communicative memory but more usually it includes both communicative and cultural memory as defined here, and this is the sense in which it is used in this book.

Historical consciousness and past presencing

In order to avoid some of the problems of the history/memory distinction and to put emphasis firmly onto questions of *how* the past is conceptualised and represented, some researchers choose to frame their investigation in terms of 'historical consciousness', as we will see in later chapters. This draws attention to questions about matters such as the 'narrative structures' or 'temporal orientations' through which the past is apprehended.[28] Although work of this kind does not always assume that people will be aware of the forms that their historical thinking takes, the term 'historical consciousness' can be confusing in that it implies active awareness. Moreover, this *is* how it is used by some theorists. In Gadamer's classical discussion, for example, he is concerned to specify the development of a reflexive – historically conscious – relationship to history.[29] Rather differently, it is also often used in discussions of history education, sometimes in laments over the lack of historical knowledge ('historical awareness') of particular social groups (see Chapter 2). Another shortcoming of the term – and of most though not all research undertaken under its rubric – is that it directs attention to cognitive process rather than to more embodied modes of engaging with the past.

In suggesting 'past presencing' as a way of demarcating the field of study, my intention is to find a broad frame that allows for as much Maussian totalising as possible; and that allows for unconscious or embodied relationships with the past as well as more conceptual ones.[30] This aims to avoid pre-defining what is involved in a wide array of social and cultural engagements with the past. It also tries to avoid the dilemma of 'analytic double-take' (Macdonald 2012: 234), where those being studied use the same language as that being used to frame analysis. That is, by using a terminology that is not part of what Gable and Handler describe as 'native discourse of memory' (2011: 43), it seeks analytical leverage on the fact that terms such as 'memory' and 'history' are part of the 'memory phenomenon' under investigation. By so doing, it aims also to avoid the usual dualisms and connotations that infuse these debates. One charge against this way of framing the debate might be that it does not perform a theoretical refinement by narrowing down and making the field more precise.[31] It seems to me, however, that what is required at this stage in research is a broad recasting of the field that does not overly constrict its scope and that conceptual refinement – for example, exploring differentiations between specific processes – can then proceed more effectively. Another possible charge is that 'past presencing' is presentist: its concern is with how the past is related to at specified moments or stretches of time. In defining the field in this way, however, my intention is not to say that historical research should be conducted in this way – historians can continue about their business as they please! I make no assumptions that the only worth or interest of the past is in its relation or use in the present – the argument is simply for looking at this. Neither do I maintain that such an approach cannot be tackled historically. Although much anthropological research does involve direct study of ongoing action, not all does so and how the past was made present in the past is as fully valid a focus for attention as is 'past presencing' in the present. The analytical 'present' of study might well be the past – indeed, it is inevitably so, if only recent.

It should also be emphasised that 'past presencing' does not entail taking for granted what will be considered 'past' or 'present' in practice, neither indeed whether a distinction will operate between these; on the contrary, part of its point is to indicate the elision and indeterminacy that is so often involved, and the disruption of linear notions of past preceding present preceding future. Ghosts, monuments, and old furniture are some of the many means by which the past may inhabit the present – and the future – or perhaps that a continuous past may embrace present and future. While linguistically differentiating between past, present and future operates widely in Europe, and all its indigenous languages, Indo-European and not (e.g. Basque, Hungarian), have a past tense, there are nevertheless differences between languages in which grammatical tenses are deemed appropriate when (for example, German often uses the present tense where English would use past or future), as well as in the tenses themselves (for example, French has many different past tenses, making distinctions such as between repeated actions that used to occur and actions that are completely finished in the past). Likewise, in social practice, though not necessarily mapping directly onto languages, there can be distinctions between kinds of pasts – variously related to as fully over, periodised, continuing or likely to return; as well as of presents and futures, and the relations between them – linear, cumulative, non-cumulative, progressive, regressive, reversible, irreversible, disconnected, cyclical, rhythmic, looping, spiralling and so forth.[32] Past-presencing, then, necessarily gives attention to temporality. Reinhart Koselleck's philosophical reflections on how 'time is historically enacted in humans as historical beings' suggests that the present is 'elusive' and constituted 'in the relationship between past and future' (2002: 111). Although the 'temporal dimension' that he calls 'space of experience' most closely maps onto what I am here calling 'past presencing' – namely, the framework 'out of which one acts, in which past things are present or can be remembered' (2002: 111) – this is tightly bound up with a more future-oriented form of temporality that he calls 'horizon of expectation'.[33] How we conceive the future has implications for how we conceive the present and the past – and vice versa. More importantly, as he argues, the relationship between the space of experience and the horizon of expectation may shift (and has shifted significantly in Europe at certain historical moments (Koselleck 2004/1979)), thus altering, for example, the significance that the past is accorded in anticipations of the future. The implications of past presencing for imagining futures is a concern that runs through many chapters that follow.

Heritage

Another way of framing the concerns of this book – and that is also part of 'native discourse' – is 'heritage'. Over the past decade heritage studies has blossomed as a lively forum for debate, moving from a predominant concern with questions of conservation to interest in the politics and, more recently, the phenomenology of heritage.[34] There is a good deal of overlap with what is also considered under the rubric of memory studies, though the connotations and framing differ to some extent. Where 'memory' entices social researchers into analogies with individual memory and the language of psychology and also prompts questions about veracity and transmission, 'heritage' directs attention to materiality, durability over time and value. In more conservative heritage approaches, this may centre on questions about how to identify the worth of different kinds of heritage and manage it accordingly; but in critical heritage study it leads to interrogation of why and how some things come to count as 'heritage' and the consequences that flow from this. Because much discussion of heritage has been concerned with material forms – monuments, buildings and the like – research conducted in its terms has contributed some sophisticated discussion of 'intangible heritage'. Indeed, the very term 'intangible heritage' – for practices that might previously have been called 'tradition' – speaks to this framing.[35]

It also speaks, however, to what Barbara Kirshenblatt-Gimblett calls the 'meta-cultural' status of heritage (2006) – the way in which once something is identified as 'heritage' it is inevitably altered. As she argues, this occurs in particular ways through 'metacultural operations' (2006: 162), such as conservation, listing and becoming part of the 'tourist gaze' (Urry 1990), which have multiple consequences for people and other things within its orbit and for its future. In like vein, Bernhard Tschofen points out that one 'banal but not self-evident' feature of heritage is that it 'can be visited' (2007: 26). Extending this, we can say that heritage turns the past into something visitable; and, as Tschofen contends, research should then consider the implications of heritage's *Präsenzeffekts* – the ways in which heritage makes the past's presence felt (2007: 29).[36] All of this contributes to making 'heritage' a productive focus of research. Heritage legislation, heritage management, heritage conventions, heritage tours, heritage sites and so on and so forth are thoroughly part of European memorylands, constituting an identifiable field of practice for investigation.

Heritage is, moreover, an especially efficacious element in the European memory complex, capable of reorganising land- and city-scapes and validating certain social groups (and not others). A manifestation of possessive individualism, heritage invariably implies ownership – at least metaphorical but usually actual property relations – and as such instantiates whosoever's heritage it is said to be. More broadly, one of the most important accomplishments of heritage is to turn the past from something that is simply there, or has merely happened, into an arena from which selections can be made and values derived. We might even put this as heritage turning the past into The Past.

As a set of metacultural operations, heritage is increasingly global. At the same time, however, what is meant by 'heritage' – and the expectations that flow from it – does not necessarily map seamlessly onto the diverse contexts in which it is put to work, even within Europe. An excellent edited collection of cultural anthropological research on heritage is entitled *Prädikat 'Heritage' (Predicate 'Heritage')* (Hemme *et al.* 2007). By using the English word 'heritage' in their German title, the editors neatly point out that it is this, English-language, term – and its specific connotations – that is being globalised, and that it acts as a predicate by asserting the very existence of 'heritage', as well as asserting as 'heritage' whatever it is attached to. As they explain, 'heritage' does not have a precise equivalent in German; and neither does it in most other European languages.[37] In German, the usual term used in relation to heritage developments such as conservation and listing is *Denkmal* (e.g. *Denkmalschutz* for heritage conservation), which also means 'monument' and speaks to an emphasis on material and public heritage. By contrast, *patrimoine* in French and *patrimonio* in Spanish have as part of their etymological root the notion of 'country' and yet can apply to personal inheritance as well as collective.[38] While the inflections may be slight, they can have consequences for heritage practice, as discussed in Chapter 5 (with reference to the Scottish Gaelic term *dualchas*). They highlight variations within the European memory complex – even while, at the same time, the various conceptions may share at least some assumptions, as well as, perhaps, coming to resemble one another more closely as a consequence of predicate heritage.

Europe and others

As the preceding discussion shows, Europe is characterised by diversity as well as by certain prevalent – but not all encompassing – patterns. In describing such patterns, my intention is neither to suggest that these are necessarily exclusive to Europe, nor that they can be used as a means of identifying what is 'truly' European and what is not. Claims of exclusivity usually founder either in light of the global diffusion of cultural forms, such as the nation-state or 'predicate heritage', or in view of the fact that many cultural patterns prevalent in Europe – such as using items of material culture as mementoes of the dead or telling linear histories – can be found in other places too. More important, however, is that my aim in discussing patterns is not to highlight Europe's uniqueness – an enterprise that is widely undertaken in service of substantiating and legitimating 'Europe'. Doubtless, Europe *is* unique – but this is just a banal fact and it is not *more* (or less) unique than any other continent.

Anthropology has often employed an opposition between Europe (sometimes glossed as 'the West') and other parts of the world in its analyses. Claude Lévi-Strauss's distinction between 'hot' and 'cold' societies, for example, characterises 'our' (European) societies as 'hot' in that time is conceived as linear, changing and unrepeatable; they are societies that 'have internalised their own historicity' (Gell 1992: 23).[39] 'Cold' societies, by contrast, conceive themselves as closed systems, and operate according to mythical, repeatable or cyclical temporality. Many commentators have been critical of this idea, mainly because it reifies an absolute distinction that they deem untenable.[40] Eric Wolf, for example, provides a robust dismissal of the supposition that any people have been left 'outside history' in his ironically entitled *Europe and the People without History* (1982). As Kirsten Hastrup (1992: 2) points out, however, Wolf's argument retains an idea of history as an especially European phenomenon in its depiction of how European expansion has long and insistently affected lives around the globe. More undermining of the distinction are examples of the historical thinking that Lévi-Strauss dubs 'hot' in other parts of the world – as John Davis provides in an article that is a neat riff on Wolf's: 'History and the people without Europe' (1992). Also disruptive of the absolute nature of the opposition are examples of alternative modes of conceptualising temporality and history – what Hastrup calls 'other histories' – within Europe. Many examples will follow later in this book but to just make the point here, and to emphasise that alternatives are not somehow 'not European', we might turn to an example provided by Marc Abélès in his study of one of the most modern central locations of Europe – the European Commission in Brussels. The predominant temporality there, he argues, is quite counter to the pervasive historicising so widely seen in Europe.

Instead, amidst a relentless sense of urgency, '"One goes ahead without looking back, as if one were driving without a rear-view mirror"', as one official said to him (2000: 32). In consequence 'Everything happens as if the Commission was not able to think about its own relation to history' (2000: 32) – a form of historical consciousness (or non-consciousness perhaps) that he sees as part of the Commission's lack of institutional self-awareness.

Despite critiques of such oppositions – provided by exceptions and post-colonial nervousness over making Europe special – they can nevertheless be 'good to think with', to borrow from Lévi-Strauss' phraseology (1963/1962). Marilyn Strathern's contrasts between Melanesian ways of doing and thinking and those she calls 'Euro-American' is a notable case-in-point; and has led to extensive productive discussion as well as criticism for much the same reasons as those raised in relation to Lévi-Strauss' hot and cold division.[41] Highlighting alterity, as Strathern does, can be particularly valuable as a means of making us aware of what we might readily take for granted – e.g. notions of persons as individual rather than dividual. In my own thinking about concepts such as identity and memorial practices, it was often cases where these are done very differently or not at all that provoked me to 'see' the taken-for-granted cultural patterns in my own field-sites. For example, the assumption that prized material products should be preserved is challenged by the assertion among the Igbo of Nigeria that the creativity of artists is only released as the physical art-works decay.[42] This means that the preservation of what might be called 'material heritage' should be avoided, thus undermining an assumption that material continuity needs to accompany remembering.

As we will see in the chapters that follow, however, we do not necessarily need to look outside Europe to find alternatives to the more widespread patterns that contribute to the fluid and multivalent European memory complex. These alternatives are thoroughly part of the reality of Europe today and it is to these, as well as the more frequently encountered patterns, that this book attends. As such, its intention is neither to affirm Europe, nor to either dissolve it into diversity or to reclaim it through the very idea of its diversity (as has been the attempt in European Union initiatives and slogans of 'Unity in Diversity', see McDonald 1996). 'Europe' here, then, is primarily a heuristic – and a fairly loose one at that – for exploration. This necessarily entails treating 'Europe' not as a self-evident category but as itself variously, and sometimes uncertainly or acrimoniously, defined and characterised. Even with reference to geography, what counts as Europe is unclear and contested: are Russia and Turkey part of Europe or not, for example? From my point of view, the anthropological task is not to adjudicate on such questions but to see these questions as part of what constitutes Europe and to explore the motives and contexts of the different positions taken. Chris Hann points out, for example, that the Urals 'were nominated for the role of boundary marker only in the middle of the eighteenth century, when Russian intellectuals were determined to prove that the Czarist empire, or at least its capital and historic core, belonged to Europe rather than to Asia' (2012: 88). Framing his own account in terms of 'Eurasia', Hann identifies various continuities and shared histories across Europe and Asia, and presents these too as challenging any taken-for-granted unity of the former (and, presumably, also the latter, though this is not stated). He also notes, as do many other ethnographers working in Europe, that what 'Europe' means to its inhabitants can vary substantially. Susan Gal has observed, for example, that 'for educated Hungarians, as for most inhabitants of the continent, "Europe" is less a geographical region or unique civilisation than a symbolic counter of identity' (1991: 444). This remains the case, though, as Hann points out, in the post-Socialist era this negative, oppositional understanding of 'Europe' may also be accompanied by a very different, celebratory and enthusiastic 'rejoining' of Europe (2012: 98).

This is probably also the place to say that this book does not attempt to survey or even refer to all of the different parts of Europe – that is not its purpose. Ethnographic research on Europe is itself uneven, with some areas long and well researched and others relatively neglected; and there are also regional variations in what themes are given attention, with research on memory being especially strong in Greece, for example. Even within this, however, my account is selective, mainly discussing work conducted within the British and North American anthropological traditions, and especially that of my own research areas; and within this still further by the narrative that I craft through what seem to me to be particularly telling examples and arguments. I also draw on my own research, which has been conducted in the UK, especially in Scotland and to some extent in England, and in Germany. This provides a range of contexts for past presencing – both rural and urban, of 'memory workers' – i.e. those officially concerned in various ways with public memory – and 'ordinary people', including tourists and 'the public'. Moreover, the UK and Germany provide contrasting national developments, with the UK 'disuniting' in the 1990s, as Scotland and to a lesser extent Wales gained greater political autonomy, while the two Germanys became reunified. In addition, they provide a contrast in terms of their relationship to 'Europe', with 'Europe' often being referred to as 'elsewhere' in the UK, whereas a sense of being 'at the heart of Europe' and of being 'European' is more usual (though by no means universal) in Germany.[43]

Preludes

This book is not a history of changing forms of memory and historiography in Europe – this would be a separate, fascinating, project. There are, however, certain shifts that have been discussed by historians that are a prelude to the current memory phenomenon. I have already noted the notion of possessive individualism, which, it has been argued, became widespread in Europe from the seventeenth century. This turned memory and the past – and awareness of the past – into crucial elements of identity, initially personal and then, especially from the late eighteenth century, national. Then, in a logic of inversion, that so often seems to operate in the social sphere, a continuous memory or history could itself become a way of proclaiming distinctive, individuated entities. Moreover, in what we might call a logic of extension, which also operates widely, this became a model ever more widely applied – or 'pirated', as Benedict Anderson has nicely expressed it (1983: 66). This was especially so from the 1970s, with the development of what is often called 'identity politics', in which there was a flourishing of demands for recognition by groups of various kinds on the basis of their identities – usually ethnic but also of other kinds, such as sexuality. Seeking out shared memory and manifesting this in some form of heritage was a 'natural' implementation of the model.

The past as a foreign country?

David Lowenthal's claim that there was a shift in Europe in the late eighteenth century which saw the past increasingly thought about as a 'foreign country' (1985) – or set of foreign countries – initially seems to suggest a development that was at odds with that of possessive individualism, which posits the past as part of the continuing (though changing) self. Prior to the eighteenth century, he claims, the past was mostly thought about as 'much like the present' (1985: xvi) – as basically a playing out of a universal and unchanging human nature. Antiquity, for example, might be admired as an exemplar of how to do things well, but this was seen as a 'better' version of the present rather than as substantively different. Towards the end of the eighteenth century, however, a new perception of the past 'as a different realm, not just another country but a congeries of foreign lands endowed with unique histories and personalities' emerged (1985: xvi). Regarding the past as a foreign place, as distinct from the present, would seem to sever the continuities that could make the past substantiate present-day identities. In *The Heritage Crusade*, Lowenthal concedes the dilemma, acknowledging that the view of the past as fundamentally alien to the present is not easily accommodated with a perception of the past as 'our own possession' (1998: xv). His response is to blame historians for the view of the past as 'foreign and exotic', as a place that 'frustrates understanding: its events seem unfathomable, its denizens inscrutable' (1998: xiv). 'I suspect', he then adds, 'that few take historians' cautions to heart': '[p]robably most people, most of the time, view the past not as a foreign but as a deeply domestic realm' and for them heritage is fundamentally concerned with 'domesticating the past' (1998: xv).

Certainly, what the compendious *The Past is a Foreign Country* seems to illustrate above all is a remarkable *range* of ways of addressing the past; and perhaps he is swayed to overstate the case for difference on account of the tempting quotation from L.P. Hartley that provides his title: 'The past is a foreign country, they do things differently there' (quoted in Lowenthal 1985: xvi). Nevertheless, he does show the growth of an idea of the past as worth looking at not just for exemplars of the present but for the more detailed and varied content that it could provide. Clearly, this is a kind of past that can be appropriated more readily to a model of distinctive histories possessed by distinctive nations. The past here is 'foreign' in that it may provide instances of practices that are no longer continued – such as stories and songs collected as part of the swathe of folkloristic collecting that swept Europe with the spread of the nation-state – and in that it can even set puzzles over why things were as they were. The past is separate and different from the present. But it is not incommensurable with it. Rather, it is seen as a precursor of particular presents and owners. Moreover, it is also increasingly understood as requiring investigation as a means not just of knowing what happened *then* but for understanding and demonstrating present day distinctiveness.

The new practices of conservation and rooting around in actual physical remnants of the past, of which Lowenthal provides ample documentation, show this well. Prior to the nineteenth century, even though Antiquity was widely admired, he explains, 'its physical remains were in the main neglected or destroyed' (1985: xvi). Only in the nineteenth century did archaeology grow as a popular practice and as a discipline.[44] So too did forms of preservation and restoration. According to Svetlana Boym:

> In the nineteenth century, for the first time in history, old monuments were restored in their original image. Throughout Italy churches were stripped of their baroque layers and eclectic additions and recreated in the Renaissance image, something that no Renaissance architect would ever imagine doing to a work of antiquity… By the end of the nineteenth century there is a debate between the defenders of complete restoration that proposes to remake historical and artistic monuments of the past in their unity and wholeness, and the lovers of unintentional memorials of the past: ruins, eclectic constructions, fragments that carry "age value". Unlike total reconstructions, they allowed one to experience historicity affectively, as an atmosphere, a space for reflection on the passage of time.
> (2001: 15)

If not wholly foreign, then, and worthy of trying to preserve both for the sense of historicity, of the passage of time itself, and as precursor of the present, the past was also in effect made into something visitable. It was, moreover, increasingly regarded as worthy of visiting for what it could 'tell'. Not an entirely foreign country, then, but a place where at least some things were done differently and that it was worth going to in order to learn from – and, moreover, to learn not only about others but also about one's self in *longue durée*.

The sciences of memory

The idea that the past provides clues to the present was also strengthened and expanded from the late nineteenth century by what Ian Hacking (1995) calls the sciences of memory. His discussion is of multiple personality disorder, of which there was an 'epidemic' in the 1980s (1995: 8) – a timing that is surely not merely coincident with the memory phenomenon discussed here. He shows how the Lockean forensic notion of personal identity was a necessary precursor to late nineteenth-century sciences of memory and that these in turn established ideas that needed to be in place for the later flourishing of multiple personality disorder. His is a detailed and nuanced account to which I do insufficient justice here. A novel notion that these sciences helped instantiate, however, was what he describes as the idea, 'dazzling in its implausibility', that 'what we have *forgotten* is what forms our character, our personality, our soul' (1995: 209, my emphasis). Today, that idea is most readily associated with Freud's concept of the unconscious – in which form it has been widely popularised throughout Europe and beyond. As Hacking shows, however, the idea predates Freud and suffuses wider scientific ideas about memory as well as Freudian psychoanalysis.

Although Hacking's account is directly concerned with a medicalised disorder suffered by individuals, the idea that the past can reveal things about ourselves that we do not yet know but that might be shaping our responses and capacities – and that there is a need to develop specialised techniques to access these – has wider resonance. It, too, is one that I suggest can be seen as part of the European memory complex – widespread but far from universally mobilised within European memory cultures.

There is much more that could be discussed as part of the prelude to the memory phenomenon within Europe. This includes *inter alia* the rise of mass production and consumption – proliferating new material forms and accompanying moral concerns about them; new forms of 'mechanical reproduction', as Walter Benjamin called them in 1955 (Benjamin 1992), playing into new concerns with the simulated, real and authentic; migration and urbanisation entangled with searches for community and roots; growing disenchantment with modernity and progress, meaning that the future could not be relied upon to provide the best answer; fissures covered over by the nation-state opening up, and becoming exacerbated by riffing on the compulsion to express distinctive identity in a politics of recognition; and the experience of mass warfare and destruction of human life – and accompanying mourning and memorialising – on a scale never previously encountered in Europe. Many of these will be addressed in the chapters that follow. In these, we turn to anthropological research to venture into what this too can tell us about the memory complex and the memory phenomenon in the memorylands of Europe.

The rest of this book

Memorylands divides roughly into two halves, the first of which introduces a range of anthropological perspectives and history of research on past presencing, together with methodological discussion. The second half, from Chapter 5, deals more directly with specific dimensions of the memory phenomenon.

The division is, however, far from absolute and there is discussion in the first half of topics, such as post-Socialist nostalgia, that are also part of the memory phenomenon – as indeed is much that is discussed throughout the book; and many topics introduced in the first half – including methodology, forms and media of narration and past presencing – are further developed in discussions in the second half.

Chapter 2, *Making Histories,* looks at the growth of anthropological interest in questions about the past amongst anthropologists of Europe, including questions of tradition and the invention of tradition, and of historical consciousness. A major focus of work has been on the making of history; and, in this chapter, this is discussed through a range of examples from both earlier work and more recent, the latter including attempts to construct European history, traditions and historical consciousness, the last drawn from my own fieldwork in Germany.

Chapter 3, *Telling the Past,* takes a more methodological tack to discussion of anthropological interest in past presencing, including exploration of similarities and differences between anthropology and history; and the difficulty for anthropologists of dealing with temporality – what I call the multitemporal challenge. The chapter gives particular attention to how the past is told and what the very forms of telling might themselves indicate. It also provides examples of various experimental anthropological work that tackles the multitemporal challenge in novel ways.

Not all past presencing, however, takes narrative form, as is acknowledged in various chapters but addressed most extensively in Chapter 4, *Feeling the Past.* This looks directly at questions of affect, materiality, embodiment and place and discusses a range of insightful ethnographic research that seeks to explore the implications of these for memory and other relationships with the past. In particular, it considers 'nostalgia' – a longing for the past; and especially the emergence of nostalgia for the Socialist past in post-Socialist Europe.

Chapter 5, *Selling the Past,* looks at one of the major memory phenomenon debates – that concerning the commodification of the past, or what is sometimes called 'the heritage industry', and accompanying concern about authenticity. To explore the questions in depth, the chapter includes an extended case-study of a heritage centre from my fieldwork in the Isle of Skye. Questions of materiality raised in the previous chapter, as well as alternative conceptualisations of 'heritage', are further developed here.

Chapter 6, *Musealisation,* looks at the memory phenomenon from the perspective of the growth of museumisation or heritagisation of everyday and folk life. It charts the growth of these forms of past presencing and engages with a range of influential theories about the museum phenomenon. Through another case study from the Isle of Skye – that acts as a partner to that in the previous chapter – it proposes some more specific concepts and an alternative, more reflexive, perspective on what is involved.

Like the two preceding chapters, Chapter 7, *Transcultural Heritage,* has a central focus on cultural agencies involved in past presencing: here, especially at monuments, public sculpture and museums. Given that these played significant roles in the nineteenth-century articulation of bounded, homogeneous identities, especially national identities, and associated histories and heritage, this chapter explores whether they are capable of addressing and even encouraging more fluid, multiple and transcultural memories and identities. The discussion here focuses especially upon the transcultural in relation to migration from outside Europe, and includes debates about heritage in relation to multiculturalism, citizenship, Islam and the veil as heritage. How far transcultural forms indicate a transformation in the nature of the European public spheres is explored through a number of innovative examples.

The transcultural theme is continued in Chapter 8, *Cosmopolitan Memory,* which addresses arguments that the nation-state is receding as a frame of memory, replaced by more cosmopolitan memory forms. The Holocaust has been a major focus for this claim and this chapter charts the expansion of Holocaust heritage as well as exploring arguments about cosmopolitan memory through a range of anthropological research. I won't give the game away here about what it concludes but will note that, as throughout the book, anthropological research throws up new perspectives and complexities, challenging existing theorising.

Culminatory narratives, ending in futurology, are a familiar strand in the European memory complex repertoire. The final chapter, *The Future of Memory – and Forgetting,* does not escape its cultural conventions … entirely.

2

MAKING HISTORIES

Europe, traditions and other present pasts

> Remembrance of things past is not necessarily the remembrance of things as they were.[1]

A central focus of anthropological research on memory is on ways in which the past is configured and reconfigured in the present. What is recalled, when and why? Whose pasts are told in the public sphere? What is forgotten, not mentioned or perhaps only told in whispers? And what notions of continuity, change, repetition or rupture shape or are expressed in recounted memories?

This chapter looks first at some of the background to interest in these questions among anthropologists of Europe, focusing on interest in the invention of tradition. It then presents and discusses a range of examples and debates about the making of histories and variations in forms of historical consciousness in Europe. This includes a sustained example from my own work on a European project whose aim was to try to identify the elusive possibility of 'European historical consciousness'. As I argue, such projects – and academic research on history and memory in Europe more generally – are not only 'meta' reflections of what is occurring in Europe but themselves play a constitutive part in producing Europe as a particular kind of space and possibility.

Inventing traditions

One spur to these questions about how histories are made in Europe, especially for anthropologists in English-speaking countries, was the attention given by some historians to what Hobsbawm and Ranger famously called 'the invention of tradition' (in their edited volume of that name published in 1983). By showing that traditions were often not as old as had previously been assumed, Hobsbawm and Ranger's 1983 volume showed clearly that not only did the past shape the present, the present could also shape the past. A main focus of their attention was on histories and genealogies created by nation-states – especially European – as part of their self-legitimation; but they also made a broader argument about tradition-making as a politicised process, serving the interests of some social groups more than others. These points were not wholly novel to anthropologists and, indeed, Hobsbawm and Ranger acknowledge that anthropological and sociological perspectives influenced their own. In Germany, for example, the way that the National Socialists had devised histories and genealogies, and created traditions and monuments – and the role that German *Volkskunde* (folklore) had played in this – meant that there was considerable awareness of how the past could be manipulated to political ends.[2] Nevertheless, the injection of the term 'the invention of tradition' into anthropological discourse, and the forthright nature of its exposition in the 1983 volume, chimed well in a Europe in which many areas were experiencing ethnonationalist revival and heritage movements and variously 'discovering' or 'inventing' traditions in the process.[3] Moreover, the interest in tradition invention and the making of nations coincided with a growth in the anthropology of Europe,[4] which at this time concentrated mainly on more rural or apparently traditional parts of Europe but where there were already questions being raised about the nature, persistence and revival of tradition. The invention of tradition thesis contributed to encouraging further research from anthropologists on the ways in which histories might be mobilised in service of present interests and interrogating how these might link with broader state developments.

The invention of tradition thesis has, however, been subject to critique.[5] In particular, it has been argued to posit a misleading dichotomy between 'real' traditions and 'invented' ones, forgetting that all traditions were made up at some point, and that they are subject to re-making and imbued with new meaning and significance over time. It was also criticised as overly instrumentalist, regarding history-making primarily as an act of elites engaged in forms of social engineering and leaving no space for the agency of those actually performing or living the traditions. In recognition of the fact that renditions of the past are always selective, more recent research has tended be framed in 'softer' terminology, such as historical 'making' or 'memory'; and has turned to more wide-ranging investigation of which accounts of the past are told, by whom, in what forms, and how these might relate to contemporary social relations or aspirations. Nevertheless, the invention of tradition perspective does seem to be productive in some contexts, especially those in which there *is* active and even instrumental tradition-making going on. Before looking at examples of these, let us turn briefly to some other perspectives on tradition, which was already a major topic in the anthropology of Europe before its invention and inventedness became a preoccupation.

Anthropology, tradition and change

A major thrust, and even the *raison d'être,* of much anthropological work in Europe before the 1980s was seeking out and documenting what were perceived as minority and peasant folkways, distinct from the nation-state and regarded as part of authentic ways of life. Salvage – gathering up information about ways of life deemed on the brink of disappearing – was a predominant ambition. Occasionally, questions of invention crept in, as they did in relation to some folktales, for example, but rather than becoming part of the study these tended to be dismissed as 'fakelore'.[6] The anthropological concern was with 'real' tradition.

This did not mean, however, that traditions were always perceived as fixed and unchanging; though the tendency was to see them, if not as stable, as adaptively responding to change.[7] Research on folktales, which was a staple of much ethnological work in many parts of Europe, was often concerned with charting changes in the stories over time (see Bendix 1997). Hermann Bausinger's influential *Folklore in a World of Technology* (1990), originally published in German in 1961, importantly drew attention to the making of traditions in modern societies, arguing that ethnologists should give consideration to matters such as how modern technologies became the subject-matter of new lore; and contending that it was as legitimate to study what he called 'second-hand traditions' – those adopted and usually altered by people who did not originally produce them – as 'first-hand' ones. Eugenia Shanklin's ethnographic study of sheep farmers in South-West Donegal – a part of the world in which it was commonly assumed that traditions were dying out – likewise pointed out that rather than disappearing, 'traditions' were changing 'in order to fit present circumstances' (1985: xiii) and that this was probably the usual rather than exceptional state of affairs. Although Shanklin's work partly fits the pre-1980s emphasis on tradition-making as adaptive, she also makes a significant move that is characteristic of the turn that begins in the 1980s. This is to treat 'tradition' not as a given or as something that she, as the anthropological analyst, is straightforwardly able to identify, but as a discursive construct. As such, her work charts how the term is deployed and what gets to be *counted* as 'tradition'. In an innovative chapter, she presents the voices of five different farmers, showing how 'tradition' could be variously opposed to 'modernity', sometimes being viewed as worth preserving and at others as something to be transcended in order to develop.

Discourses of this type amongst those studied, together with self-evident change, were also part of what prompted attention to questions about what was 'traditional', what kinds of 'past' persisted into the present or what aspects of the present came to be inscribed as part of a longer, more enduring temporality. The development of cultural tourism and the marketing of tradition and heritage also brought to the fore questions about 'tradition' as a resource for selling places and the consequences for localities of the marketing of the past, as in the example below and as I discuss further in Chapter 5. In some of these cases 'tradition invention' seemed a useful lens, in part at least, through which to examine what is going on.

Inventing quality French wine

Aware of criticisms of the invention of tradition thesis, Robert C. Ulin (1995) nevertheless argues that it is analytically useful because of the attention that it directs to how traditions may be actively created in the service of particular sectors of society. Working historically, but informed also by his ethnographic work as an anthropologist, he directs his attention to the making of *Grands Crus* wines in Bordeaux. Although the status of wine regions is typically seen as a consequence of the 'natural facts' of soil and climate, he shows how elites in certain regions have worked to elevate the status of their wines through various practices, self-promotion, legislation and the construction of a history. In particular, elites lobbied for legislation – beginning with the 1855 classification of wines that ranked them by 'crus' (e.g. *premier cru* – first growth) – that would both distinguish their wines from those of others and ensure that only their wines would be eligible. As he explains, criteria such as yield, length of ageing and also being produced from a château, all worked to favour elite producers and exclude both smaller, non-château wine-makers and cooperatives. Even if the châteaux were no longer owned by aristocrats, and even if new methods of wine production were used, the elite vineyard owners drew on the imagery of age and tradition associated with the aristocracy.

In a more recent study, in Burgundy, Marion Demoissier comes to similar conclusions in her investigation of the concept of *terroir* – a term with no direct English equivalent (though sometimes rendered as 'soil' or 'country'), subject to different definitions that 'nevertheless share an appeal to notions of unchanging place and enduringness' (2011: 689). As she shows, this concept is used especially to the advantage of wine-growing elites in Burgundy, who typically are 'third or fourth generation … inheritors of the best plots in Burgundy' (2011: 699). By emphasising the 'unique attributes of a specific site' (2011: 702) – understood as manifest in the resulting distinctive taste of the wine produced – elite wine-makers confirm 'their own individual economic and social status and sell… their uniqueness at global level' (2011: 702). This will be further consolidated, she argues, if Burgundy and Champagne succeed in becoming recognised by UNESCO as world heritage.

Invented traditions as ideology in Communist Eastern Europe

The legislation and manoeuvring involved in the making of French wine culture have taken place over more than a century – though certain moments were especially busy, notably the 1855 classification, which was announced at the Paris Universal Exposition, itself a hotbed of performative creation of national culture (Ulin 1995: 522). Hobsbawm's original formulation of 'invented traditions' included that they are established rapidly ('a matter of a few years perhaps', 1983: 1). This, together with active and even self-aware production of tradition, does characterise some situations well. One such is Socialist Eastern Europe. Here, ethnographers were inevitably confronted with newly created practices that had been introduced as part of the state restructuring of the social along Marxist-Leninist ideological lines. Typically, new official histories were written and traditions either invented or adapted in order to 're-educate, to transform practice and consciousness' and generally to integrate localities into the socialist state, as Deema Kaneff describes it for the village of Talpa in Bulgaria (2004: 14).[8]

Unlike in the 'invention of tradition' contexts described by Hobsbawm *et al.*, what this also often produced were high levels of awareness among citizens about how history and tradition might be used to political ends. In some cases too it led to sophisticated folk taxonomies of different kinds of history and tradition serving different social functions. In Talpa, for example, Kaneff explains that villagers themselves make distinctions between

> history [as] the embodiment of political-economy; tradition [as] a potentially oppositional way to conceptualize the human order (primarily through religious/mystical practices); [and] ... folklore [which] provided a state-sponsored notion of national identity.
>
> (2004: 10)

This did not mean, however, that villagers necessarily rejected the newer, ideological forms. It was contrary to what various studies elsewhere in Eastern Europe – including Martha Lampland's in Hungary (1988, 1995), Kathryn Verdery's in Romania (1983, 1991) and Chris Hann's in Poland (1985) – had shown. In these, state ideology and its associated history and traditions were cast primarily as an alien imposition (Kaneff 2004: 16). In Talpa, however, the new rituals and frameworks ('folklore' in local terminology) were mostly taken up widely and enthusiastically. Small numbers of people engaged in minor forms of resistance by ignoring the socialist rituals and valuing 'tradition', which was seen within the official ideology as a retrograde clinging onto the past. For the most part, however, Kaneff argues, local 'officials and others were skilled at using these [state sponsored] pasts ... in strategic ways to achieve their political ambitions' (2004: 15). And they largely succeeded in enlisting the majority of villagers to support them.

Clearly, then, there was here active invention of pasts and traditions in service of particular political ends. But this does not mean that the new pasts – here called 'folklore' – are less meaningful than the older ones. Neither, in Kaneff's analysis, is 'tradition' simply defined as the true and authentic bedrock of practice that had pre-existed socialism. As she shows, the status of 'tradition' changes within new socialist system, not least in it becoming a site of opposition.

As such, she avoids the problematic a priori distinction between invented and non-invented traditions, in which the latter were assumed to be outside political process and somehow more authentic; and instead presents a more nuanced picture that leaves space too for the reflexivity of participants.

Anthropology, tradition and Europe

Investigations of the invention of tradition also drew attention to the role of experts, including folklorists and anthropologists, in the invention process.[9] While this identified some cases of out-and-out fabrication of folktales and traditional practices, for the most part what was involved were more subtle processes of overly enthusiastic search, 'discovery' and selection. In addition, the very fact of *what* anthropologists of Europe directed their attention to and where they carried out their research played a part in configuring Europe as a particular kind of epistemological space. In particular, the concern with non-modern ways of life that was the mainstay and *raison d'être* of much anthropological research on Europe until the 1980s, imagined Europe as sharply divided between, on one side, the modern, central and urban, and, on the other, the rural, peripheral and traditional. This effectively conjured up a Europe of two distinct temporalities: one, of rapid forward momentum and ongoing change; and the other, of static tradition, waiting for the probably inevitable invasion by the former. By focusing on the traditional and seeking this in the peripheries of Europe, it was argued, anthropologists of Europe contributed to what Jeremy Boissevain famously called its 'tribalisation' (1975: 11).[10]

During the 1980s, spurred on too by the *Writing Culture* debates following (and to an extent preceding) publication of an edited volume of that name later in the 1980s (Clifford and Marcus 1986), anthropologists of Europe became more reflexive about how their own research selections and emphases might contribute to particular representations of Europe, and also to how they might best tackle their subject – and the various pasts they encountered. As we see in the next chapter, this also contributed to various methodological explorations and innovations.

Historical situating

One way in which ethnographers of Europe sought to tackle the criticism of their ignoring of history was by emphasising how supposedly marginal areas were *part of* wider historical and political processes. The ethnographic present, in other words, was situated *in* history instead of sealed off from it. In research in Communist countries, this generally happened inevitably as the role of the state and historical situation was so pervasive and visible. Elsewhere, however, historical situating was sometimes against the grain of earlier, more romantic, perspectives that had tended to see villages and rural areas as bastions of only slowly changing tradition (see Boyes 1993; Rogers 1991). For example, researchers (including myself) in the Scottish Hebrides showed how an apparently traditional practice such as crofting – a form of landholding in which people have small amounts of land in order to be able to undertake small-scale farming – was not the ancient way of life that some romanticised accounts presented it as being. Rather, it was a product of nineteenth-century capitalist development that served to bind local populations into unfavourable labour relations that maximised profits for landlords.[11] While it had taken on other meanings since, ethnographers saw part of their task as to look beyond the immediate romantic descriptions to try to see where ideas about traditionality and community came from and what this might also say about the present. My own experience of this kind of work was that reading historical materials – and especially primary sources – helped me to better understand some of the selections (and silences) involved in official or better known accounts of Scottish Highland history, and thus meant that I was aware of what was *not* recalled or was only referenced in relatively subtle ways that I might not have noticed otherwise. For example, in everyday speech in the area of the Isle of Skye in which I worked, there were sometimes subtle allusions to people whose families had gained from the redistributions of land following the nineteenth-century land wars. I would have been less likely to have registered these if I had kept in mind only the oft-told popular account of local togetherness and community, and not the more complex situation that the primary sources revealed (Macdonald 1997). This was not to imply that my aim was to dismiss popular or romanticised accounts: on the contrary, I attempted to explore how they were variously mobilised and put to work – for example to distinguish different kinds of people or moral positions – in everyday life.

As part of this work of historically situating ethnographic accounts, some anthropologists of Europe also turned their attention to wider nationalist discourses, using anthropological techniques to analyse their structuring. Michael Herzfeld's considerable body of ethnographic research, for example, often gives attention to the relationship between state or nationalist histories and those he encountered in his various fieldsites, ranging from Cretan shepherds to bureaucrats in Athens. In *Cultural Intimacy* (1997), for example, he coins the term 'structural nostalgia' to describe how the Greek state and also 'its most lawless citizens' (1997: 109) deploy an 'image of an unspoiled and irrecoverable past ... an Edenic order – a time before time – in which the balanced perfection of social relations has not yet suffered the decay that affects everything human' (1997: 109). While both the state officials and the 'lawless citizens' share the same idealised vision of a pre-state past – and this 'provides ... the common ground of their continuing mutual engagement' (1997: 109) – they mobilise it to very different ends. For the lawless, it shows that things were better without state interference. 'For the state the model legitimizes its intervention as an act of restoring a formerly perfect social order' (1997: 109). While his argument is drawn from close ethnographic observation of the Greek case, he also suggests that such 'structural nostalgia' – for social states of 'originary perfection' (1997: 112) – is widespread in both nationalist and religious (especially Christian) narratives. It is so in part because it can act as a 'strategic resource' (1997: 115) to provide 'a spiritual basis' for claims and actions and also to 'disguise the strategic manipulation of present time' (1997: 113). As such, it is a pattern that we can expect to find widely in Europe.

Anthropological work of this kind, then, took on board the notion of histories and traditions as made but instead of viewing this as a feature of only *some* histories and traditions, it regarded history-making – and present-making – as more ramifying ongoing processes with continuing implications. Histories, nations, and cultures are not imagined once and for all, went the argument, but were in a continual process of reimagining.[12] In highlighting this, anthropological work also showed that making histories was not the preserve of political elites – though getting to hear other kinds of accounts, which were typically relatively inaudible both in the historical record and in the present, posed a greater methodological challenge, as we see below. At the same time, it also showed that 'local' accounts were not necessarily separate from national or state ones but thoroughly entangled with them.

Anthropologists also tackled the question of how Europe was imagined by their discipline by looking at other topics, more urban locations and what were at that time unconventional sites. For example, Françoise Zonabend, who had published an exemplary detailed ethnography about time – including, significantly, ideas about change – in a Burgundian village (Zonabend 1980), turned her attention to looking at workers in nuclear installations (1989). Today, it is hard to think of a site in which anthropologists of Europe would not work.

Making European history

As part of growing attention to anthropological practices, George Marcus and Michael Fischer in the US called for what they called the 'repatriation of anthropology' (1986). This entailed anthropological research on the US in order to help fulfil anthropology's promise of a 'cultural critique' capable of 'disturbing cultural self-satisfaction' (1986: 111). Looking at institutions involved in constructing the nation was one dimension of this. In Europe, in a similar spirit, anthropologists increasingly turned their attention to European institutions.[13] Some of this work included attention to their mobilisations of history and, in particular, the way in which history has been produced in attempts to forge a European identity.

EU invented traditions

In *Building Europe* (2000), Cris Shore documents some of the policy initiatives by EU institutions to create new, shared traditions and, as he quotes from an EU official document, 'affirm the awareness of a common cultural heritage as an element in the European identity' (2000: 45). The former included creating 'a new set of symbols for communicating the principles and values upon which the [European] Community is based (2000: 46). Most of these were modelled on those that were part of the earlier 'identikit' of ways of symbolising national identity (Macdonald 1993). They included a flag, with 12 gold stars on a blue background. According to the official account by the Council of Europe, this was chosen because:

> Twelve was a symbol of perfection and plenitude, associated equally with the apostles, the sons of Jacob, the tables of the Roman legislator, the labours of Hercules, the hours of the day, the months of the year, or the signs of the Zodiac. Lastly, the circular layout denoted the union.
>
> (quoted in Shore 2000: 47)

This seems like a capacious casting around for symbolic attributes of the number 12, though it also shows a predominance of Christian and classical references – the two main pillars in attempts to create a European history – with some more universal ones thrown in for good measure. Marc Abélès also makes the following, rather different, observation about the choice of the number:

> Most people think that the twelve stars correspond to the twelve member states at that time, but the symbol was chosen for more negative reasons. Fourteen or fifteen stars raised the problem of the status of Saarland, and thirteen was a bad omen. From an aesthetic point of view, a circle of twelve stars represented harmony and left enough space for introducing in its centre the particular emblem of the various European organizations.
>
> (Abélès 2000: 38)

Other constructed symbols of the new Europe – part of a self-aware invention of tradition that mixed pragmatics with historical inspiration – included a European anthem ('taken from the fourth movement of Beethoven's Ninth Symphony – the "Ode to Joy"' (Shore 2000: 48)); a European passport; and 'new celebratory calendrical markers, such as festive "European weeks" [and] "European Culture Months (to accompany the "European city of culture" initiative)' (2000: 49); and 'proposed new Community-wide public holidays commemorating decisive moments in the history of European integration – such as the birthday of Jean Monnet and the date of signing of the Treaty creating the European Coal and Steel Community' (2000: 49–50). The new currency, the Euro, showed some of the struggle for, on the one hand, linking the new Europe to its history and, on the other, avoiding giving precedence to the history of some nations. Debates about what imagery to show were lengthy and in the end, rather than select particular images of persons or sites, the decision was to put abstract generalised 'European' architecture on the new coins and notes. The new currency thus features imagined bridges or other buildings in various 'European' architectural styles – 'Classical, Romanesque, Gothic, Renaissance, Baroque, and Rococo, the age of iron and glass architecture, and modern twentieth-century architecture'

FIGURE 2.1 Euro currency. Photograph by Sharon Macdonald

(Shore 2000: 112). This decision was both fascinating and bizarre, speaking to the significance of place in the European imaginary but at the same time defusing its real situatedness.

Writing European histories

This creative and somewhat perverse strategy was not, however, so readily available for the production of European public histories that addressed Europe's past(s). Making up generalised abstract histories of Europe was not perhaps totally impossible but it was more challenging for media such as school textbooks and public exhibitions. Reviewing some of the possible 'historical building blocks on which to construct a European identity' – 'the classical tradition, Christianity, the Renaissance and European humanism, the Enlightenment, the Holocaust and the European Union itself' (Berger 2009: 29), historian Stefan Berger points out the exclusions and other dilemmas that each of these raises. Having led a major European Science Foundation project, *Representations of the Past: The Writing of National Histories in Nineteenth and Twentieth Century Europe* (2003–8),[14] he concludes that: 'History is what divides Europeans, not what unites them' (Berger 2009: 29) and that, therefore, it cannot and should not be used as a foundation for European identity building. This robust view is not shared by all historians.[15] Neither is it by the numerous initiatives that have been instigated to try to foster European identity through history. These include commissioned histories and film (Shore 2000: 56–60), networks of history teachers (van de

FIGURE 2.2   Europeans: individuals in *'It's our history!'* Photograph copyright Tempora/ Musée de l'Europe

Leeuw-Roord 2000), European Cities of Culture and city twinning initiatives (Sassatelli 2002; Lotterman 2009; Patel 2012), European pavilions at World Fairs and a wide range of exhibitions.[16] The last includes the Museum of Europe project, which was influenced by the ideas of Pierre Nora and officially devised to 'be the "place of memory" that Europe needs'.[17] Its first temporary exhibition, opened in 2007, was entitled *'C'est notre histoire!'/'It's our history!'*

There is not space here for a review of these but it is worth briefly pointing out some of the difficulties with these histories that some have identified. First, there is the point repeatedly raised, as by Berger above, concerning the diversity of Europe and the fact that history is as likely to divide as unify. As such, common histories of Europe have been accused of skating over differences or making unwarranted assumptions of what is shared. In a thoughtful analysis of *'It's our history!'*, Steffi de Jong notes that the exhibition – which seeks to create a shared memory for Europe – begins in 1945. World War II is referenced but not in any detail. It acts, rather, as a shared 'memory' but one evacuated of the detailed content that could highlight antagonisms between different European countries (see also Chapter 8). As de Jong puts it, World War II 'is remembered; but it is remembered as a pan-European catastrophe in which all Europeans appear equally as victims' (2011: 378).

There is also the dilemma that identity-building often works by creating an oppositional 'Other' (see also Chapters 7 and 8) and that this can have the effect of creating exclusions – as has been the case especially in relation to Muslims in some European projects.[18] In many respects *'It's our history!'* takes thoughtful and innovative approaches to avoiding presenting a singular European identity. It does so, for example, by presenting variety through the display of life-stories of 27 individuals, representing what by 2007 were 27 member-states. Those chosen mostly symbolise contributions to the European project, including:

> an Erasmus student, a Swedish scientist working for the European Organisation of Nuclear Research, a Portuguese entrepreneur running a transportation and logistics company, a Finnish interpreter at the European Parliament, a Bulgarian farmer producing organic yoghurt, a Greek and a Maltese civil servant at the European Commission and the

Austrian founder of SkyEurope... a Belgian worker who fought for equal payment in the Belgian national weapon's factory, a Czech co-signatory of the Charter 77, an Estonian participant in the 'Phosphorite War', a Polish fellow campaigner of Lech Wałęsa in the Solidarity movement and a German couple who fled from the GDR through the tunnel dug underneath the Berlin Wall.

(de Jong 2011: 377)

As de Jong observes, however, all of the 27 individuals who are pictured in the exhibition – and who tell part of their own life-histories – are white. A kind of European diversity is displayed, then, but not one that includes visible 'racial' difference and that might reference histories – of migration and colonialism – beyond the European Union.

In search of European historical consciousness

How to write histories of Europe – and whether these could be done in 'inclusive' ways and that would foster senses of being European – were questions discussed as part of a project on European Historical Consciousness of which I was part during the late 1990s and early 2000s. The project was led by Professor Jörn Rüsen, a charismatic and internationally renowned theoretician of history, based at the Kulturwissenschaftliche Institut (Institute for Advanced Study in the Humanities) in Essen, of which he was director. It was funded by the Körber Foundation, a private organisation that is involved in a wide range of projects concerned with history and with multiculturalism.[19] The most famous of these is the 'President's history competition' – a competition held for school children and young people every year since 1973, on a particular theme. This is the competition which is the subject-matter of Michael Verhoeven's excellent fact-based film *Das schreckliche Mädchen –The Nasty Girl* – about a schoolgirl who unearths all sorts of unsavoury details about the public worthies in her small town as she researches its recent history. Central to the Körber Foundation's funding of the European Historical Consciousness project was that they were involved in extending the competition to other countries, including at that time to many in Eastern Europe and the former Soviet Union; and they were also planning a pan-European version of the competition, which was launched as EUSTORY – the History Network of Young Europeans – in 2001.[20] One outcome that the Körber Foundation wanted from the European Historical Consciousness project was assistance with drafting a 'Charter' – a set of principles of what would constitute 'good history' in this context – for this new network.[21] A particular concern – reflected in the Charter's wording – was over nationalistic histories being produced in post-Socialist countries as part of the enthusiastic embracing of national independence. Germany's experience of nationalism under the Nazis had made many historians wary of nationalistic history. The dilemma was how to articulate this without engaging in dictatorial laying down of rules by the German organisers. Setting up the accompanying academic project and bringing together scholars from a wide range of countries to hopefully provide a robust scientific perspective was intended as a means of helping to find a way of doing so.

I was invited to participate, initially as a guest speaker, as an anthropologist and expert on Scotland, and later to become part of the steering committee.[22] This met regularly over several years and contributed to reports, publications and the Charter. Seven of 12 members of the steering committee were German, more specifically West German, and the others were from the Netherlands, Russia, Norway, and Hungary. All other than myself were trained in history, working either in academic history, or in the field of history pedagogy, or in organisations working with history (e.g. providing information for history teachers). Over the course of the project we heard talks by many presenters, including from those running history competitions in East European countries. These often highlighted dilemmas such as recalcitrant teachers, or the discomfort of young people discovering alternatives to the histories that their families or schools preferred to tell. Certain lines of difference – between some of the participants, including some members of the steering committee – and assumptions also became apparent as I discuss below. First, however, I offer some brief comments on the notion of 'European Historical Consciousness' that was our project's rubric.

What is European historical consciousness?

In the previous chapter, I introduced the term 'historical consciousness' as a possible analytical focus for investigation of modes of historicising. Some of the most extensive and subtle theorising has come from Germany, where it is usually called *Geschichtsbewusstsein*. Developed especially by Jeismann (1985) to draw attention to the ways in which cognitive and cultural factors may structure the learning and teaching of history, and more broadly to how past, present and future are understood in relation to one another, it has been further developed in Rüsen's sophisticated theorising to include conceptualising historical consciousness as a fundamental part of the human condition – the process of 'orientation in the course of time which has to be brought about by remembering the past' (2005: 1). This posits historical consciousness not so much as a particular and contingent way of structuring the past and of configuring time (as, in common with most other anthropologists, I use it below), but rather as a faculty allowing individuals and groups to escape senses of contingency and give meaning to the passage of time. Rüsen is also much concerned with the ways in which different historiographic modes variously help satisfy the need for temporal orientation, arguing, for example, that postmodern approaches fail to do so (2005, especially Chapter 8).

Despite Rüsen's own subtle thinking about the term, there was often dispute in the group about what might be meant by it, and more specifically what was meant by *European* historical consciousness.[23] Rüsen's conceptualisation of historical consciousness was universalistic. So what could European historical consciousness be? Sometimes, especially in the early days, we talked past one another, employing different assumptions without always being aware of doing so. At others we debated whether it concerned ways of structuring history and temporality (a configurative conception of 'historical consciousness') that might be found in Europe – and, if so, across all parts of it or only some? Or was it about particular knowledge (a content conception) – and then, knowledge about Europe or knowledge held within it? Although we often agreed in our more theoretical discussions that our emphasis was not on knowledge content, in practice, in the detail of debate, it often was. Shocked discussion of teenagers not knowing about this or that historical event or person was recurrent, for example. Most often, however, 'historical consciousness' seemed to relate to *forms* of historical narrative, and particular attention paid was to 'national' and 'nationalistic' (the two sometimes being regarded as synonymous) structuring of history. Such structuring was frequently talked about as involving potentially dangerous degrees of patriotism and negative sentiments towards other nations and minority groups. A 'European historical consciousness', by contrast, was normatively conceived as a mode of historical narration that would avoid these problematic nationalistic dimensions of national historical consciousness.

In the throes of our actual work, our discussion mostly focused on the following: (1) how to write a *common* European history – what should go in, what should be avoided and how should it be disseminated; (2) whether there was history that could give people in different parts of Europe a consciousness of being European. The question of why and even whether these should be done was rarely raised and, when it was, felt like breaking a taboo or being rather politically incorrect, as I found when I did so. (My crassness was readily explained either as being from Euro-sceptic England or as my anthropological peculiarity.) For the most part it was taken for granted that a common European history could act as a basis for a common European identity; and that a sense of a shared past could transcend the potential divisiveness of national histories. This is not to say that Europe's differences were ignored. On the contrary, there was considerable and sometimes heated discussion of how to recognise 'diversity' and allow for 'multiperspectival' history that would not fall into what Rüsen frequently denounced as the postmodern 'anything goes' quagmire.

National differences and cultural models

Not all participants, however, were as ready to so thoroughly castigate 'national' history. (This was especially evident at some of the bigger meetings, involving history teachers from around Europe.) Participants from post-Socialist countries often embraced national history as an escape from socialist and Soviet-dominated history; and my own consideration of Scottish nationalism and history did not lead me to be quite so unequivocal about the need to transcend the national past.

Our Russian colleague, Michail Boytsov, was also concerned that the implicit positing of 'Europe' and 'European' as superior to 'nation' and 'national' was an evolutionistic schema that reinforced a distinction between 'modern' and 'non-modern' parts of Europe, the former being those who accepted 'Europeanness' and demonstrated 'European historical consciousness', the latter being those who did not.[24]

Another 'given' was that bad – usually nationalistic – aspects of the past needed to be addressed. This was based on loosely psychoanalytical ideas that suffuse much discourse about the past in Germany, in which an adequate and healthy relationship to the present (and the future) is seen as premised on having come to terms adequately with the past, and in particular not having repressed anything which will cause continuing trauma or difficulties in the present. Drawing on ideas that are part of a broader European memory complex, the repression model is one that has been adopted especially in relation to the Nazi past in Germany, having become widespread since the 1960s.[25] The past becomes something that must be faced, addressed, worked through, mastered, overcome or otherwise tackled as summed up in the German term *Vergangenheitsbewältigung*. In project seminars, I noticed that this understanding of the past – which is coupled with a perception of the past as inherently problematic, as dangerous if not properly managed – was one which (West) German steering committee members (there were none from the GDR) were especially likely to bring to bear on the cases which we discussed. As such, they were particularly likely to perceive the past as intruding into the present; and they tended to use language such as 'coping with' history, and individual-psychologised terms such as 'guilt' or 'shame', in their discussions of society to a greater extent than, say, East European members. The latter were more likely to talk about the politics and structures of history production, and to cast particular ways of doing history as bound up with particular regimes in a way that did not so readily depict history as likely to cause eruptions into a later period. On one occasion, a scholar from the Netherlands was given a rough ride when he presented a paper to the European Historical Consciousness project which contained research concluding that the Dutch have not accepted their role as collaborators (nearly all imagine themselves as part of the resistance) and that he suggested was 'healthy' by comparison with the German constant dwelling on their own guilt and culpability. A Norwegian colleague also wittily questioned the German determination to keep confronting their guilty past when he recounted having turned on the television in his hotel room in Essen to find a British-made World War II film featuring Michael Caine, dubbed into German, in which Germans were so clearly and stereotypically depicted as 'baddies'. 'Why do you do this to yourselves?' he asked. Nobody had an answer.

Yet, it was a question that some of the German participants acknowledged as relevant to the ambitions of the European Historical Consciousness project. In particular, would framing histories in terms of 'Europe' lead to a playing down of national histories and affiliations – or would Germans still have to come to terms with a specifically German past? Or – as was explicitly raised in discussion on more than one occasion – would a more developed *European* history make us think about the Nazi past and the Holocaust less within a frame of *German* culpability? Was the concept of 'European Historical Consciousness', as a German participant reflected to me at one point, a matter of German 'flight' or 'refuge' (*Flucht*) into Europe – a way of not having to think about that burdensome German history any more?[26] If at any level it was, it also was not: for we often found ourselves addressing it. Indeed, it seemed to me – and the other participants that I suggested this to generally agreed – that there was a profound ambivalence over the Nazi past. On the one hand, Germans often resented (understandably) that they were so often identified with it – and that it seemed to them to be mentioned so much (this was often a source of remorse expressed to me – why were the British so obsessed with stereotyping Germans as Nazis?).[27] On the other hand, they were determined that the Nazi past and the Holocaust should remain at the centre of any thinking about the past in Europe – and they often brought discussion back to this even when we were talking about other topics. Interesting here too was how persistently notions of nationality – 'Germans' – kept re-emerging in this attempt to forge European historical consciousness.

During the project, I noted other instances of what seemed to me to illustrate culturally specific forms of historical consciousness. For example, there was often talk about 'generation', with German participants often presenting themselves by noting that they were 'second generation'. This is based on a reckoning of history beginning with World War II – the time from which the clock starts ticking and social relations and present-day German identities are reckoned. As a mode of narration it collapses national and personal, thus deeply implicating individuals in collective relations with history.[28] Yet the clear-cut division into different age-bands that this use of 'generation' implies, does not map out so unequivocally on the ground, and individuals classified as of one particular 'generation' might have diverse relationships even to the 'past of reckoning' – never mind other histories or experiences. Furthermore, this generationalism – thinking about social relations through the lens of generation – is not ubiquitous across Europe.[29]

By identifying some of the culturally specific modes of historical consciousness at work during the European Historical Consciousness project, I do not wish to detract from the value of the project or from the EUSTORY initiative. Discussion was sensitive and sophisticated and the resulting Charter weaves a careful course between some of the issues that the project highlighted. The Charter itself was presented to the European Commission in Brussels and has been used in the President's History Competition, helping teachers across Europe to better articulate dilemmas that they faced in the teaching of history. I personally learnt a good deal during my participation and my observations are in part a consequence of how the high-level debates attuned me to questions of historical consciousness. Moreover, my interest in questions that shape this book owes much to my time on the project. This included an interest in questions of relatively inaudible histories or modes of historicising also present within Europe.

Other histories

Within the anthropology of Europe there has been increased attention, especially since the 1980s, to local memories and ways of telling the past in everyday life. This has helped to highlight 'other histories', that is, as noted in the introduction, accounts that differ from more mainstream or official ones, thus 'demonstrating the inherent plurality of history in Europe... [and] breaking down modern European history's alleged uniqueness and unity' (Hastrup 1992: 1). In some cases 'other histories' constituted major challenges to official accounts, prompting wider revisionism or even political outrage. In others, it exposed not just differing memories of the past but also alternative ways of conceptualising the nature of history and temporality.

Work of this kind has been carried out in many parts of Europe. One particularly productive location, however, has been Greece, ethnographers of which have contributed especially rich studies drawing attention to questions of history-making and historical consciousness. That Greece became the location for such significant work is in some ways not surprising, as Michael Herzfeld argues, in that it had occupied an ambivalent position of being, on the one hand, the historical 'ancestor' of Europe and thus in a sense the most 'European' of Europe's countries, and, on the other, of being relatively marginal within the newer European economy and polity (1987). In addition, the complex history of the Ottoman Empire, World War II occupation and Civil War, of strong nationalism coupled with strong regional and island identities, ethnic minorities, and several and shifting borders with other countries, all contribute to Greece being an especially fertile ground for exploring questions of relations between past and present, and what is 'remembered', why and how.

Nationalist narratives and hidden histories

One theme in past presencing research in Greece, as indeed elsewhere, is the construction of national histories and the ways in which these intersect with local or regional accounts of the past, sometimes differing from these and at other times being mutually reinforcing. Inevitably, this raises questions about nationalist historical narratives, as, for example, in Anastasia Karakasidou's *Fields of Wheat, Hills of Blood: Passages to Greek Macedonia 1870–1990* (1997). Karakasidou began her research with a model – rooted in her own upbringing and education in Greece – of a clear-cut distinction between 'local Greeks' and 'refugees' (who had arrived later from elsewhere). Her historical and ethnographic research showed, however, that rather than there being a 'pure Greek' historical trajectory back to the ancient kingdom of Macedon, Slavic-speakers had continually been present in Greece, and in greater numbers, than usually acknowledged. This presence had, however, been written out of the official national historical record and Slavic-speakers and their descendants generally concealed their Slavic identities in everyday life. Her work thus showed revision of histories at national, regional and even personal levels. Conducted at a time when the question of Macedonia was becoming even more politically contested – namely, in the aftermath of the break-up of Yugoslavia and the establishment of an area of North of Greece as the Former Yugoslav Republic of Macedonia, an independent, Slavic, country – her work was widely seen as unpatriotic, to such an extent that she even received death threats. In macabre fashion this showed the significance with which history was imbued. It also highlighted some of the particular challenges that might be faced by anthropologists working on such questions in their own countries – though others could experience these too (e.g. Cowan and Brown 2000: 2).

One analytical difficulty Karakasidou faced was the fact that the model of identities of which she was critical was widely held by the people with whom she worked. Alternative, or 'other', histories that showed a different reality were relatively muted not only in the official historical record but also in daily life. This did not mean that they were absent but rather, as other researchers of Greece also found, that they were rarely addressed directly. In fieldwork in central Greece, for example, Anna Collard was puzzled to discover that villagers would make 'constant comment' (1989: 95) about the late eighteenth- early nineteenth-century 'Ottoman period' as though they had directly lived through it; while mostly ignoring the more recent traumatic period of German occupation in the early 1940s. On the one hand, reference to the Ottoman period – 'celebrated as a time of freedom fighters (and brigands), of national resistance, of patriotism and heroic deeds' (1989: 96) – fostered links 'with a national culture of patriotism, Greek heroism, and ideas about a untied Greek nation' (1989: 97). Equally, however, it allowed an indirect way of talking about 'a less officially acceptable past' and 'the "forbidden" topic of self-government in the occupation period' (1989: 97). As well as showing how selective 'social memory' (as Collard called these mobilisations of the past in daily life) could be used to morally evaluate the present, Collard's work also showed 'other historical consciousnesses' or forms of 'past presencing'. For the Greek villagers not only made their own particular selections from the historical record, they also flouted usual temporalities, as in their collapsing of certain distant time-periods together or talking about a period before they were born as though they had directly experienced it.

Other historical consciousnesses

Other work too has shown not just other histories but other historical consciousnesses. Michael Herzfeld's extensive Greek ethnography has often addressed such questions. In *A Place in History* (1991), for example, he explored how the people of Rethemnos, in their fight to resist bureaucratic controls on the alterations to their homes that they were allowed to make, attempt to 'reclaim their lives from a detemporalised past and a desocialized present, and to develop other kinds of historical consciousness' (1991: 9–10) than that of the 'monumental conception of history' – or 'monumental time' – produced by the modern bureaucratic nation-state. These other historical consciousnesses are rooted instead in what he calls 'social time'. As he explains:

> Between social and monumental time lies a discursive chasm, separating the popular from official understandings of history. Social time is the grist of everyday experience. It is above all the kind of time in which events cannot be predicted but in which every effort can be made to influence them. It is the time that gives events their reality, because it encounters each as one of a kind. Monumental time, by contrast, is reductive and generic. It encounters events as realizations of some supreme destiny, and it reduces social experience to collective predictability. Its main focus is on the past – a past constituted by categories and stereotypes.
>
> (1991: 10)

By exploring the contests over restoration and conservation of property in Rethemnos, Herzfeld was able, then, not only to illustrate the fact that people chose different historical periods to preserve or obliterate but also how these selections were thoroughly embedded in ongoing social relations and specific ways of conceptualising time and the nature of history. Importantly, this shaped not only the town's present but also its future – creating a physical heritage that would endure into the future and, in the process, making certain other histories less visible in the future townscape (see also Herzfeld 2009).

This attention to physical and embodied dimensions of the past or memory is another major theme of anthropological research, as I discuss further in Chapter 4. It expands upon the more discursively focused aspects of historical consciousness, highlighting that the ways in which the past is apprehended and mobilised are not necessarily only linguistic. As David Sutton puts it, in his *Memories Cast in Stone: The Relevance of the Past in Everyday Life* (1998), a detailed ethnography of the island of Kalymnos, discussed further below, 'historical consciousness … comes in many forms other than articulated written or oral histories' (1998: 10). Moreover, these other forms do not necessarily 'say' the same thing as the verbally articulated. 'Discursive, narrated historical consciousness is sometimes supplemented by, sometimes contradicted by, ritual and kinship practices' as well as by other embodied practices, such as the ritualised throwing of dynamite (which is as dangerous as it sounds) at Easter, which 'subtly bring[s] to mind different periods of the island's past' (1998: 10). These are periods that 'often remain unarticulated in everyday conversation because direct articulation would explicitly question the relationship between Kalymnos and the local and national authorities' (1998: 10).

This 'indirection', so often found in anthropological work on Greece but also elsewhere in Europe,[30] is in part due to the fact that those involved 'see the past as alive and active in the present', and, as such, as potentially 'dangerous' (Sutton 1998: 203). Sutton suggests that this can be distinguished from 'cut off history' (a notion he adapts from Collingwood 1939) – that is, pasts that are 'commodified for tourist consumption, museumified, made an object of nostalgia' (1998: 203). At the time that he was writing, such pasts seemed to be becoming increasingly prevalent in Europe (and indeed elsewhere), as we will explore further in Chapter 5; though we should note here that not all anthropologists have found apparently commodified pasts to be as 'cut off' from the present as is often imagined.

Here, however, I present some brief case studies in order to show further some of the varieties of ways of conceptualising history and its significance, of modes of recounting it and otherwise making the past present that have been highlighted by anthropologists working in a variety of countries in Europe. All were based on long-term ethnographic fieldwork and involved the researchers encountering past presencing in a wide variety of contexts, including ones in which they had not expected the past to be of such significance.

The first example, by David Sutton on Kalymnos in the 1990s, already introduced, is from a location that is on the peripheries of 'Europe' according to some of the EU ideas about Europe, though also the 'cradle of European civilisation' according to classical ideas and some Greek self-perceptions (Herzfeld 1987). The second is from Latvia, based on research also carried out in the 1990s, as the country became independent from the Soviet Union. Latvia is a country which is seen as even more marginally part of Europe, though is now part of the new expanded Europe – winning the Eurovision song contest in 2002, hosting it in 2003, and joining the European Union in 2004. The third is Berlin, Germany, in the years before and shortly after the coming down of the Wall dividing the two Germanys. This concerns a country and a history closer in many European imaginations – and in European policy-making – to the centre of Europe today.

The everyday life of long histories – Kalymnos, Greece

In *Memories cast in Stone* (1998), David Sutton explores multiple contexts in which history is invoked in everyday life on the Greek Island of Kalymnos. In doing so, he emphasises that islanders may hold different perspectives on historical events and that these events are not even perceived as equally relevant by all islanders. Moreover, individuals may express different perspectives in different contexts. Also posing a challenge for his understanding was the fact that some forms of 'memory' were expressed indirectly, as noted above, through 'casting stones' and use of dynamite rather than through verbal or written accounts. At the same time, however, Sutton was able, on the basis of his lengthy fieldwork, to highlight certain commonalities or recurrent patterns in the way that inhabitants of Kalymnos think about themselves and the past, as well as to analyse when particular kinds of accounts were mobilised.

One common feature of Kalymnian historicising, he explains, is to conceptualise national and global history within the same model as family histories. 'At a local level', he tells us, '"histories" are disputes, quarrels or acts of shame (sexual infidelities, stealing) that alter the normal pattern of life in predictable ways' (1998: 121). While these may alter the course of events, however, 'histories' are also regarded as revealing of underlying character that remains constant over time. For this reason, Kalymnians talk of the 'history' of particular families and interpret current behaviour, and even potential behaviour, in light of the behaviour and character of previous generations. Conceived as familial, history is often emotionally charged. To illustrate this, Sutton describes a man called Manolis who explains the strong feelings he experiences on seeing ancient pots in museums by referring to his feelings about his grandfather. '"My hair stands up on end!"' Manolis exclaims, describing the emotional impact of seeing the pots, and asks the ethnographer to imagine what it would feel like if one's own grandfather had actually made them (1998: 143). The grandfather had no direct relationship with the museum pots but the relationship is conceived of through the analogy – as of the same order and having the same senses of affect and duty attached. The pots, even though they are from a very distant past, are felt by Manolis to be connected to him through the same kind of relationship that he shares with his grandfather.

The same familial model of conceiving relationships with 'heritage' is also applied at national level. Kalymnians are aware, however, that other countries do not necessarily see things in the same way as they do. They complain, for example, that 'Europeans' – a category that they generally invoke as an 'other' – tend to forget history, and fail to read contemporary events in light of their historical, and character-revealing, precedents. Sutton gives an insightful analysis of the Greek support for Serbia during the 1990s Yugoslav wars in this light, showing how Greeks tend to view events within a longer historical time frame than commentators from many other parts of Europe. In addition, they draw on their own historical experiences, and interpretation of those experiences in light of their contemporary marginal position within the European Community, leading them to support Serbians, partly *because* Serbians were being condemned by much of the rest of Europe. He also shows how this dispute and that over Macedonia are interpreted partly through senses of continuity and property manifest in familial practices of inheritance of land and of naming of children. As he explains, these 'local-level practices' create 'a sense of historical connectedness', and, moreover, they naturalise 'the connections between history, property and intergenerational continuity,… making disputes over the past seem inevitable' (1998: 193).

Many aspects of how Kalymnians think about the past – and also their strong feelings about certain aspects of it – can be seen as part of the European memory complex. This includes their invoking of notions of history as property, and as fundamental to identity. It makes sense too in terms of their analogies with family relations. Yet, their own contrasting of how they see things with how the past is conceived elsewhere in 'Europe' – especially in the strength of their feelings about the past and their 'long memories' – also show that there are more specific renditions and variations within that complex. It is also worth noting that they contrast their strong senses of continuity and long temporal perspective even more strongly with North American perspectives on history, noting that Greeks had 1,500 years of civilisation behind them by the time that America was 'discovered'. The US anthropologist, Sutton, does likewise in his efforts, from a country where 'history is toast' (1998: 210), to understand the very tangible connection with a distant past that his subjects describe. While on the one hand critical of the shallow historical consciousness of Americans (and, to a lesser extent, 'Europeans'), Kalymnians also ambivalently regard this as a positive attribute, seeing it as responsible for the prosperity and success of America. Involved here too are different conceptions of what is involved in 'making history'. As Sutton explains, in the US this 'means doing something that has never been done before: setting a record' (1998: 135). By contrast, 'on Kalymnos, history refers to unusual events which can nevertheless be incorporated into a pattern' (1998: 135). This partly accounts for the frequent invoking of analogies between events – of talking of some through the frame of others – that he and other anthropologists of Greece encounter.

Narrating the self and the past – post-Soviet Latvia

Like Kalymnians, the post-Soviet Latvians interviewed by Vieda Skultans in *The Testimony of Lives* (1998) may also invoke long histories and collapse temporally distant times together. One of her interviewees, for example, spoke seamlessly of the fate of a thirteenth-century warrior and the menfolk in her family in an account that drew 'no temporal distinctions between the deaths of husband, brother and son, and the medieval chieftain' (1998: 18). In formulating such accounts, Latvians draw on modes of story-telling that are rooted in what Skultans calls 'European literary traditions' but which are used in specifically Latvian ways. In Latvia, as in most other East European countries, 'the development of a national literature has been particularly associated with the shaping of national identities' (1998: xiii), and has resulted in ways of talking about the past, at an individual as well as a collective level, that employ literary terminology – such as 'destiny' (*liktenis*) or forms of emplotment. Moreover, national literature offers particular plots through which individual accounts may be storied. As she explains: 'The moment people talk about the past they remember it in the way stories are told; they are unable to ignore the conventions of story telling. One such convention is the quest' (1998: 130). The quest positions the teller (usually – or more occasionally some other main character) as having to undergo battles and journeys to achieve their ends, and along the way experiencing 'chance meetings, coincidences and recognitions' (1998: 131). In its post-Socialist Latvian rendition, this narrative is usually a vehicle for stories about overcoming the past repressions of the Soviet era and coming to full recognition of the importance of being Latvian and of the Latvian homeland – return to which, literally or metaphorically, is usually part of the tale (1998: 132).

This does not, however, mean that individuals simply mould what they have to say to fit these narrative 'paradigms' (as she calls them) but, rather, the paradigms 'are actively and selectively enlisted because they help to make sense of the past' (1998: 125). At the same time, '[m]emories of individual suffering derive meaning from their positioning within national history' (1998: 47). While national literature is important to many post-Soviet Latvians in crafting their own self-narratives and understanding the past, written sources are not accorded a greater value than oral accounts and personal memories. This is a legacy of the Soviet period when 'the spoken not the written word was the bearer of truth. ... If history books lie, memory acquires a central importance for the preservation of authenticity and truth as well as a peculiar poignancy' (1998: 28).

Skultans' research was not originally intended to be about the past. A medical anthropologist, her interest was in 'neurasthenia' or 'nervous exhaustion', a category used by Latvian physicians and psychologists. But as she tried to investigate how patients recounted their medical symptoms, she found herself 'pulled ineludibly by people's memories of the past' (1998: xi):

> The past could not be laid to rest and left people little motivation to talk about the present. The brutal and chaotic events following the Second World War did not release their hold on memory... Eventually I let myself be carried by the narrative flow. In this way I found myself listening to accounts of events central to Latvian and, indeed, Soviet history.
>
> (1998: xi)

In listening attentively in this way, she pays attention to variations in ways in which narrators may mobilise the various paradigms. In particular, she notes a difference among older and younger narrators. The former tend to cast their lives 'in a legendary, mythical mode, whereas the lives of younger narrators are told as a sequence of unconnected happenings' (1998: 143), a difference which, as she explains, 'is not merely one of style, but of literary packages which carry social meanings and which position the individual in relation to a culture' (1998: 143). One reason for the difference, she suggests, is the congruence or lack of it between 'public and private scripts' (1998: 142). Older people had attended school during or before independence, were more likely to have been steeped in nationalist literature, and had generally experienced more 'concordance' between the public and the private, and, thus they adopted elements of literary styles which enabled them to configure their own lives as meaningful. For the younger interviewees, however, who were schooled in the Soviet period, 'there was a conflict between the public and the private' (1998: 142), and they were educated instead with texts that 'failed to supply form and structure for personal memories and accounts of lives' (1998: 156). This did not mean that they were unable to articulate their feelings or memories but it did seem to make it more difficult for them to do so. Moreover, it contributes to what Skultans describes as senses of conflict and loss of meaning that are part of the 'neurasthenia' that she set out to investigate.

State and individual historical narrations – the two Berlins

Like Skultans, John Borneman, in his study of Berlin (mainly) before unification, is concerned with the ways in which wider social and cultural experiences can shape individual life histories and their narration, as well as forms of historical consciousness (1992). His historical and ethnographic study considers the state policies and laws concerned with kinship, that is, through which citizenship and the life course were defined in different periods since the 1930s in the two Germanys, with particular emphasis upon family policy, including issues such as child-bearing and bringing up children. He brings this together with accounts by Berliners, primarily from the West. In doing so, Borneman's aim is not to try to suggest that either personal narratives or documented ones are fuller or more accurate than the other. Rather he seeks to look at the structuring of both kinds of 'narratives' in order to understand both the particular tropes that each employ and the ways in which they relate to and diverge from one another. Both play a part in what he calls the 'constitution of meaningful subjects' in the two Berlins.

Borneman analyses state kinship-related policies as a means to understand the ways in which the two German states propose – and in effect try to shape – particular accounts of temporality. In brief, this entails the post-war West struggling to assimilate while simultaneously denouncing the past; and the East configuring itself as the result of a radical break with the past, the full yields of which were still to come. As with the studies by Sutton and Skultans, Borneman acknowledges individual variation and seeks to present a range of perspectives rather than some mythical mean or mode. At the same time, however, like them, he highlights certain patterns, or 'experiential tropes', as he calls them, which shape the construction of state policy and (to varying extents) the narration of life stories in different generations. The point is not to universalise these but to understand their particular historical and social situatedness. For example, he suggests that the gap between state and individual narrations was greater in the German Democratic Republic (especially for his Generation 1 – those born 1910–1935) than in the West. In the latter, individuals more readily recount their own life histories – or more specifically, their accounts of child-bearing and rearing, within a narrative that he calls 'satiric' – that is, concerned with reflecting on the vices of contemporary society and making improvements rather than wholesale transformations (1992: 78). The narrative is also lapsarian – it harks back to ideas about the past and tradition, justifying, for example, certain qualities of motherhood in terms of tradition and religion. This is not, however, just about the continuity of a tradition. Rather, it relates to the contemporary situation of West Berliners. As he explains, this 'lapsarian appeal to tradition, virtue and assimilation into a prosperous community of Germans served for most West Berliners precisely as an antidote to their sense of victimization' (1992: 235). Marooned from the rest of West Germany, West Berliners, before the unexpected fall of the Wall, recounted their own lives primarily through narratives that accepted their own state and anticipated only small-scale changes. The state narrative in the German Democratic Republic, by contrast, was less congruent with the experiences of East Berlin citizens. In this case, the state narrative that shaped family policy was what Borneman characterises as 'romantic' and 'utopian', 'aimed towards a future Communist destiny' (1992: 79). Over time, fewer and fewer East Berliners subscribed to this mode of temporalising, culminating dramatically in the events that brought the state to an end.

The concern of the anthropologists whose work is described here was not just to understand the uses of the past in the present, then, but to analyse how both the past and the present were interpreted through models or forms of consciousness that themselves have histories. This is not to say that the models were themselves unchanging. All examples also describe struggles faced by people to try to accommodate the social changes underway. This could lead to the demise of some forms of historicising, with, perhaps, school or public histories becoming more dominant or, perhaps, what were previously voiced accounts becoming expressed in more indirect ways. It could also result in different periods becoming the focus of attention; and of a phenomenon that often accompanies change – nostalgia for past times.

★ ★ ★

This chapter has introduced some of the forms of past presencing that have been described and discussed by anthropologists of Europe. In particular, it has sought to highlight some of the diverse ways in which the past is conceived, experienced and put to work in different parts of Europe – and as parts of projects to create European history and identity. At the same time, it has attempted – in a pattern that will continue throughout the book – to identify some of the forms of past presencing that we find repeatedly if not necessarily universally or in invariant form. These include trying to define senses of self with reference to the past and through creating traditions for the future; pitting different histories against one another – perhaps regarding a distant past as idyllic; and thinking of 'big' histories (such as those of the nation) through more intimate ones, such as those of family and kinship. Many of the themes highlighted here – such as the mobilisation of different pasts, nostalgia, affect and questions of the authenticity of particular accounts – will be discussed further in subsequent chapters. In the following, however, I extend discussion of modes of narrating history to the 'multitemporal challenge' that past presencing sets for anthropologists.

3

TELLING THE PAST

The multitemporal challenge

> What is memory? Do we hunt it with a questionnaire or are we supposed to use a butterfly net?
>
> James Fentress and Chris Wickham[1]

This chapter looks further at the relationship between history and anthropology in the study of Europe, with a focus on questions of methodology. How should anthropologists investigate a field replete not only with people capable of giving oral testimony but one also filled with documentation and other kinds of evidence of the past – that is with a multiplicity of forms of telling the past? What are the challenges of working with different accounts of the past – and of different modes of historicising?

One development within social and cultural anthropology, introduced in the previous chapter, is an increasingly 'multidirectional' approach to considering the relationships between past and present. This can be seen as a methodological correlate of 'past presencing'. If past presencing is the empirical phenomenon of how people variously experience, understand and produce the past in the present, the challenge for anthropologists is how to approach it. This can be seen as a multitemporal challenge. In this chapter we will look at approaches – some experimental – that seek to explore the potentially multidirectional relationships between pasts and presents; and that investigate the intersection or gaps between individual and various forms of collective memory. This investigation involves more specific methodological challenges too, such as those concerning the status and veracity of different historical tellings; finding ways of hearing 'quiet voices', that is, accounts that do not readily become part of the wider public sphere; and representing multitemporality.

Anthropology and history: towards an entanglement

As noted in the previous chapter, Europe's various anthropological and ethnological traditions have taken a range of approaches to history. In the anthropologies of much of continental Europe, a historical approach has been and often still is taken for granted, with ethnology sometimes regarded as a sub-branch of history, dealing with 'present-day' peasant histories on the brink of disappearing. Across Europe, however, there have been increasingly sophisticated and multi-directional approaches to the past over more recent decades. In Anglophone anthropology, the expansion of ethnographic work in Europe in the 1970s and 1980s came together with, and in part propelled, a growing and sometimes overstated critique of various existing, especially structural-functionalist, conventions. These included synchronism: the tendency to focus on a particular moment in time as though it were an enduring reality. Enshrined also in the ethnographic present (the use of the present tense in ethnographic accounts), synchronism entailed an assumption of stability that was clearly at odds with the emphasis on social change that characterised most social scientific work on Europe.[2] Political economy perspectives also highlighted the need to take macro, as well as micro, structures and transformations into account, and this demanded use of documentary sources beyond those concerning localities themselves. The emergence of questions of identity, belonging and change as key problematics within the anthropology of Europe added to the demand that anthropologists pay attention to history, particularly in the context of 'ethnic resurgence' – a version of what was later to be called 'identity politics' – in which identities and rights were often articulated through claims about the past.

Developments within the discipline of history also encouraged some anthropologists to take a more historical perspective. In addition to the invention of tradition work, discussed in the previous chapter, the fact that historians such as Emmanuel Le Roy Ladurie (e.g. 1979/1975) and Keith Thomas (e.g. 1973/1971) were using and praising the perspectives offered by anthropology, perhaps helped bolster anthropologists' confidence to use historical materials and fostered the development of historical ethnography in particular.[3] Historical ethnography employs anthropological concepts and perspectives to study a period of time in the past, generally focused on a small locality, the archive thus forming the field site (Des Chene 1997: 76). While historians, such as Le Roy Ladurie, have used this approach to construct detailed and essentially synchronic accounts of past times, anthropologists have more often taken larger time periods and undertaken historical ethnography also in order to highlight transformation, change and degrees of continuity (Silverman and Gulliver 1992: 17). On the whole, these anthropological studies have been unidirectional in the sense that they take a stretch of time and show forward-plotted change. In some of its most sophisticated hands, however, such as those of Kirsten Hastrup in her work on Iceland (1985, 1990, 1992a), the ways in which conceptions of history and time themselves play into historical change are part of the account.

As anthropologists of Europe also came to tackle topics such as national and regional identities, as well as more local ones, they faced a wide range of available materials – including numerous written histories that might be brought to bear on localities and topic. There were also typically ample historical records available at local levels in archives, local history societies, libraries and museums, many local areas of Europe having their own strong historiographic traditions (Silverman and Gulliver 1992: 3). Increasingly this also involves kinship-based histories that are part of searches for family ancestors – 'roots tourism' (Basu 2007), 'ancestral tourism' (Darieva 2011), 'popular genealogy' (Cannell 2011), or 'family-treeing' as those in a Northern English town studied by Jeanette Edwards call it (Edwards 2010, 2012). Sometimes this is strongly linked with identification of particular places as 'homelands' of certain surnames; and these can become the centre for 'roots tourism' as Paul Basu (2007) has discussed in his work on diaspora visiting of the Scottish Highlands, or as occurs in 'ancestral tourism' as Tsympylma Darieva (2011) writes of US Armenians returning to Armenia. All of this has provided not simply large amounts of potential historical evidence but has raised questions about the status of different sources and how to bring these together with each other and with other kinds of ethnographic data.

Multitemporal approaches

While a focus on present uses of the past was an important corrective to the previous temporal directionality which had tended to regard the past teleologically as leading inexorably to, and shaping, the present ('culminatory history' as Davis has called it, 1992: 16), there was a risk that this would simply replace one form of unidirectionality with another – in the opposite direction. This was 'presentism' (e.g. Peel 1989). By working uni-directionally from the present, a 'presentist' perspective was only concerned with the past that was being consciously used in the present day. 'The past', therefore, tended to be depicted as something largely 'made up' in the present, with the emphasis especially on the manipulation of history. What it ignored was both the intrinsic interest of the past – and the possible contribution of anthropology to understanding this – and less overt or self-conscious relationships between past and present. Some ethnographic work, as discussed in the previous chapter, tried to move beyond this by looking both at appropriations and recastings of history. In my work on the Scottish Hebrides I borrowed the notion of the past 'sourcing' the present from the philosopher Charles Taylor (1989) to capture this idea, and to explain how the past might shape the present in ways of which present-day actors were relatively unaware (Macdonald 1997). By trying to look simultaneously at the ways in which the past was multiply encoded, recorded and transmitted at different points in time, as well as at the various ways in which the past could inform the present, and the present use the past, anthropological work offered multidirectional possibilities which went further than 'history' as generally performed by historians, or than 'historical ethnography' or the 'anthropology of history' as normally conceived.[4]

A multitemporal approach, then, is not only about how the past is referred to in the present. The following are all dimensions that can be taken into account:

(a)   Ways in which events, persons or whatever, were perceived and experienced at the time.
(b)   Ways in which events or experiences were encoded at the time; i.e. how they were materialised or documented. Both a and b may also involve attention to historiography – that is, to the ways historians may have perceived and recorded events; and to notions of time and change (including perceptions of past, present and future).
(c)   Ways in which past traces survive over time, including attention to why these and not others may endure and to the structuring of historical evidence (as text, trace, material, verbal account and so forth) at different moments in time.
(d)   Ways in which past events and experiences are perceived, experienced, used and recast today, including the notions of time, change, identity etc that are implicated.[5]

This schema, based upon that developed by Edwin Ardener (1989), is, perhaps inevitably, a little crude but it is intended as a useful point of reference in order to develop a multitemporal practice, and to move beyond a purely documentary approach to find ways of dealing with and theorising various kinds of 'past presences'.

The term 'multitemporal' alludes to George Marcus's advocacy of what he calls 'multisited fieldwork' – conducting fieldwork framed not by place but by 'following' particular actors, ideas or processes into multiple locations; an approach that has been highly influential in anthropology since it was propounded in the mid-1990s.[6] Multisited fieldwork offers the potential to unsettle not only assumptions of bounded units of study but also easy moral and political affiliations; and it can highlight links and movement that are typically obscured by a single site focus. More generally, multisited fieldwork provides ethnographers with a more mobile and plural set of viewpoints from which to try to depict a world of partial connections, flows, and boundary crossings.

Multitemporal 'fieldwork' is anthropological research that considers a range of time frames in its attempts to follow particular ideas, actors and processes. It can be considered a particular type of multisited fieldwork, similarly unsettling assumptions of boundedness – temporal in this case – by highlighting movement over time. Like multisited fieldwork, it can unsettle the certitude of any one site or period by showing it in relation to partially connected others, which is also a useful relativising strategy, and, as such, perhaps especially valuable to anthropologists working in familiar contexts. If, as Bernard Cohn has argued, a temporal perspective helps avoid objectifying culture by showing it in transformation (1990: 43), a multitemporal perspective does so even more effectively. Like the multilocale imaginary, the multitemporal also helps us to better access and depict a world in which multidirectional movement seems to be increasingly complex. Thus, narratives of the traditional simply being replaced by the modern don't work when we need to take into account not only possible tradition invention but also self-aware nostalgia, retro-fashioning, alternative traditionalities, memory work, and multiple ways of being modern, some of which involve being traditional in new, or even old, ways.[7]

Field and archive

To use the term 'fieldwork' in relation to historical materials is to deploy the term loosely and perhaps is not fully justified. It is nevertheless worth reflecting on some of the similarities with ethnographic research with contemporary subjects. These include the delving into another life-world, an archaeological sensibility of 'digging into' the past and piecing together fragments of experience, and 'following clues' as the eminent Frankfurt anthropologist Ina Maria Greverus puts it (2002), echoing Carlo Ginzburg's (1980) description of pursuing clues in historical research. Importantly, it also involves dealing with materials that can 'speak back', upsetting our presuppositions. There are also experiential parallels. In *Dust,* historian Carolyn Steedman has written evocatively of the experience of working with archives in ways that are surely familiar to ethnographic fieldworkers – the anxiety of knowing 'I shall never *get it done'* (2001: 18), there always being that other file to check, the periods of boredom, the sometimes uncomfortably voyeuristic sense of glimpsing into other lives, and the exhilaration over discovered details that would seem of such little consequence to others. She writes too of accompanying physical dimensions of archive work that resonate with those of the field: the lying awake in 'the bed of the cheap hotel ... [amidst] the dust of others, and of other times' (2001: 17), the exhaustion of bus journeys, routes that become routine, the smells of the papers and places. Her observations show that historians, like ethnographers, also fetishise 'being there' (as Geertz famously put it, 1989; Steedman 2001: 70), even if they do not, perhaps, do so quite so much or in quite the same ways.

Working with historical materials – which may or may not form 'an archive' – is not, however, entirely like working with living subjects, though the experience of both, of course, can be extremely varied. While historical material – in the form of documentary records or material culture – undoubtedly has the capacity to surprise, to redirect the ethnographer's gaze or to be blankly obstinate, the nature of interaction is in general less mutually interactive. The historian is not usually the subject of their materials' gaze in the same way as is the case for the fieldworker. Reflecting on this, Mary Des Chene suggests that using historical materials is more like 'overhearing' than it is like 'conversation' and explains:

it is from conversations among engaged and positioned subjects that one conjures answers to one's queries. The materials of the archives are a lacunary deposit from records of the past. Of what is missing, one only sometimes knows that it is missing at all. One may 'ask new questions' of documents, or discover a document that answers one's query. But one cannot ask that the archives fill silences or that they comment on the fact of silence itself.

(1997: 77)

Learning how to effectively 'overhear' documents, how to place them in relation to one another so that some help shed light on the silences – and possible motives for the silences – of others, is a skill that the historical ethnographer must acquire. Context must be generated from text, a process that Bernard Cohn suggests occurs simultaneously, and perhaps without its practitioners being fully aware of it, in ethnographic fieldwork (1990: 48).

Using multiple kinds of documents – such as official reports, newspapers, diaries, letters, novels – requires sensitivity to medium and genre; and so too does the use of other kinds of traces of the past – material objects and buildings, photographs and film, music and art.[8] Moreover, as Des Chene points out, the use of historical materials raises the same questions about locale, and how far to spread the net or follow connections, as does an ethnography of the present (1997: 73). If anthropology has traditionally focused upon small-scale locales, historians have more often taken the nation-state as their frame; though it is worth noting that international history provides a basis for work that does not constrain itself to single locales, even if it usually operates with a model of nation-states as relatively autonomous players. Increasingly, historians too use alternative frames, including the small-scale, such the village or estate. One 'locale' that has 'attracted the attention of entire battalions of historians in the past twenty-five years', according to Jay Winter, is the 'site of memory', which he defines as 'physical sites where commemorative acts take place' (2009: 252), such as battlefields. Such sites attract for their moral significance as 'topoi with a life-history' but also because they allow for attention to commemorative practices, as well as archival work, that draw in 'the local, national, and transnational' (2009: 252).

All historical materials inevitably incorporate an interplay of pasts and presents: there is the present of their original production in the past, the past-presents in which they survived over time, the pasts to which they refer and which they may reconstruct, and the present in which they now live. Anthropologists will usually work at least partly with some present-day accounts of the past – oral histories of some form. As we saw in the previous chapter, these might be presented in relatively storied form, perhaps already looking like historical narrative or heroic quest, or they might be more fragmentary, overheard in snippets and sotto voce remarks. Both despite, and also to some extent because of, the fact that oral history opens up the possibility of direct questioning by the researcher it poses particular methodological problems, including those of relationships between the researcher and interviewee, and over issues of veracity and representation.[9] Writing of historians' use of oral history, Tony Kushner claims that it was initially used to provide what was perceived to be unproblematic reporting, with 'no need for an "anthropological gap" – the self-doubt and awareness of what could not be grasped by the participant-observer that has characterised the discipline of anthropology since 1945' (2006: 282). Growing awareness of the fact that oral histories were shaped through narrative conventions and that matters such as presumed preferences of the listener could shape them, led some historians to dismiss them as inherently unreliable (ibid.). Oral history was, in this view, 'mere memory' and, as such, not the realm of 'proper history'. But, as he notes, what has since developed is a more sophisticated understanding of oral history that recognises and seeks to also explore the ways in which these are structured in order to understand the shaping motivations and representational genres, as well as to gain a fuller understanding of the subject both in the past and the present.

Shaping memories

Questions about oral histories have been especially fraught in relation to World War II and the Holocaust.[10] The following three cases illustrate well some of the issues raised and collectively illuminate the complexities of conducting research in this field. Each example is from a different discipline in turn – history, anthropology and social psychology respectively; and all are exemplary in their sensitivity. While the three cases demonstrate some differences of approach, collectively they also show common concerns and the potential for multidisciplinary approaches.

The past in hiding

Historian Mark Roseman's *The Past in Hiding* (2000) insightfully reveals dilemmas involved in Holocaust testimony. The book recounts his research, beginning in 1989, with Marianne Ellenbogen, a Jewish woman who had escaped the Gestapo in 1943. The research was initially based on face-to-face interviews; then, after Ellenbogen's death in 1996, Roseman continued to work through her substantial collection of papers (of which he was largely unaware at the time of the interviews), to contact some of those who knew her and to generally follow through the threads that the interviews and other sources raised. What this made evident was that her account was not simply a reflection on her own experience but that she 'had subtly changed some incidents, forgotten others or "appropriated" memories that in fact belonged to other people' (2000: 13). He does not conclude, however, that this renders her testimony unreliable but instead tries to understand how and why she shaped it as she did. He found, for example, that 'The most striking and consistent pattern was the reworking or obscuring of episodes of separation and loss' (2000: 477). The changes were often subtle – such as altering the route by which she escaped the Gestapo. These could sometimes slightly alter the degree of agency or possibilities available – for example, making it possible that her brother might also have managed to escape. But for the most part, what was involved, he surmises, was a 'defusion' of

> traumatic and guilt-ridden partings by amending them ...The important thing was to impose some mastery on the moments that caused such pain ... The stories had gently been changed into metaphors. As 'parables' of her and her family's fate they were slightly more bearable.
>
> (2000: 477–8)

It is as though the act of turning them into some kind of story itself helped her to narrate them; and at the same time, perhaps, it also helped her to keep at bay the memories that she did not want to address – the 'past in hiding' (like the vast cache of documents in the garage) of Roseman's title. This insight into a probably unconscious motivation for the storying of traumatic memory may also help shed light on a phenomenon recorded by other scholars, namely, the structuring of Holocaust memoirs through powerful existing narrative genres.[11]

Creative recollection of Tuscan trauma

Francesca Cappelletto's ethnographic research on memories of World War II massacres in Tuscan villages provides insight into the collective shaping of narratives and 'adoption' as memory of events experienced by others (2003, 2005). In the villages where she worked, brutal killings – carried out by German Nazis and Italian Fascist partisans in 1944 – were still being described by villagers more than half a century after they occurred.[12] The tellings were both by those who had witnessed the events as children and also people who had not been born at the time. The memories were maintained partly through dedicated commemorative events, especially on annual anniversaries of the murders (2005: 108). The repeated telling of the stories – with different individuals contributing to the accounts – gives them what she calls a 'choral quality' (2005: 121).

What sustains them too is the 'emotional density' of the trauma described (2005: 117). This in turn is linked to the strong and detailed visual imagery of the massacres themselves – of houses being burned, of horrible bodily suffering. In the communal tellings – as well as in more private ones – the massacres are graphically described, with the narrator visibly emotionally affected. One consequence of this is that listeners enter the experience of the teller:

> The repeated evocation of visual pictures prepares the listener, including those who were not eyewitnesses, to relive a narrated event as if he had actually experienced it. It is as if the story 'stays with' the listener and makes him suffer, as one woman ... said, because the strong visual imagery

> has such a strong visceral content ... In descriptions of episodes, the past perceptual experience of some individual, a sort of sensory memory, is communicated and reified in a 'text'.
>
> (2005: 118)

When people recall events that they did not live through as though they had been there, this is not, Cappelletto argues, some kind of questionable appropriation. Rather, it is because the memories have become part of communal identity and a 'felt' history that villagers share: 'Other people's stories are internalized and re-lived ... This is a "creative", but not fictive, aspect of one's memory' (2005: 124). Indeed, she also suggests that the collective nature of the process of sharing memories has helped to ensure their veracity: 'the description of events, put together like stone chips in a mosaic, seems to have been minutely sifted and subject to careful examination by the group' (2005: 107).

Contributing to the sense of a shared experienced past is also the fact that villagers feel that theirs is a history that the outside world has insufficiently acknowledged and that is at risk of misrepresentation by outsiders. They thus have a sense of collective ownership of it, which also legitimates their telling of stories that they regard as their own even if they did not see them with their own eyes. Both the sense of continuity with the past experience and of ownership are also mediated by place. Villagers live with visible reminders of the past – the church where people were killed, houses that were burnt out, woods to which people fled. These are, in effect, mnemonics – inscribed by past events – in the landscape.

Grandpa wasn't a Nazi

The work by Roseman and Cappelletto both concern what can be called survivor or victim memories. To some extent these have come to be a genre, with their own narrative conventions, conveyed through media and throughout Europe, even if they may vary locally.[13] Perpetrator narratives are less commonly recounted and in many ways are more problematic. This is evident in research conducted in Germany by social psychologist Harald Welzer and colleagues.[14] This research also provides a striking example of how narratives may change over generations. Interested in the way in which accounts of activity during the Third Reich were transmitted within families, Welzer's team conducted interviews across three generations: (1) grandparents who were adults during the early 1940s; (2) their children – the parent generation; and (3) grandchildren. What they found was a transformation over the generations such that grandchildren's accounts of their grandparents played down or eliminated any pro-Nazi activities and sympathies. Instead, they recounted instances of resistance – sometimes constructing these from scant or even contrary evidence in a process that Welzer and colleagues call 'cumulative heroization'. For example, their interviews include a recollection by a grandmother who gleefully describes how she prevented Jews and Russians (who were displaced persons wandering the countryside in the immediate period after the war) from staying on her farm. At one point, she says, she found a Jew hiding in a barrel and turfed him out. In her grandchild's narrative, the incident is related as the grandmother hiding a Jew during the war in order to protect him from the Nazis. In another case given by Welzer *et al.*, a dead grandfather, who was almost certainly unsettled by his experiences of having shot a child during the war, is transformed by the grandchild generation into a hero who shot the officer who had shot children. Welzer and his team also showed how, when asked to repeat a narrative that the researchers had prepared, respondents tended to omit parts of the narrative that did not fit their expectations or revise them to fit stereotypes about how particular people (e.g. Russians) would behave. Furthermore, the researchers' accompanying large-scale survey, asking about the activities of grandparents and parents during the war, showed considerably lower responses acknowledging grandparents or parents as having been sympathetic to or involved in Nazism, and considerably higher levels of reported resistance, than accords with other historical sources. Their book reporting on this cross-generational restructuring of memory sums up the main tendency in its title, *Opa war kein Nazi* (*Grandpa wasn't a Nazi*).

All of these three examples highlight themes that are likely to be found in other contexts too – if in less marked form. The tendency to turn grandparents into heroes, for example, may be widespread, as is imbuing landscapes with mnemonic significance, recounting events in ways that fit preconceptions and stereotypes, and indeed the very 'storying' of pasts and lives. All of the authors draw on a range of sources in addition to individual oral histories. These include the use of documents by all three, collective interviews and participant-observation by Cappelletto, and the survey by Welzer. In all of the different disciplinary examples here, the mixing of sources is not conducted in a positivist triangulation spirit of corroborating the true and eliminating the false – though the latter is important in relation to the Holocaust especially, in a world containing Holocaust denial. The researchers' primary interest, however, is to show what particular accounts – individual and collective – reveal about people's understandings of themselves and the ways in which they invoke the past. Through different sources they are able to identify effects of genre, positioning and framing. While for many historians, though not those such as Roseman, the interest in genre, positioning and framing is mostly directed at better figuring out 'what happened', anthropologists, and social psychologists like Welzer, are more often interested in these frames and so forth in themselves, as instances of possible modes of experiencing and telling.

Quiet voices

One of the most important questions raised by the concerns above, and one of the most important concerns more generally for anthropologists, is what we might call the 'audibility' of accounts. Neither all voices, nor all accounts, are encoded in forms which are equally likely to be heard by others. The 'reach' of some genres and media – and thus of some people's utterances – is greater than others. One motive for carrying out ethnographic fieldwork – for spending a considerable period of time looking, listening and learning *in situ* – is to try to come to be able to hear and understand those who do not easily, for one reason or another, get their voices heard.

Mutedness

A classical anthropological articulation of the relativities of audibility is Edwin and Shirley Ardener's discussion of 'mutedness' (E. Ardener 1975, 1975a; S. Ardener 1975). Originally discussed in relation to gender relations among the Bakweri of Cameroon, the Ardeners sought to alert anthropologists to the danger of accepting men's descriptions of the nature of Bakweri social relations as *the* Bakweri account. This was likely to occur, they pointed out, because men's forms of expression were more likely to conform to the ways in which Westerners expected to find matters expressed than did women's. Bakweri women, unlike the men, did not typically provide narrative verbal accounts. Nevertheless, the Ardeners argued that women did express themselves but through symbolic action; and, moreover, that when they did so they expressed a different version of social reality from that articulated by men. In particular, women's rituals showed, according to the Ardeners' analysis, women to be critical of the male authority that Bakweri men seemed to assume women to completely accept. In women's ritual, however, men were symbolically associated with rats and the phallic edible plantain banana was jettisoned in favour of the feminised 'inedible, seed-filled, wild banana' (E. Ardener 1975: 12). Because of the non-verbal, and inherently more ambiguous, form of symbolic expression, men could ignore this alternative account – and so, unwittingly, might researchers.

In the Ardeners' formulation, Bakweri women are relatively 'muted'. This does not mean that they do not speak, neither that they do not express themselves. Rather, the form in which they do so is less likely to be heard on a wider stage, and, also significantly, is also less likely to be heard by those carrying out research. While the Ardeners' initial example concerned gendered differences, they point out that many groups are likely to be 'muted' to varying degrees, and that men are neither necessarily 'audible' nor women 'muted'. All kinds of other factors may also be involved – class, ethnicity, occupation – and to varying degrees in different contexts.

Although the Ardeners' example here concerned West Africa, the difficulty of hearing 'quiet voices' that they identify is a more general one, and one faced equally by anthropologists in Europe. Within Europe, those whose voices are likely to be less audible include many minorities and even majorities: in some situations perhaps almost all of those who sit in the classrooms where history textbooks are being used will not be hearing accounts that they feel are their own. Numerous examples in this book highlight quieter accounts that are not typically recognised in the public domain but that are part of the quieter diversity of Europe.

Questions raised by a concern with quiet voices in relation to history include whether certain 'key events' will be regarded differently or even registered as relevant at all. Which pasts and histories matter – and which do not – and how, if at all, are they related to one another? Is history conceived of as culminatory, unique, repetitive, progressive or regressive? Are collective memories of different groups conceived of as battling for mutually exclusive presence in the public domain? How do understandings of the past relate to the present and to the future? And how is the past used, performed and embedded in everyday life?

Methodological approaches

Addressing these questions requires further attention to method. Any researcher inevitably begins with assumptions that frame the questions that they ask. Difficulties arise, however, when there is little space in the research methodology for recognising and addressing this. Questionnaires and closed-format interviews can undoubtedly be useful in research – not least as a legitimated format for asking questions – but in themselves are relatively inflexible and may trigger certain kinds of response. In my research in the Scottish Hebrides I carried out a semi-structured questionnaire as part of my research. This began with questions about place of birth, and places of birth and habitation of parents and grandparents. For a number of respondents, and especially those whom I interviewed in Gaelic, this triggered a remark to the effect: 'Ah, so you want my life story then?' Such respondents were well able to recount their lives in this form that has come to be a dominant way in which inhabitants of late modernity conceptualise our selves;[15] and more specifically in a form which was very commonly used on Gaelic radio to which most of my Gaelic-speaking interviewees listened. That this genre was so resonant, especially for Gaelic-speakers, was itself of interest, of course. This conventionalised genre was also, however, liable to be associated with certain conventionalised constructions of content, and these could differ from what I learnt in other contexts. For example, one woman told me when I recorded her 'life story' on tape that she spoke Gaelic at home with her daughters. Because I knew her well, and she had told me at other times that she rarely spoke Gaelic at home and because this was what I had witnessed myself, I expressed surprise. This clearly disconcerted her and she was unsure how to reply, for she had been giving me the kind of account that I should surely want – a story, as might be heard on the Gaelic radio, that expressed her deep affinity to the Gaelic language. That affinity was not to be doubted but my clumsy questioning was expressed in the wrong register and made her unclear about the kind of performance or event in which she was engaged. Were I to have relied only on such interviews, my overall understanding would have undoubtedly been more partial than it was. But contextualised within a broader frame of research it also made me aware of the genre-effect of certain kinds of interviews, which included potential for performing an emotional attachment to language. The 'life story' was also an opportunity to express one's love of the Gaelic language and way of life. What was needed, then, was to find an approach in which the relatively audible form of the taped interview did not wholly obscure the quieter versions of reality expressed in everyday practice and conversation.

In trying to access quiet modes, researchers need to understand the relationship between utterances and context. Again, in my work in the Scottish Hebrides, accounts familiar from the popular media tended to be recounted if individuals were asked specifically about 'history'. In the course of more everyday interaction, however, other kinds of accounts of the past would emerge. In popular accounts, for example, the idea of 'the people' and 'community' would be emphasised, depicting Hebridean 'crofters' as a single group united against landlords. This kind of account could also be employed to articulate opposition more generally to interference from outside organisations – past and present. In other contexts, however, stories of past fission within 'the community' would be told, highlighting the fact that sentiments and goals were not necessarily shared. Such stories were nearly always mobilised in relation to disagreements in the present, and especially in order to indicate particular groups (e.g. certain churches or families) as not sharing a common project and therefore not able to speak 'on behalf of the community'.

An implication of studies such as this is that to hear quiet voices, research needs to take place within everyday practice rather than only through more actively interventionist, and inevitably more predetermined, techniques such as interviews. Such work also indicates the interweaving of past and present, highlighting the fact that 'history' is not necessarily restricted to discussion of 'the past'. Indeed, sometimes what matters most to people about 'the past' is encoded in talking about other things. Anthropologist Wendy James has written of how when she was trying to understand the history of the Uduk people (of the Sudan-Ethiopia borderlands) she was initially frustrated that they would keep interrupting the historical narrative that she was trying to piece together and would tell anecdotes about what seemed to be irrelevant matters (1979: 60; see also Hoskins 1998, discussed in Chapter 6). Later, however, as she worked longer with the Uduk, she came to understand the relevance of these anecdotes to their understanding of history, and importantly to their sense of the continuing relevance of this past. Likewise, history may intrude where it was not initially expected, as we saw with research on illness by medical anthropologist Vieda Skultans in the previous chapter. It may be expressed in ways or in modes that do not 'sound' like history, and perhaps not narrated verbally at all.

Non-narrated memory

The past might, for example, be performed through practices of restitution of property (see Chapter 4); restoration (or not) of buildings (e.g. Herzfeld 1991, 2009;

Hodges 2009); through rituals – such as 'mumming' in Bulgaria (Creed 2011), dawn bell-ringing in Andalucia (Driessen 1992), visits to family graves in Istria (Frykman 2004) or the forms taken of weddings of Italian migrants in Britain (Fortier 2000). It might be expressed through comments about the body's aches and pains and the problems of not having a pension, as Tomasz Rakowski describes in an industrial Polish town (2002) or views on whether or not 'finching, a sport played almost exclusively in Flanders, [in which] male finches are made to compete for the highest number of bird calls in an hour' should be banned (Ceuppens 2011: 165). History may also be commented on indirectly – being told, perhaps, through other historical periods or events, as we also saw in the previous chapter. There might be an emphasis on some kinds of past to the exclusion of others – as Jaro Stacul (2005) argues for the Italian Alpine valley in which he worked, where World War II was never mentioned, his informants saying that it did not occur in their locality, and instead mainly recounting 'repetitive' pasts associated with nature. This serves, he argues, to 'give historical foundations to the widely shared view that [the valley] is different' (2005: 825) and to depict the past – in contrast to the present – as stable (2005: 828).

Certain histories may only be revealed to very close acquaintances, in 'trusted, private encounters' (2010: 102), as Stephanie Schwander-Sievers writes of certain positive memories of the Tito-regime by Albanians; or as Elsa Peralta discusses of recollections of social difference and hardship involved in cod-fishing during Portugal's Salazar regime (2009). Or perhaps they might only be revealed at key-life moments, after long acquaintance, as in the death-bed testimony, revealing a 'Slavic' rather than 'Pure Greek' identity, as told to Anastasia Karakisidou, in research described in the previous chapter.

It may also be the case that some memories are too traumatic to express in words but that the silence that surrounds them itself expresses the depth of emotional response. This was the case, for example, for some of Anselma Gallinat's respondents (2006, 2009). Former political prisoners of the East German Stasi regime, many of her respondents felt marginalised in everyday life in a context marked by a reluctance to dwell on that past or a tendency to do so in nostalgic terms. Being interviewed by her was for many of her respondents a novel and sometimes uncomfortable – and sometimes liberating – occasion for talking in ways that they did not normally do. There was, however, much that they found difficult to articulate and about which they said little. As she writes, however: 'it appeared to me that those passages which used the fewest words were actually very telling in their silence' (2006: 354). Of a former prisoner called Herr Jone, for example, she recounts the following about his response to her question to tell her about his time in a notorious jail in Halle:

'The time in prison? Well, you can imagine that' and [he] paused. This small insertion conveyed more than an elaborate monologue could have expressed. From his silence and the expression on his face, I fathomed

that Herr Jone lacked the words and the emotional power to describe in a
structured and directed text what this time had been like for him.

(2006: 354–5)

Gallinat believes, however, that she is able to 'feel' and 'fill' the unsaid – the
'heavy silence' – not only by interpreting his facial expression but also because
of her knowledge of the 'dehumanising conditions and degrading treatment'
(2006: 355) that she has learnt from others, including those who worked in the
prisons, and from literature.

No memory or commemoration? Roma

These 'quiet' modes of expression could not have been readily accessed through
relatively noisy, or quick, methodologies such as questionnaires. Researchers
bring considerable resources of wider knowledge as well as sensitive and self-
reflexive interpersonal relationships to their investigations. But are there people
who do not narrate – or possibly do not even remember – their pasts at all? As
Michael Stewart (2004) discusses, this is a claim that has been made by some
who have studied Roma. In his own long-term ethnographic fieldwork among
Hungarian Roma, he too found that the past was neither commemorated in any
ceremonies nor recounted through narratives; and he sums up as follows:

> it is clear that Romany peoples lack many of the mnemonic devices which
> ground shared memories of European societies. The built environment
> in which they live … is so temporary that it hardly bears a trace of the
> past …This is a world without nostalgia, inhabited by people who seem
> to 'celebrate impermanence' (Kaprow 1982). The institutional practices,
> calendrical rituals, for instance, by which others reproduce the past in the
> present, are almost totally absent.

(2004: 566)

For some scholars, such as Isobel Fonseca (1995), he writes, the lack of explicit
mention of this past, especially of Roma Holocaust, is part of a problematic
forgetting that should be rectified by a 'recovery of memory' that 'will be an
act of cultural empowerment, and hence the route to cultural self-discovery'
(Stewart 2004: 573). His own argument, however, is that despite the lack of
conventional commemorative forms, Roma do not wholly forget their past; but
that their particular relationship to it – including a resistance to chronological
narrative and the materialisation of memory – are part of the way that they
form their own sense of identity. In his fieldwork he found that although
Roma did not talk about explicitly about the past, they did nevertheless make
references to it in singular moments – short references to a particular event.
This was usually triggered by an analogy with the present, as when, referring
to the rise of neo-Nazi threat in late 1980s Hungary, they use phrases used for

the Roma Holocaust (2004: 565). More often, though, he argues, the past is recalled *implicitly* through Roma dealings with others, especially those they refer to as *gazé* (non-Gypsies), particularly through experiences that bear continuities with the past, such as continued experience of repression and humiliation (2004: 576). Rather than fashion these events into a chronological narrative, they become part of a 'continuous present' (2004: 573) in which their identity is maintained through continual opposition to *gazé*. What is involved here, he suggests, is 'memory' not as an identity-defining possession but as distributed through social relations – including through those who they self-define against (2004: 574). Perhaps part of the problem here is the term 'memory', which usually refers to some kind of explicit recollection. In the terms of this book, Roma past presencing is dissimilar to that of the European memory complex but not because they 'have no memory', in Stewart's terms, but, rather, because of the alternative way that they conceptualise the relationship between past, present and identity.

Repertoires of past presencing

'Quieter' accounts are a useful caution to generalisations we otherwise might make, sometimes highlighting how different from 'dominant' historical representations, historical consciousness 'on the ground' may be. They can help us to understand not only the kinds of historical themes and events which engage local populations but also the variety of everyday structures of historical narration (or non-narration) and awareness.

At the same time, there are patterns that we find repeatedly, though rarely universally within Europe, as part of a repertoire of possibilities sourced by partially shared histories. The development of nation-states in Europe, the models of identity implicated and the consequences of this are undoubtedly crucially important to understanding certain aspects or formations of historical consciousness within Europe. So too are partially shared literary forms, religious motifs and kinship formations. It is notable, for example, that many ethnographic studies of communities within Europe describe a *local* concern with 'the nation'. However, rather than this just being a matter of national issues being talked about locally, what this work shows is how even topics like *national* identity are recast and expressed in *local* idioms. In other words, this is how the nation is *done* in Europe. The nation, then, may be conceptualised within local (or regional) notions of kinship, personhood or home. Shared nationhood may, for example, be expressed through terms such as brotherhood, the Fatherland or Motherland, something that typically naturalises it, though whether the nation is conceptualised as a father or mother may be reflective of a partially different set of duties and expectations, and precisely what is entailed may vary. In a discussion of notions of kinship and personhood in conceptualisations of the nation and politics in Greece, Michael Herzfeld tells us that '[n]ot only are national and international conflicts often perceived in terms of agonistic interpersonal relations (e.g., 'the *eghoismos* of the prime ministers') but the very notion of the nation is often expressed as *yenos* (patriline)' (1992: 67). By contrast, Czech notions of nationalism involve metaphors of kinship that do *not* explicitly involve ancestry or agonistic ideas – something that is very important to their sense of having a non-aggressive way of being nationalist. As Ladislav Holy writes:

> The concept of home enables the Czechs not only to imagine the nation as a family writ large but to imagine it as such without talking about it as sharing blood and soil or as a community of people linked together through common ancestry.
>
> (1998: 129)

At one level, then, anthropological work on Europe has shown that there is more variety within Europe, and even within nation-states, than is commonly assumed. At the same time, however, because of shared historical experiences there are certain areas of contestation that are found in study after study. These historical experiences include modernisation, industrialisation and nation-state building and the associated development of 'centres' and 'peripheries', of state agencies and bureaucracies, and of common transformations in the social structure (especially increased social mobility and numbers of 'incomers') of many localities. What we also see is that in the business of trying to comprehend and deal with these transformations, 'the past', or various pasts, are often invoked. Thinking historically seems from most of the accounts to be something that 'Europeans' do; and there are similarities as well as differences among them in the *ways* that they do this. For example, we find in many accounts a dualistic pitting of 'past' against 'present', together with an exaggerated 'golden age', 'pastoral idyll' or 'dark abyss' vision of that past; we find examples of past solidarity often being used as an exemplar for the present, perhaps with more complicating details 'forgotten'; and we find 'life stories' to be an increasingly common form of historical narration. At the same time, however, there are differences in the historical 'depth' of past-present contrasts – as between the 'long memories' of the Greeks and the episodic ones of the Roma, for example; differences in the kinds of collectives for which examples of solidarity are mobilised; and different kinds of emphases in the way in which lives are narrated.

Many of these modes of historicising are not, of course, restricted to Europe; and increasingly we see models for how to represent the past travelling internationally. Literary scholar Michael Rothberg's recent characterisation of 'multidirectional memory' draws attention to this, with particular reference to current attempts to commemorate slave history being enacted in part through models that were established for Holocaust remembrance (2009). As he argues, we need to consider 'memory as *multidirectional*: as subject to ongoing negotiation, cross-referencing, and borrowing; as productive not privative' (2009: 3). By the latter, he is addressing what he regards as a particular problem in contemporary public memory – its 'competitive' nature. That is, the ways in which different groups battle for representation in the public sphere, fearing that their histories will be blocked out by those of others. In a normative argument, he hopes to persuade that rather than these existing in a 'zero-sum game' they are stronger in concert, precisely because they can borrow from each other. From an anthropological perspective, what his discussion also highlights is the strength of proprietorial models of memory, and understandings of distinctive identities being bound up with discrete histories, that shore up the memory competition that he identifies.

No cheese, no heritage

Identities are not, however, necessarily articulated through the idea of a distinct 'heritage' of this kind. The work of Paola Filippucci in the rural Argonne region of France shows this well. In this region, which has repeatedly seen major devastation, especially during World War I, it is common for local people to make comments such as '"Here we have no old stones", and "We are not rooted"' (2004: 72). So strong is their sense that they are different from parts of France that *do* 'have heritage' that they state their deficit with reference to a key marker of French distinctiveness: '"In the Argonne, there is not even a cheese"' (2004: 72). Her argument, however, is that although local people do not have a *patrimoine* (a cultural heritage) in the standard form promoted by cultural policy agencies, they do nevertheless express senses of attachment to place – in which, moreover, the past figures. Rather than evoking a linear 'inward-looking' history that supports a coherent bounded community, as Filippucci argues is expected by cultural heritage agencies, Argonne people instead emphasise the disruptions in their past, the lack of continuities and roots that this causes and the fact that people move in and out of the area. This can be said to form part of their sense of a distinctive identity. It is, moreover, held together by place – as a kind of node – even if actual spatial presence is transitory (see also Filippucci 2004a and 2010).

An initiative by a government department to restore a village cemetery and turn it into a statue park in order to give the villagers '"a bit of identity" (*un peu d'identité*)' (2004: 75), shows well some of the different ideas held by officials and locals. Against the official stipulation that the grave-stones themselves should not be restored but instead left with their patina of age – as part of a generalised positive valuation of what looked old – villagers cleaned and mended stones enthusiastically, effectively making them part of the contemporary landscape rather than of a discrete past. Involved here, as manifest also in how they talked about names on headstones as they worked, was making the past and the place part of 'ongoing history'. This history was conceptualised, however, not as necessarily integrated and continuous but also as containing 'moments of fragmentation and loss, absence as well as presence, returns and departures and … the pull of other places as well as the attachment to this one' (2004: 82).

FIGURE 3.1 Villagers at work cleaning a grave in the pre-World War I cemetery of Neuvilly, Argonne (France), in 2001. The graves were damaged by artillery when the village was in the immediate vicinity of the frontline in 1914–18 (marks of gunfire are just visible on the gravestone in the left foreground). In the background, housing dating from the almost total reconstruction of the village in the 1920s. Photograph and caption courtesy of Paola Filippucci

Filippucci describes this as a 'relational' conception of space and time; and points out that while official heritage policy claims to be 'valoriz[ing] local forms' it is in effect denying them by not recognising the different, relational, form that local temporalising (and spatialising) takes (2004: 82).

Filippucci also makes a strong case for the value of ethnographic approaches to 'heritage' – not least for highlighting the potentially problematic nature of this as an analytical category (2009). Although people in the Argonne are viewed by the authorities as lacking in 'heritage', and although local people largely concur with this in their spoken statements, Filippucci's in-depth fieldwork shows that local people *do* care about much that might be associated with 'heritage' – e.g. matters of identity, place and past – but that it nevertheless differs in important ways from the more usual, and increasingly widespread, heritage-identity complex.

Multitemporal experiments

In the final part of this chapter, I continue and further develop the methodological discussion by turning to some examples of research that take up the multitemporal challenge – that of trying to understand and represent some of the complexities of past presencing – in relatively experimental ways. As we will see, ethnographic research remains important here but it takes various forms and is sometimes supplemented with novel techniques or approaches. All of the examples that I have selected for this section are by researchers in the Department of Social Anthropology at Manchester University, though they were not produced as part of a common research project or methodological school. Rather, they are specific innovative responses – in very different contexts and with diverse overall aims – to trying to deal with what we variously encountered as struggles with aspects of the past in our contemporary fieldwork.

Clashing memories of Bosnian conflict

In an article about recollections of the conflict in Bosnia, Stef Jansen takes what he himself describes as an 'experimental' and 'unconventional' approach. This is to present his arguments through a detailed discussion between himself and three other men. The reason for this choice, as he explains it, is

> to deploy the critical impact of a vivid description of one specific event against the sterile simplification that often comes with the more sweeping journalistic and scholarly accounts of contemporary Bosnian life. I believe that many such accounts tend to underestimate the complexities of everyday life, while overestimating the importance of national identities at the expense of other (non-national) factors.

> (2007: 193)

To this end, he invites the reader to accompany him as, one evening in October 2000, he joins three other men in the house where he is staying, in the town of Tuzla in Bosnia, to take a drink and participate in the ensuing conversation. The reader is introduced to the three men, former colleagues in an engineering company, two of whom – Samir and Hasan – are Bosnian Muslims and the third, Robi, is Serbian. Samir was originally from a neighbouring village but resettled to Tuzla after having worked in Germany for several years. Hasan and Robi are from Tuzla, Hasan having remained in the village through the years of shelling, Robi having recently returned. Hasan, fired by the shared alcohol, insists that Robi knew when Serb attacks were due to begin in 1992 and that this was why he left. Jansen takes us in detail through Hasan's accusations and Robi's rebuttals, showing how other dimensions of discontent get drawn into the argument, such as Hasan's anger with Samir for having left to get a higher standard of living, and criticisms of 'the occupying forces', which are voiced pointedly towards Jansen himself.

While it is clear that ethnic identifications are mobilised in the argument, Jansen's research and mode of representing it shows that how this occurs is not straightforward and from a fixed position. At first, the three men are behaving as colleagues, neighbours and drinking companions. What we see in microcosm, however, is a process of fissures being prised open. But even here, the lines of division are not unambiguously or exclusively 'ethnic'. Hasan's rage begins with Robi but is also, and increasingly, directed at Samir – a fellow Bosnian Muslim who was (like so many others) – out of the country during the war for reasons that, it seems, had nothing to do with it.

Jansen's experiment, then, is directed especially at providing insight into how the past might be experienced and mobilised by individuals in an everyday – if specific – context. He conveys how the past has shaped particular villages – in ways that may be dissimilar from others in matters such as their particular ethnic mix and the degrees of war and ethnic cleansing that they experienced – as well as how that past can be brought into the present and fought over. Different particular events – such as the particular date on which Robi left the village – hold different significance for Robi and Hasan; what for one was chance or coincidence, is to the other evidence of knowledge, complicity and untrustworthiness.

What Jansen's experiment also achieves is a recovery of some of the individual agency of what Cornelia Sorabji, in a discussion of Sarajevo Bosnian post-war memories, calls 'memory management' (2006). She points out troubling implications of some of the models of memory transmission that are often invoked in the Balkan post-war scenario. These typically remove individual agency, either regarding ethnic hatred as transmitted automatically from one generation to the next through recollection of war – and therefore as deep-rooted and only possible to shift by active therapeutic intervention; or seeing memory as politically produced and therefore as fairly readily manipulable through education programmes. Like Jansen, she also looks at individual case-studies to show how individuals themselves may steer their own way through the various accounts of the past that they encounter – thus 'managing' their memories.

Layering histories in Nuremberg

My second example is from my own research on the Nazi past in the city of Nuremberg, Germany. The research was based on historical sources and on interviewing and participant-observation (Macdonald 2009a). It focused especially on the former Nazi party rally grounds – a vast complex of buildings and marching grounds built in the 1930s as a stage for Nazi rallies, left largely intact post-war and variously neglected, reconstructed, preserved and put to multiple uses ever since. Its uses have included commemoration of victims of fascism and war dead, pilgrimage by neo-Nazis, tourism, exhibition, artwork, education, and numerous forms of leisure, such as motor racing and sun-bathing. Methodologically, my focus on such a contested site aimed to provide a lens into diverse ways in which the Nazi past had been approached since 1945. I wanted to avoid concentrating on one particular group of people and to deploy instead James E. Young's idea of 'collected' rather than 'collective' memory (1993). That is, I aimed to investigate how different people and memories and practices were gathered and sometimes collided at this site.

In conducting archival and historical research, I sought to understand better how the site had come to be shaped into its present form over time – why, for example, certain parts of buildings had been destroyed – as well as to examine how they were discussed and represented in the sources available at particular times. One dimension of the latter was to try to grasp what was involved in what appeared to be major changes of approach over the years. Some of these, I found, turned out to be less marked than they were usually represented as being in recent historicising. Original sources showed, for example, more attempts to address the Nazi past through public education in the post-war years than later commentators usually credited. What I also found, however, was that there were other changes that seemed to make more fundamental shifts – such as a psychologisation of approaches to buildings in the 1980s that reconfigured *not* publicly acknowledging the site into an act of 'repression'. My research across different time periods, then, provided me with materials to relativise both the present and other periods – that is, to throw the specific constellations of each into relief. It also highlighted multidirectional relationships between past and present, as the physical past – in the form of the buildings themselves – shaped actions and interpretations in the present (sometimes setting up new challenges or puzzles), and was itself altered; and as earlier interpretations of the past were revised by later ones; and later ones by earlier historical accounts.

In my plans to represent this multitemporality I was influenced by the work of the artist Anselm Kiefer – including his Nuremberg paintings (Macdonald 2002, 2009a). As in some of his other work, these paintings are heavily layered with materials – in this case, straw, ash and paint. Beneath the layers, earlier images can be detected – images of Nuremberg's skyline, and words alluding to Wagner's *Meistersinger von Nürnberg* and perhaps to the rally grounds (*'Festspielwiese'* 'festival ground'*)*. In German, the word for layers is *Schichte,* which is part of the root of the word for history, *Geschichte,* a word that also means 'story'. This compelling semantics prompted me to experiment with juxtaposing historical moments and commentaries upon them. In doing so, however, I faced a difficulty not shared with Kiefer, of wishing to provide explanation, discussion and analysis rather than cryptic allusion. In the monograph that I finally produced, therefore, I chose to retain a broadly chronological framework in order to trace through how later periods had – sometimes literally – built upon earlier. But I also interspersed this with discussion and reflection concerning other times and with what I called 'interventions' – comments or descriptions that were not part of the chronological narrative intended to 'supplement, and sometimes disrupt or complicate, the main account, and sometimes to lay clues and traces for later arguments' (2009a: 22).

AIDS, personal memories and staged fieldwork in London

In research carried out in Africa and New York, as well as in London, with volunteer 'buddies' of people who had died of HIV/AIDS related illnesses, Andrew Irving has experimented with methodologies to help him access individual – and often deeply painful – memories. In an article on his London research, he describes what he calls 'staged "fieldwork" encounters to create a type of ethnographic-mnemonic context through which the past – in this case London from the mid-1980s to mid-1990s – can be relived and interpreted' (2006: 9). This was conducted as follows:

> I asked persons, who I had previously worked with, to return to significant streets and buildings in their personal biography and history, and then asked them to narrate past events and experiences into a tape-recorder while another person took photographs, interjected with comments and responded with their own ideas and memories ... The two informant roles were then reversed so that the narrator became the photographer and vice-versa in the attempt to further uncover the layers of memory and emotion that have been sedimented into London's pavements, streets, parks, paths and buildings.
>
> (2006: 9)

The approach produces highly individual memories of the city – for example, a bus stop is important to one volunteer as it is where she last saw a friend who later died. This shows vividly the way in which even mundane landscapes can be imbued with deeply emotional significance. What is also evoked by the photographic selections and the commentaries are wider senses of fear and loss surrounding AIDS/HIV in the city during those years. This is a past that might otherwise be easily forgotten.

Irving's approach is also representationally experimental in that he presents much of his account through photographs accompanied by descriptions of, and stories about, those with whom he worked. This creates a purposefully fragmentary impression, itself conjuring up the disconnected nature of many of the memories and the processes of remembering.

Chorographies and sensory remembering in Bucharest

Alyssa Grossman, who completed a PhD in Social Anthropology with Visual Media in Manchester in 2010, also conducted a form of 'walking' research, which she describes through the term 'chorography' (originally deployed by Ptolemy and developed also by cultural geographers), and recorded through the medium of film as well as written account. Like Irving's, her work is also city-based – in this case, in Bucharest. Unlike his, her walking research was most often conducted alone and centres upon her observations of the city. Her

FIGURE 3.2   The last goodbye. Bus stop outside Marks and Spencer's, Kensington High Street. Photograph and text courtesy of Andrew Irving

This bus stop is the place where the volunteer saw Isabel Collins alive for the very last time. Often words and gestures possess little significance in their own time and place and they are only retrospectively inscribed with meaning. Throughout history small words and tiny gestures are made resonant and meaningful by a later event, and a forgotten smile, casual wave or trivial comment subsequently becomes infused with intense emotions say in knowledge that this was the last time a friend or family member was seen alive. This reminds us that meaning is never completely wrapped within its present context but remains unfinished and open to later re-signification. But what is distinctive with regard to HIV/AIDS and other terminal conditions, is that events are already and routinely ascribed with their potential future signification. Saying 'see you later' is not the same casual act of ordinary everyday speech but an unresolved statement or question that can be seen in people's eyes, heard in their voices and felt in handshakes which are all too often interpreted as an invitation to collude with a particular vision of the future where life goes on. Both Isabel and the volunteer knew this was likely to be the last time they were going to see each other as the volunteer was leaving for a job abroad. Fifteen years later whenever the volunteer walks past the bus stop arresting memories of things that were unsaid at the time emerge alongside the hurt of saying goodbye in a public place and the shared unspoken and moribund knowledge of finitude. This was it, a goodbye that recalled Schopenhauer's suggestion that 'every parting gives a foretaste of death'.

(Irving 2006: 16–17)

FIGURE 3.3 Cabinet in Dorel's living room, Bucharest. Photograph courtesy of Alyssa Grossman

overall aim was to try to access 'everyday sites and practices of memory' in what she describes as 'post-Socialist, EU accession-era Bucharest'. She seeks to do so through chance encounters and in unexpected settings rather than through more conventional techniques. Chapters of her thesis are thus focused, for example, on the eclectic contents of a chest of drawers of an elderly couple and display cabinets in people's homes; objects in the basement of the Romanian Peasant Museum; and everyday uses of, and discourses about, money. Through these, she is able to highlight ways that the socialist past is approached that are not usually considered within more conventional accounts of post-Socialist transition. For example, in relation to money, she identifies various continuities with the socialist past rather than only the differences that are the usual subject of academic commentary.

Like Irving, Grossman also deploys forms of staged fieldwork. In an inspired staging, she set up what she calls a 'memory meal' to which she invited acquaintances to bring foods that reminded them of the socialist era. This created an ephemeral encounter in which recollections of the past, and the taste of the past, were exchanged and evaluated. She uses this as a basis from which to describe and discuss the embodied and sensory qualities of memory, the power of certain substances to evoke remembrance, and the often ambivalent and partially individualised and partially shared character of the memories of socialism produced.

FIGURE 3.4   Food brought to the memory meal. Photograph courtesy of Alyssa Grossman

Grossman's accompanying film provides a further medium for experimental representation. In it, she takes the viewer on her own chorographic route round the central park in Bucharest, allowing us to see the mixed life of the city that collects here, lingering over particular scenes or individuals and eaves-dropping on snippets of conversations underway. The film is also self-consciously constructed to evoke different time periods through some of the characters of various ages and generations, and also by its use of music from different time periods. In this way, it seeks to evoke the past in the present of the city and to provide the audience with a 'feel' for remembrance as well as to provide them with a supplement to the more discursive understandings offered in the text.

★ ★ ★

This chapter has explored dimensions of and approaches to the multitemporal challenge. Both the more conventional methods of doing fieldwork and representing it, as well as the more experimental ones described here, are only some of the possibilities for trying to address questions of past presencing. In subsequent chapters we will encounter others, designed to tackle particular aspects of remembrance and historicising in Europe. All, however, share a commitment to trying to understand specific practices and forms of past presencing in particular contexts. And all show alertness to how different forms of mediation and representation may shape accounts of the past and of its significance in the present. The aim in much of the work by anthropologists is to try to understand 'the stories of ordinary people' (Comaroff and Comaroff 1992: 17). As Comaroff and Comaroff note, in relation to similar approaches in Africa, these 'stand in danger of remaining just that: stories. To become something more, these partial, "hidden histories" have to be situated in the wider worlds of power and meaning that gave them life' (1992: 17). What we have seen in the examples here is the attempt to do just that. Providing that situating – which is likely to be local, national and European in various measure – is a further part of the challenge that we will encounter in the chapters that follow.

4

FEELING THE PAST

Embodiment, place and nostalgia

> I see the hands of the generations
> That owned each shiny familiar thing
> In play on its knobs and indentations
>
> Thomas Hardy[1]

The past is not only discussed and thought about, it is also materialised in bodies, things, buildings and places. It is felt, experienced and expressed through objects, such as ruined buildings, monuments, flared trousers or the marks of wear on old furniture; and practices, such as commemorative rituals, historical re-enactment, eating a sun-warmed peach or hearing a familiar melody. It is so in ways that may run counter to, or be in excess of, verbal articulations; the 'feel of the past' can be hard to express. Specific and embodied constellations of affect accompany some forms of past presencing – perhaps sadness and a feeling of loss in the commemorative ceremony; an uplifting sense of connection with people who lived long ago during a historical re-enactment; a sense of awe and even fear in encountering an embalmed corpse. Others are harder to characterise – the mix of melancholy and pleasure in touching, and being touched by, the indentations on an old chest of drawers or spade handle left by years of use; or the sense of being pulled into wistful recollection by the scent of hyacinths or notes of a street piano. Individual memories can prompt senses of joy, amusement, shame or grief, which in turn can have consequences for how they are addressed in ongoing life; and emotions may contribute to processes of remembering and forgetting, of feeling compelled or unable to speak about the past.

In dedicating a chapter specifically to embodiment and emplacement, materiality and affect, I do not intend to imply that these can be separated out from other aspects of past presencing. On the contrary, remembering and forgetting that reach beyond the individual are inevitably externally materialised in some form,[2] be this speech, text, rituals or objects; and we experience them through our senses and in, and usually in relation to, specific places. Moreover, they are inevitably imbued with particular, more or less strong, feelings. Remembrance may be embodied in practices, perhaps collectively repeated as ritual. Objects and places are widely recognised as capable of triggering recollection; and the attempted preservation of memory through forms of materialisation is embedded in numerous practices throughout Europe. As such, many other chapters, as already evident in the previous ones, also consider aspects of 'feeling the past' both in relation to particular topics considered here and others that might have been included. Addressing the embodied (including affective and sensory), emplaced and material dimensions of the past more specifically, however, allows more in-depth consideration of some of the anthropological research on Europe that explores and theorises these.

In this chapter I first outline some of the theoretical background to the increased emphasis in anthropology – and in studies of memory more generally – on the embodied, emplaced, sensory, material and affective.[3] Discussing these together makes sense partly because they are so intertwined – discussions of embodiment, for example, almost inevitably give attention to the body's materiality, sensory capacities and affective experiences – but also because, even where the emphasis is upon one in particular, researchers typically draw on broadly shared theoretical resources. As I argue below, while theoretical positions often rely on an either/or stance in relation to more discursive approaches, or on a form of universalism, neither of these is either necessary or adequate for tackling the kinds of questions that arise in relation to memory practices in Europe – nor, perhaps, for much else.

What is needed instead is to couple some of the insights from phenomenological and related approaches – as they have come to be understood within much social and cultural study – with attention to the historical, socio-cultural and political-economic. In the second half of the chapter I argue this largely through attention to 'nostalgia' – a form of past presencing, originally designated as a particular bodily/affective affliction formed in relation to displacement, which has been discussed in numerous ethnographies in Europe. As in other chapters, what we see here is a set of practices that is widespread in Europe – yearning for the past, for home, for place, and a cherishing of objects from times now passed, at the same time, considerable variation – in effect, manifold nostalgias – that need to be understood in relation to particular historical, socio-cultural and political-economic contexts.

Turning to embodiment, materiality and affect

In the pirouettes of innovation that disciplines like to claim, giving attention to embodiment, place, materiality, affect and the senses have all been hailed as 'turns' in a wide range of social and cultural studies over the past decade or so. Commonplace in these claims is what Margaret Wetherell, in this case addressing 'the affective turn', bluntly calls a 'rubbishing' of the discursive (2012: 18). Words are dismissed as of lesser social and cultural significance than what is embodied, materialised or felt. The implication, and sometimes the explicit claim, is that domains of experience 'beyond discourse' are somehow more 'real' or 'authentic' than those expressed in words. This has the effect of separating 'the felt' from the linguistically expressed, and regarding these as relatively autonomous domains, only one of which deserves in-depth attention. As Wetherell argues, however, this cuts off investigation of the relationship between discourse and affect (and also embodiment and materiality) and does not recognise how language might, say, trigger, crystallise or intensify particular feelings and, more generally, denies or at least downplays, meaning-making, sometimes even to the extent that 'new' theorising looks close to older psychological theories of 'instinct'. In addition, it rests on a mind-body distinction that it generally decries; and its privileging of the non-verbal as (explicitly or implicitly) more 'authentic' replicates a set of divisions involved in constituting memory as 'a romanticized object' (Lambek 2003) as discussed in the introduction. Moreover, in its most linguistically-dismissive forms it is analytically self-defeating in its own use of words to try to explain what it has deemed 'beyond words'.

Dismissing discourse can only mean that we ignore much that matters. We have already seen that how the past is told and written, and the particular words and linguistic constellations used, can be highly significant. The past is often the subject of intense debate or of poetry. Moreover, these are never 'purely' verbal – debate happens in particular locations and may be accompanied by shaking of fists; poetry may be inspired by affectively intense experiences and lead to them. At the same time, as we saw in the last chapter and discussed in terms of the Ardeners' notion of 'mutedness', not all forms of past presencing are expressed through language, and there may be a 'gap' between what is said and what is articulated or performed in other ways. The notion of 'mutedness' itself, however, is not entirely helpful here as it implies that a lack of verbal expression is centrally at issue, whereas the Ardeners' main point is that it is researchers' privileging of this mode of expression that limits attention to other, more embodied, forms. To those involved – Bakweri women in the Ardeners' example – their embodied and materialised ritual performance is not 'mute' but highly expressive. Embodied and material forms, then, need attention; and neither language nor the embodied/material should be seen simply as supplement to the other. Not only do the discursive and the embodied/material not necessarily 'say' the same things, however, they do not necessarily work in the same ways or produce the same effects.

Part of the critique of discursive approaches is that these sometimes assume that all aspects of experience can be analysed in the same terms, as though they all work in essentially the same way as language. This is an important criticism, though sometimes overstated. Approaches that make analogies with language and draw on concepts from literary theory to tackle a wide range of cultural forms – from art to food to clothing – have often been insightful and subtle; and the use of analogies and concepts does not mean that what is being considered is being 'reduced to' language. At the same time, such approaches do not usually help convey people's actual experience of, say, eating a fruit or hearing a melody. Such experiences merit consideration in themselves but also for understanding social action and its motivations. There is here too a question as to whether other cultural forms necessarily work in the same way as language and whether, therefore, the 'decoding' approaches of linguistics and literary theory are most appropriate or insightful. Assemblage and 'non-representational' theorising, which put more emphasis on what particular forms do than what they mean, and also theorising drawing from phenomenology, have been influential here, as we will see further below. Certainly, different cultural forms – or media – have different capacities, or in this case what we might call 'memorizing capacities', in relation to their durability, mobility and so forth; though attending to this does not necessarily mean that meaning and the symbolic need to be abandoned altogether. Indeed, attending to temporality – for example, how the past may be enfolded into the present – may provide a means of bringing them back in.

Phenomenologies

In all of these related 'turns', phenomenology has been an important alternative theoretical source of inspiration to more semiotic approaches. Phenomenology encompasses various strands of philosophical and theoretical work, not all of which agree and not all of which have been widely taken up in social and cultural studies. This is not the place for an extended account but in broad terms social and cultural studies, including anthropology, have characterised phenomenology as emphasising subjects' perception and experience of the world.[4] Experience here is generally understood as going beyond that which people might verbally articulate to include, indeed, often to concentrate upon, bodily and sensory experience. Phenomenologically-inspired anthropological research typically entails paying careful attention to people's actual practices (e.g. walking, cooking) as part of their 'being in the world' – to use a phrase from Heidegger that often features in such work; as well as trying to convey how they feel about it. Attempts to find more adequate ways to convey experience have also inspired experimental, evocative approaches, including use of visual and other sensory media, such as those of Irving and Grossman described in the previous chapter.

A significant strand of phenomenology in anthropology, and even more so in other disciplines, is concerned with commonalities in human perception and experience.[5] The shared experience of embodiment is the primary basis for the supposition of common human experience – and includes the 'life-events' of birth and death, as well tendencies to perceive scale and spaces through analogies with the body. In addition, hypothesised shared human urges and responses, such as a longing for a place to be 'home' (a need to 'dwell' in the Heideggerian lexicon)[6] or being moved by the experience of certain natural phenomena, have also been variously theorised as central to human experience, and, in the work of anthropologists, fleshed out in ethnographic description. In its quest for what is humanly shared, however, such work risks paying insufficient attention to cultural and historical specificity. Moreover, as has been a criticism of Heidegger, some of the phenomenological language and oppositions seem to reproduce a particular romantic vision that should, perhaps, be seen as part of a specific European complex rather than sought out and substantiated.[7] Certainly, notions of dwelling and being-in-the-world bear a strong resemblance to ideas involved in musealisation that we will discuss in Chapter 6, and they have been influential in 'compensation' theorising of the memory phenomenon – that is, seeing it as primarily a response to loss. And, as we will see below, they may be used in explanations of nostalgia. While much research carried out in this vein is interestingly suggestive, my contention here is that its further investigation merits coupling with attention to the historical and cultural specificity of sensory/bodily/affective 'regimes'. This should, furthermore, include reflexive attention to the potential analytical dilemmas of shared frameworks (the 'analytical double take' discussed earlier).

Materialities

Anthropological phenomenology typically emphasises the 'materiality of sociality' (Hsu 2008: 437). It is sometimes coupled with an emphasis on the 'agency' of materials or objects, which has been central to a range of theorising including actor network theory, assemblage theory, non-representational theory, the influential theorising of Alfred Gell (1998) and the new material culture studies.[8] These variously overlap and in their 'strongest' versions are sometimes hyperbolically referred to as 'post human' in that they seek to avoid giving privileged position to human beings and meaning-making in analyses (e.g. Latour 2005). While this might seem to be incompatible with a phenomenological approach, which attends foremost to the human experience of the world, it is sometimes brought together by theorists in an interest in how certain objects or materials might shape that experience.

While a researcher might not want to go the whole hog on the de-privileging of human agency for which strong versions of these approaches argue, they might nevertheless wish to draw on some of its insights about how materials work on and in us. That is, while they might want to give attention to questions such as when and why people choose to roast hogs, the symbolic meanings with which it is attributed, how the labour of cooking and carving are allocated and how the eating is distributed, they might also consider phenomenological and material questions about how the smell of the roasting hog might get our stomachs rumbling and whether there is something about hogs that make them suggestive to certain uses. Giving attention to materialities not only recognises the inevitably material nature of human existence but also opens up investigation of how the differential properties of particular materials, objects or technologies interact with human endeavour and understanding; in other words, what difference do the differences between things make?

In relation to past presencing, this can be unpacked into questions such as those posed by Elizabeth Hallam and Jenny Hockey in their exploration of death, memory and material culture:

> why it is that certain objects are infused with the capacity to endure time, persisting and rejuvenated *in* memory, whereas others are constrained in their temporal reach as ephemera, as *only* memories, barely present as fading traces that may be cut adrift by the passing away of certain generations or individuals.
>
> (Hallam and Hockey 2001: 8)

How, in other words, do particular media forms – such as writing or monuments – make a difference to what persists over time and its relative openness or resistance to reinterpretation? In trying to grasp some of these material distinctions we might consider relativities of *durability, mobility, singularity, labour of production* and *size*. How readily something persists or perishes over time, how easily it can be transported, whether it can be replicated, how much effort is needed to create it and how large it is, all play into the work that particular material forms do in relation to memory – though not in neatly pre-determinable ways. Here I only note these relativities and suggest that the moments of shift from one medium to another – e.g. as when a photograph is taken of a mountain – can act as productive entry points for analysis of mediation in past presencing. In addition to these relativities, and in interaction with them, are also other, metaphorical resonances that, likewise, may give them specific 'expressive potency' (D. Abram 1996: 80), as we will see below in examples such as gardening or things left in abandoned houses.

Studies giving weight to materiality tread a difficult line between identifying properties of things that may widely evoke certain responses or share 'affordances', to use a term (from psychologist James J. Gibson 1979) that has come to be widely adopted in such discussions, and recognising the potential variability of responses or attributions of meaning that people may make. This is dealt with well in the studies that are discussed in more detail below, which on the one hand show how certain material properties – e.g. of the dead body – can lend themselves to certain affectively charged ritualisation, and on the other alert us to 'other' ways of responding (or not responding at all). So while, for example, carrying around a piece of a dead person's body – as in the hair jewellery that was popular in Victorian Britain – might be seen as a natural way to preserve the memory of a loved one in some contexts, it is not currently in favour in most parts of Europe – and might, indeed, be viewed with distaste (Hallam and Hockey 2001). The ideas of Robert Hertz

(1960/1910) are insightful here.[9] He notes that positive associations of the right side (e.g. the term 'right' referring to both a direction and a positive value in many languages) are found widely across the world and argues that this is prompted by the statistical prevalence of right-handedness. What we see here is certain physical features of the natural world, in this case the 'sidedness' of the human body, acting suggestively, but not deterministically, to prompt certain apprehensions. Paul Connerton argues likewise in relation to bodily morphological features of verticality and the distinction between inside and outside, which, he suggests, are frequently the mode through which place is apprehended (2011: Chapter 4). However big the hints that bodies and the natural world may give, however, these are inevitably incorporated into socially and culturally particular life-worlds and will bear their specific inflections. This is evident in many of the examples below, beginning with Katherine Verdery's brilliant investigation of what she calls the 'political lives of dead bodies' in post-Socialist Europe (1999). What we see here, alongside an insightful analysis of the 'bodily hints' that dead bodies may make, is also how these become enmeshed in the historically, politically and culturally specific – in this case, Eastern Europe post 1989.

Post-Socialist dead bodies

Bodies, dead as well as alive, Verdery argues, are especially symbolically effective and emotively resonant because they are capable of, on the one hand, evoking human commonality – the shared fact of inhabiting bodies – and, on the other, of evoking human particularity. It is 'because all people have bodies that any manipulation of a corpse directly enables one's identification with it through one's own body, thereby tapping into one's reservoirs of feeling' (1999: 32–3). As well as this 'ineluctable self-referentiality' (1999: 32), the fact that dead bodies 'suggest the lived lives of human beings' – death is a time for reflecting back on a life – also means that 'they can be evaluated from many angles and assigned perhaps contradictory virtues, vices and intentions' (1999: 28). A corpse is also that of a *specific* individual, and so, while on the one hand a corpse might be invested with numerous identifications and meanings, its particularity simultaneously creates 'the illusion [that is has] … *only one* significance', a singularity that is further emphasised by its discrete physical form (1999: 29). This dual referentiality – general *and* particular – is why the dead body is potentially so resonant for use in political ritual, allowing a playing with both generalising and more specific motifs. Moreover, the body's 'deadness' contributes to imbuing ritual with powerful affect both by indexing other rituals – the funeral and the commemorative ceremony – and by the more general sense of awe and of connection with 'the sacred and the cosmic' (p.32) that surrounds death.[10]

    If these are commonplace 'affordances' of corpses, they have specific inflections in the wake of the collapse of communist regimes. According to

Verdery, this collapse produced 'a problem of reorganisation on a cosmic scale ... a reordering of people's entire meaningful worlds' (1999: 35). In the face of this, dramatic ritual acts moral regeneration (a notion she takes from Durkheim) – such as the return of dead bodies and their ceremonial reburials – abound. But where Durkheim would see these as acts of consensus-making, Verdery observes that they are frequently 'sites of political conflict' (1999: 36). Nevertheless, by reburying the bodies in their 'homelands' – another evocative notion, and one that sometimes entails selective memory (Gal 1991) – the new political regimes also conduct 'proper burial', which symbolically helps to restore cosmic order. As Verdery describes and others have also documented, ideas about risks that may follow from improper or non-existent burial are widespread in Europe, especially Eastern Europe.[11] Such improper burial risks incurring the wrath of the spirit of the dead, who may even become a vampire or other vengeful spirit, as is the case in Transylvania (Verdery 1999: 41–2). Exhumation and proper burial, thus, are not only general but are also locally charged material and symbolic modes of trying to effect a 'proper' social order in which bodies are, literally, re-rooted into place.

In addition, the metaphorical resonance of the return of dead bodies for reburial also helps to fortify unified national visions – even if these are contested. Returned bodies are widely conceived as 'ancestors' or 'sons' of the nation, thus mobilising kinship metaphors that are widespread in conceptualising nations and their continuity over time. Repatriation of bodies thus plays into a reaffirmation of nations, and national distinctiveness, that is especially salient in the immediate post-Socialist years as countries strive to perform their national independence – frequently turning to the past, including past heroes, in the process. Not only are the returning dead bodies conceived as ancestors, and as national figures returning to the fold, they are also described as forms of 'cultural heritage' or 'national treasure'. This not only further substantiates the nation's possessive individuation, but also emotively invokes globally increased calls for the repatriation of property to 'those to whom it properly belongs' (1999: 48–9). The new post-Socialist nations are thus also positioned as heritage-possessing actors in a global scene in which repatriation claims are part of an identity-performing currency. Repatriating dead bodies is simultaneously a reproduction of persons and things, and, as such, it also acts to equate these; and in the process it reinforces the idea that the nation may have property and members elsewhere – but that these should, ideally, return 'home'.

Verdery does not discuss the post-Socialist 'repatriation' of dead bodies as a manifestation of nostalgia, and this would be to stretch the term. But as we will see later in this chapter, forms of nostalgia have been widespread in post-Socialist countries, with a looking back and calls for reviving aspects of both pre-Socialist and Socialist pasts. Moreover, the affective and epistemological constellations of nostalgia – a positive gaze and longing for aspects of the past and for home – are also entangled in the necro-rituals that Verdery describes. In the rest of this chapter I turn to various nostalgic practices that have been documented in

Europe over the past 30 years, some of which can be seen as part of the memory phenomenon that is the focus of the chapters that follow. In exploring this, I am concerned too to consider further how subjective experience and the 'prompts' or affordances of bodies or materials are articulated in particular ways in specific times, places and circumstances.

Nostalgia

As Svetlana Boym, among others, has discussed, the term 'nostalgia' was coined in the seventeenth century by a Swiss medical student to designate an illness – 'the sad mood originating from the desire to return to one's native land' (Dr Johannes Hofer 1688, quoted in Boym 2001: 3) – that he identified as being suffered by 'various displaced people … [including] freedom-loving students from the Republic of Berne studying in Basel, domestic help and servants working in France and Germany and Swiss soldiers fighting abroad' (Boym 2001: 3). Since then, Hofer's Greek neologism has found its way into various European languages, sometimes supplanting and sometimes existing alongside, or perhaps eclipsed by, local variations. Mostly, 'nostalgia', and what are deemed its cognates, is used to indicate a more or less general longing for the past, often, but not necessarily, including the longing for home indicated by the Greek ('*nostos* – return home, and *algia* – longing', Boym 2001: xiii). While 'nostalgia' is no longer a medical diagnosis in most countries and medicines, it still often retains a taint of the pathological, and, as we will see, is frequently moralised; though it also has other connotations, not least in Greece.

Nostalgia emerged as a focus among anthropologists working in a wide range of countries in Europe during the 1990s and 2000s, though studies were not usually brought together for comparative analysis.[12] In most cases, nostalgia was not part of what the researchers had initially intended to research but its significance in the locality in which they were working, as well as in wider debate, drew their attention. In many but not all cases discourses of nostalgia were entangled in the growing memory phenomenon, and specifically the expansion of 'heritage'. For some commentators, as we will see further in following chapters, the memory phenomenon – or specific renditions such as 'the heritage industry' – was a manifestation of a rather naïve nostalgia, a rose-tinted looking back to a time of 'safety' in the face of disruptive change and dislocation. Nostalgia from this perspective was a foolish sentimental view that the past had been better and might somehow be returned to. What anthropological research brought to the debate were on-the-ground perspectives, based on lived experiences, which contributed to a more informed as well as nuanced picture of the kinds of relationships to the past involved in the booming of heritage and tradition. In addition, anthropological research highlighted different understandings and experiences of 'nostalgia' and its relatives – such as 'home', 'the past', 'return'; and some also sought to bring this together with an attempt to grasp the sensory, affective and material dimensions involved.

The breast of Aphrodite, sensory memory and the historical unconscious

The difference between the connotations of the Greek-rooted 'nostalgia' as it is widely used in the English language and its meanings in Greek is one spur of C. Nadia Seremetakis's compelling argument for attending to the entanglements of language and experience, and to memory as sensory and embodied.

> In English the word nostalgia (in Greek *nostalghía*) implies trivializing romantic sentimentality. In Greek the verb *nostalgó* is a composite of *nostó and alghó*. *Nostó* means I return, I travel (back to homeland); the noun *nóstos* means the return, the journey, while á-nostós means without taste ... The opposite of ánostos is nóstimos and characterizes someone or something that has journeyed and arrived, has matured, ripened and is thus tasty (and useful). *Alghó* means I feel pain, I ache for, and the noun álghos characterizes one's pain in soul and body, burning pain (*kaimós*). Thus *nostalghía* is the desire or longing with burning pain to journey. It also evokes the sensory dimension of memory in exile and estrangement; it mixes bodily and emotional pain and ties painful experiences of spiritual and somatic exile to the notion of maturation and ripening. In this sense, *nostalghía* is linked to the personal consequences of historicizing sensory experience which is conceived as a painful bodily and emotional journey.
>
> (1994: 4)

This dense semantic complex maps an affective and moral constellation that is significantly unlike the romantic 'freezing' of the past that 'nostalgia' is often seen to imply in English. Nostalgia in the Greek context instead 'evokes the transformative impact of the past as unreconciled historical experience' (1994: 4).

Seremetakis shows this well through poetically crafted cameos that seek to evoke as well as to represent the sensory and affective experiences of *nostalghía* and of memory more generally. In Proustian fashion, her account begins:

> I grew up with the peach. It had a thick skin touched with fuzz, and a soft matte off-white colour alternating with rosy hues. *Rodhákino* was its name (*ródho* means rose). It was well rounded and smooth like a small clay vase, fitting perfectly into your palm. Its interior was firm yet moist, offering a soft resistance to the teeth. A bit sweet and a bit sour, it exuded a distinct fragrance. This peach was known as 'the breast of Aphrodite' (*o mastós tis Afrodhítis*).
>
> (1994: 1)

The nostalgia here lies not only in looking back at childhood, now gone, but also in that this kind of peach is no longer available, having been supplanted by more watery, á-nostós, varieties.

Seremetakis' nostalgic memory of the breast of Aphrodite is also a basis for her argument for attention to the sensory dimensions of memory. She regards the senses and memory as thoroughly intertwined: 'The senses are … implicated in historical interpretation as witnesses or record-keepers of material experience' (1994: 6). Indeed, memory, she suggests, might be understood as

> a distinct meta-sense [which] transports, bridges and crosses all the other senses. Yet memory is internal to each sense, and the senses are as divisible and indivisible from each other as each memory is separable and intertwined with others.
>
> (1994: 9)

This does not mean that the senses are outside culture – or history. On the contrary, she emphasises how these are thoroughly mutually implicated. The peach that she remembers has all but disappeared, a consequence of European 'economic and social transformations' (1994: 3) – it has become history, in the sense of no longer extant. New trade-routes and transportation technologies have brought new products, with new sensory qualities – such as the kiwi fruit – and these too are embedded in the lived, embodied experiences that form 'the historical unconscious' (1994: 4). A starting point of an object, and the embodied and sensory experiences of it, thus leads into questions of remembrance, personal but also, inevitably, entangled in wider socio-cultural and political-economic histories.

Seremetakis' essay is partly a methodological exemplar: beginning with accounts of various powerful embodied memories and using these as a journey – *nóstos* – into a specific cultural history, one in which the senses themselves are historicised. It is also a manifesto for recognising the significance of the sensory, embodied and material in how we apprehend history and historicity. Rephrasing one of her questions (which her essay surely answers in the affirmative) as a statement, her argument is that 'memory [is] stored in specific everyday items that form the historicity of a culture, items that create and sustain our relationship to the historical as a sensory dimension' (1994: 3).

Proustian perspectives – food memories

That Seremetakis' plea for a sensory approach to memory begins with a peach is not, perhaps, surprising, for food is often a powerful trigger for nostalgic remembrance – as Proust has shown so ineluctably. Her essay contains several other examples that also centre on her own food memories from her childhood in Greece. The small cups of strong aromatic coffee that serve as temporal 'decompressions' in daily rhythms, allowing moments of reflection and recollection, inform an argument about how moments can be created for bringing 'the senses and memory … into play' (1994: 14). Her experience of discovering, after years living away in America, that she knows which wild greens to pick, even though she has only eaten and not gathered them before, illustrate her claim that embodied memory is also transferable between different senses: 'When I went out to collect them, the sensory memory of taste, order, orality stored in the body was transferred to vision and tactility. My body involuntarily knew what I consciously did not' (1994: 16).

This 'sensorial transfer' is also discussed by David Sutton, in *Remembrance of Repasts* (2001), as a form of 'synaesthesia'. Food, he argues, is particularly powerful in memory not only because it is embodied but because of its synaesthetic qualities – taste, smell, vision, touch and sound.[13] This creates an 'experience of "returning to the whole"' (2001: 17), which can be important for creating senses of identification as well as being the object of nostalgic longing. The capacity of food to sensorially link to a wide range of other aspects of experience – as well as for eating to be an important social experience itself – also contributes to its prevalence in nostalgic recollections, sometimes even being their starting point. Its mnemonic resonance for exiles has been shown in a wide range of research in Europe, including that of Lynn Harbottle with Iranians in the UK (2004), Regina Römhild with Cretans in Frankfurt (2002), Elia Petridou on Greeks in England (2001), Elia Vardaki with returnees to Kythera, Greece (2006), Andrea Smith with Algerians in France (2003) and Marta Rabikowska with Poles in London (2010). In addition, it can act methodologically as an entry point for a wide range of other, sometimes nostalgic, memories, as in Alyssa Grossman's memory meal in Bucharest, described in Chapter 3, or in Carole Counihan's use of what she calls 'food-centred life histories' to explore 'the largely missing voices of the consumers' (2004: 2), especially those of women, in her Tuscan research. As we will see in the following chapter, it may also be entangled with the nostalgia-entangled notions of tradition, heritage and authenticity. In addition, food's material properties mean that food comes from *somewhere* – it is grown and produced in particular (not necessarily singular) locations. This can create affectively and sensorially powerful links with *place,* perhaps generating longings for locations as well as times when a particular food was consumed. While some foods are highly perishable, others are more mobile or reproducible, and thus available for creating senses of connection – and perhaps sparking recollections or new longings – over space as well as time.

Re-rooting memory

Depending upon the climate, one possibility for exiles to create material connections with 'back home' may be to grow produce from their homelands in their new locations. Doing so may carry the metaphorical resonance of people themselves also putting down new roots in a new place, roots being a commonplace notion invoked in nostalgic and diasporic discourse, and also in the memory phenomenon more widely.[14]

Anne Jepson's study of gardening in Cyprus (2006) provides an interesting commentary on this idea – at once highlighting the fertility of metaphorical affordances and actual capacities offered by plants and gardening, but at the same time highlighting its cultural, historical and political situatedness.[15] As

FIGURE 4.1 Elemental rooting practices: planting potatoes in Cyprus. Photograph courtesy of Anne Jepson

she writes, gardening involves 'direct and sensual interaction with the soil, the immediate stuff of a place, as well as an immediate sense of physical integrity' (2006: 159), which constitute what she calls 'elemental rooting practices' (ibid.). Yet, although gardening brings people into direct sensory engagement with the place whose soil they are tilling, it does not necessarily 'root' them to that place.

Those she studies are mostly Greek Cypriots who, since the 1974 division of the island, live in houses that still formally belong to the Turkish Cypriots who were evicted from them (2006: 166). As such, they consider themselves refugees, who may at some time in the future have to give up the properties in which they live. Despite – or as Jepson suggests, perhaps partly because of – this sense of fragile residence, such refugees often create gardens even while they may resist carrying out work on the houses that they live in. Moreover, many expressed to her how important gardening was to them, doing so through phraseology of 'a need to grow' (2006: 166). Although gardening would seem redolent with metaphors of setting down roots, of becoming one with the land in a particular territory, she suggests that it also affords other notions that are mobilised in this case. While rooting, locating and the resulting flourishing do seem to be important to those she describes, the rooting is not prioritised and is, perhaps, seen as relatively 'shallow'. Instead, she suggests, it is 'the very provisional, transient, cyclical nature of the garden that draws them towards this work' (ibid.). This is different from – and less political than – work on the house, which is regarded as 'investment in concrete' (ibid.). Gardens require constant tending and renewal if they are not to return to wilderness; buildings deprived of human attention are relatively durable. Gardens will disappear once people vacate them; buildings will remain. Moreover, plants can be dug up and moved or replicated through cloning or gathering seed for re-sowing. As such, they allow for the possibilities of a future re-rooting elsewhere. At the same time, they also invoke a 'sensual memory' through the growing – and smelling and sometimes eating – of plants that were grown 'back home'; the creation of 'something that is both new and connected with the past through identical sensual experience' (2006: 173).

The importance of plants in sensory memory and for creating connections with place is also vividly evident in Andrea Smith's insightful ethnography of visits to Malta by *pieds-noirs* – settlers from Algeria living in France – with Maltese ancestry.[16] These former inhabitants of Algeria talk longingly of Algeria, often slipping into the present tense as they do so, and dwelling on richly sensual memories of foods and places. They have even coined the term *nostalgérie* to describe their self-recognised affective practice (2003: 340). While this is often dismissed by non-*pieds-noirs* French citizens as a form of 'colonial nostalgia' – a misplaced longing for the colonial order of French-ruled Algeria – Smith argues that the longing is more to do with *pieds-noirs'* intense sensory evocation of *place* and sense of not fully belonging, of being unable to 'root themselves', in France. As one woman struggles to explain to her:

> You see, in France … I don't find the *plains,* the, the *mountains*, the, the, the same *landscapes* (paysages), the same *smells* … the same colors …Thus, I get the feeling that I am always traveling (en voyage) in France. I'm floating.
>
> (2003: 341; original emphases)

On visits to Malta, however, even though this is a place where most of the *pieds-noirs* who visit have never lived, they manage to find landscapes, smells, colours – and especially plants – that evoke their nostalgically imagined Algeria. Smith describes the excitement and sensory delight of the *pieds-noirs* during one such visit when they discover prickly-pear cactuses, and enjoy eating their tasty, red-juiced fruits. In a sense, what these *pieds-noirs* of Maltese ancestry are doing is re-rooting their memories of Algeria in Malta; a process in which Malta in effect becomes a sanitised substitute for an Algeria to which they either cannot return or that would likely bring disappointment if they did. The 'pilgrimages of nostalgia' to Malta thus act as sensorially intense visits to 'an Algeria without anti-Maltese discrimination' and in which being a European settler makes one no less Algerian – that is, to 'an Algeria that never was' (2003: 354).

Varieties of nostalgia

What these studies show is that natural materialities, such as plants, and commonplace practices, such as gardening, may be richly metaphorically suggestive – they may make big hints – but that this is still woven into culturally specific and historically contingent interpretations. In the cases above it is the particular predicament of the semi-rooted Greek-Cypriot 'refugees' that shapes the symbolic import with which they imbue gardening; and of the peculiar double displacedness of the *pieds-noirs* that flavours their delight in the Maltese landscape and its fruits. Also highlighted here is that there may be different kinds, and intensities, of nostalgia – as of other affective constellations. This, indeed, is one of the most strongly emerging themes from research on nostalgia in the anthropology of Europe.

For researchers in the 1980s, working in areas caught up in the heritage boom, they faced questions being asked in other disciplines, and the media, about whether this was just a nostalgic looking back to a time that was, in the words of critic Robert Hewison, 'past, dead and safe' (1987: 144). Was nostalgia basically a longing for a past in order to escape an increasingly unprepossessing present? In post-industrial northern England, for example, Jeanette Edwards, working in a former mill-town, documented local people's new-found concerns with preserving their industrial past – a major form of the new heritage expansion. Confronting arguments by Hewison and others, she argued that what was involved was not a romantic nostalgia for that period – people were well aware of its negative dimensions. Rather, it was a means by which local people could – variously and in particular contexts – make claims of belonging through knowledge of local history (1998; see also 2000).[17] While some forms of preserving or restoring the past (such as in the town's museum) would be enthusiastically supported, others (such as to erect 'Victorian railings' in the town centre) would be soundly rejected. What was involved was not some blanket nostalgia for the past or wish to return to it but a select discourse embedded in ongoing social relations. Elsewhere in post-industrial Northern England, Susan Wright (1992) likewise argued that the flourishing of 'galas' – traditional mining festivals – in towns in which collieries had been closed was not just a romantic recollection of a time imagined as better than the present – a world of full-employment. Instead, she showed, these forms allowed the performance of a critical historical perspective and contemporary political commentary, and perhaps also subterfuge emotions, albeit often in coded form.

This seems to call for distinguishing between forms of nostalgia, as does Matt Hodges in his discussion of how villagers in Monadières, southern France, periodise the past. Pointing out that nostalgia is in effect a form of periodisation – typically making a sharp divide between a certain 'then' and 'now' – he shows how, even within one village, and even within one person, nostalgia may operate variously. He draws especially on discussions with local 'amateur ethnographer', Guy Cadas, who collects stories of 'the old days', making a sharp distinction between the past and today, and describing the pain that he feels in recollecting all that has gone as 'the knife', so physical is his sense of loss (2010: 121). Yet, in looking back in this way, Guy Cadas not only engages in what Hodges calls 'palliative nostalgia' – 'searching out a blissful if temporary shelter from the demands of the present' (2010: 120), but also in 'critical nostalgia' – 'critically … subjecting the present to comparison with remembered or invented pasts' (ibid.).[18] In doing so, Guy Cadas draws upon, and tries to make sense of, his lived experience of the considerable change that the village is undergoing, not least from the growth of heritage tourism, which has also given a new validation to his self-appointed work collecting up and commenting on the locality, tradition and change.

Returning to the case of Cyprus provides further illustration of how distinct affective sensibilities embedded in different socio-political situations that may co-exist – in this case, between the different populations on the island. According to Papadakis *et al.* (2006), after the 1974 division of the island, 'nostalgia ... became a patriotic duty' for Greek Cypriots who had been displaced from their original homes in the North and continued to long for them (2006: 13). (These are the 'refugees' of Jepson's study.) Turkish Cypriots, however, faced 'an official rhetoric that the past was all negative and that the north was now their true and only "homeland"', which meant that they were not supposed to 'feel nostalgic towards the homes they left behind in 1974, as that could imply that they wished to return or that life there was not always bleak' (2006: 13–14). Papadakis *et al.* draw on Aciman (2000), in what is perhaps an over-stated opposition, to characterise the Greek Cypriot position as *nostomania* and that of Turkish Cypriots as *nostophobia* (Papadakis *et al.* 2006: 14).[19]

Below, I return to differentiation of nostalgias and their playing out in particular histories and locations through an examination of post-Socialist nostalgia.[20] First, however, I turn further to the theme of place, which so often also figures in nostalgic longing, as well as informing the original definition of the term.

Touching places

Place is bound up with a wide range of affects, not only nostalgia; and it is central to heritage – which is always emplaced.[21] In heritage it is through place – and its specific physical elements, such as buildings or natural features – that the past is made present. According to Edward Casey's phenomenological perspective, place is central to human experience: 'To live is to live locally, and to know is first of all to know the places one is in' (1996: 18). This perhaps informs the capacity of places to 'touch' those who come to them – and thus the affective resonance of history presented as heritage; as well as, sometimes at least, their capacity to exert a pull of return.

The idea that pasts that are not known to those who visit or inhabit certain places can nevertheless be somehow sensed is widespread in European cultures; and is often expressed through forms such as ghostly presences and ideas of haunting, as we will see below.[22] If 'memory' is understood as not only cognitive but as embodied or emplaced, such traces may be transmitted through, say, sedimented bodily movements or sculptural and architectural forms. Chris Tilley's phenomenological exploration of various prehistoric remains in Europe – Breton menhirs, Maltese temples and rock carvings in Sweden – suggests, not uncontentiously, that there are various common human structurings of perception that we will bring to any actual encounter and that our embodied experience of this, while inevitably interpreted through 'a contemporary cultural frame', can nevertheless allow the stones to 'exert their muted agency in relation to us' (2004: 219) in ways that are likely to echo those of prehistoric peoples.

Where an anthropologist has shared in the way of life of a people over time, they may come to share not only narrated memories but also embodied ones, including senses of longing for particular places and times. This is illustrated in Judith Okely's research with the rural aged in Normandy. In the local authority 'home' (her inverted commas) to which the rural aged move once they can no longer work their farms, they choose to sit in a 'cold and draughty' corridor from which they can catch a distant glimpse of the fields beyond the town (2001: 106). Although they do not verbally explain their reasons for sitting there, Okely draws on her shared tacit experience of having helped them in their fields to suggest that they are engaged in longingly recalling their lives on the land.

In research among older people in a former mining and steel-working village of Dodworth in the North of England (2005), Cathrine Degnen likewise shared embodied experiences and everyday recollections with those she studied. This included walking the changing local village-scape with its residues of past times, and talking about it – the village past being a topic of relentless enthusiasm among local people. The effect of this everyday mundane chatting and walking the locality was that she was tacitly taught how to populate the village streets with names and histories of former inhabitants. The past thus became locally and spatially present for her, as it was for local people, in what she calls 'three dimensional memory'. This is a kind of 'place memory' that Connerton (2009) would designate the *locus*, a lived taken-for-granted emplacement, and that he contrasts with the *memorial* – more active and conscious designation of some places as significant for remembrance. While Connerton's discussion of this distinction implies that the locus is a more important form of memory than the memorial, much of his other work highlights the significance of both, as of the embodied practices that variously characterise them. A more productive approach, therefore, is to consider the cultural work that they variously achieve. Furthermore, while the distinction is useful, it should be noted that these 'types' may blend into one another or become transformed over time, as for example, when everyday knowledge and memory become recorded into official memorials and heritage, as Jane Nadel-Klein describes of the fisherfolk of Ferryden, Scotland (2003); and sometimes these in turn become the focus of everyday sociability, as Angela Janelli discusses in relation to amateur – or what she calls 'wild' – museums (2012; see also Chapter 6).

Home

Many of the studies already discussed in this chapter have illustrated the significance of 'home' in some form, perhaps especially for those who feel exiled from it; and the anthropology of Europe is rich in further examples.[23] 'Home', we have seen, may variously refer to particular countries, regions or villages; and it may be indexed by particular foods, smells, bodies and practices. Nigel Rapport and Andrew Dawson (1998) rightly caution that we should be wary of thinking that 'home' is necessarily emplaced and static; but at the same time it is clear that ideas about 'home' as rooted in particular places are widespread – and highly affectively and politically charged – in Europe. Indeed, Stef Jansen notes that 'the war that tore Yugoslavia apart was precisely a war about the notion of "home"' – who had the right to use it and with precisely what reference (1998: 86). The very fact that 'home' readily encompasses different scales – referring either to the whole country or possibly even continent as well as to familial domestic space – affords this affective and political charge. While there are particular renditions within Europe, as in the German notion of *Heimat* discussed in Chapter 6, an idea about home as a significant locus of our identities and senses of well-being, and as existing as part of a set of nested realisations, especially that of the domestic house and the nation-state, might be seen as part of a European complex. Certainly, it is multiply challenged – by mobility, migration, those with 'homes' in more than one place and those with no homes at all; but it is also, simultaneously, multiply reinforced by memories of, and longings for, 'home' by those who feel its lack.

The sensory and affective density of domestic homes, coupled with the fact that these are often locations of life intimacies and developments over more or less lengthy periods of time, shapes the particular emotive and symbolic resonance of 'home' – and its significance for past presencing. Many anthropological studies have explored the significance of the particular spatial arrangements of houses and their contents, many, especially in Europe, highlighting the salience of the idea that the home and home possessions act as carriers of personal identity and memory.[24] Daniel Miller's *The Comfort of Things* (2008) does so in a particularly compelling fashion by focusing on a London street and exploring the meanings of 'things' – which range widely from furnishings to clothing to internet images – for the street's various inhabitants. By doing so, he paints a vivid portrait of the multiple memories, affects and capacities with which they are invested.

As an illustration of how the sensory experience of the house may furnish nostalgic memories of home, I turn to Anat Hecht's account of the home in Croydon, London, of 'Nan', a Scot in her sixties. Hecht describes Nan's house as a 'private museum of memory' (2001: 141; Hecht 2013), packed with numerous everyday items that she has collected over time; and she describes how these are used by Nan for narrating her life and linking it to the wider histories through which she has lived. Nan's narrations are often nostalgic, as engrossingly conveyed through her use of words and descriptions of the places in which she has dwelt: 'the warmth, light and shininess of the interior [that Nan describes] grants it an almost magical quality, regardless of its modesty. The glowing fire illuminating the multitude of objects in the small family room, creates a sense of warm enclosure, intimacy and care' (2001: 126). At the same time, it is through the everyday possessions that surround her that Nan 'feels

FIGURE 4.2   Display of family photographs and ornaments in Nan's home. Photograph courtesy of Anat Hecht

at home' (2001: 141). These, as well as the stories that she tells, enable Nan to make her past homes present to her; or, as Hecht puts it: 'By "housing" the material and sensory evocations of her narrated memories, Nan symbolically revives the past homes she has left behind' (2001: 141). Interestingly, not only does she do so in her everyday life but also in 'Memory and Smell reminiscences sessions' that she runs at her local museum in London – organised events in which she uses objects as a starting point for memory conversations with visitors (2001: 140).[25]

Dispossessions and repossessions

Houses, even homes, are not, however, always places in which their inhabitants feel 'at home'. As a final area of discussion in this section I briefly turn to cases in which people find themselves living in houses in which they do not feel they fully belong. This is a departure from my focus on nostalgia except insofar as these residents long to be elsewhere, perhaps in a less troubled past, or in a more homely relationship with the places that they occupy. What these studies show is the powerful affective resonance of houses and their contents; as well as the historical and political situatedness of 'dwelling'.

Yael Navaro-Yashin's research on Turkish-Cypriots' experience of living in houses that, before the war and partition of the island, belonged to Greek-

Cypriots, details a particularly intimate uncomfortable presence of the past. These homes – and the things belonging to previous householders with which they are often filled – are described by their inhabitants as generating a 'state of mental depression, deep and unrecoverable sadness, and dis-ease', called '*maraz*' in the local dialect and glossed by Navaro-Yashin as 'melancholia' (2009: 4). The objects and spaces of these houses seem to carry something of the loss experienced by their former owners, and this then penetrates their new owners' bodies through powerful and disconcerting affect. Perhaps this is an especially troubling feeling and needs to be kept subterfuge if, as Papadakis *et al.* suggest, the official affective script of rehoused Turkish Cypriots advocates that they should now feel 'at home' in their new locations (2006, discussed above).

In other post-conflict contexts of homes being occupied by new inhabitants, senses of discomfort among the new owners have been recorded. In many parts of the Balkans, houses have been reallocated post-war, as in the village of Knin, in what is now Croatia, where houses that previously belonged to Serbs now have Croatian owners (Leutloff-Grandits 2006: 117, 122–3). As among the Turkish Cypriots, some of these new inhabitants report senses of depression, guilt and fear. However, Carolin Leutloff-Grandits also observes other, different, emotional dynamics in play. These include a sense of righteous entitlement, the houses being viewed as a form of 'compensatory restitution'. Among some inhabitants this is fuelled not only by ethnonationalism but also religious conviction: 'I think that the houses were given by God' explains one new settler to the ethnographer (2006: 122).[26] In post-Socialist countries more widely there has also been considerable dispossession and reallocation of houses, sometimes to relatives of former owners, as well as contests over ownership, generating mixed and unsettling emotions, and also encounters with ghosts inhabiting the properties. In Estonia, for example, there has been an escalation of ghost stories in the media and everyday life since 1990 (Valk 2006). As Ülo Valk discusses, while these ghosts generally take forms familiar from Estonian folklore, their variable prevalence historically is also bound up with issues of property distribution; and it is also perhaps not surprising that similar kinds of ghosts – human presences continuing to inhabit specific locations after their death – should be widespread in Europe as 'ownership is such a powerful relationship between the self and material objects that it is often projected beyond the grave' (2006: 49). Even so, the 'affecting touch' of ghosts is not necessarily always disquieting; as Valk reports, in some cases the ghosts return to quell the anxieties of the new owners, usually vanishing after they have done so.

This section has attempted to show 'place' – and some of its specific renditions, especially 'home' – to be an important and constitutive element in the European memory complex, not least because of the affect with which it is so often entangled. As a prime mode through which the past can be experienced as a powerful physical presence, 'place' is variously 'made up' not only in rooted locations but also through memory and imagination and the various media that enable them. That the term *nostalgia* might be interpreted as longing for, and yearning to return to, either the past or home is, perhaps, a significant elision, for it is the past as potentially suitable 'home' that nostalgia summons up; and it thus also makes sense that forms of nostalgia emerge and proliferate at times when people are challenged by displacements of various sorts. As we see below, however, and discuss further in Chapter 6, this is does not complete an explanation of nostalgic practices in Europe.

Post-Socialist nostalgia

In the rest of this chapter I continue the discussion of nostalgia through what has emerged as one of the most interesting and extensively documented and debated examples in Europe – nostalgia for aspects of the Socialist past in many post-Socialist countries. That nostalgia for the Socialist past has generated so much interest and discussion speaks partly to the surprise that the phenomenon generated, especially but not only among those who had never directly experienced living in a Socialist country. According to dominant accounts, the demise of socialism should, surely, be viewed entirely positively, especially by those who had 'escaped' it. Given the deprivations and abuses of the Socialist period, why should anybody look back with any longing whatsoever?

Ostalgie

Germany – where post-Socialist longing goes under the name *Ostalgie* ('nostalgia for the East') – was probably the first country in which the phenomenon emerged; and this looking back by former East Germans was in sharp distinction to the future oriented temporality that Borneman argued characterised most citizens of the German Democratic Republic (see Chapter 2). Daphne Berdahl provides one of the most insightful accounts of the phenomenon. Like Verdery, she describes the post-Socialist context as one of 'profound displacement' – summed up in East Germans' 'popular saying that we have "emigrated without leaving [home]"' (2010: 55). While she suggests that *Ostalgie* 'can be an attempt to reclaim a kind of *Heimat* (home or homeland)' (ibid.)*,* she also argues that there have been different phases of *Ostalgie*, none of which has as its object or objective 'recovery of a lost past' (ibid.). The first phase arose in the early-1990s, after an initial rejection of all things eastern. It was mostly a low-key minority movement, instances including middle-aged women wearing the work-smocks that they had discarded in the immediate aftermath of the *Wende* (transition) – thus literally re-embodying their vilified past. But this was not out of a wish to return to that past – to all aspects of lives lived in those smocks. Rather, according to Berdahl, it was about some of those from the former German Democratic Republic asserting 'identity as East Germans' and in effect refusing the relentlessly negative associations that others typically made of their former lives (2010: 43).

By the mid-1990s, however, there was a move to a new phase in which a 'nostalgia industry' developed, with increased production and consumption of

FIGURE 4.3 Display of popular culture in the Olle DDR Museum, Apolda, 2007. Photograph by Sharon Macdonald, reproduced courtesy of the Olle DDR Museum

East German products, such as particular brands of beer or detergent, and also special East German ('Ossi') discos and television shows. This was commonly reported in the press as a rather retrograde romanticisation of the Socialist past engineered by capitalist entrepreneurs; and many waxed vehement against the way that it sanitised the past, forgetting the brutalities of the regime in its shallow concentration on consumer products and popular culture. Acknowledging that this move did entail a degree of knowing forgetting, Berdahl argues, however, that it nevertheless allowed East Germans to share and express their knowledge of the former East, 'of a period of time that differentiates Ossis' (2010: 44). Rather than a purely commercial phenomenon, creating a tidied up past, it was, she claims, a mode of self-identification for East Germans as 'Ossi'. In addition, the focus on consumer products, she suggests, 'reveal[s] a certain mourning for production' (2010: 44), expressive of a sense of real loss.

The new millennium saw the continuation of some of these themes, especially that of shared knowledge, but also – in what she sees as a new phase – 'a playful appropriation and ironic parody of Ostalgie [in which] East German things became "camp" rather than objects of nostalgic longing or counter-memory' (2010: 121–2). This was exemplified in the film *Goodbye Lenin!* On the one hand, she claims, the film's own irony, parody and playfulness exemplify a dimension of Ostalgie that 'celebrate[s] and naturalize[s] capitalism as the inevitable outcome of socialism's demise' (2010: 131). On the other, however, the film also offers an alternative to relentless capitalism, Ostalgie thus providing 'a means of assessing and critiquing global capitalism' (2010: 132).

Evident here is that dealing with 'the past' is neither a once-and-for-all process nor uniform (see also Berdahl 1999). 'Transition' was not encapsulated only in the immediate before and after – although it was often thought of as such, as in the idea of it as a 'turn' or 'new beginning'. In practice, however, it was a longer-term ongoing process in which the past was continually reconfigured in the changing present; and in which different phases were accompanied by different predominant affects and materialisations. My own observations over many years of Germany-observing and especially the academic year 2006–7, that I spent largely living in the former East Germany (mainly Jena), support this too. In addition, though new forms of Ostalgie – the consumerist and the camp – emerged over time, the previous versions did not necessarily vanish; everyday low-key assertions of an Ossi identity – exhibited perhaps in choices of words or jokes – existed alongside the noisier publicly mediated ones. Post-Socialism was also characterised by diverse processes that did not always act in concert. So, for example, while there were manifestations of Ostalgie on the one hand, there could be a simultaneous embracing of capitalism and hurtling future momentum on the other. As everyday furnishings of homes in the Socialist East were lovingly salvaged and put into museums, citizens flocked to the newly opened IKEAs for the globally ubiquitous Swedish replacements. Perhaps other languages, such as Bulgarian, which used plural terms, such as 'changes', captured better what was underway (Creed 2011: 15).

It seemed to me that the dominant and most enduring feature of GDR Ostalgie was an imagined time of greater communitarian solidarity – often refracted through notions of shared willingness among ordinary people to 'make do' with few consumer goods (even if their leaders were behaving otherwise) and to seize other forms of enjoyment; and that this sometimes played itself out through continuing forms of leisure (willingness to sit in bars) and (generous) hospitality. At the same time, however, there was also often a deep ambivalence among former GDR citizens about 'Ossiness', sometimes also seen as a kind of complacency and lack of drive that, it was feared, could lead to them being 'trodden on' as in the past. Likewise, there was considerable ambivalence – about the West and the new Germany (often regarded as more or less synonymous), providing opportunity on the one hand and an 'elbow society', pushy and selfish, on the other. The material culture of the former East could act as a site for the playing out of ongoing identifications and differences, not always in ways that followed along predefined or straightforward identity-categories – not least because so many Wessis ('West Germans') were acknowledging kinship or other links to the East. The burgeoning DDR museums – especially the smaller ones, usually begun by enthusiasts – sometimes provided space for encounters of this kind. Offering the material culture of the former East Germany up for public viewing – museumising it – was itself an ambivalent enterprise. On the one hand, museumisation provided an affirmation of worth. On the other, however, there was a risk that those coming to view would simply confirm their stereotypes of the German Democratic Republic as backward. While I noted this in various things told to me by museum staff, a visit as a tourist to the newly opened Haus der Geschichte in Lutherstadt Wittenberg provided an illustration in practice.[27]

As my husband and I began visiting the museum, we were greeted with suspicion, verging on hostility from one of the museum staff members, who followed us from one room to another of the museum – set out primarily, as with so many others of this type, into different 'rooms' of a house. As we entered a living room, my husband pointed to some plastic crockery and exclaimed: 'We had those!' The woman laughed at his enthusiastic identification and a friendly conversation followed about how fashionable these had been in the 1960s and how the GDR had produced lots of very smart things. She opened cupboards for us to see more items, many of which were very similar ones to that we had also had at the same time. Elsewhere in the museum too, there were lively conversations underway with visitors – mainly East Germans – also sharing memories of the items, and times, displayed. Not so much about a wish to return to those times, the Ossi material culture provided a valuable focus for shared memories and for forging conversational links mainly between those who had directly shared the East German past but also, to some extent, to those who were willing to judge in the same terms as Ossis themselves.

FIGURE 4.4 Site for shared reminiscence. Exhibition of everyday life in the Haus der Geschichte, Lutherstadt Wittenberg, 2007. Photograph by Sharon Macdonald, reproduced courtesy of the Haus der Geschichte Wittenberg

Other post-Socialist nostalgias

Post-socialist nostalgia, at least in its public versions, seems to have emerged later in most other countries than it did in Germany. Gerald Creed suggests that the variation can be explained by the fact that it requires two conditions to do so: (1) the impossibility of return to a Socialist system; and (2) actual economic improvements in people's lives (2010: 37). While the re-unification of Germany rendered going back to any kind of Socialist system unthinkable and also led to quicker economic gains than was the case elsewhere, it is among those who have been disadvantaged by the new political-economic system – especially those who are unemployed – that Ostalgie is especially strongly felt. Elsewhere in Eastern Europe, Creed's two conditions seem to provide part but not all of the explanation for the different timing and different forms of post-Socialist nostalgia that have emerged. In Albania, for example, where the socialist period was especially brutal and marked by extreme hardship, and where there is still considerable poverty, there has been little such nostalgia – at least expressed publicly (Schwander-Sievers 2010).[28] In Romania, where there was 'continuity in the Communist and post-Communist elites' (Gille 2010: 282), nostalgia does not seem to have emerged until there were prospects of EU accession, and it has remained restrained (Grossman 2010). Creed's own study is of Bulgaria, where, he notes, it was only in the twenty-first century, as prosperity grew and the prospect of joining the EU began to look likely, that nostalgia for socialist times began to blossom.

Hungary is an interesting case here, for it seems to contravene Creed's conditions, but perhaps what is involved is not in fact 'nostalgia' even though it takes some of the same forms. In the immediate wake of the collapse of Soviet control, 'even before [the country's] first democratic elections took place' (Nadkarni 2010: 194), there was a revelling in things Soviet. These included a booming market in Soviet memorabilia, and setting up 'Socialist-themed parties, happenings, and even a pizzeria ("Marxim")' (ibid.). This was too soon for there to have been any material change in people's lives – and indeed Hungary was one of the most prosperous of the Eastern bloc countries – and before it had even been decided which party would control the country. Characteristic of the 'nostalgia' was that it was mostly expressed through Soviet materialisations. In some ways this was peculiar, for from the 1960s Hungary had managed to gain more autonomy than most other countries under Soviet rule, in what was sometimes called 'Goulash Communism'. Equating the Socialist past with Soviet rule, however, suited the political Right – by equating Socialism with its more repressive face; and also the Left – by depicting the Socialism of the past as unlike their new, freshly renamed version. What was involved here then was not in any sense a longing to recuperate any aspects of the Soviet past. Rather, as Maya Nadkarni argues, it entailed a commodification of Socialist 'historical relics as humorous kitsch'; and in doing so managed to 'demonstrate not only… emotional distance from the recent Socialist era – but also the success of Western

FIGURE 4.5 Soviet sausage. Photograph courtesy of Neringa Klumbyte

capitalism in Hungary' (2010: 195). This, then, was a kind of 'meta-nostalgia' – a strategic and ironic playing with the nostalgic form to demonstrate its opposite.

In Lithuania too, in a splendid discussion of 'the renaissance of the Soviet sausage', Neringa Klumbyte argues that the growing popularity of this sausage – and various other 'things socialist', including some populist political parties – should not be equated with a wish to 'return to oppression' (as some journalists complain) or to not have democracy. In this case what is involved, however, is not so much ironic meta-nostalgia as an attempt by a politically and economically marginalised population to reclaim themselves as being and having been 'honourable citizens'. Imagined as a healthy, non-contaminated product, 'Soviet' sausages (reintroduced in 1998) do not signal a desire for all aspects of the Soviet system but rather for a 'new postsocialist utopia, successfully consumed in the literal and metaphorical sense, which mixes the imagined Soviet past and the European present in people's imaginations to produce a distinctive fantasy of their reconcilability' (Klumbyte 2010: 33). Many consumers claimed, simply, that the sausages tasted good (2010: 24).

These examples, and especially the possibility of ironic nostalgia, illuminate the fact that the same practice may be invested with different meanings and affects. This is well illustrated in the countries of the former Yugoslavia, with their various, and sometimes absent, nostalgias. Zala Volčič argues that the fact that most of these countries suffered 'destruction and ethnic cleansing in the wake of the collapse of socialism' meant that it was *post*-Socialism that was linked with 'brutality and the subsequent rekindling of ethnic and religious hatreds' (Volčič 2007: 27), leading to a more fertile ground for the growth of nostalgia for Socialist times. Yet, Svetlana Boym recalls visiting *Nostalgija Snack Bar* in Ljubljana in 1997 and being told by one of her friends in Zagreb that there could never be such a place in Zagreb or Belgrade, because 'Nostalgia is a bad word … Nostalgia is Yugo-nostalgia' (2001: 51). From a country that *had* suffered post-Socialist brutality, unlike Slovenia, it was precisely this – the suffering that had gone in to achieving a redrawing of the maps – that made Yugonostalgia 'bad' and only possible in places outside the war zone.

Since then, however, there has been a flourishing of Yugonostalgia across most of its former countries – with it now 'perhaps loudest in Bosnia-Herzogovina' (Burić 2010: 227). One reason for this may be that Yugonostalgia has since come to be seen as a way of 'not talking about the war'. In ethnographic research in long-term ethnically mixed villages in Croatia, on the border with Bosnia-Herzogovina, in the late 1990s, Stef Jansen (2002) shows that it was Serbian villagers who mostly articulated Yugonostalgic sentiments. Not wanting to draw attention to Serbian violence of the war, Yugonostalgia allowed them to express willingness to exist peaceably alongside their neighbours (see also Jansen 2009; further discussed in Chapter 8).

Yugonostalgia takes a wide range of forms, however, and is unevenly embraced not only by different ethnicities but also by different generations and genders. A particularly 'noisy' form is a cult of former President of Yugoslavia, Josip Broz Tito, which includes the turning of his (luxurious) home into a holiday resort, the use of his image in advertising, opening of *Café Tito* in Sarajevo, and restoration of his official train by the Serbian Railway company for themed trips.[29] While some of this looks like ironic nostalgia, and to some may well be, Fedja Burić describes how it also includes visits to his birthplace, and a Tito 'homepage on the Internet, which has generated thousands of emails addressed to the deceased Marshal' (Burić 2010: 227). Her interviews with Bosnian Muslims in Chicago show them to differ sharply on the question of whether Tito 'got the Muslims their nation'; however, their reference to Tito as a father figure (an image that was propagated during his regime) helps them to straddle this difference and their own potentially conflicting positions. At the same time, however, Burić notes that this father figure image appeals less to her younger, female interviewee, so highlighting potential variations of nostalgic affinity along gender and age as well as ethnic, political and individual lines.

Transnational or other 'external' players, such as tourists or Western media, have also influenced the shapes and strength of post-Socialist nostalgia. Dominic Boyer argues that *Ostalgie* in Germany, especially as manifest in a film such as *Goodbye Lenin!,* is a 'West German…naturalizing fantasy', that allows West Germans to 'claim a future free from the burden of history' (2006: 363) – it is turned instead into harmless kitsch. As such, it also speaks to the fantasies – and historical consciousnesses – of those who never lived under Socialist regimes. Certainly, souvenirs of Socialist times – like the gas-masks, fur-hats, currency and Lenin statuettes on sale in a Berlin market – and the chance to eat at a Communist-themed café, visit a museum of the Socialist past or even stay in an 'Ostel' (a GDR-themed hostel) have proved popular tourist draws throughout the former Eastern bloc.[30] While much of this is infused with an ironic, playful affect – very different from that surrounding Holocaust tourism (see Chapter 8) – it remains open to more complex interactions and historical awareness, especially in its museums, some of which detail brutalities as well as consumer goods.

In an argument based on fieldwork among young far-Right-supporting East Germans in Berlin, Nitzan Shoshan argues that their nostalgic affect 'exceeds' the specificities of German memory politics and also 'the broader story of post-Socialism' (2012: 44). His argument is that a nostalgic sensibility towards commodities from the past – which may be Nazi memorabilia as well as the cheaper beer of pre-*Wende* times – is also part of a more global waning of a forward-looking temporality exemplified by material accumulation. Shoshan's study is also a reminder that not all of the new forms – or intensities – of nostalgia in post-Socialist countries have been for the Socialist past. Indeed, most have been for other, especially pre-Socialist, times. Among Slavic Muslim Pomaks in Bulgaria, for example, Kirsten Ghodsee has described the rise of more orthodox forms of Islam – perceived as more traditional (especially in terms of gender relations) – alongside nostalgia for a Socialist past in which standards of living are claimed to have been better (2010; see also Parla 2009). Other examples include many of the returned dead bodies, as discussed above, as well as traditional and folk heritage (Chapter 6) and Jewish heritage (Chapter 8). This turn to the pre-Socialist variously offers a means of claiming temporal integrity of identity over time, perhaps 'skipping' the Socialist period; as well as ground for debating and affectively engaging with the present via the revisited past.

★ ★ ★

This chapter has sought to make clear that memory does not only occur 'in the head'. It is also distributed in practices, materials, bodies and interactions with others; it is sensory and affective experience, including talk. Ethnographic research on past presencing in Europe has begun to pay greater attention to the embodied (affective and sensorial) and material (especially objects, food, homes and place), describing the sensory and affective experiences of recall, and showing how these may involve material 'prompts' and widespread human experiences but at the same time take shape in specific times and places. Research also explores how particular kinds of objects – such as the furniture of others or foods from childhood – may be especially memorially or affectively affecting; that which is strongly felt seemingly being more likely to be remembered.[31]

Nostalgia has repeatedly emerged in this literature. It can, I suggest, be understood as part of the European memory complex, as one of its elements, or

FIGURE 4.6 Market with Socialist-era-style souvenirs, Berlin, 2011. Photograph by Sharon Macdonald

FIGURE 4.7 DDR café and exhibition in a popular tourist area of Berlin, 2011. Photograph by Sharon Macdonald

perhaps shapes, repeatedly occurring, available for 'borrowing', and morphing into different forms. While nostalgia might be felt acutely by an individual – perhaps rendering them listless and unable to concentrate on their task at hand – the research discussed here shows nostalgia to be social and cultural, and about the here-and-now as much as the past or elsewhere. This does not mean that it is not expressive of real changes that are underway (Heady and Miller 2006). The chapter has highlighted variations in nostalgias – including post-Socialist and meta- or ironic nostalgia – though has not attempted a taxonomy. Distinctions are useful, as that between 'restorative' and 'reflective' (Boym 2001), but the aim should not be to try to fulfil the collector's dream (or is it nightmare?) of the full set. Rather, the task is to probe into what is going on, explore subtleties and nuance, as well as to grasp any commonalities. In the end, 'nostalgia' might not be the right characterisation of a particular phenomenon. Its role is that of entry point rather than object to be pinned down.

Nostalgias do seem to have increased alongside the wider memory phenomenon. Maybe this is almost a tautology, for the memory phenomenon is so centrally concerned with 'looking back'; nostalgia is just one of the modes in which this is done. Precisely what this mode is, however, has become less clear the more closely 'nostalgia' is examined. Typically seen in English-language discussions as looking at the past or distant home through rose-tinted spectacles, seeing only the nice parts and ignoring the rest, the anthropological studies show both that the word or its 'translations' often carry other connotations and also that what is called 'nostalgia' can be very different from this characterisation. Certainly, there are forms of looking back that *do* fit the description – the shiny, glowing interiors of Nan's recollections or juicy fruits in the memories of the *pieds-noirs*. But even here, what the anthropologists show, is that these are not simply uninformed or naïve understandings of what the past was like but are part of people's ongoing articulation – not only in words but also in actions – of their relationships to the present and to each other. These are themes too of the chapter that follows, which explores them further in relation to questions of commodification, authenticity and that noisy form of memory materialisation: heritage.

5

SELLING THE PAST

Commodification, authenticity and heritage

> Figuring out how to stop or stave off forgetting is becoming a huge business.
> Eric Gable and Richard Handler[1]

An anxiety repeatedly voiced in the memory phenomenon is that the past is being commodified. History is becoming business; money is being made out of memory; and Europe is turning into a market of heritage attractions. Welcome to *Memorylands,* the European heritage theme park!

Central to this concern is not just that there is money to be made from marketing the past, but that, deluged by a proliferation of standardised historical forms produced for tourists, Europe's populations will lose their sense of their own identities as they are manipulated into putting on performances of themselves or their pasts for commercial ends. Real diversity will be swept away in a barrage of predictable forms of superficial difference. Historically themed places will be manufactured as part of an essentially standardizing identity industry. Heritage, by these accounts, is a noisy cultural form, an artificially manufactured memory practice, dominated by the market, which risks drowning out 'authentic' relationships with the past.

We have already seen the contours of this debate in previous chapters, especially in concerns about invented traditions and the commercialised dimensions of nostalgia; and will meet them again in discussions of 'musealisation' in the following. They are also reflected in wider debates central to the anthropology of tourism,[2] in which tourism is conceptualised as a kind of 'cultural contamination' (Meethan 2001: 90), with 'commodification' cast as the principal pollutant, and heritage or cultural performance that requires payment to view regarded as inherently inauthentic. In this chapter I explore some of the arguments and assumptions involved in this position through anthropological research on Europe. While giving attention to the ways in which the past is being marketed and to consequences of this, I am also interested in the fact that anxieties about the memory phenomenon – in academic analyses and local discourses – so often centre upon commodification. To couple terms such as 'industry', 'business', 'commerce', 'market' and 'money' to 'heritage', 'history', 'the past', 'identity' and so forth seems itself a kind of sacrilege. Certainly, strong arguments have been put forward about the commodification of the past and why it might be cause for concern, and anthropologists of Europe have reported cases of standardisation and a loss of diversity, as we will see below. Nevertheless, I suggest that the prevalence of commodification anxiety discourse also merits attention as an ethnographic phenomenon in itself. The opposing of the 'spheres' or 'assemblage elements' of heritage/memory/identity, etc., on the one hand and commodities/industry/the market on the other is itself a distinctive feature of the European memory complex.[3]

The axis of this opposition is authenticity. Put overly crudely, the market is typically considered inauthentic – as concerned only with profit; and heritage is valued for its promise to provide 'something more', 'something real' – the authentic. So when the two come together, this is oxymoronic and unsettling. It is worth noting here that if authenticity is indeed about 'objective' qualities of a thing, such as its origins and age, then the idea that it becomes less authentic when it is treated as a commodity is rather odd. Why should it be considered any the less 'genuine' just because it can be bought and sold? As we will see, there is a lot ravelled up in this, not least, both specific and variable ways in which 'authenticity' is understood and performed. These contribute to particular effects, dilemmas and paradoxes involved in heritage practice, including techniques such as official heritage listing – something which is both part and not part of marketing the past and which is also proliferating in the contemporary memory phenomenon.

Commodification and inauthenticity

A classic account of cultural commodification is Davydd Greenwood's ethnographically-based account of a ritual called the *alarde* in the Basque town of Fuenterabbia (1989/1972). The *alarde* is a commemoration and celebration of a seventeenth-century siege that the town successfully endured. In the ritual, the townspeople come together, ignoring status differences that might normally divide them, and collectively perform a sense of equality and of Basqueness, in opposition to outsiders. As Greenwood emphasises, '*it is a performance for the participants*, not a show' (1989: 176, original emphasis). Nevertheless, during the expansion of tourism in the 1960s the *alarde* increasingly became a magnet for tourists seeking out 'local color' (1989: 172). Indeed, so popular did it become that the town could not accommodate all those wishing to view it. In response, the municipal council decided to charge tourists and to stage the ritual twice on the same day. As Greenwood reports, however, this was highly detrimental to local people's sense of the meaningfulness of the ritual. Outsiders became a legitimate presence at the event rather than its symbolic other. They had, in effect, bought the right to view it. Something that had been part of an authentic culture, thus, became instead a commodity, 'rob[bing] people of the very meanings by which they organise their lives' (1989: 179).

This loss of meaning was not, however, simply the result of making the viewing of the ritual available for a price. Also at issue was a transformation involved in the shift from performance to show; a shift that Greenwood casts as a transformation in the nature of 'culture' itself. Prior to becoming a show for tourists, the meanings of the ritual were encoded in its practice – they were *implicit*. Greenwood regards tacit meaning as characteristic of authentic culture. In performing the ritual for paying tourists, however, the meanings became *explicit*. For Greenwood this means that 'culture' loses its significance – it is, we might say, 'de-meaned'. Generalising from this, Greenwood argues that tourism almost always and inevitably involves a loss of meaning for those who put their culture on display.[4]

Dean MacCannell's celebrated work on tourism is similarly concerned with the ways in which display may render practice inauthentic. He employs the notion of 'staged authenticity' (1989) to highlight what he sees as the ersatz nature of that which the tourist is offered. He regards tourism as a quest after the authentic – a quest that is inherently doomed because, as soon as anything is presented to tourists, it is necessarily 'staged', so rendering it inauthentic. If this is a dilemma for the tourists avidly seeking 'the real thing' it is even more so for those putting their cultures and heritages on display for touristic consumption. The latter involves what MacCannell calls 'a kind of going native for tourism' (1992: 159), which puts its performers in danger of 'a distinctive modern form of alienation, a kind of loss of soul' (MacCannell 1992: 168). This alienation stems, according to MacCannell, from commodification, a process in which phenomena such as ethnicity or authenticity cease simply to 'be' and to have *use-value* in everyday life-worlds but instead come to have *exchange value* in a cultural system that peddles numerous formulae for translating between, or exchanging, things and categories that would normally be thought incommensurable. The market and market-values subsume everything 'to the exclusion of all other values' (MacCannell 1992: 169). Nothing is valued in itself but only as currency. Moreover, he suggests, there is a standardisation that accompanies this process. Although standardisation may adopt a veneer of variation – such as a superficial appearance of cultural difference that is presented to the tourist – it works in fact to iron out real, authentic, difference.

In a more recent work, *Ethnicity, Inc.*, (2009) John and Jean Comaroff offer a similar argument along slightly different lines. Observing people around the world seeking to market themselves and their culture through distinctive ethnicity, they argue that this does not mean a weakening of cultural identity, as MacCannell assumes, but that it has become its means of affirmation. Gaining more 'sales' – literal and metaphorical – of their 'ethnic' products and selves, is a means by which those marketing their culture in these terms accrue rather than lose value. Although the Comaroffs claim that this gaining of value from circulation makes the 'ethno-commodity' 'a very strange thing indeed' (2009: 20), it is surely not so unusual in commodity terms – there are other products that become more desirable as they become more widely known about (this is the point of advertising). It is only strange if we think that it is ethnicity (and its manifestation as heritage) that is up for sale and that it will, therefore, have new owners once it is bought. But we do not usually assume that selling a product is also selling the people who made it – even if qualities about them are used to sell the product. So, to return to an example from Chapter 2, when French wine is sold there are not concerns about this as an alienating selling of people, even though the qualities of Frenchness and *terrain,* or specific châteaux, may be used in selling. Although the Comaroffs add cautions about historical contingency and 'material exuberance' (2009: 146, 23; after Mazarella 2003), like MacCannell, they too regard what they call 'the identity industry' (2009: 24) as producing greater sameness, working according to a common, if not invariant, neo-liberal logic. This involves subjects operating according to self-directed economic calculation as choice-making consumers or entrepreneurs – 'ethno-preneurs' as they put it for those engaged in 'the ethnicity business' (e.g. 2009: 27).

Below, I address these arguments by looking at some anthropological research on heritage and tourism in Europe, including a sustained example from my own fieldwork in the Scottish Hebrides. As we will see, there undoubtedly is much evidence of marketing places and products through forms and ideas about heritage and the past; and local people as well as academics may be concerned about commodification and authenticity. But to interpret these concerns straightforwardly as evidence of commodification and a loss of authenticity does not get at all that is involved.

Culture and enterprise in *The Skye Story*

Like a number of anthropologists working in Europe in the 1980s and 1990s, I found that the making of heritage and museums, and debate about whose history should be displayed and how, was going on around me – and, as such, demanded attention in relation to my focus on identity and history.[5] A heritage centre or museum can be seen as an instance of what John D. Dorst refers to as an 'auto-ethnography' (1989: 4) – a text that 'culture' has produced about itself (1989: 2). It is a formalised and self-conscious cultural account, though one that inevitably bears the imprint of more than its makers' conscious intentions. By looking at both the 'text' – the finished exhibition – within the surrounding cultural context, and also discussing its making and aims with its makers, an auto-ethnography of this sort can help to highlight the preferred histories that are being told and also the particular conceptions of history, identity, commodification, authenticity and related elements that are in operation.

In 1993 a new heritage centre opened in the Isle of Skye's capital, Portree. Called *Aros: The Skye Story*,[6] I chose to look at it as it seemed a telling case for ongoing debates about heritage, as well as being part of the fieldwork context in which I had worked for a decade. At first sight, it was a typical example of the kind of tourist-oriented heritage centre that was springing up at the time, and had various features that suggested that it might well be an epitome of the commodification and inauthenticity that critics such as MacCannell were decrying. It employed exhibitionary technologies that were often regarded as part of a relatively ersatz or even fake heritage: namely, models and reconstructions, bought from specialist heritage companies that were also proliferating at the time, and that were supplying many of the new heritage centres springing up around Europe and beyond. It contained very few 'old things' – in contradistinction to the museum of folk-life that I will discuss in the next chapter; and it was located in a prefabricated building, erected specifically for the purpose. Tourists were an intended audience – its audio commentary was available in French, German, Italian, Japanese and Spanish as well as in English and Gaelic. But, as I learnt, tourists were not the *only* ones at whom it was aimed.

The centre had been established by two men in their thirties who had been brought up on Skye – Donald and Calein – both of whom were Gaelic-speakers and had been involved in various Gaelic revival projects on the island. This revival had taken off during the 1980s, with a wide range of developments aimed at preserving the Gaelic language and community. It included educational projects, such as increasing the use of Gaelic in schools, cultural projects, such as community history initiatives, and economic projects, such as the establishment of community cooperatives. This was part of the broader ethnic revival – sometimes called 'ethnic resurgence' or 'ethnonationalism' – underway in many parts of Europe, especially the peripheries with longstanding minority languages.[7] Donald and Calein were part of a generational group who would previously have had to leave the island to find work but who now, with the expanding Gaelic revival, were able to tap into some of the new possibilities, including new funding sources, to become revival entrepreneurs – or what the Comaroffs call 'ethno-preneurs' (2009: 27). As Donald described it to me, he and Calein were 'looking around for something new' to do in the late 1980s and a visit by Calein to the Jorvik Viking centre in York – one of the most renowned and successful of the heritage developments of the new 'heritage industry' at that time – inspired them to investigate doing something along those lines in Skye.

Donald's account of making the centre and of his own wider experience of the revival made it clear that he did not see a gulf between enterprise and Gaelic culture. He referred, for example, to 'the revival or business or whatever you call it', taking them as synonymous; and he accounted for his own participation in the revival in terms of the life experience that turned him into an enterprising person. He was aware that some – such as an older generation or those who looked at the Hebrides as a repository of qualities lacking in the urban, industrialised and rational world – did see calculated business activity as running against the grain of local, Gaelic, culture; and perhaps he was also aware of a wider critique at that time of entrepreneurial activity as at odds with 'authentic culture' (e.g. Corner and Harvey 1991). But he regarded this as a view that needed to be challenged. Challenging it also meant refusing to locate Gaelic culture and language just in the past, or as separate from wider socio-political developments. The heritage centre – and its exhibition, *The Skye Story* – were a means of doing this.

Inalienable heritage

One running theme of the exhibition was about the survival of the Gaelic language and culture over time in the face of oppression. This was a direct counter to a widespread discourse about Gaelic decline; and it served to depict the current revival and its various developments as part of a longer history of popular struggle and resistance. At work here was also an interesting conception of *heritage*. The Gaelic subtitle for the heritage centre was *Dualchas an Eilein,* which can be translated as 'heritage of the Island' (*An Eilein,* 'the Island', being used colloquially to refer to Skye). However, *dualchas* means heritage in rather a specific sense. Most Gaelic-English dictionaries list *oighreachd* as the standard translation of *heritage. Oighreachd* refers to material property that is inherited from generation to generation. *Dualchas,* by contrast, refers to more intangible matters of nature, character and duty. The following glosses are given in Gaelic's most comprehensive dictionary, which also notes the difficulty of translating the term into English:

> 1. Hereditary disposition or right. 2. Imitation of the ways of one's ancestors. 3. Bias of character. 4. Nature, temper. 5. Native place. 6. Hire, wages, dues. 6. [sic.] Duty.
>
> (Dwelly 1977/1911: 367)

Dualchas is something to which one is obviously and undeniably connected and for the most part from which one is inseparable. It might manifest itself in various ways (a child is not identical to its parents), and might be put to various uses, but at root it is inalienable: it is kept even while it is passed on (as from one generation to the next).

According to anthropologist of Melanesia, Annette Weiner, this idea of the inalienable, and its embodiment in material form, is a very different kind of relation to objects than that of commodity relations (Weiner 1992).[8] In commodity exchange, ownership is transmitted from seller to buyer. 'Inalienable possessions', by contrast, are kept for as long as possible or, if they are passed on, stolen by or lent to others, are not fully disconnected from their original owners but remain 'imbued with [their] intrinsic and ineffable identities' (Weiner 1992: 6). Her main examples are drawn from Melanesia, especially the armshells and necklaces that are exchanged in the system known as *kula*, famously described by Malinowski (1922), but she also notes the Crown Jewels, the Elgin Marbles, heirlooms and art works among Western instances. Such objects are what she calls 'symbolically dense' (1993) to varying degrees: that is, they are regarded as rich in significance and many stories are told about them. Over time, this symbolic density, and their value, usually increases. This means too that inalienable possessions are likely to play roles in what she calls 'cosmological authentication' (1992: 9) – asserting the legitimacy of the social identities of their owners. In addition, because of their relative persistence over time and resistance to the movement of exchange, 'inalienable possessions' act, she says, as 'stabilizing forces' (ibid.). This does not mean, however, that they are necessarily uncontested. On the contrary, others might want to possess them, especially as they may accrue particular value from the fact that they are kept out of the market. In addition, because of their role in cosmological authentication, they may become a focus of struggles for change. This does not mean that inalienable possessions never change hands; but just that even if they do so they are somehow still partly 'kept' due to the link with their original owners. Neither does it mean that they exist in settings that are fully outside the market. On the contrary, they may be surrounded, and even sustained, by accompanying exchanges of alienable things.

Heritage would seem to be an inalienable possession in these terms (cf. McCrone *et al.* 1995: 197). It is dense in history and symbolic significance and tightly bound to the identity of a particular people and/or place. It is properly kept, though its ownership may be contested. What are called the Elgin Marbles in the UK and the Parthenon Marbles in Greece are a clear example of this, Greece putting more emphasis upon origins and the UK on subsequent aspects of the sculptures' history.[9] More widely, however, the notion of inalienable possession opens the possibility for non-owners to come to learn and admire, and to take away souvenirs, knowledge, images and memories, without this leading either to a diminishment of what is 'kept' by the people nor to its recasting in commodity terms. This, we should note, is very different from the argument of the Comaroffs who regard heritage as 'identity in tractable, alienable form, identity whose found objects and objectifications may be consumed by others and, therefore, be delivered to the market' (2009: 10).

Dualchas: *inalienable dispositions*

Inalienability in the sense described by Weiner does seem to be characteristic of *dualchas*. It is what endures – what keeps its identity – over time, through any exchanges (such as inheritance) that occur. As such, it is not conceptualised as a commodity and nor does it have 'commodity candidacy' – i.e. the likelihood of becoming a commodity (Appadurai 1986: 13). It is less clear, however, that *dualchas* is a 'possession'. First, it does not refer to specific objects or a body of material culture. Second, rather than being something owned by persons –

and thus separable from them – it is, rather, in the words of Dwelly (above), a 'disposition'. That is, it is a quality of persons – their 'character', 'nature', 'temper'. As such, it hardly seems to be the kind of thing to be available for sale or exchange.

This distinction – between possession and disposition – might seem slight, especially in light of the argument that I made in Chapter 1 that in Europe persons are widely conceptualised in terms of a Lockean forensic model in which property is thoroughly entangled with personal identity. Yet, I suggest, it is precisely because property can be detachable that certain predicaments of the European memory complex occur – such as the Estonian ghosts discussed in the previous chapter; and it also accounts for some of the often rather bizarre arguments of economic anthropology. In addition, it is part of the reason why commodification is such a concern, as I discuss further below. What the example of *dualchas* shows, however, is that heritage does not need to be understood and acted in this way.

Dualchas, then, is a particular way of being or going about things. As such, it might be manifest in particular social relations and encounters. This includes in relations of contact with 'outsiders', about which there is a good deal in *The Skye Story*. However, rather than corrupt or dilute 'heritage', as a proprietorial model might have it, these interactions manifest or even produce *dualchas. The Skye Story* has no problem with showing Gaels making use of outside agencies or practices. Primary origins are not what matter. What does matter is the disposition involved, and how other things or events are related to through it. Note here too that one meaning of *dualchas,* according to Dwelly, is 'hire, wages, dues'. From a perspective that sees heritage and economics in different, and even opposing, spheres, this appears strange – a mere homophone perhaps. If we understand it, however, as a particular way of going about things that endures over time, and that looks to past practice as a model for the future, then it is explicable that one term might cover both of these. It is also perhaps not so strange if we follow Keith Hart's argument that money should be recognised as a means of forming and maintaining social relations, and also carrying symbolic values, rather than reified into a distinct, supposedly impersonal realm (2005). At least some concerns over commodification stem, then, from beginning with a model in which money/the market/commodities are regarded as antithetical to other kinds of supposedly less superficial values. Hart provocatively suggests that this model is widely held by anthropologists because 'they don't like money and they don't have much of it. It symbolises the world they have rejected for something more authentic elsewhere' (2005: 160). It is, of course, not only anthropologists who hold this model – though we are perhaps especially susceptible to the lures of alternative rewards (cf. also Bendix 2008). Indeed, as Hart observes, it is part of a dualism between market and home – one the space of wage-labour and the other of more personal relations – that is widespread in the West (2005: 166). As we see here, a version of this dualism thoroughly infuses debates about commodification and heritage in the European memory complex.

History, myth and story

Thinking about heritage as a disposition also opens it up to questions about who is relating to it and from what particular position: of whose disposition is a particular account a manifestation? This is evident, I suggest, in an emphasis on *positioning* – or vantage-points – in Donald's carefully differentiated use of the terms 'history', 'story' and 'myth'. As he explains, the exhibition was not only aimed at tourists but also at:

> the people. It's for the ordinary person who lives on a croft, really… It's aimed at a lot of people, you know, whoever's interested in their history and in their culture who wants to get a wee bit extra from what they would get in most of the story books… We find that a lot of [local people] are not well versed in their history… There's an awful lot of myths told about their history. So we feel that … somebody had to deal with them.

History, according to this account, is told through different 'stories' – accounts from different vantage-points. He says:

> The story we tell is very different from what is told elsewhere in Skye, especially Dunvegan Castle [ancestral home of the MacLeod chiefs] and Clan Donald [home of the MacDonald chiefs]… It is a very different story, told from a different point of view.

Although he expresses some respect for these centres, and although his description of all of the different versions of the past as stories might appear relativist – each manifests its own particular disposition – his use of the term 'myth' shows that he does not regard all equally. Myths are incorrect histories in his account; and part of the aim of *The Skye Story* is to provide *truer* alternatives to those told in Skye's more aristocratic heritage venues. All might be products of their dispositions but some can still be factually wrong.

One example of this is how the popular topic of Bonnie Prince Charlie is represented in *The Skye Story*. Rather than depicting the Jacobite rebellion of 1745, led by the Prince, culminating in the Battle of Culloden (1746), as a near triumph of Scotland over England, with the Prince a Highland hero, it is portrayed as a disaster for Highland people. A reconstructed scene of the Prince's sojourn in Skye shows him at the inn where his identity was revealed. This happened, according to the exhibition's account (which Donald tells me is based on some of the little sound evidence available), because the Prince refused to share a drinking cup – as was Highland custom – thus betraying his aristocratic and foreign identity.

In its revelation of usually untold 'stories', the exhibition goes further still. It argues that the Clan chiefs – MacDonald and MacLeod – failed to support the Jacobite rebellion because they had been bribed into inaction for fear of

FIGURE 5.1 Pages in a leaflet about *The Skye Story*. The image in the lower left of the leaflet shows the innkeeper MacNab recognizing the Prince's true identity as he refuses to share the drinking cup. The image to the right is of the slave ship. Copyright: Aros; reproduced courtesy of Donald MacDonald, Aros

the revelation of their complicity in a 'slave trade' – in which Skye peasants were sent to America as slaves. The most dramatic section of the exhibition is a reconstructed part of a slave ship – referred to as 'The Ship of the People'. The choice to focus on activities labelled 'slavery' is an especially powerful means of conveying the reprehensible nature of the activity to visitors, partly because of the parallel historical cases elsewhere – 'multidirectional memory' as Michael Rothberg (2009) would put it – which are thereby evoked. Countering the image of the Clan chief as a paternalistic benefactor is not only a historical matter, however. The role of such chiefs as major landholders, sometimes in conflict with local people (most of whom are tenants of such landholders) over how land should be used, is a continuing one. As such, it is clear that heritage here is far from 'dead and safe', as Hewison characterised it (1987: 144; and see previous chapter) but is, rather, part of a continuing playing out of certain dispositions that have also manifest themselves in the past.

This aim and conception of history also has bearing on the conceptualisation of authenticity. As with the idea of *dualchas* and manifest in the lack of attempt to include real old objects in the exhibition, authenticity here is not about origins or provenance. Instead, it is concerned with the truth to a disposition and to the story – and vantage-point – that deserves to be told. As Donald emphasised to me, the quality of the *research* undertaken for telling this story – for providing this particular history – was especially important. This, and its capacity to tap into a popular but usually relatively hidden history, is what constitutes authenticity here. Authenticity is a kind of integrity of being and doing things in a certain way. As I argue further below, this is a central way in which authenticity is understood in the European memory complex, though it is not the only one.

Authenticity

According to Gilmore and Pine, authenticity is 'what consumers really want' (2007). It is also remarkably stretchy. As I noted above, the idea that commodification *in itself* renders heritage inauthentic is odd, for usually marketing, advertising and so forth are considered *extrinsic* to the objects, events or persons that authenticity claims are being made about. More commonly, authenticity is thought of as *intrinsic* to the thing – about actual origins, factual histories and the fabric or stuff from which it is made, all of which might be 'authenticated' (the verb itself highlighting this particular understanding). This is an 'objective' conception of authenticity. When Donald emphasises the importance of 'getting the facts right' and the role of research and expertise, he is attempting to set this objective model as the frame for judging authenticity. He does so in awareness both of the fact that this is a dominant, respected means of judging authenticity and also that *The Skye Story* might be judged in other ways – as an inauthentic, commoditised cultural form.

The ethnography of Europe is rich in examples of battles over the authenticity of heritage. These make it abundantly clear that what is at stake is rarely just incorrect facts. They also show that commodification is only sometimes what is at issue. Rather, if heritage is shown to be inauthentic – if it is not what it purports to be – then this throws the authenticity and legitimacy of the related social identity into question. To question the authenticity of somebody's heritage is generally regarded as equivalent to casting aspersions on their identity claims and usually too, on other qualities, such as their truthfulness. Disputes over the authenticity of heritage – which are often bound up with questions of what is worthy of conservation – are, thus, almost always simultaneously identity contests, battles over whose identity will be projected into the future. This often leads to high passions over matters such as whether a particular building or site should be preserved or not, as shown by examples such as disputes over the restoration of buildings to Venetian or Turkish styles in the Cretan town of Rethemnos (Herzfeld 2001), whether and how to restore parts of the villagescape in Monadières (Hodges 2010) or whether to restore or reconstruct back to pre-Socialist times in post-Socialist Europe, as for example, in the case of the rebuilding of the former *Schloss* on the site of the GDR Palace of the Republic in Berlin (Binder 2009).[10] Such disputes variously mobilise ideas about origins – which is older or 'who got there first' (one version of authenticity), or about aesthetics – what is more 'in keeping' with the 'atmosphere' of the place (another version of authenticity). But they are all simultaneously also political:

which past – and whose – will endure? Moreover, they can also determine access to resources – and tourists – as Mary N. Taylor argues in an analysis of Hungarian folk dance revival movements (2009). This is not to say, however, that 'authenticity' is simply a label that can be instrumentally applied however participants wish, with the most powerful group winning out. As we will see further below, there is more to authenticity than this, which is why it is so central to the memory complex and memory phenomenon.

Real versus fake heritage in Pogoni

An important first point to make here is that it is not necessarily the case that each ethnically distinctive group will seek to make its mark on the city or landscape – that all will want *their* pasts to predominate and be judged as most authentic in order to assert their identity with place. This is a particular, if common, model of heritage and authenticity that is not universally deployed. Sarah Green's intricate discussion of considerations of heritage and authenticity in the town of Delvinaki in the Pogoni region of Greece, close to the Albanian border, shows this well. Although the town was divided into three different neighbourhoods, each of which consisted predominantly of one particular group – Vlachoi, 'ordinary Greeks' and gypsies – there was a shared 'strong disinclination to mark differences' (2005: 237) as this might be socially divisive. A result of this, however, was that the town was unable to make claims based on the more locally distinctive cultural heritage that is usual in applications to the EU for cultural heritage developments. Rather than applying to the EU for money for a specific cultural heritage, then, Delvinaki made an application for general restoration of 'a generic kind of cultural heritage… It was a "just Greek" kind of cultural heritage' (ibid.).

That did not mean, however, that the authenticity of cultural heritage was uncontested. On the contrary, there was much disagreement over developments to make the town appear more 'traditional' and thus more appealing to tourists. For some inhabitants, including the town's mayor, to do so was 'fake' (2005: 243). This stemmed partly from a mixed set of understandings about modernity and modernisation more generally, which, for some, including the mayor, entailed 'progress' and 'radical change', whereas for others would be slower processes that would, finally, 'emerge from the pores of those who had lived their "authentic" traditions' (2005: 247). For the latter, authenticity and tradition were precursors to proper modernizing development. For the mayor, however, 'possessing "authentic" tradition depended … on people's being "properly" modern: only such people would be able to recognise the "real tradition"' (ibid.) – as opposed to the 'fake' versions being put in place by heritagising programmes.

Here authenticity acts as an axis between 'tradition' and 'modernity' – a dualism related to that between 'heritage' and 'market'. Modernisation that entails restoration to an apparent past seems to be especially unsettling, resulting in the considerable reflexivity over authenticity among Delvinaki inhabitants.

FIGURE 5.2   Church in the Pogoni region having plaster removed to restore it to a more 'traditional' state. The plaster was applied in earlier years to 'modernize' the church. Photograph and caption courtesy of Sarah Green

What we see here too is a struggle over identity and authenticity, played out not through 'ethnic' or related categories but through ideas about tradition and modernity themselves. Only some people, according to the mayor at least, will be sufficiently modern to recognise the authentic, which includes the legitimately ersatz. The detail of this struggle shows that what is involved is not a straightforward instrumental use of the term 'authenticity' but a more complex attempt to comprehend and shape what is involved in the unsettling social changes underway, and the new forms of authenticity and of social differentiation that emerge in the process.

Reflexivity – re-living the Indian in Europe

It is not surprising that there should be so much reflexivity over authenticity as the memory phenomenon throws up dilemmas of what might or might not be considered genuine. Rather than being a definition ready-made for application, 'authenticity' is itself shaped, nuanced and often repeatedly contested in relation to the specific contingencies of practice that people face. This is an ongoing process in which these various understandings themselves have consequences – for social differentiations, practice and the heritage produced. Nowhere is this more so than in the case of historical reconstructions or re-enactments.[11]

Petra Tjitske Kalshoven shows this with particular insight and subtlety in her in-depth ethnography of Indianist groups in Germany, Belgium,

France, the Netherlands, the Czech Republic and the UK (2010, 2012). While reconstructions of this sort are often thought to be about an attempt to copy or imitate Native American life, Kalshoven shows that more complex calibrations of authenticity are practised. Indianists know full well that any kind of complete replication of Native American life would be impossible, but authenticity remains important to them. How they understand this is in terms of attempting to 're-live and re-experience' that life. (The German-speakers use the terms *nacherleben* and *nachempfinden* (2010: 66).) This 're-living' is understood as more authentic than imitation, which would be a surface, 'mere dressing up' activity, regarded as 'insincere' by serious Indianists, who locate authenticity instead in an honest and serious 'quest for knowledge' (2010: 69), and 'a feeling of connectedness to these [Indian] cultures' (2012: 168). Differentiations between Indianist groups, and members of groups, still take place, as they variously engage in this quest. For one group, for example, the wearing of Wellington boots in wet weather may be an acceptable compromise within the larger aim of reliving Indian life in a field of teepees, while for another it is evidence of that group's not taking the aim seriously enough. Importantly, Kalshoven emphasises that these matters are not just argued about but for the most part are embodied in practice. Indianism itself entails 'sensuous practice' in which the body 'becomes a prime tool for enquiry into the material cultures of the past' (2010: 61). For this reason, there is often

FIGURE 5.3 Dog Soldiers Society, Indian Council, 2004. Photograph courtesy of Petra Tjitske Kalshoven

considerable striving for accuracy in learning traditional craft techniques. While as far as possible this also entails using natural materials of the kind that Native Americans might have used, compromises are made and modern substitutes sometimes made. But this does not compromise their quest for a sincere attempt to seriously engage with the past. This possibility is what attracts Indianists to become Indianists. Authenticity thus matters to them deeply.

Kalshoven's work puts strong emphasis on the sensory, embodied and material dimensions of engagement with the past, showing authenticity as thoroughly embedded in practice. It shows too that Indianists cannot – in their own terms – count whatever they please as authentic. They must also contend with what is known about the traditional life that they try to relive and the materials that are available to them. In the next section, I continue this interest in the place of the material and sensory in relation to authenticity, returning also to questions of commodification and standardisation.

Real food

What we might call 'edible heritage' is the subject of a growing ethnographic literature, some of which has been mentioned in Chapter 2 (in relation to wine) and Chapter 4. As discussed in the latter, food is materially and sensually evocative, a powerful 'conveyor' of memory through its synaesthetic effects. Moreover, the fact that it is produced in a particular location gives it a charged link with place. Yet at the same time it is often relatively mobile, though this depends in part on what it is made from and the availability of techniques such as refrigeration and transport. All this makes it a form of heritage that is potentially especially available for the market – and for struggles over authenticity both as part of what might sell a product and as 'something else'.

Artisanal authenticity: Grand Cru chocolates in France

In a lively account of the way in which makers of Grand Cru chocolates in France disparage Belgian and mass-produced chocolates for their lack of authenticity, Susan Terrio highlights the way in which certain qualities – such as relatively low sugar content – come to be defined, in contradistinction to the other kinds of chocolate, as characteristics of 'authentic' high quality chocolate. She includes discussion of her own induction by a master chocolate-maker into appreciating the qualities of the authentic product and becoming able to distinguish these from those that the Grand Cru makers count as inauthentic. Her nervousness about getting this wrong and showing herself up as lacking proper taste and discernment, and her search for clues as to what the correct responses would be, show well how shared understandings of what is authentic can be transmitted. She also shows how features of the making of the chocolate become part of notions of authenticity. In particular, she argues that craft products,

> unlike mass-produced commodities … do not require significant cultural
> work on the part of consumers to be moved from the realm of the
> standardized, impersonal commodity into the realm of personalized gift
> relations … Craft products do this cultural work for consumers; they
> make visible both a particular form of production (linking the conception
> of a product to its execution) and its attendant social relations… Produced
> in limited quantities, using traditional methods and/or materials, they
> evoke uninterrupted continuity with the past.
>
> (Terrio 1996: 71)

In other words, there are certain qualities of the production methods of these
particular chocolates – or, as she also refers to it, of the 'historicities of these
goods' (ibid.) – that make them especially amenable to becoming part of
authenticity discourse. What is at work here is a contrasting of different kinds
of *things* as carrying different kinds of histories and social relations – and an
attendant relativity of authenticity. I will return to this point below.

First, however, let me note that Terrio's account helps to articulate what it is
about craft and artisanal products that makes them especially appropriable into
discourses of authenticity. This is widespread in Europe, and indeed elsewhere;
and more recently has become part of the 'Slow Foods' movement too – as part
of what Grasseni refers to as 'the timescape of authenticity' (Grasseni 2005).
As Terrio explains of the chocolates, it is because they are positioned as part
of a mode of production that is regarded as somehow separate from – and
even counterposed to – the world of the market and mass-production that
they readily fit authenticity criteria. Rather than being part of the cold, rational
relations of the market, they are presented as coming from a different world of
more personalised forms of exchange. Of course, they are in fact thoroughly
part of the market but there is enough in the way in which they are made, and
in their actual histories, to position them as though they are not. How much
this is invented or draws on actualities varies considerably and the image and
discourse of authenticity – for example through presentation as artisanal craft
products –are drawn upon in the marketing of numerous types of products.
In UK supermarkets today many fruits, vegetables, eggs and cheeses, come in
packaging which names the particular farmer whose farm the product comes
from; and this is often accompanied by a photograph of him (the farmer is
always a rugged male, usually wearing a waxed outdoor jacket, perhaps with
cows in the background) in an outdoor setting. The consumer is thus presented
with an ostensibly more personalised relationship with the producer. This
personalisation is a performance of the authenticity of relationship between
producer and consumer.

Ironies of authenticity: slow foods and the standardisation of local products

There are, however, often ironies in the production of the appearance of the craft or personalised product. UK supermarkets are notorious for making life hard for many smaller farmers, wielding such financial power that they are able to offer very low prices for goods; and they often prefer to buy stock from larger suppliers who are able to ensure more continuous, large-scale and cheaper provision. Both Alison Leitch (2003) and Cristina Grasseni (2005) have identified some of the ironies of the Slow Food movement, founded in Italy in 1996 (Grasseni 2005: 80). Focusing on *lardo,* cured pork fat produced in the village of Colonnata in the Carrara marble-producing area of Italy, Leitch traces the transformation of what was previously a peasant food, despised by sophisticates, to gourmet delicacy as part of the wider European and Slow Food prizing of local and traditionally produced foods. As often happens with a rise in status, commercial copying ensues – and this has been the case with *lardo.* To protect their product, traditional producers attempted to acquire European Denomination of Protected Origin (D.O.P.) status. This required, however, that they use certain standards of hygiene, including non-porous implements in the production process; but to do so would require abandoning the use of marble, due to its porosity. And marble is locally understood as vital to preparing *lardo,* not only for perceived material effects on the pork fat but also, in an interesting material analogy, as its symbolic correlate – white and hard and produced in the area. *Lardo* is simply not *lardo* if not made using the local white stone. In local terms, it is made *inauthentic* if severed from its traditional production in the way that the European Denomination status requires.

In the Auvergne, France, Simone Abram (1996) also observes how EU hygiene requirements alter the production of Cantal cheese in ways that make it less 'authentic' to its producers. In Cyprus too, Gisela Welz and Nicholas Andilios (2004; Welz 2007) chart how EU hygiene standards and procedures, and rules about what 'authentic' halloumi cheese should contain (in terms of proportions of different types of milk) have driven out small-scale producers in favour of factory production. Ironically, the new 'guaranteed regional-typical' halloumi is no longer typical of different parts of the island but a standardised product of Cyprus as a whole.

Even in contexts in which the aim is to reclaim *regional* diversity, as Bernhard Tschofen (2008) discusses, the workings of the EU food quality assurance systems may have the effect of both reducing intra-regional diversity and also standardizing how regional difference is presented. In fieldwork in Italy among Alpine dairy farmers who make taleggio cheese, and also among participants at many events connected with the Slow Food movement, such as food fairs and exhibitions – including 'the Milan "Expo of Taste" [and] the Turin "Slow Food Salon"' (2005: 79), Cristina Grasseni charts the 'great amount of *creativity* [that] is required to restore "tradition" and to transform it into a commodity-heritage' (2005: 83). As her fieldwork shows, the ways in which distinctiveness is marketed are increasingly 'through *visual* and narrative strategies' (2005: 84), especially the presentation of locality. This itself, however, is often standardised into clichéd images of, for example, the alpine valley. Far from reclaiming diversity, what results is what Grasseni describes as a 'standardisation of sensory experience' (2005: 86).

Evident in these cases, then, is the market, in conjunction with hygiene regulations, reshaping products, often not in ways that their producers (and sometimes even their consumers) might wish. This is a complex and contradictory process that can lead to differentiation, as when 'heritage foods' are 'rediscovered', or/and standardisation. As we have also seen here, it is a field in which versions of the market-heritage dualism come into play, as in contrasts between craft- and factory-production. They frequently do so, moreover, as local producers themselves emphasise the caring personal, work and material conditions in which their products – unlike those of mass-production – are crafted. At the same time, however, the authenticity value of being outside the market is itself a marketable resource, deployed not only by the local producers but also larger corporations as part of ongoing appropriations and reappropriations that contribute to the dynamism of 'tradition'.

Authentic ethnics

As a final example in this section, let me take the case of 'Turkish' products in Germany, for these show well some of the complexities involved, including relocations of authenticity and related shifts in social relations. The *döner kebap,* as it is usually called there ('donner kebab' being the usual English transliteration), is widely regarded in Germany as the archetypical – and authentically traditional – Turkish food. Introduced by a growing Turkish population into Germany in the 1960s, the *döner* (as it was often abbreviated to) quickly became 'the number one fast-food' (Çağlar 1995: 216), Germans were attracted to it partly by its qualities, but also by its marketing as traditionally Turkish. Stalls selling *döner* would present themselves as Turkish and exotically ethnic, through 'touristic Turkey posters, … souvenirs from Turkey, and colorful lights' (1995: 217). Yet, as Ayşe Çağlar points out, the food product sold in Germany was not quite like anything on offer in Turkey; the revolving spit of meat was a new innovation and eating meat in bread in this way was not common in Turkey. Moreover, the sort of bread, *pide,* used was normally only available at Ramadan. For Turks living in Germany this prompted a shift in the kind of *pide* that they themselves used at Ramadan: a novel variant being produced only at this time of year (1995: 214).

For non-Turkish Germans the *döner* (symbolically and literally) fed into their pre-existing readiness to seek out and consume authentic ethnic food, partly as an enactment of multicultural openness. Indeed, *döner* came to fill this role to such an extent that the term could be used to express multiculturalism

FIGURE 5.4   Döner and pizza and pasta: multicultural snack food outlet in Berlin, 2012. Photograph by Sharon Macdonald

(1995: 221). There is, of course, an irony in the fact a product specially adapted to the local market becomes the symbol of acceptable difference. Ironies continue too, as Çağlar argues, as the Turkish population seeks to mark its difference less, through use of English names for their snack-bars – such as McKebab – or seek to move their product up-market, perhaps through more generalised marketing as middle-Eastern, as part of attempts to avoid derogatory images of Turkishness.

In more recent years, there seems to have been further diversification. On the one hand, *döner* have become just one foodstuff in snack outlets that offer a range of foods, as shown in Figure 5.4. At the same time, however, there has been an emergence of more up-market Turkish restaurants sometimes presenting themselves as 'Anatolian' or choosing personalised names (e.g. *Osmans Töchter – Osman's Daughters)* that will not necessarily register as Turkish by possible customers. Other anthropologists have also reported a more recent recasting of Turkish products. Berlin's Kreuzberg area has a substantial population with Turkish roots and its Turkish Market has begun to be included in tourist guides as a place to visit to see the 'real life' of contemporary multicultural Berlin. In 2008, however, the market's name was changed, to *Bi-Oriental Markt,* thereby managing to tap into ideas about Turkish food as 'healthy' that Çağlar also discusses ('bio' means 'organic') as well as their exoticism (Kaschuba 2008: 41). As Wolfgang Kaschuba observes, this self-referential use of 'Oriental' is not, however, just conforming to tourists' fascination but is also

FIGURE 5.5 Oriental ambience in a Berlin café. Photograph courtesy of Silke Helmerding

a purposeful reappropriation of an originally 'othering' term (ibid.). Using the term 'Oriental' is also more usefully encompassing of other kinds of migrants – 'Arabs' and 'Russians' in the case of Berlin – than is 'Turkish', as Alexa Färber points out in a rich discussion of the expansion of water-pipe – *hookah* or *shisha*– cafés in Berlin over the past decade. Some of these present as 'authentically Arabian', as one owner emphasised to her, explaining that this meant no alcohol and no belly dancing (Färber 2012: 340); and they cater especially for their local Muslim populations in areas which lack chi-chi coffee shops. Others, however, especially in more mixed and fashionable areas, such as Kreuzberg, make no claims to traditionality or authenticity. Within a generalised 'Oriental ambience' they serve up new flavours of tobacco alongside alcohol to their mainly young cosmopolitan clientele (p.342).[12] As Kaschuba argues, this ethnic hybridity is what is now considered authentic urban culture (2008: 39). No longer located in the unchanging tradition of bounded communities, this is authenticity short-term-memory style. For a better grasp of how and why such new forms can also be considered authentic, and more widely how the term authenticity can encompass so much (but not just anything), I make a brief journey into its own history.

Authenticities of things and persons

The Greek word, from which the current term, as used in many European languages (including English, German, French, Spanish and Italian), originated, meant somebody who does something by their own hand. Initially, this included, intriguingly, suicide or the killing of a relative (Knaller 2007: 10). This sense of 'original do-er' or 'perpetrator' later became partially broadened to incorporate notions of both wider authorship and also authority, though the specific sense of suicide or murder of relatives was lost. According to Susan Knaller, who tracks the use of the word across several fields and centuries, it came to mean genuine, as opposed to counterfeit, only in the eighteenth century, when it was initially used especially in relation to music. Later that century, its relatively juridical senses were supplemented by a use of 'authenticity' to refer to expressions of 'sincerity, naivety, intimacy, transparency, sensitivity and moral sense' (Knaller 2007: 18, my translation). In a conceptual rather than etymological exploration, Lionel Trilling suggests an understanding of authenticity as not simply encompassing or supplementing 'sincerity' but as partly displacing it in what he sees as a significant 'revision of moral life' (1971: 1). Where sincerity entailed a 'congruence [of] avowal and actual feeling' (ibid.) – the sincere person would speak and act in accordance with what they truly felt – Romanticism, compounded later by psychoanalysis, opened up the possibility that one might not know one's 'deep', possibly 'dark', inner self. The authentic, thus, might be 'dark' or even 'mad'. What resulted was an often tortured concern with how to fulfil the requirement to seek, know and express this self; as well as with what form of social and political life could best encourage and accommodate this (Berman 1970/2009). This was all even further pressing, as Marshall Berman argues in his exploration of writings on authenticity in the late eighteenth century, in the face of social change, especially social mobility, and especially as prompted by the growth of capitalism.

An examination of past uses of 'authenticity' highlights, then, a range of meanings, including: the author of, being undertaken with authority, not counterfeit, and a particular moral sensibility. They also apply, variously, to things – for example, to music and art works – and to persons. Susan Knaller argues, however, that it is only in the late twentieth century that there comes to be a use of 'authentic' as part of a mutually reinforcing application to things and people; as in, for example, 'this is an authentic Picasso' and 'Picasso is authentic' (2007: 23).[13] In a blurring of subject and object, the authenticity of the painter reinforces the authenticity of the painting, and vice versa. In addition, 'authenticity' can also refer both to human generality – which makes it attractive to normative and universalizing discourse – and to 'the incomparable individual' (2007: 21). This allows for the paradox of claims both that authenticity is a general quality and that it is always unique. This stretchiness, together with the fact that a use of the term in one context may carry inflections of its use in others, has contributed to what Knaller calls an 'authenticity industry' (2007: 7). It also, we might add, makes it especially likely to be subject to dispute; those arguing perhaps not being fully aware of the different senses in which they are deploying the term. The synchronicity of the authenticity industry with the heritage industry, as part of the broader memory phenomenon, speaks to the fact that heritage has not only been an especially active domain of authenticity discourse, but also been a key mode of relating and making comparable unique people and things, past and present identities, and, as such, a major producer of 'authenticity'.

The ethnographic studies above variously show the mutually reinforcing traffic between authentic people and authentic things that Knaller describes. The idea that Alpine farmers have produced taleggio cheese as part of a longstanding tradition and that the cheese contains particular kinds of milk (in this case, from the 'tired' cows that give it its name) mutually reinforces the authenticity of both; as does the idea that people with their roots in Turkey are producing an authentic product, using distinctive techniques and ingredients. For the most part, authentic things or practices are invested with long histories and seen as embedded in either continuing or past ways of life and social relations. In the case of the new urban authenticity, however, the bi-directional mapping of people and things still operates – this cultural mixing of people and products is the real Berlin. These new senses – allowed by authenticity's malleability – do not, however, displace those concerned with tradition and 'old things' (see Chapter 6) and they still seem to promise ways of life and objects that are superior to their 'less authentic' alternatives.

Social and object relations of authenticity

In an interesting analysis that tries to understand why people are still drawn to what they consider authentic – and why it cannot be just anything – Siân Jones suggests that we think about it in terms of 'networks of relationships between people, objects and places' (2010: 195) – networks that can extend back into the past too. This contention is based on her in-depth archaeological-anthropological research on the Hilton of Cadboll monument, a late eighth-century Pictish cross-slab in the village of Hilton of Cadboll, Easter Ross, Scotland. Since 1921, the upper part of the cross-slab has been in what was then the National Museum of Antiquities in Edinburgh, now absorbed into the Museum of Scotland. Following unsuccessful campaigns by people in Easter Ross to have the stone 'repatriated' to them from Edinburgh, a full-size reconstruction was carved and erected in the village in 2000. In the following year the original lower part of the stone was unearthed close to where its replica counterpart stood – and debates ensued about whether or not this join the rest of the cross-slab in Edinburgh. Not surprisingly, perhaps, authenticity was frequently invoked in these debates, as in earlier ones. It was so both through direct uses of 'authenticity' and related terms such as 'genuine' as well as through affectively charged references to the meaningfulness of the slab, which might be made through talking about it as a person and referring to its social relationships – e.g. as an 'ancestor' (2010: 199; 2011).

Authenticity, she suggests, is attributed especially to things or relationships that are able to make connections – not only social but also material (e.g. the identity of the stone in the museum and in the village) and historical, linking past and present. In the case of Easter Ross, she argues that the historical experience of dislocation, especially during the Highland Clearances of the late eighteenth

FIGURE 5.6   Lifting the rediscovered base of the Hilton of Cadboll cross-slab in the village of Easter Ross. Photograph courtesy of Siân Jones

and nineteenth centuries, contributes to local people's desire for a locally placed monument that endures over time. The monument, in other words, affords the particular kinds of connections – especially, though not only, temporal – that those she studied were predisposed to seek. Although she does not put it in quite these terms, we might conceptualise this through Weiner's notion of 'symbolic density' (1993)[14] – the authentic is, perhaps, conceived as part of dense networks of meaningful connections. But not anything can do this. Only some objects have sufficiently rich histories and also material qualities – in this case, for example, the cross-slab's intricate designs that are open for comparison and also artistic emulation – to do so. And only some are likely to be able to make the specific connections that particular people might seek or be pleased to discover.

This discussion also raises the question of the particular qualities of different kinds of materials. The fact that the monument discussed by Jones is made of stone means that it has a particular kind of materiality – it is relatively durable, capable of persisting over time.[15] Stone is a substance at once thoroughly natural, from a particular location and often easily identified with a specific geography; and it is usually ancient. Yet it can also be shaped and weathered by natural processes; and cut and inscribed – usually requiring substantial effort – by human ones. Once altered, stone is not easily altered back. In consequence, natural and human shaping and inscriptions endure over time. Smaller stones are transportable, though relatively heavy, compared with many other substances, for their size. Larger stones are more cumbersome to move and may be immobile if part of a cliff or building. As such, stone is often resistant to moving far beyond its original location (though sometimes it does so). All of these various features of stone's materiality make it physically and practically amenable to certain authenticity practices (e.g. scientific dating; presence in a landscape over time); and also metaphorically resonant in particular ways (e.g. notions of durability or immobility). The fact that monuments are so often made of stone is not only a practical matter. At the same time, however, it is important not to assume that forms made of stone are necessarily regarded as monumental tangible heritage by those involved. Jones's study highlights that it is as much the relationships and stories brought together by the cross-slab that she discusses that matter to those involved. Likewise, in a discussion of Sámi sacred stones, Stein Mathisen (2010) points out that although these look like durable monuments to outsiders, to the Sámi they are sacred spirits with whom Sámi engage in ongoing relationships.

Relativities and authenticating authenticity

While durability – a particular form of temporality – of materials is undoubtedly one significant feature that is drawn on in many European discussions of the authenticity of things, it is certainly not an invariant, as examples above, such as the qualities of food, make clear. In heritage debates, the Japanese emphasis on the continuity of form rather than material durability – at least in relation to buildings – has become an iconic (and perhaps not entirely accurate) case of an alternative conception of authenticity (Cox and Brumann 2010); and this has been significant in informing more complex understandings of authenticity and heritage in heritage management. The challenging case was Japanese temples made of wood, which were usually substantially restored annually, meaning that their materials were certainly not ancient or original (see also Jones 2010; Meyer-Rath 2007). The temples' authenticity lay instead in their location and being reproduced true to form, by traditional methods. At a conference organised by Japanese heritage officials and held in Nara, Japan, in 1994 to discuss the World Heritage Convention definitions of authenticity that had prevailed up to that point – and that put emphasis upon originality and persistence of materials – this example contributed to prompting a more expansive approach to authenticity, recognising that 'it is … not possible to base judgements of values and authenticity within fixed criteria', and declaring instead that 'heritage properties must be considered and judged within the cultural contexts to which they belong' (Nara Document on Authenticity 1994).[16]

This relativistic stance struggles, however, with the fact that heritage management – in matters such as selecting for World Heritage listing and so forth – requires some sort of basis on which to operate (see also Strasser 2007).[17]

At issue here too is what Knaller describes as a central 'paradox' of authenticity, namely that on the one hand it relates to that which is supposed to be unique and, as such, incomparable, and on the other that it is a universally applicable attribute, and thus capable of being deployed across many cases (2007: 20–21). The fact that it allows this theoretically impossible comparing of the incomparable (unique) is, she suggests, a further reason why 'authenticity' has come to be so widely used. But it still does not eliminate problems in operationalising that comparison through lists and rankings. What the document proposes to do so is to refer to the 'credibility and truth of related information sources' (Nara Document on Authenticity 1994). In other words, authenticity is to be established through the expert knowledge attached to an object or practice. This need for expert substantiation to make heritage valid has led to a growth of experts engaged in producing documentation. Anthropologists too sometimes find themselves called upon to provide further expertise (see the Tauschek example below), especially with reference to intangible heritage, where evidence of networked relations into an 'authentic' community and tradition may be sought.

The other difficulty that the Nara document acknowledges is that while the cultural diversity of evaluations of authenticity and of heritage is recognised, one feature of heritage management, especially since the second half of the twentieth century, is a globalising, transnational development in which heritage is regarded as not just belonging to the specific group of people where it is located but to humanity as a whole. As the Nara document puts it: 'the cultural heritage of each is the cultural heritage of all' (ibid.). To accommodate this potentially awkward dual or multiple ownership (and responsibility), the Nara document proposes the following scaled approach:

> Responsibility for cultural heritage and the management of it belongs, in the first place, to the cultural community that has generated it, and subsequently to that which cares for it. However, in addition to these responsibilities, adherence to the international charters and conventions developed for conservation of cultural heritage also obliges consideration of the principles and responsibilities flowing from them. Balancing their own requirements with those of other cultural communities is, for each community, highly desirable, provided achieving this balance does not undermine their fundamental cultural values.
>
> (Ibid.)

Making this work in practice, however, is part of the difficulty here. In part this is due to the prevalence of the model of distinctively individuated heritage and identity – heritage as 'cultural property' that signals individual distinctiveness (Welsh 1997) – as discussed in previous chapters. Markus Tauschek (2007, 2010, 2010a) provides discussion of this in relation to the successful attempt by the Belgian town of Binche to have its carnival listed by UNESCO on its 'Masterpieces of the Oral and Intangible Heritage of Humanity' list – an

FIGURE 5.7 Masked figures in the Binche carnival. Photograph courtesy of Markus Tauschek

achievement that it announced to the world with a neon sign. Following the listing, a proposal was made by some of the presidents of societies that had been involved in the carnival to remove the stipulation that participants should be Belgian citizens. Their argument was that as the world was now globalised, town inhabitants of other nationalities, who might well have lived in Binche for decades and participated in other town activities, should not be excluded. The fact that the carnival was now official *world* heritage was evidence of the fact that the heritage was *global* and that it had received UNESCO accreditation as such. But the president of one organisation, who contacted Tauschek to request his assistance, argued that this would run counter to the 'nature' – and 'purity' – of the tradition itself. Insisting he was not xenophobic, this president argued that 'carnival had "always" been "protected" from outside influences and that must remain so' (2007: 217). In the language of the Nara document, the exclusion of outsiders was part of a 'fundamental cultural value' of carnival – an argument that is similar to that made by Greenwood about the Basque *alarde*. In the end – at least, by the time that Tauschek completed his research – this argument that the ethnic integrity of carnival should be maintained had won out.

As Tauschek notes, however, in practice exceptions had long been made, usually without this even being remarked upon. This is a useful reminder too, as ethnographic work is unusually able to reveal, that what goes on in quieter contexts, outside the noisier world of disputes or public pronouncements, may be rather different from official pronouncements. This does not mean that the public or official does not matter – on the contrary, it often does and deeply, and it may shape and constrain what goes on elsewhere. But it is not the whole story, and without knowing what else might be involved we may easily misunderstand what else is at stake.

★ ★ ★

In this chapter we have looked at some of the concerns over commodification and authenticity that have informed heritage debates, and have given attention to some of the insights that ethnographic studies in Europe can bring to these. Questions of economics are never far from discussions of heritage (see also Eriksen 2004). As Barbara Kirshenblatt-Gimblett puts it: 'The moment something is declared heritage, it enters a complex sphere of calculation', in which processes of *valorisation* (e.g. heritage listing) are followed by those of *valuation* (e.g. working out the income from increased tourism) (2006: 193), which can in turn lead to further valorisation, further valuation and so on (2006: 195). Regina Bendix discusses this in terms of 'the elaboration from cultural practice to resource' (2008: 116) and argues that this is not necessarily negative – local actors, as we have seen in some of the cases above and as she discusses with reference to examples including Corsican polyphonic singing, may be well aware of this and seek it out (see also Bithell 2003). Doing so, as Donald at *The Skye Story* discussed above, argued, does not necessarily mean a diminution of meaning and significance for those involved. The presence of the market does not itself necessarily bring a loss of authenticity. But awareness of this risk – a risk of who will control what happens with heritage in future – is what so often leads to heightened authenticity discourse and practice as a means of enabling participants to establish and demarcate a boundary between what they count as 'true to itself' and what they do not. How and where this is drawn is not constant – though certain features, as we have seen, recur – and may be the subject of disagreement. That being able to make this distinction matters to people is shown by the ubiquity of concerns – in relation to numerous diverse practices – with authenticity.

The successful expansion and marketing of heritage brings people from elsewhere – either to become inhabitants or as visitors. This is part of heritage's 'sticky' quality (Macdonald 2008). Many ethnographic studies in Europe have described a preoccupation with questions of *belonging,* which is typically played out through discourses of insiders and outsiders, and that is especially prevalent in localities in which long-term inhabitants feel that they are being forced to change their ways to meet the demands of tourists or when they fear they may be supplanted due to processes such as gentrification.[18] Encounters at a local level are often structured through the memory of past histories of relationships with 'others' of various kinds. In the Isle of Skye, for example, locals (variously self-referred to as 'Skye people' or by the name of the locality) might make reference to the history of bureaucratic intervention in the area ('the Highland Board') or even to the eighteenth- and nineteenth-century Highland Clearances in dealing with those they dubbed 'strangers' (which included tourists). The original article that I wrote about the *Aros* centre on Skye began with the following joke, versions of which I heard told many times by local people:

> There was an old woman [or man] living in township X. One day a couple of tourists come by and start asking her questions. 'Have you ever been outside this village?' they ask. 'Well, yes. I was at my sister's in [neighbouring township] not so long ago.' 'But you've never been off the island?'. 'Well, I have, though not often I suppose.' 'So, you've been to the mainland?' She nods. 'So you found Inverness a big city then?' 'Well, not so big as Paris, New York or Sydney, of course ...' she explains, going on to reveal that she has travelled to numerous parts of the globe.
>
> (Macdonald 1997a: 155)

A longstanding experience of feeling patronised by those coming from other places informed such jokes. As I wrote then:

> This is one of a large repertoire of jokes which highlights local people's awareness of touristic images of themselves, their ability to play along with those images, and their enjoyment of subtly disposing of them. It also highlights the conceit of tourists who assign local people only the role of object of the tourist "gaze" (Urry 1990).
>
> (Macdonald 1997a: 155)

I haven't heard this joke in more recent years, however, though this may be just because I have only spent shorter amounts of time in Skye. But it may also be because it has been dated by an explosion of popular travel that means that we are more likely to expect everybody everywhere to have spent time away from their birthplaces. Cosmopolitanism in the peripheries is no longer a surprise, either to those who live there or those who visit. Questions about the structuring of relations between different kinds of inhabitants, and the relatively mobile and relatively, perhaps temporarily, immobile remain pertinent, however, as do those of the economics of authenticity and cultural tradition. What heritage presents is the paradoxical promise on the one hand of a world that can transcend economics, and, on the other, a hopefully golden economic opportunity. This is, in part, what makes it such an expanding and compelling presence today, as we will see further in the chapter that follows.

6

MUSEALISATION

Everyday life, temporality and old things

All these old things have a moral value.

Charles Baudelaire[1]

This chapter takes up the debate about the proliferation of heritage in Europe by looking especially at the 'musealisation' of everyday life. That is, it looks at a specific dimension of the memory phenomenon: the collection and display of objects and sites of banal, if vanished or disappearing, daily domestic and workplace existence. Why, we might ask, should people decide to gather up, preserve and display the ordinary stuff of mundane everyday life? Here, I present a range of theoretical perspectives that, I suggest, can complement those we have discussed in previous chapters and that can help shed light both on the memory phenomenon more generally as well as this particular, widely found, heritage-memory-identity formation.

I begin with theories of musealisation. Although these were not developed specifically to address the topic of everyday life, this is a major, though often implicit, theme; and these theories deserve attention in any case for their attempt to characterise and explain the growth of popular interest in the past. I then outline the development of museums of rural, folk and everyday life in Europe – highlighting both commonalities of form and motive as well as some more spatially and temporally specific developments – before turning to analyse a specific folklife museum in more depth. My aim in the latter is to further examine musealisation theories and also to complement them with further theorising, especially that concerning temporality, and the affordances and potentials of objects.

Musealisation

The notion of 'musealisation' is used most frequently in German scholarship –
Musealisierung – though it has seen increasing use in other European languages,
including English. In German, the first use of *Musealisierung* is usually said to
be Joachim Ritter's essay 'Musealisierung als Kompensation', first published
in 1963 (Ritter 1974; see also Sturm 1990: 99). A philosopher, Ritter employed
the term to describe how pasts that were once tradition and part of organic
Lebenswelten (life-worlds) come in modernity to be institutionalised. From
the late nineteenth century, he argues, the humanities and organisations such
as historical societies and museums increasingly take over roles of cultural
memory in a functional compensation for the erosion of tradition.

Taking up this thesis, another German philosopher, Hermann Lübbe, sees
an intensification of musealisation underway since the publication of Ritter's
essay. Writing in the 1980s, in work that has been very influential in German
heritage and museum debate, Lübbe notes a 'dramatic increase' in numbers
of museums in Germany, and over much of the Western world, occurring
especially over the previous decade (Lübbe 1982, 1983). This increase, he
argues, is just one symptom of an accelerated institutionalisation of the past
that is articulated to changing temporal sensibilities (*Zeitverhältnisse*). New
technologies, rapidly changing city-scapes and the fact that many fewer people
live lives connected to the land, contribute to a relentless experience of change
in which the past becomes markedly different from the present much more
quickly than ever before. This means that there is *more* past than there used to
be – events and practices become history sooner – and so there is ever more to
be musealised, and ever more immediately. Lübbe notes this as constituting a
particular challenge for technology museums.

Another consequence of this temporal acceleration and sense of unexpected
change, argues Lübbe, is that the future becomes less predictable and less
rooted in the present. The combined effect of the burgeoning past and the
unruly future is a 'squeezed present', relatively disconnected from past or
future. This is unsettling for individuals, especially as it is coupled with other
associated changes, such as greater difference and conflict between generations,
and having to put more trust in formal systems rather than direct knowledge of
individuals. Lübbe argues that the sense of past values vanishing or being on the
brink of doing so prompts responses such as the proliferation of regulations and
practices of heritage protection (*Denkmalschutz*). These act as forms of 'cultural
compensation' for the dwindling of social trust: we rely on explicit rules and
regulation as we cannot do so on direct personal knowledge. Musealisation,
thus, can be seen as a form of temporal anchoring in the face of loss of tradition
and unsettlement brought about by the increased tempo of technological and
related change.

The agony of the real

Also writing in the 1980s, Jean Baudrillard discusses some of the same phenomena under the label of *museumification (museification* in the original French) – a term that he prefers due to its allusion to 'mummification' (1983). His characterisation is broader than that of Lübbe in that he includes not only phenomena such as the historical theming of townscapes but also simulations more widely, such as the creation of a perfect replica of the caves of Lascaux, with their prehistoric paintings, and Disneyland. Museumification for Baudrillard is about what he calls 'the agony of the real': it is the creation of the apparently real in the face of a breakdown of the distinction between the authentic and the simulated. This breakdown is partly a consequence of a technological capacity for accurate reproduction but is also of a postmodern dwindling of faith in the superiority of the real and in any sense of progressive futurity – there is, he claims, only a belief in imminent catastrophe. For Baudrillard, then, museumification is an afunctional symptom of the turmoils of the real in which people are likely to feel either disturbed or exhilarated by the instabilities of the real and the simulated. There is none of the sense of soothing compensation that Lübbe regards as the core function of musealisation.

In *Twilight Memories* (1995), German cultural studies scholar Andreas Huyssen discusses the compensation and simulation accounts of Lübbe and Baudrillard respectively in relation to a set of arguments that he calls *Kulturgesellschaft* – 'culture society'.[2] In these, the museum is not positioned as standing *against* modernisation – as a kind of bulwark against change or a freezing agent – but as part of the culture industry, serving late modern society by offering opportunities for individuals to create distinctive lifestyle choices and gain experiences through consumption. The proliferation of museums – and the proliferation of their provision of different kinds of consumer experiences – is part of an expansion and diversification of what German sociologist Gerhard Schulze in 1992 theorised as the *Erlebnisgesellschaft* – the experience society. From this perspective, as Huyssen develops it, what museums offer as part of their distinctive niche, is an experience that is distinguished from the less material, more ephemeral media of television and film. At the same time, however, it is able to satisfy the 'scopic desire[s]' of an audience brought up on the visual. The museal, thus, offers a distinctive experience in a changing media landscape, and is capable of incorporating other media (such as film or computerised exhibits) as part of its specific offer. The quest for this experiential difference is why the number of museums and other three-dimensional representations of the past have expanded rather than – as anticipated by many – retracted in the face of the increase of other media such as television.

Registers of reality

Huyssen draws insights from each of these positions. He rejects compensation theory as unable to account for many of the developments in museums as well as beyond them – theirs is a rather traditional vision of the museum, perhaps one full of old tractors rather than the dynamic, varied heritage 'scene' of today's Europe. Nevertheless, he concludes that 'the popularity of the museum is ... a major cultural symptom of the crisis of the Western faith in modernisation as panacea' (1995: 34). This motivates the emphasis on *the past,* providing an alternative vision of how the world might be and also an illusion of remembering in the face of cultural amnesia. Where his argument differs from the compensation theorists, however, is in seeing the museum, or musealisation more generally, not so much as the provision of a settled vision to calm our modern unease, as a site offering up opportunities for reflecting upon, and commenting upon, issues such as change and unsettlement. As he puts it: 'the museum [is] ... a site and testing ground for reflections on temporality and subjectivity, identity and alterity' (1995: 16). Although he does not say so, presumably there may well be differences between different kinds of museums here too – some offering more reflective and provocative accounts and others relatively cosy ones. This is something to which our next levels of theorising need to be increasingly attentive.

What Huyssen takes from Baudrillard and the Kulturgesellschaft theories is a concern with questions of authenticity, the real, our experience of them and the relationship of the museum to other media. What museums offer through the museum object – and what musealisation encodes – is what he describes as 'a register of reality' (1995: 33). As such, he writes, the 'gaze at museal things ... resists the progressive dematerialisation of the world which is driven by television and the virtual realities of computer networking' (1995: 34); and in this way it 'revokes the Weberian disenchantment of the world in modernity' (ibid.). But if we see the museum too as a site of (often implicit) commentary, we can understand its own uses of such media as not simply an aberration or distraction but, at least sometimes, as part of an offering of opportunity to reflect upon the differing affordances and implications of the media themselves.

These theorisations are useful for understanding what Huyssen describes as the 'relentless museummania' that has been underway as part of the memory phenomenon since the 1970s especially but not only in Europe. They supplement attempts to explain the phenomenon in terms of the rise of identity politics, in which groups variously seek recognition through the medium of the museum.[3] This analysis is certainly relevant to many cases, as evident in other chapters in this book, but the expansion of heritage is over-determined and as such needs to be understood through a range of possible theorisations. Another of these is the 'heritage industry' thesis, formulated in relation to the heritage boom in Britain in the 1980s, discussed earlier. This saw increased musealisation as a consequence of the marketing of safe pasts of stable social relations in the face of industrial decline and increased social unrest. Putting it crudely, the past was being sold, and being used to sell places as tourist attractions, as manufacturing industry had declined and there was not much else left to flog.[4] Again, this perspective seems to have at least partial validity for some cases. It also helped explain some of the particular forms that the heritage boom was taking – in particular, an emphasis on industry and community. The heritage industry critique was also insightful on the way in which these themes were often represented in romantic and nostalgic ways that ignored or downplayed some of the harshest aspects of life and class conflicts. Its emphasis on the managed and manipulated dimensions of heritage production for commercial ends can also provide insight into other cases, as, for example, Sybille Frank argues and demonstrates well in an analysis of conflicts over tourism at Checkpoint Charlie in Berlin (2007). More generally, it usefully brings political-economic dimensions of the display of the past to the fore. But it does not work for all or at least it does not exhaust all of the relevant dimensions – as we saw in examples in the previous chapter. As such, it needs supplementing with attempts to grasp the shifting temporal and ontological sensibilities that theorising such as that of Lübbe aims to provide. This also helps to refine further understanding of the particular *forms* that musealisation may take.

The musealisation of folklife

Here, the form that I explore further is that of the everyday life of 'ordinary folk'. This is not a conventional museum designation, at least not in English, and my use is intended to be fairly loose, to incorporate museums that are concerned with the stuff of everyday domestic and working life – the kind of subject-matter that challenges ideas of the museum as selector and preserver of a culture's most singular and valuable items.[5] In a discussion of the notion of 'everyday life' in Norway, Marianne Gullestad makes the important point that this concept should not be taken for granted, and that its meanings may change over both time and location (1991; see also Bennett and Watson 2002). In the case of Norway, she argues that popular and academic discourses about everyday life changed during the 1980s from distinguishing everyday life from that of the festival to demarcating it from a wider socio-political 'system' (1991: 481). In what follows, it should, therefore, be noted that while museums of past or passing everyday life clearly have something in common, there are also differences in their detail and significance in different times and locations.

Across much of Europe a 'first wave' of museums dedicated to this form began in the late nineteenth century – a period of wider expansion of museums more generally and also of the formation of the nation-state. These museums were part of a broader institutionalisation of the past. More specifically, however, they were also part of a materialisation that helped make the new nation-states imaginable. As has been discussed by many scholars, museums helped to furnish the new nation-states with histories and shared national property, as well as providing a venue for a visiting public of new 'citizens'.[6] In the case of museums of folk life, these often had the explicit aim of salvaging ways of life within the nation that were seen as on the brink of disappearing. As Mark Sandberg – in a detailed analysis of the development of Scandinavian folk museums – insightfully points out, the notion that 'culture is the sort of thing that can vanish ... should not be taken as obvious' (2005: 159):

> it is only one of many possible ways to conceptualize cultural change. In contrast to these images of cultural 'dilution,' 'dispersal,' and 'extinction,' alternative metaphors of change are possible, such as 'translation,' 'hybridization,' 'transplantation,' or 'cross-fertilization.' The particular metaphor that dominates the discourse in a particular time and place thus keys into some very fundamental assumptions about the way culture is perceived.
>
> (Ibid.)

In the late nineteenth century, he goes on to suggest, Darwinian ideas 'helped to conceptualise the competition between cultural forms, especially between the old and the new, as a struggle for survival in which only one outcome was likely' (ibid.). In some ways what was involved, therefore, was that some features that ensured the success of the nation – its modernity and rationalisation – were also conceptualised as responsible for extinguishing its distinctive culture. This was a deep dilemma and helped set up an enduring ambivalence about modernity and rationalisation themselves. It also helped fuel quests to salvage traditional culture and restore them to the nation. As such, folk-life museums were also part of broader patterns of salvage and attempts to 'hold on' to and even reclaim traditional forms. They were thus a museological counterpart to the turn to vernacular languages, to the collection of folk tales and music, and to using these as inspiration for new compositions, which in many European countries were intended to be part of a new (already old) national heritage. Within this complex, however, not all forms operated in quite the same ways or played identical roles. What museums allowed, for example, was a particular kind of 'visitable' three-dimensional experience in which traditional life could be both viewed and entered but also exited, and left behind.

Many of the museums that developed in the late nineteenth century took conventional museum form, collecting and displaying objects such as craft and costumes in glass cases; others, such as Skansen (founded 1891) in Sweden, were open-air, recreating and displaying different styles of buildings. Some newly forming nation-states developed a national version of such a museum. The Austrian Museum of Folklore, for example, was founded in 1895 and the Hungarian Museum of Ethnography – which concentrates on Hungarian peasant life – was a specific section of the Hungarian National Museum from 1872. Interestingly, the possession of a national folk-life museum did not seem such an essential part of the new national identikit as other kinds of museums, such as a national art gallery; and in many cases folk-life museums came later and sometimes not at all. For example, the Museum of the Romanian Peasant was opened in 1906; Latvia founded its Ethnographic Open-Air Museum in 1924, and Lithuania founded its open-air Museum of Folk Life in 1966. In

FIGURE 6.1   The Village Hall (Folkets Hus) in Skansen open-air museum in Sweden. Photograph by Marie Andersson, reproduced courtesy of Skansen Museum

FIGURE 6.2   Domestic interior in the Latvian Ethnographic Open-Air Museum, Riga. Photograph by Sharon Macdonald, reproduced courtesy of the Latvian Ethnographic Open-Air Museum

France, where the Musée des Arts et Traditions Populaires was only founded in 1937, Martine Segalen points out that nation-formation entailed a centralising impulse that sought to eradicate difference and that unlike in Scandinavia, where 'national identity could be embodied in the collection of rural houses' (2001: 77), peasant cultures were equated with 'the savage' (2001: 77–78).[7] Britain or England never formed such a museum at all, as I discuss further below.

Heimat

Alongside the national versions of such museums were also smaller local rural or urban ones. In Germany, for example, which unified as a nation in 1871, there was a proliferation of museums of *Heimat* in the subsequent years – 357 such museums being founded by 1914 (Confino 1997: 134 and p. 244: fn.33) – in what was, at the time, referred to as a 'mania' (1997: 134). These were museums of the 'homeland' locality – museums that collected items relating to the history and natural history of the village, town or community and displayed them in 'a mode of exhibition, a humble space crammed with exhibits, that was informal, unpretentious, and did not impose strict manners or etiquette' (Confino 1997: 139). As Confino argues, and as is surely the case for similar such museums in other countries too, these museums should not be seen as necessarily expressing identities at odds with the new national ones. Neither is it simply the case that local museums of *Heimat* straightforwardly represented 'the nation writ small' (1997: 136). Rather, he contends:

> the fundamental aspect of the Heimat museum phenomenon [was ...] that it articulated, based on the metaphor of whole and parts, the relationship between the locality and the nation, between hundreds of divergent local histories and one single national history ... As a national phenomenon, Heimat museums constructed a particular local Heimat identity that could be placed within the national Heimat. The fundamental factor of Heimat museums was that although they represented hundreds of different local pasts, their representation shared basic common denominators in terms of objects displayed, content, and meaning. Heimatlers, by displaying everyday life instead of big historical events, ordinary people instead of elites, and the historical origins of the community, constructed a pattern to understand national history, a national narrative. By reclaiming the local pasts, they in essence represented the locality as the location of the origins of the nation.
>
> (1997: 136–7)

Heimat museums were, therefore, part of a new memory cartography in Europe in which the local and everyday were regarded as integral – but not reducible – to the nation-states. The whole–part relationships were of a particular kind: neither microcosmic nor fractal nor divided by function.

Rather, the numerous parts demonstrated a lived belonging on which the whole – the nation – implicitly depended, and which acted indirectly to bring the nation 'home'. These relationships, and folk-life museums, were replicated throughout Europe, producing numerous instances of specific local memories and belonging within a broadly common model.

Museums of everyday life

Like Germany, many countries experienced particular periods of relatively intense activity. In Britain, for example, the 1920s and 1930s saw an increased museological 'turn to the everyday' (Kavanagh 1990: 22). Kavanagh sees this as evidence of the public's desire 'to put behind it, or at least out of its mind, the war, the depression, social division, industrial strife and the frightening changes taking place in Nazi Germany' (ibid.). In an interesting recent analysis, Bridget Yates sees the expansion as 'one manifestation of a trope of Englishness that saw the rural community as the embodiment of the nation' (2011: 204). The same trope, she suggests, was bound up with 'the continual failure of attempts to set up an English Folk Museum' (Yates 2011: 215). This was despite numerous attempts over the years, including by figures such as the Egyptologist Sir Flinders Petrie in 1896 (2011: 165), Pitt-Rivers Museum Curator Henry Balfour, for example in his 1903 Museums Association speech (2011: 169), and many since. It was only after World War II, 'when the rural community was no longer seen as the embodiment of the nation' (2011: 277), that the Museum of English Rural Life was opened (in 1951), though still not as a national museum. Both Wales and Scotland also opened museums of rural life soon after the war: the Welsh Folk Museum, St Fagan's, in Wales in 1948 and the Scottish Agricultural Museum in 1949 (which became the National Museum of Rural Life in 2001). That each country created its own museum – rather than some central 'British' one – spoke also to the fact that *everyday* and *rural* life made more sense at these more intimate national levels.

From the 1970s the numbers of museums of some kind of 'ordinary, everyday life' have escalated in most European countries, the great majority of which are local – of village, town or region. Museums of everyday (*Alltag*) and village life opened in Germany at an even greater rate than in the first wave (Schöne 1998; Janelli 2012: 16–17); as did their counterparts in Britain (Yates 2011: 363). In France, the idea of the 'ecomuseum' was formulated in the 1970s (Segalen 2001; Poulot 1994). This partly characterised an ongoing movement – of locally run museums concerned with preserving a community's heritage and identity – but also served to propagate it still further both within France and in other European countries. While rural life has been the focus of some of these developments, the 1970s boom also saw a turn to the more industrial, as noted above. Communities in towns and cities looked to their industrial past; and old mills, pits, canals and factories were turned into sites of heritage.[8] There were also shifts of interest towards the industrial past, as Jeanette Edwards observes in her 1980s fieldwork in 'Alltown', a town in Northern England, where the locally-run museum shifted its original principal focus on natural history to the industrial past:

> The museum opened in 1873 with a natural history collection (including, among other things, blown bird eggs, stuffed small mammals, pinned butterflies, and glass-encased birds, insects and reptiles). By 1987, this collection had been relegated to the margins of the museum, and the paraphernalia from a more recent industrial and post-industrial era had taken pride of place. Today, the museum is filled to bursting point with artefacts. Machine parts, gadgets, items of clothing and jewellery, household furniture and fittings, kitchen utensils, gas masks, wooden toys, pharmaceutical, dental and medical instruments, postcards, cigarette cards and letters, slippers, shoes and clogs manufactured in Alltown factories, models, ornaments, and embroidered samplers made in Alltown homes, are just some of the things that jostle for space in drawers and in cases, hanging from the ceiling and on every available surface.
>
> (1998: 151)

If in the period of industrialisation, preserving the natural landscape – or, elsewhere, peasant and folk-life – were the priorities, by the 1970s, in the face of de-industrialisation, it was life in the industrial age that had itself become the focus of musealisation.[9] The sheer plethora of what was deemed collectable was also characteristic of this turn to the more recent past. It was at once part of the democratisation of the past that the turn to 'ordinary things' represented but also a reflex of the massive expansion of 'things' that industrialisation itself produced.

This kind of development was the case not only in Britain but across many other parts of Europe. It sometimes took specific inflections, as in museums dedicated to particular forms of working life, or as in the museums of everyday life under socialism that grew up in many post-Socialist countries and that have been seen as expressions of post-Socialist nostalgia (discussed in Chapter 4). Implicated in the development was the spreading of the model of museums as modes for articulating identity and as venues for 'collecting' – especially in relation to ideas of community, locality and place; and also a valorisation of ordinary forms of life – especially those deemed as having recently vanished. Typically crammed with objects, museums acted as densely material reminders of how much stuff was disappearing, as well as repositories for its preservation. In addition, they were, and are, *concentrated* spaces, in which everyday objects are separated from existing everyday life, and offered up for a different form of experience.

Objects

Objects come to museums such as these after a previous life of regular use. In one folklife museum in Scotland, the man running it directed my gaze to the

FIGURE 6.3 Traditional Heritage Museum, Sheffield. Photograph by Sharon Macdonald, reproduced courtesy of Professor John Widdowson, founder of the Traditional Heritage Museum

handle of a peat-cutting implement where a shinier and slightly indented area of wood indicated years of use. As he did so, he told me to think of the back-breaking labour, out on the moorland in maybe poor weather, that this tool would have experienced. It was as though it was a witness, telling me, if I had the will to listen imaginatively, about what it had lived through. This prior existence is a key aspect of their specific 'aura', to use a term from Walter Benjamin (1992/1955). As in Marcel Mauss' discussion of the Maori concept of *hau* – a spirit of the giver that is carried by an object that is given as a gift – the aura of an object is an ineffable quality gathered during its history (1967/1923). This idea informs Annette Weiner's concepts of 'symbolic density' and 'inalienable possessions' discussed in the previous chapter; but unlike most of the 'inalienable possessions' discussed by Weiner, these things do not begin their lives as special and neither, for the most part, is this specialness slowly accumulated: rather it is effected by their movement to the museum. Furthermore, paradoxically perhaps, it is their very 'ordinariness' that allows them to be special in this specific context.

Although museums of rural life contain many craft items, most of these, as well as the mass-produced goods (e.g. Staffordshire pottery, Sheffield cutlery, Oxo cube tins) that also, and increasingly, populate them, would at some point have been commodities. All museums remove objects from circulation and daily use, and from their 'candidacy' to participate as such (Appadurai 1986: 13). They only occasionally sell or gift objects from their collections, and this is nearly always accompanied by unease, criticism and self-justification (perhaps involving claims that this is being done out of dire necessity and to help preserve remaining objects in the collection or some such). Demonstrating the use of their objects – of a spinning wheel or steam engine – is not itself generally taboo for folklife museums; and indeed some are to varying extents what are called 'living museums', where previous activities are acted out for visitors. But to return something to ordinary daily use – to lend a farmer a scythe from the collections to help with the harvest, or to borrow a cup from the dresser to drink tea – should not really be done.[10] Once objects are in museums, they are in a sense sacralised. Their disconnection from use not only stabilises them but also, as Weiner argues of inalienable possessions more generally, enables them to act as 'stabilising forces' in social relations (1992: 9). As many of these were objects that were once part of the swift cycles of mass production and consumption, this act of stabilising is, I suggest, particularly significant, and is part of what has made these museums a compelling form.

To explore the role of objects further I turn to Janet Hoskins' discussion of 'biographical objects' (1998) for this shows well how objects can act as modes of telling about people's lives. Hoskins' interest in objects in her fieldwork among the Kodi of Indonesia began when she found that people did not tell 'life histories' – or respond to requests to produce these – but they did talk at length about objects, effectively narrating their concerns and lives through material things. As she puts it: 'stories generated around objects provide a distanced form of introspection … and a form of reflection on the meaning of one's own life' (1998: 2). Although the Kodi did not story their lives into 'life histories' of the form that have become familiar in modern Europe, Hoskins argues that they nevertheless seek some kind of narrative completeness in their object-focused story-telling. In doing so, they equate certain objects, especially those that can be categorised as 'possessions', with persons, individuating both through the analogy and through their biographical accounts of the objects. While on the one hand this looks similar to Western notions of possessive individualism, it also diverges in that a major preoccupation of the biographies is gender differentiation and the bringing together of male and female in the narrative closure of the stories.

Hoskins' notion of 'biographical objects' is derived from the work of French sociologist, Violette Morin (1969), who was concerned with a distinction between kinds of object relations that she saw as significant in 'this society of abundance' (Morin 1969: 132–3), namely, between the *biographique* – a personalised form of subject-object relations, in which an object may indicate the subject's identity – and the more formulaic *protocolaire,* in which the object does not form a personal relationship with the subject. The distinction here is a version of that encountered in the previous chapter between objects as commodities (indeed, Hoskins renders the *protocolaire* through the notion of 'public commodity') and other kinds of things, variously characterised as gifts, inalienable possessions and, in this case, biographical objects. As we saw earlier, making such a distinction is widespread in past presencing in Europe as well as analytically (see also Carrier 1994). While the characterisation of certain objects as gifts or inalienable possessions understands them primarily in relation to exchange – being removed from market relations – that of biographical objects especially emphasises their role in storying persons and social relations. As we will see below, both of these are significant in museums of everyday life – institutions that essentially salvage what were once commodities and otherwise more or less ordinary things and make them the centre for story-telling. To further explore this, and the capacities of such museums more generally, I examine a particular case from my fieldwork in the Isle of Skye, Scotland. In doing so I consider the museum and its objects, and also how it is talked about by its creator; framing this through what Morin variously refers to as 'fields' or 'levels' of 'mediation' through which objects may be 'recomposed' and their consumers mutually 'recomposed through them' (1969: 134). These are, loosely expressed, time, space, and ownership/consumption.[11]

The Skye Museum of Island Life

Opened in 1965, the Skye Museum of Island Life is a precursor to the bigger museum phenomenon that was to follow, though it was also considerably expanded over the years since its opening. It was established by a local Gaelic-speaking man, Jonathan Macdonald, who was born in the 1930s. Like many islanders, Jonathan Macdonald made a living from a range of occupations, one of which was running a craft shop, specialising in sheepskin goods. As he tells the story – and he is an excellent storyteller, with a poetic turn of phrase – he kept a small collection of local items in the shop, including those that could illustrate the processes of craft production, and this expanded over the years. At some point he visited the Highland Folk Museum at Kingussie. This had opened in 1944, founded by the eminent folklorist of Highland life, Isobel Frances Grant (1887–1983). She in turn had been inspired to create the museum after visiting other such museums in Europe, especially Skansen.[12] Jonathan Macdonald's museum initially consisted of his collections in a single 'blackhouse' – a one-storey thatched-roofed stone dwelling of a style that was then beginning to vanish from the landscape as people moved to more modern dwellings. Over the years he added more blackhouses to his site, carefully disassembling local houses that were condemned for demolition and moving and rebuilding them 'stone by stone'. By the 1990s there were five such houses, each packed with what Jonathan Macdonald repeatedly and lovingly refers to as 'old things'. These include old agricultural implements – stacked in profusion, some rusting; tools for weaving or blacksmith work; domestic household items – crockery, cutlery, furniture; photographs and books; and reconstructions using mannequins (made by Jonathan Macdonald himself) depicting scenes

FIGURE 6.4   Skye Museum of Island Life. Photograph by Christine Moon. Reproduced courtesy of Christine Moon and Jonathan Macdonald, Skye Museum of Island Life

of everyday life and work. Some of the numerous objects are historically unique and even precious – such as some mementoes of Flora MacDonald, of Bonnie Prince Charlie fame, who lived in this area – but the great majority are the ordinary things of the daily work and domestic life of the majority of the population.

So how are these ordinary things mediated or 'recomposed' by this museum – and others like it? And what are the effects of such mediation or recomposition? In considering these questions in relation to the museum, I look both at the materiality of the museum itself and at Jonathan Macdonald's commentary on it.

Time

While 'biographical objects' age along with their owners, and 'public commodities' remain 'youthful', according to Hoskins and Morin, museum objects have previously aged as part of everyday lives but in the museum come to a temporal standstill. Sometimes, museums seek to 'return' objects to their earlier state, to remove the rust or to repaint, though others leave them as they were found, even if this state is a consequence of years of neglect rather than of use itself. It should be noted, however, that a specific historical consciousness cannot simply be 'read off' from whether objects are restored or not. As Jane Nadel-Klein observes in a fishing museum in Anstruther in North-East Scotland, the cleaning and restoration of certain objects did not signal its temporal isolation but, rather, the fact that these had remained constantly in use and would, therefore, have been cleaned and repaired. Such cleaning was, moreover, a matter of pride, and to display them dirty was seen by fisherfolk as 'wrong' (2003: 197).

At the Museum of Island Life, there is evidence of both of restoration and purposeful neglect – houses have been rethatched and repaired but tools have an ever increasing patina of rust. There is a mix of reasons entangled here: if roofs are not repaired they will quickly become further damaged, as will their contents; repaired roofs still look old, as thatch is no longer used; keeping rust off metal items is relentless and shiny rust-free tools are not easily distinguished from new ones. From the way in which Jonathan Macdonald talks about the objects it is clear that what is most important to him is the fact that they are *old*: they have lived through time and been part of an earlier way of life. The word 'old' – and especially 'old things' – beats through his narration like a metronome. Here, for example, is how he describes how he started to collect and form the basis of the museum:

> Many, many years ago when I had just left school I started off doing weaving in the local weaving factory and ... after that, around 1950 ... I started a craft shop, a little craft shop down the road, and I had to buy crafts from various people. And part of that shop I put aside for old things because I had an interest in old things. And I began collecting around that time and it was an interest I had all my life – collecting old things, and hearing old stories and history and old songs and so on. And anything old interested me and I began a collection in a corner of that shop. And in 1965 ... I moved the lot of the artefacts in here and it started from there. And of course ever since then I have always collected old things, collecting all the time. I never seemed to be far from old things and collecting more.

The 'old things' that Jonathan Macdonald collected were not confined to a very specific time-period and the museum itself contains artefacts ranging from several hundred years ago (as with some of the Flora MacDonald memorabilia) to fairly recent (e.g. coronation memorabilia of Elizabeth II). The majority, however, are from what he describes as 'the period before the white houses and the comforts that we have'. This is a world that he caught glimpses of as a child – for example at the ceilidh house (house for meeting, singing and telling stories) that he sometimes attended when young – and that his parents and grandparents had lived through. Gathering the artefacts of this period was a means of salvaging a way of life that was on the brink of vanishing:

> It was firstly a case of trying to keep together something that I saw disintegrating and *fast* disappearing. Because when I was a young boy growing up people were very, very anxious to get new things – new houses, new comforts, everything new, piped water, roads, cars, tractors.

> Everything they could find, they were striving hard to get them so that they could get out of the old way of life and into a better and more comfortable way. And this [the museum] was something here that I believed would keep the best of what we had lost or were about to lose.

The attempt to salvage a way of life that has just been swept away by gathering up its material remains is characteristic of many such museums, whether they deal especially with rural life or with industrial heritage. This fits well with Lübbe's cultural compensation thesis. By maintaining the objects of such lives through time – musealising them – the ways of life themselves in a sense live on. This idea is often explicitly expressed in the making of the museum, as variously observed in ethnographies of local museums and museum-making by Marta Anico in Loures, Portugal (2009), Jane Nadel-Klein in North-East Scotland (2003) and Elsa Peralta in a Ílhavo, Portugal (2009) – though the latter especially also points out what is forgotten amidst the ambition to materialise remembering. As Jonathan Macdonald puts it in talking about generations and the effect that he hopes his museum to have on young people:

> I thought of it as being a museum that people, young people of Skye, you see, who were coming through a major change, would see how their parents and their grandparents, and their forefathers lived. And I was hoping very much that people in Skye would come here and say this is how my people lived earlier on. And that would be something for them to keep alive, keep alive their history.

Evident in Jonathan Macdonald's account, and in his museum and so many others, is an attempt to rescue certain ways of life from transience. Rapid social change has rendered whole ways of life ready to be discarded like so many commodities. The constant emphasis on the 'new', which Jonathan Macdonald sees in the desires of so many people around him and which Morin sees as typical of 'public commodity' relations, risks, in this account, failing to hold on to anything of value from the past. By literally preserving 'old things' – artefacts which would otherwise be thrown away – it is as though the way of life and the people of that time are 'de-alienated', removed from the kind of social relations that are imagined as typical of a more modern 'consumerist' society. To be forgotten is conceptualised as a kind of death; but by employing objects as mnemonic devices, capable of 'carrying' the past, the past is brought into the present and, with the 'young' generations who are part of the museum creator's hoped for audience, into the future. The museum and objects in it thus act as a denial of ephemerality – as a symbolic counter to the transience of a world in which 'the new' threatens to predominate and even overwhelm. In a period in which it is widely perceived that 'all that is solid melts into air', as Marx and Engels so famously expressed it, museums of everyday life, rather literally, 'resolidify'.[13]

FIGURE 6.5   Croft House in the Skye Museum of Island Life. Photograph by Christine Moon. Reproduced courtesy of Christine Moon and Jonathan Macdonald, Skye Museum of Island Life

FIGURE 6.6   Dresser in the Croft House. Photograph by Christine Cassanell. Reproduced courtesy of Christine Cassanell and Jonathan Macdonald, Skye Museum of Island Life

Space

Museum space is also a time-space: its layout and contents typically evoking a frozen moment of time or a historical progression. Its spatial organisation also bears a distinctive relationship to the locality in which it resides. At first glance, the Skye Museum of Island Life appears to emulate a community of dwellings – it could almost be a continuation of the nearby township. But it is also marked off from its surroundings, by its own boundary and by the fact that it is relatively self-contained, its buildings relating to each other in a perfect mini-community, rather than to those outside. Likewise, its internal organisation could *almost* be that of a 'real' village – its five houses divide by function into the croft house (a domestic space, containing a kitchen and bedroom); the barn (full of agricultural implements); the weaver's cottage; the smithy; and the ceilidh house (full of photographs and text about the history of life in the area).[14] As such, it is a representative space of the functional division of life in the locality – tokens of particular types – though no township itself would have just five buildings of this kind, or with quite these contents.

This subtle but nevertheless apparent distinguishing from outside space is partly what enables the transformation of objects that cross its boundary. Paradoxically, however, their removal from their previous life in the locality and recomposition in the museum renders them *more* emplaced into the locality rather than less so. This is because the museum acts as an emblem of a particular place. In the case of the Skye Museum of Island Life, that place is Skye, as the

FIGURE 6.7   Weaver's cottage. Photograph by Christine Moon. Reproduced courtesy of Christine Moon and Jonathan Macdonald, Skye Museum of Island Life

name of the museum implies, and as the museum's creator often invokes in his accounts, though place is also conceived at a still more local level, as when he talks of the specific townships from which particular objects have come. As is characteristic of the discourse of place in the Scottish Highlands and in many parts of Europe (and some anthropology of Europe), place is to a degree conflated with community.[15] To be 'of the place', as would be said in Skye, is not simply to live in a particular area but to be bound into a set of social relationships. To be 'of the place' is to 'belong' – to use a possessive term that is both used indigenously and has been the focus for some insightful anthropological accounts of identity especially in areas of Britain (Cohen 1982).

The objects in the Museum of Island life are 'of the place' not so much because they have been made there – very many have not – but because they have been implicated in social lives in the locality. Ploughs have furrowed the nearby soil, tea cups have been drunk from in former homes nearby, bibles taken to churches in the vicinity. As such, the objects in the museum evoke (usually in general and unspecific ways) these lives and social relations; and in the special, concentrated, place-flagging space of the museum they simultaneously demarcate the objects that are there as *of* the place – as things that belong – wherever their origins may be. In this way, a mass-produced object, produced perhaps in China, comes, through the mediation of the museum, to be primarily *of* the locality instead. The profusion of objects that is typical of such museums speaks partly to this too – each helps to instantiate the locality, more things meaning more place and more history. As Maleuvre writes of another context of museum clutter, it is only ownership that unifies it (1999: 97).

One aspect of narratives of belonging, exemplified in such museums as well as in the anthropology of Europe, is an attempt to reclaim both difference and independence in the midst of changes that are widely believed to threaten both. In popular discourse this threat is often envisaged particularly in relation to material culture: mass-production and mass-consumption being cast as obliterating distinctive identities, as, for example, regionally distinctive clothing is replaced by jeans and tee-shirts, and local foodstuffs by burgers and cola. In Jonathan Macdonald's account, 'new' products and 'comforts' 'from outside' are regarded as threatening local integrity. He tells me that he wants his museum to tell local people:

> that it is always a good idea to hold on to the good things of the past. And to really show them, you see, how people were so ingenious and how they did things for themselves. They weren't dependent on the outside world. They were dependent on their own resources. But they relied on themselves, you see, and what was around them. You see, even in the building of a house there was nothing brought in except pieces of wood, perhaps, from the shore. Everything else, you see, was there and they used it. They had to be resourceful. I think that this is something that young people have to learn nowadays – to be more resourceful and to use what

is available to them – to be more concerned really, not to really look to the outside world for everything. They should be more looking to themselves, to create and to use and to establish things from what they have ... You see, I'm *ashamed* when I look at the island that we live in now. Even all of the milk that we drink every day is from outside; all our vegetables brought in, everything – butcher meat, bread, whatever, brought in from outside. And we do so very little for ourselves. We are so *reliant* on *other people*. And this is the example and lesson I think that this portrays, that people were very versatile and could put their hand to everything. [Italics indicate words that he emphasised]

As is done in the museum, then, presenting a locality's 'own' objects – especially those which demonstrate local production (the looms, the ploughs, the sheep-shearing clippers) – stands as a testament to local resourcefulness and independence from the 'outside' which is regarded as threatening to engulf the local.

At another level, however, museums of this type often simultaneously refer to a way of life that is broader than the locality – e.g. 'island life', 'rural life', 'the industrial age'. This has two dimensions. First, it metaphorically extends the significance of the local in a process of 'semantic reach'. Second, moving metonymically and 'intensionally' (as opposed to extensionally), it makes broader ways of life and social processes visible and 'grasp-able' at a local level. The museum – located in a discrete and 'over-see-able' space – presents itself as a partial microcosm; and the visitor is invited to enter not just a few old houses from a local township, or a mill from this particular industrial town, but something conceived as representative of a broader way of life. At the same time, this spatial mediation can serve to help 'de-alienate' those wider processes by inserting locality and the idea of human presence into them, reminding us that we are not dealing with 'mere' objects or 'mere' technologies but with people's lives.

The fact that museums themselves occupy a terrain helps to convey this idea: the visitor literally becomes present in the space and by physically moving through the space of the museum – strolling from one black house to another – is brought into proximity to past lives. The recreation of domestic interiors, with their carefully constructed *Marie Celeste* impression of being only temporarily vacated (knitting still on the chair, a half-eaten meal on the table), is one of the most powerful ways in which this sense of proximity is effected. As in many parts of Europe, especially since the nineteenth century, the domestic interior has become a private, 'inner sanctum' – a spatial correlate of the 'inner depths' of the 'modern identity' (Taylor 1989) – allowing access to this is a particularly effective, and affective, way for museums to exhibit the everyday as special.[16] Moreover, it presents a relational 'layering' of spaces in terms of belonging, with domestic space as the most intimate, followed by locality or community, and layering out to national and then global space. The depiction of an anonymous domestic interior in the museum – an interior which acts as a token of many such interiors – is thus also one of the ways in which we are enabled to think layered space; and thus bring wider spaces 'home'.

Ownership/consumption

Who is the 'owner' of the museum object? Part of the museum effect is to move objects from individual ownership into what is conceived as a more collective ownership – ownership by the locality. Although the Skye Museum of Island Life, for example, has been executed largely by one person (with no external funding, as he repeatedly notes), he talks about doing this as though on behalf of 'the people of Skye'; and when people bring him artefacts for the museum, they do so not as a personal gift but as contributions to a local resource.[17]

In museums, ownership and consumption are potentially separate. However, they are almost always conceptualised as to a degree overlapping, and the imagined collective 'owners' are nearly always claimed as the most important audience. Talk of 'the community' and attempts to involve 'the community' are very widespread in these kinds of museums. Jonathan Macdonald, for example, recognises (and values) that the Skye Museum of Island Life attracts tourists but he emphasises that it was not *for* tourists that he began the museum: it was 'for the people of Skye'. And although the museum is a public space, it acts as a biographical object in just the way described by Morin: as a witness to the unity of its 'owners' and as a making of their everyday experience 'into a thing' (quoted in Hoskins 1998: 8). As a collection of objects that are 'kept', the museum is a manifestation of the very existence of the locality to which it 'belongs'. Moreover, it literally 'objectifies' the everyday experience, and very existence, of the locality by representing it through a collection of things in a manifestation of 'possessive collectivism'.

In museums of everyday life, then, objects are to some extent contrasted with the relationships that are stereotypically regarded as characteristic of 'public commodities'. Ownership is collective rather than individual, objects are salvaged and preserved rather than bought, sold and thrown away, and those who come to 'consume' – i.e. visit – the museum do not literally take the museum's objects away with them. In this way, the act of collection and the very institution of the museum act as important symbolic counterpoints to – and as a cultural commentary upon – other kinds of relationships to objects that are perceived as alienating and ephemeral. Moreover, because objects are associated with personal and collective identities, museums of everyday life can also intimate the possibility of retaining personal and collective values in an increasingly 'throw-away' society. Museums offer the promise of 're-enchantment' in the face of social processes that are widely perceived as 'disenchanting' (in Max Weber's terms).[18]

The elision of 'owners' or 'producers' with 'viewers' or 'consumers', so important to the rhetoric of museum creators and managers, is important to this attempted re-enchantment. So too, I suggest, is an emphasis on *experience,* so often privileged in advertising leaflets and museum-makers' accounts. Experience is not just looking: it is 'being in touch with', transcending the boundaries between past and present, viewers and viewed. The spatial layouts of such museums, entailing not just gazing upon a scene set out in a diorama behind glass but actually entering an original black-house, mill or factory – placing oneself *within* – configures the audience not as 'outside' (as in the 'window-ethic' mode of seeing; Adam 1995: 131) but as 'implicated' (ibid.).[19] The presence of *everyday* objects, and the representation of 'ordinary' lives ('we' as viewers would probably have lived or worked like this), is a further dimension of the mutual implication of subjects and objects. Viewers are being invited here not so much to gaze upon 'others' but on themselves as they might have been: they are being asked to *identify* rather than to position themselves as distanced subjects. The domestic interiors, and perhaps especially those artefacts that visitors remember from their own childhoods or from those told by their grandparents (those Oxo-cube tins, inhaling devices for Vick's Vapour-rub, an advert for Birds' Custard Powder, the mangles, the irons), are particularly effective in generating a sense of semi-familiarity and thus mediating the divide between subject and object. And even in unfamiliar contexts for most visitors, such as a mill or pottery factory, the exhibitionary strategies, accompanying text or guide will probably work, with varying degrees of success, at trying to generate a sense of imagined implication ('You lad, how old are you? Ten? Well, you'd have been working here, then. Up at six, not knocking off until six or after ...'). Telling stories about and around the exhibits – stories that may change according to the particular interlocutors – is central to the experience of some kinds of museums, according to Angela Janelli in her in-depth ethnographic study of a selection of small, amateur museums. In a distinction from what she calls 'scientific' museums, she uses Lévi-Strauss' notion of 'wild' to characterise museums whose form of knowledge-formation is 'non-scientific but not irrational' (2012: 24, my translation). The talk generates a profusion of meanings; and also itself constitutes part of the sensory, community-evoking, convivial experience of such museums.[20] The cluttered style typical of such museums is also part of this, seeking not to provide indicative 'types' or neatly pre-packaged narratives. When some local people told me of their preference for the Skye Museum of Island Life over *Aros* (discussed in the previous chapter), it was this open-endedness, which meant that no visit would be a repeat of that before, which attracted them.

The Skye Museum of Island Life began its own life as a collection in a craft shop, as noted above. The presence of 'old things' that were not available to be bought or sold within a shop, the main purpose of which, by definition, was buying and selling, can itself be seen as an attempt to mediate some of the usual connotations involved in commodity relations. In her account of 'inalienable possessions', Weiner suggests that their presence can alter the meaning of other kinds of exchange or relations in their vicinity (1992). So too, the 'old things' in the craft shop helped to transform this from being a site of 'mere commercial exchange' and the objects for sale from being 'mere' ephemeral goods. With their symbolic weight of age, stability and locality, the 'old things' helped to suggest that visitors too could buy something which might one day become an 'old thing' – unlike most mass-produced fast-discarded artefacts – as part of the personal collection of its purchaser perhaps.

Museums today nearly always have a shop, and museums of everyday life, including the Skye Museum of Island Life, are no exception. Within the perspective that has been pursued in this chapter, such shops can be seen not as a separate subject for analysis but within the same framework (Macdonald 2011). It is notable that such shops do not contain just any objects: rather, these are specially selected and generally play upon the similar sets of ideas to those represented in the museum, perhaps also within similar presentational styles. At the Skye Museum of Island Life, for example, the shop is also contained in a black house, and a dresser – similar to that in the reconstructed domestic interior – is used to present a selection of pottery, jams, shortbread and other products for sale. Almost all of the items displayed are in some sense 'local' even if this is construed here as more generically 'Scottish Highland' (as in the tartan-boxed shortbread). They may have been locally-produced, or may depict local scenes (postcards and watercolours of nearby landmarks), or at the least (as with key-rings, pencils, purses, miniature tool-kits) have the name of the museum printed on them.[21] In some museums of everyday life, reproduction – or in some cases real – 'old things' are on sale; as, for example, with bobbins in many mill towns in the North of England and crockery in museums in the Potteries; and occasionally products of the museums themselves can be bought (e.g. flour from a windmill in Nottinghamshire, scissors from a workshop located in a Sheffield industrial museum). This could, of course, be seen as a cynical marketing ploy but even if it is (and I suggest it only sometimes is), it draws nevertheless on a powerful popular drive to make consumption meaningful, to remove it from alienating social relations, to 'sacralise' it, to endow it with the *subjective*.[22] Museums, which transform objects of everyday use into objects of devotion, are a key space for effecting this; and their shops, which invite visitors to buy artefacts of the locality – objects which can themselves act as mementoes, carrying one time into another, even turning their owners into collectors – are another space in which objects can be rescued from the fate of being 'mere' commodities.

The fetishisation and musealisation of everyday life

Taking 'ordinary', 'mundane' objects of the recent past and putting them on display in museums might be seen as a kind of fetishisation of past everyday life. Collecting such ordinary things and displaying them, typically in densely massed profusion, speaks to a profound and affectively meaningful relationship with objects. According to Freud, fetishism involves desires that should be directed at people being misplaced onto objects instead; and he sees this as a 'pathology of everyday life' (1990/1901). Marx too views fetishism as a problematic relationship with objects, not as a focus only on their *material* nature, as he is sometimes misunderstood as saying, but a relating to them only in terms of their abstract, de-materialised values, that is, as commodities (Marx 1976/1876; see Stallybrass 1998). Anthropologists, however, have more usually sought to understand what is involved in these 'irreducibly material' objects of apparently 'irrational' devotion (Pietz 1985: 7; Spyer 1998).

Putting familiar everyday objects and everyday lives on museological display has flourished especially in parts of Europe that are relatively marginal within late capitalism, though which were often once more central. In providing a close-reading of one particular museum in a now marginal part of Europe, my aim has been to approach it both from 'within' (i.e. from the point of view of some of those involved) and comparatively (i.e. in relation to various other kinds of object-practice), rather than to try to read off the practices involved off from wider contextual change as does Lübbe's compensation theory. One consequence of this close approach is that it enables understanding of the practices not simply as *outcomes* of certain broader developments but as active commentary upon them. This commentary may entail familiar romantic allegories of resistance to potentially alienating social change, but this makes it no less deserving of anthropological attention. This attention – involving a comparative approach – highlights the web of knowledge and practice, entailing culturally-specific ideas about time, space, objects and identities, involved.

The idea that the post-war period has entailed considerable and dislocating social change is widespread; and has been the subject of extensive social and cultural theorising. Many of these accounts have suggested that this period (be it described as post-Fordist, post-Modern, late-Modern, liquid modernity, the time of flows or whatever) is one in which our very conceptions of time, space and identities – the foci of this chapter – have been transformed. In a period in which time and space have been claimed to be 'compressed' or 'distanciated' and identities 'fragmented' or 'disembedded', an increase in cultural practices seeking to provide existential anchors is not surprising, as Lübbe and others have argued.[23] Of particular interest, however, are the forms that this has taken. In the case of museums of everyday life this has involved the 'irreducible materiality' of object fetishism – a form that, I have suggested here, should be understood at least partly in relation to other kinds of object relations, particularly 'commodity fetishism' and 'materialism' (as popularly understood, as an undue concentration upon superficial material things). The emphasis on *everyday* things (and lives) is an ultimate extension of this idea – *everything* can be salvaged, everything turned into a collector's item, and all lives given recognition (in an appropriate identity-displaying agency such as a museum). It is witnessed too in the massive expansion of what Gregson and Crewe call 'second-hand worlds' – car-boot sales, antiques shops, jumble sales, flea markets, charity shops and so forth (2003). It is also a function of the rapidity of commodity obsolescence which generates ever more 'old things'; a phenomenon which also has a practical dimension in that it is now possible to start a museum with little more than a garage-full of 'junk'.

Many elements are implicated in the musealisation of everyday life – more, as I have tried to show, than have been discussed in the theories of musealisation with which this chapter began, and even more than included here. Some of them are relatively longstanding (such as possessive collectivism, the interiorisation of identity and the idea that objects can act as repositories of memory), and others are more recent (such as the salvage of newly 'old' things and the attribution of all kinds of social ills to the lust for 'new' things). My analysis of this cultural practice has sought to highlight further assumptions involved. These include storying personal and social identities and lives through stories of and around objects; presencing the past as something that can be 'experienced'; expressing senses of belonging in material form; regarding 'culture' as something that can 'vanish' or 'be preserved'; valuing 'thing-knowledge' of a form that is neither conventionally scientific nor economic; and believing that it is possible to 'de-alienate' commodities (and that they are 'alienated' in the first place). Some of these are widespread in both time and space; others flourish especially at particular moments and locations. The museum of everyday life is but one location in which these operate. It is nonetheless a particularly distinctive and powerful medium that is not only a reflex of wider developments but itself an active ongoing intervention into past presencing. The following chapter turns to another, expanding, museum interventions and thus probes further the workings and potentials of specific forms of past presencing within Europe's memory complex and memory phenomenon.

7

TRANSCULTURAL HERITAGE

Reconfiguring identities and the public sphere

> For our house is open, there are no keys in the doors, and invisible guests come in and out at will.
>
> Czesław Milosz[1]

Given that historically heritage has been entangled with attempts to forge and maintain bounded, homogeneous identities, especially of the nation-state, a major question is whether heritage is capable of accommodating other kinds of identities, especially those that might be considered, variously, 'hybrid', 'open' or 'transcultural'. This question has arisen especially in the face of recognition of heterogeneity within nations arising from immigration – from other parts of Europe and, especially, from outside. This has prompted further questions concerning whether it is possible to draw on memory and heritage to form new identity stories that include rather than exclude cultural diversity and 'mixed' culture. Is it possible to have a common heritage and a 'multi-heritage' simultaneously? Are some forms of past presencing more or less amenable to incorporation within a more 'inclusive' national identity? And can or will new identity formations and memories displace or be felt in the same ways as those that preceded them? These and similar questions arise too in relation to European identity and formation of a European public sphere, as noted in Chapter 1. Can and should a 'European heritage' be identified that transcends national and other diversities within Europe? Are there alternatives to replicating national-style models at another scale? In many ways, these questions probe at the very nature and significance of heritage, for they open up examination of the usually assumed consonance between past, people, location and culture, especially material culture, and draw attention to possible alternative ways of past presencing.

In this chapter I explore these questions primarily in relation to debates concerning migrant minorities within nation-states. Numerous projects and initiatives, including exhibitions, that variously address migrant identity and its relationship to memory and heritage, usually with a view to forging greater 'tolerance' and senses of 'inclusion', are currently underway in cities throughout Europe. As we will see, these may operate within the existing identity-heritage model and may even unwittingly confound the 'inclusion problem' that they set out to address. Others, however, seek to rework heritage to create new possibilities for affiliation. In the chapter I look at a range of forms of heritage but pay particular attention to tangible material heritage in public space, especially that of museums and monuments. I do so partly because these were such significant forms in the earlier formation of national identities and are distinctive assemblages – with their own particular 'shapes', possibilities and limits – that deserve attention in their own right. In addition, they are not just forms but are also persisting physical presences in – and even constitutors of – public space, and in the case of museums are often repositories of existing 'heritage' whose very existence can have implications for future configurations of the past. Furthermore, they have been and are sites of some significant experiments and contests concerning transcultural heritage in the new Europe.

Transcultural and other terms

The term 'transcultural' is not unproblematic and before continuing I should explain my use of the term and consider some others that I also use or that might be employed. 'Transcultural' denotes a crossing and mixing of cultures. In assemblage terms, it involves bringing together elements from different cultures and fusing these in what becomes a new form, though it may retain identifiable elements of previous assemblages. Problematic here is the assumption of already existing 'cultures'. The idea that the world is divided into distinct, relatively autonomous 'cultures' has been widely criticised, especially in anthropology – a discipline that historically has also played a key role in forming this conception. Regarding culture as divided into a set of 'islands of difference' in this way has been argued to be a particular construction, born especially out of a nation-statist way of viewing the world that became dominant in Europe in the eighteenth century, as noted in earlier chapters.

Clearly, it is methodologically important to be able to perceive ways of forming values, organising lives and forging senses of belonging and so forth that do not map onto 'cultures' as they are often popularly talked about, which frequently means those of nationality or ethnicity. At the same time, however, this particular way of thinking about 'cultures' is widespread within Europe (as indeed elsewhere to varying extents) and, as such, is part of its lived reality, shaping events, contests and futures. It is an element in the European memory complex – a particular constellation of intermeshed ideas and practices – that also shapes the memory phenomenon. One of the difficulties that anthropologists have faced when trying to avoid using the term 'cultures' is that of finding ways of still talking about differences encountered and the often recurrent patterns and congruences that may coalesce around what they would previously have more comfortably referred to as 'cultures'.

In using the term 'transcultural', then, I want to give recognition to developments that seek to move across and between what are in everyday European practice perceived as significant cultural differences. This may also include the 'transnational' – that which crosses national differences, though it should be noted that the term 'transnational' may also refer to particular political or economic developments. Within Europe, then, the transcultural includes that which seeks to mix, fuse or transcend national cultural differences, including developments that seek to identify cross-border regional or pan-European similarities. We saw some examples of this in Chapter 2, especially, and will see more in the following chapter. Also, however, and as I focus on in particular in this chapter, the term can refer to – and is used in initiatives concerning – the mixing and fusion of 'cultures' within nation-states resulting from migration. Here I look at this especially in relation to migration from outside Europe. I do so largely because this has become such a major focus of interest and anxiety in contemporary Europe. Many of the issues that it raises, however, also apply to varying extents to other kinds of transcultural concerns and initiatives.

Also used to describe processes of cultural mixing and the new cultural forms that may emerge are terms such as 'syncretic'/'syncretism', 'creole'/'creolisation', 'fusion' and 'hybrid'/'hybridity'. Again, there has been criticism of their presupposition of pre-existing 'pure' or 'non-creolised' cultures and identities that exist prior to their mixing. The term 'hybridity' has been subject to particular critique for its biological origins, which some see as giving legitimacy to biologised understandings of race or find unsuitable given that 'hybrids' in biology are usually defined as sterile – as the end of a line. Others, however, seek to recuperate it as a term to describe mixing that transgresses established boundaries, producing challenging new forms in the process.[2] Here, I treat these terms as broadly synonymous with 'transcultural', and seek primarily to examine cultural initiatives and forms that set out to mix – to varying degrees – what are seen as 'cultures'.

In European public cultural policy and practice, the term that is in most widespread use is 'multicultural'. This has been widely adopted to describe and give recognition to the fact that many parts of Europe, especially its larger cities, are home to people who themselves, or whose parents or grandparents, came from other parts of the world and who may have various different cultural practices. Often used with the suffix 'ism', 'multiculturalism' describes a political position in which cultural differences are given recognition and allowed to flourish within the nation-state. The idea of multiculturalism has received significant criticism, as I will discuss further below. Even more strongly than 'transcultural', 'multicultural' contains a premise of distinct cultures – but unlike the former, 'multicultural' contains no suggestion that mixing is possible but further confirms the notion of cultures as comparable to separate species, as Ghassan Hage suggests in his description of multiculturalism as 'zoological' (2000). Yet the political philosopher Charles Taylor (1992) points out that the idea of cultures (like individuals) as being distinct and in need of expressing their distinctiveness has, since the eighteenth century, evolved as the taken-for-granted way of being in modern societies; and that the politics of multiculturalism seek to create conditions in which this is permitted to all, or the majority of, self-identifying cultural groups rather than just to a single national identity.

'Transcultural' and 'transnational' are sometimes used more or less as substitutes for 'post-national'.[3] This is based in an idea that the national is declining in significance for people's identification in the face of increasing cultural mixing. Yet, as we will see below, in this chapter and more directly still in the next, transcultural developments do not necessarily lead to a fundamental unsettling of the national, and for this reason it is important not to conflate these terms. In recent discussion, 'cosmopolitan' and 'cosmopolitanism' have come to dominate discussion, and these too are often understood as challenges to nation-statist forms of identification, as I discuss further in the following chapter. In choosing to frame this chapter in terms of the transcultural, however, and the following in terms of the cosmopolitan, my intention is to look here particularly at developments that are articulated as a mixing and fusion of cultural forms, and in the following at developments that have been understood as oriented to more commonly human concerns, seeking to further escape anchorage of nation and location. This is not to say, however, that they either succeed or that there is not a good deal in common between them.

National identity, monuments and museums

Previous chapters have already discussed the spread within Europe of a model of single 'person-like' national identities, with identifiable heritages and memories of their own. Key cultural forms assisting in performing this – both of which proliferated alongside the spread of the nation-state in Europe in the late-eighteenth and nineteenth centuries – were national monuments and museums. Given their importance in helping to instantiate particular models of identity and heritage, they deserve attention, not least as a basis for exploring how far they might be capable of operating otherwise.

The term 'monument', according to Andrew Butterfield,

> comes from the Latin noun *monumentum,* which is derived from the Latin verb *moneo.* The primary meaning of *moneo* is 'to bring to the notice of, to remind, or to tell of.' *Monumentum* consequently is something with this function, specifically something that stimulates the remembrance of a person or an event.

(Butterfield 2003: 28)[4]

The national monuments that proliferated during nation-making thus served to demarcate particular events, individuals and locations as especially significant to the nation's memory; and to materialise this in durable form. Some took the form of sculptures of individuals – almost invariably national heroes whose qualities were taken as iconic of those of the nation itself. This personification simultaneously substantiated the idea of nations as having distinct, person-like identities.

The museum – whose modern publicly-open form only began at the same time as the nation-state – also acted as an agency and site for identifying worthy heritage, in effect, creating three-dimensional identity-stories for the public. It also helped make the very idea of singular, bounded national identities, with their own heritages and cultures, imaginable. This not only operated through the display of things produced by, or discovered within, the nation, though these generally took pride-of-place, but also, typically, through objects from many parts of the world. This was the case in national museums of many kinds, including the encyclopaedic (generalist) museum, as well as more subject-specific kinds of museums, such as those of natural history or art. In ethnographic museums it was usually *only* the stuff of others on display. In part, this display of objects from other parts of the world served to illuminate the nation's 'mastery' over a large geographical area, thus substantiating the nation as a significant international player.[5] In addition, however, the material culture from other places was usually displayed in a manner that exemplified – and substantiated through objects – the discrete diversity of peoples, thus making 'objective' a particular model of the world as largely divided into territorially and culturally distinct peoples.

Another important capacity of heritage, monuments and museums was to gather people – to attract people to come to them. Of course, not all succeeded in this as well as those involved in their making might have hoped. As Jonas Frykman writes, 'Monuments are a strange kind of material culture with lives of their own' (2004: 110) and much the same can be said of museums. But what monuments and museums nevertheless helped effect was the assembling of a public, an act that has been argued to be central to both forming the idea of a collectivity of citizens and to creating senses and accompanying affects of national belonging. In the case of monuments especially, this may operate in conjunction with rituals – affectively dense collective events that help individuals to feel connection with the nation or other demarcated collectivity. But even the looser, though orderly, gathering of people by museums could encourage a sense of having common interests and ambitions with those of other unknown visitors. This was also fostered by the museum's capacity to put the viewer into a privileged distanced relationship with the displays – as an objective spectator of 'an external object-world' (Mitchell 1988: 21) that Mitchell, drawing on Heidegger, describes as 'the world as exhibition'.[6] Capable visitors were, thus, envisaged as able to step outside of culture and view it with detachment, even while feeling strongly attached to their own. In doing so, they also became part of a self-aware collective of fellow citizens.

Given how much the form of monuments, and perhaps even more so of museums, was entangled in shaping a particular kind of identity, public and even certain notions of objectivity, perhaps they, and the heritage that they preserve, are too inextricably entangled in 'old' forms of identity and ways of seeing and feeling to be able to express 'new' ones. Are they too solid and static to express more fluid or volatile identities? If museum collections are in a sense the materialisations of memories as heritage linked to specific identities, then this also raises the question of whether museums and the heritage inevitably serve as 'brakes' or 'limits' on identity reconfiguration. Before exploring this in relation to some examples, we need to turn briefly to debates about how and why there might be – or need to be – changes in identity formations.

Identities, culture and heritage

The idea that existing identities and/or models of identity might be becoming obsolete or inadequate to contemporary realities has been widespread in social and cultural theory, especially since the 1990s.[7] Generally, the idea forms part of an argument about social and cultural transformations glossed by the label 'globalisation'. Put simply, the argument is that existing identifications and perhaps even the bounded, homogeneous model of identity itself are challenged by increased global movement – of people, goods, bads, symbols, ideas, images and so forth – enabled and even provoked by modern information and communication technologies, and also by the movement of people around the world, either temporarily through tourism and travel or more long-term through migration. In some theorisations, this contributes to greater identity-fluidity, as individuals are increasingly enabled or forced to sever themselves from the contexts of their birth; and in some it leads to increasingly fragmented or fusion identities as individuals selectively make themselves up in the changing and multiple worlds that they encounter – materially and virtually. Culture, in these perspectives, usually becomes less organically connected to particular groups of people – as it does in the identity-heritage complex that we have discussed in earlier chapters – but becomes instead more 'mixable' or 'hybrid', or even a set of symbols or lifestyle choices from which individuals make their own particular selections.

National identities have been a focus of much discussion of this sort, with some arguing that the multiple various allegiances of migrants and those whose parents or grandparents were migrants – who may, variously and depending on the particular national laws, become national citizens – challenges the idea of a nation-state as mono-cultural or populated by those who share a single heritage. National mono-culturalism has also been challenged by social history, pointing out the heterogeneity of heritage and expanding definitions of heritage, especially in class terms.[8] The expansion of the local, industrial and 'everyday' heritage discussed earlier is linked to this. Furthermore, ethno-nationalism – demands ranging from increased recognition to autonomy and separatisms by self-claimed 'indigenous minorities' – has also been argued to be a return of difference previously suppressed or unacknowledged by existing nation-states. Examples in Europe include the Basques, Welsh, Catalans, Sami, and Bretons. Yet, while these show the existence and/or persistence of difference within nation-states, they do not challenge the national model fundamentally. On the contrary, as shown even more dramatically by the many ethnonationalist groups that have succeeded in gaining national sovereignty, as have those of the former Yugoslavia and Soviet Union, they are premised upon models of bounded nations with their own distinctive culture and heritage. As we saw in Chapter 2, European identity is also often modelled on that of the nation-state and so does not necessarily challenge the identity-heritage model itself.

The extent to which migration leads either to shifts in individual identities of migrants, as they seek to forge an identity in relation to their various 'homes', or identities of non-migrants or society as a whole, surely varies according to particular circumstances, including specific longings, opportunities, hostilities and resources for imagining alternatives. It is by no means assured, however, that either greater cultural mixing or a revision of existing identity formations will result. In an influential argument in 1995, Verena Stolcke argued that what she calls 'cultural fundamentalism' – 'a rhetoric of inclusion and exclusion that emphasises the distinctiveness of cultural identity, traditions, and heritage among groups and assumes the closure of this culture by territory' (1995: 2) – has increased in Europe since the 1970s. Deployed especially by right-wing politicians, she sees this as largely a function of, and certainly as supporting, 'mounting animosity against immigrants' (ibid.). In other words, an outcome of the increased movement of peoples is *increased* demarcation and separation of cultures rather than cultural mixing or weakening of boundaries. Moreover, this analysis highlights the memory phenomenon – a phenomenon that we have already seen is over-determined – as giving service to this maintenance of boundaries and the status quo, thus supporting racism and xenophobia. While 'culture' and 'heritage' are sometimes used synonymously, especially in these debates, heritage is potentially a still more powerful tool of exclusion. Culture is usually considered learnable, at least over generations, whereas heritage is much more emphatically something that stretches back, that speaks of where you have *come from*.

Multiculturalism

Stolcke's discussion of the rise of culturally fundamentalist rhetoric, which she sees as motivated by existing European nations (and also Europe as a whole) asserting their own boundaries, rights and cultural exclusivity, can also be usefully considered in relation to policies of multiculturalism and subsequent developments. As she notes, governmental policy on cultural diversity varies markedly between European countries; in particular, she compares what she calls 'the French model', which aims at 'assimilation and civic incorporation' and the 'Anglo-Saxon' one, which allows cultural diversity within a broad aim of ethnic integration (1995: 9). The latter has also formed a base for official policies of multiculturalism that not merely tolerate diversity but encourage the idea of the nation as constituted by a mosaic of different cultures.[9] On the one hand, this gives official recognition to cultural difference and grants a degree of cultural autonomy to the variously recognised 'cultures'. On the other, however, it is often argued that multicultural policies only recognise *some* elements of culture – usually an identikit of 'safe' cultural markers, such as dress and food, rather than potentially divisive differences of practice or difficult heritage.[10] Moreover, it can be said to be an extension of cultural fundamentalism itself, albeit usually without the territorial dimension, though the latter is sometimes realised through an idea of particular 'communities' or urban neighbourhoods. As such, multicultural fundamentalism also excludes more untidy or complex identity formations and memories.

Multicultural policies, enacted through a multitude of local practices, vary widely across and within European countries as ethnographic research has shown.[11] Such research has often highlighted contradictions of practice. In Berlin, for example, which as we saw in the Chapter 5 is increasingly being marketed as 'multicultural', Kira Kosnick argues that 'the management of its "really existing" ethno-cultural diversity' (2009: 162) often belies its ambitions. Her examples include those who look to be of immigrant backgrounds being turned away from using the toilets at the House of World Cultures – toilets that many others who are also just visiting the nearby park but are 'stereotypical embodiments of non-immigrant Germans' are permitted to use (2009: 161). In a study of a multicultural project to bring artists from Istanbul to Berlin, Banu Karaca describes them feeling frustrated to be 'put in the position of social workers' rather than artists, and to be treated as 'representatives of their supposed communities, and by extension "their cultures", rather than as individual artists' (2009: 35). Several told her they would avoid taking part in such projects in future.

There have also been many moments – some long – of 'backlash' against multicultural policies, including recent proclamations by the German Chancellor, Angela Merkel, and the British Prime Minister, David Cameron, that multiculturalism has failed.[12] Instances of unrest in areas of high proportions of the population with immigrant backgrounds – as in riots in Paris in 2007 and several summers since – have fuelled heated debate across many parts of Europe about which approaches hold most promise for generating senses of 'inclusion'. In some countries, most notably the Netherlands, which long held a reputation for being especially accommodating of difference, there has been a marked turn to attempting to reinstate senses of affiliation to the nation. Oskar Verkaik dates the questioning of multicultural approaches in the Netherlands to 2000, propelled partly by politicians such as Pim Fortuyn, who opposed further Muslim immigration into the Netherlands, arguing that Muslim refusal to recognise gay and women's rights threatened Dutch society, and its very liberalism. The assassination of Fortuyn in 2002, and then of film-maker

Theo van Gogh – who was also highly critical of Islam – further fuelled debate and the generation of what Verkaik calls 'the new nationalism'. Unlike earlier nationalisms, he suggests, this form of nationalism is 'primarily directed against internal migrant Others, especially Muslims' (2010: 71).[13] It strongly emphasises 'Dutch culture', seeking out and defining this through 'state-led projects, such as the creation of a Dutch historical "canon" and a new national history museum' (2010: 70) and the creation of a 'naturalisation ceremony' for those seeking to become Dutch citizens. As Verkaik describes, creating this ceremony involved 'invent[ing] key symbols for the elusive concept of "Dutchness"' (2010: 74) – a tricky task as the Dutch do not attach much significance to their flag or national anthem and 'symbols like the tulip were felt to be so commercialised as to no longer have any cachet' (ibid.). The job was largely left to local bureaucrats who came up with many creative solutions, including the following.

> In various places new citizens were treated to licorice – not always a big success – or sandwiches made with peanut butter. One municipality served Brussels sprouts and *boerenkool* – a peasants' dish made of kale and potatoes. Another took three new citizens – members of a family from Afghanistan – to a dairy farm; elsewhere there was a visit to a windmill … In one place, a box of various flowers was brought in and all guests were invited to pick a flower to his or her liking, a gesture symbolizing the multifaceted nature of Dutch national identity. Elsewhere one could have one's picture taken standing next to a life-sized image of the soccer hero Johan Cruyff …
>
> (ibid.)

While many of the bureaucrats involved in both creating and implementing these ceremonies had left-wing and pro-immigrant sympathies, and often began with an ironic stance on the naturalisation processes, Verkaik shows how the repetitive nature of the ceremonies and their affective dimension came to make the bureaucrats themselves much more accepting of the new nationalism than they were previously. As for the new citizens, what the procedures primarily taught them, he argues, is 'Dutch people's preoccupation with their own culture' (2010: 79) and also 'that culture, in its essentialist form, matters' (2010: 80).

If multicultural practice, then, may end up reinforcing essentialist and fundamentalist visions of culture, are there other approaches that might transcend this? One possibility is to focus on that which crosses cultural boundaries, mixing, fusing and hybridising in the process – or to create situations and practices that encourage this. Below, I examine some selected attempts to do this, especially through the cultural forms of the museum exhibition and what might possibly constitute a modern monument, and at the same time discuss the ways in which certain practices – in this case that of Islamic veiling – may become a focus for debates about the possible flexibility or inflexibility of heritage itself.

Veiling and unveiling heritage

In 2007, a new statue was erected in the public park of the Kunsthalle (Art Gallery) in Vienna. While calling the statue a 'monument' is a partial misnomer, in that it was not produced as part of a clearly instrumental civic process of remembrance, it nevertheless served as a reminder of a particular presence and associated history in public space. As a statue on a plinth, it partly shared the monumental format of the solitary hero – though in this case it was not elevated as were most nineteenth century monumental figures – as well as that of the classical nude statue. Created by German sculptor, Olaf Metzel, the statue was a nude of a veiled woman (Göle 2009). Its title, *Turkish Delight,* indicated its intended ethnic reference, if this was not already sufficiently clear in a city with a significant Turkish presence. If nineteenth-century national monuments were largely publicly uncontested, community-affirming insertions into public space, however, that of this statue was rather different. It immediately generated considerable public controversy and after just a few months was pulled down and subsequently removed from the park.

FIGURE 7.1   *Turkish Delight*, by Olaf Metzel, 2006, in the park of Kunsthalle Wien, 2007. Photograph by Wolfgang Woessner © Kunsthalle Wien public space

In a detailed analysis of the events, Nilüfer Göle argues that 'a new European public culture is emerging as a result of the encounter with issues concerning Islam', in which 'what is at stake is the "indigenization" of Islam, its re-territorialization in Europe' (2009: 278) and 'cultural struggles over memory and visibility' (2009: 291). Debates beginning in 2002 about Turkey's possible accession to the European Union intensified these struggles over Islam's re-territorialisation, bringing out a usually implicit but sometimes explicit 'equation between Europe and Christianity' (2009: 282), with Islam – and often specific symbols such as the veil – acting as an 'amplifier' of cultural difference more generally (2009: 292). Göle argues that neither multiculturalism, which has problems such as those discussed above, nor post-colonialism, which does not sufficiently grasp the mutuality of the processes involved as well as being not literally historically correct in the case of the Turkish presence in Austria, provides a conceptual handle on the processes involved. Instead, she uses the term *Anwandlungen* to describe what she argues are the mutually interpenetrating 'sense[s] of change of the self, and other, [and] the metamorphoses that ensue from proximity' (2009: 285). In the case of *Turkish Delight,* what is involved is not only change amongst the Turkish migrants but a reworking of Viennese, and broader European, public space, in which art constitutes a 'privileged interface' between 'different publics and cultures' (2009: 278). In addition, art allows for the production and consumption of aesthetic forms that may themselves seek to express, explore or provoke the transcultural and hybrid.

Turkish Delight is a hybrid form in its mixing of the classical nude with what has become one of the most visible and contested markers of Islam – the veil. Sculptor Olaf Metzel intended to provoke in his depiction of woman, naked except for the veil covering her hair – a depiction that affronts Islam's prohibition on public revelation of the female body – and thus, as the Kunsthalle's website explains, to draw attention to 'the precarious relationship between Orient and Occident … and the commercial exploitation of the feminine body in Western media-driven mass society'.[14] As Göle notes, the statue is not sexually provocative (2009: 288) but, with its downcast eyes, is rather demure and understated, though its title suggests orientalised sensory temptation. She argues, however, that despite the fact that the sculptor is male and not Turkish, and although the representation of a veiled woman naked, alone in a public park, is not a depiction of literal reality, the statue nevertheless expresses some of the contradictions and tensions experienced by Turkish women in European cities, who may feel alone, 'caught between past and present [and] conflicting symbolic orders' (2009: 290). As such, the statue should not be dismissed as a Western artist's perhaps rather crass or naïve provocation but understood as a more complexly transcultural form. Likewise, the toppling of the statue by two men (probably) from Vienna's migrant Turkish community should not necessarily be seen as a straightforward act of rejection of an 'outside perspective' by that 'community' as a whole. *Turkish Delight* can be regarded, then, as an expression of *Anwandlungen* – a 'cultural intermingling' in which there is an attempt to convey the new cultural fusions and contradictions of contemporary European heritage. Turkish women *are* now part of Vienna's public space and *Turkish Delight* more or less officially acknowledges this, inscribing it into the city's sculptural public heritage. At least, it did until the statue was toppled and removed. In this sense, the sculpture performed a monumental function. But this was a rather different performance from that of the nineteenth century monument, both in its attempts at cultural fusion and lack of stylistic grandeur; and in its form of a generalised, though gender and ethnically specified, figure rather than a particular hero or icon for 'everyman' emulation. While traditional monumental sculptural forms continue to be built for public space within Europe today – as we saw, for example, in the second of the monuments built for the 1956 Uprising in Budapest (discussed in the Prologue) – there is also a search for new forms, that partly borrow from earlier forms but also specifically strive to avoid certain features of earlier monumentality. Often abstract, and perhaps also defying enduring physical presence – as with many 'counter-monuments', discussed in the following chapter – and sometimes more muted and provocative figurations, as in this case, these not only question the idea of who and what should be remembered in public space but also the role of public art. Rather than seeking to establish, confirm and celebrate, or perhaps even, as some argue, contribute to forgetting and 'glorious anesthesia' (Stewart 2005: 336), new memorial forms are as likely to question, unsettle and provoke.[15] In doing so, they constitute public space as one of debate rather validation, as 'made up of, and constituted by and through, the articulation of different perspectives' (Göle 2009: 291).[16] Within this, memorial forms in the cityscape – newly created heritage – become important stimuli for bringing interlocutors together, not necessarily to agree but to engage in some kind of transcultural interaction that in effect creates a public sphere, and in which the role of public art, memory and the very nature of public – and European – space themselves become the subject of debate.

The veil as Islamic heritage

Continuing the debate, in the year after the erection and then toppling of *Turkish Delight,* an exhibition was shown in Vienna's Kunsthalle: 'Footnotes on veiling: *Mahrem'.* Partly organised by Nilüfer Göle, the exhibition came from Istanbul and included work mainly by women artists from a wide range of different countries reflecting in many different ways on veiling. Its title, *Mahrem,* means 'interior, sacred, gendered space' (Göle 2009: 286), thus invoking the veil not as a generalised symbol of Islam but as part of a more subjective experience. As Pnina Werbner points out, references to '*the* veil', understood as a symbol of Islam, are widespread in public debate, so homogenising veiling practices and failing to acknowledge alternative and often more complex motives for veiling among women (2007). Not only does the term 'veil' carry a different semantic load than does 'headscarf', it also obscures variations between the different forms that it takes, ranging from the light *dupatta* – usually of chiffon and only partially covering much hair – to full covering of the face and body, as in the case of the *burqa*.[17] While the 'meaning' and 'significance' of the veil are most often discussed in public policy in terms of the submission of women to strict tenets of Islam – with the degree of veiling being equated with the degree of submission – and, as such, as a matter of whether 'tradition' or 'modernity' prevails, Werbner explains that the subjective motivations may be otherwise, and often 'complex and ... situational' (2007: 173). In general, she argues, the significance of the veil for women is more concerned with the articulation of modesty and piety than a religious statement. As such, bans on its presence in public space – as in French schools – become matters of individual human rights. Moreover, she argues, veiling can accord women more rather than less agency. On the basis of her fieldwork with Punjabi women in England, she writes about how some of the younger women adopt 'stricter' forms of veiling than their mothers, and that this performance of greater religious observance gives them greater agency in choosing their own marriage partners and determining their own destinies more generally. Many such younger women argue that traditional Islam allows women greater freedom and they use their veiling as a way of entering public space in ways that allow them to do so with fewer restrictions than they could otherwise (Werbner 2007: 175–6). Likewise, in Germany, Ruth Mandel reports some Turkish women choosing to take up wearing headscarves to signal their identity as Turkish – and not German, an identity that also carries significance as a statement of what they see as more honourable sexual mores (2008: Chapter 11).

As is evident from examples provided by both Werbner and Mandel, 'tradition' is frequently invoked in these debates. This is often 'tradition' as an outmoded, unreflexive practice (see also Ghodsee 2008, 2010 for Bulgaria). Not only is this sometimes deployed in public debate, especially in relation to women's agency, it may also be used, as Werbner shows, by the younger 'more Islamic' women who argue that their parents are just following rural traditions rather than 'more correct' forms of Islamic heritage (2007: 171). At the same time, however, describing veiling as a matter of 'tradition' or 'heritage' can be effective in contexts in which even a weak form of multiculturalism operates, for 'tradition' and 'heritage' are automatically regarded as worthy of respect and retention. It is perhaps partly for this reason that the European media often contain commentaries about veiling among certain communities as relatively recent or as not fully endorsed by the Qur'an. Similarly, fashionable veils – the market in which has massively increased (Navaro-Yashin 2002) – or the wearing of them with fashionable clothing, are also sometimes taken as a sign of inauthenticity, and, therefore, as not requiring the respect that heritage should usually be accorded (Mandel 2008: 309). What might otherwise be regarded as a form of transcultural accommodation, then, is often excluded by the invocation of heritage discourse. Yet as various scholars point out, veiling practices and meanings have long been subject to change, not least across generations,[18] as indeed is so often the case for traditions more generally.

The unwillingness to acknowledge the veil as legitimately changing, however, is to regard it as part of an inflexible tradition, characterised by an outmoded and repressive gender relations. It is an element of the same processes of demarcating sharp boundaries around Islam that Karin van Nieuwkerk describes in her analysis of the experience of Dutch women converts to Islam. These women all related experiences of being defined by non-Muslims as 'foreign' – in myriad, sometimes stark and sometimes subtle, ways – despite their Dutch citizenship and upbringing. Veiling, in particular, intensified the reactions to them; van Nieuwkerk arguing that for most Dutch 'the veil is the symbol of foreignness' and 'of female degradation' (2004: 242). She sees this as understood by the Dutch not just as a contravention of 'Dutch' qualities but of 'a kind of universal non-identity…consisting of tolerance, freedom and emancipation with which converts are evaluated and considered to fall short since they are Muslim' (2004: 244). Likewise, in an analysis of public discourse surrounding 'Islamophobic' incidents involving veiling in Germany, Beverly M. Weber observes that the women's agency as citizens is underreported in the media: '[t]he headscarf [thus]… acts as the marker of cultural otherness that prohibits their participation in a democratic public sphere' (2012: 114). The result is that '[t]he subject of democracy remains abstracted and unmarked but firmly "European"' (2012: 114).

While veiling acts as an *object chargé* (Mandel 2008: 294) and an 'amplifier' of difference (Göle 2009: 292), and is paradoxically condemned on the one hand for its inflexibility and on the other for changing, there are cultural initiatives to highlight its variability, multiplicity, and emotional as well as religious significance, as in the *Mahrem* exhibition. Such an exhibition was just one of a growing number of interventions in public space that seek to address questions of cultural difference – framed variously in terms of providing greater knowledge in the hope of fostering greater understanding, or personalising abstract issues as a means of generating empathy. In the next section, I look at one of these – a new museum gallery – framed explicitly as *transcultural*.

Transcultural heritage in the museum

The *Transcultural Galleries* opened in Bradford, in the city art gallery – Cartwright Hall – in 1997. It is, perhaps, not surprising that this early and unusually explicit attempt to both represent and encourage particular – 'transcultural' – identity formations should open in a city with one of the highest population proportions of extra-European migrant background within Europe. The collection on which the galleries were based was what its curator, Nima Poovaya Smith, refers to as 'the first non-colonial collection of its kind in the country' (Poovaya Smith 1998: 112). Appointed in 1986, her remit was to build and display a collection of art from the Indo-Pakistan subcontinent. Cartwright Hall is a purpose-built public art gallery, opened in 1904, in a Baroque style building set in a public park. Much of its internal space is fairly typical of a nineteenth-century public museum, with most of the art on display being European, with a strong emphasis on British work (including art with a local and regional emphasis). The new exhibitionary identity 'experiment' thus took place within a space designed for an earlier civic, largely monocultural, identity project.

Bradford's largest migrant population is from South Asia, having developed during the 1960s and 1970s, and, by the early 1990s, constituting approximately 81,000 out of a total of a population of 484,000. The largest group of these migrants came from Pakistan and Kashmir but with many too from other parts of India and Bangladesh, and so including a range of religious affiliations – Islam, Hinduism and Sikhism – and languages: Urdu, Hindi, Bangladeshi and Gujarati.[19] In addition, the city has significant minorities from Africa and the Caribbean; and within the city's 'white' population, Bradford has a history of immigration beginning with the Irish who came from the 1820s and the Germans, Poles, Ukrainians and Italians who followed them. During the 1970s racial tensions – usually framed as either 'Asian' or 'black' versus 'white' – grew, partly in relation to growing unemployment; and the early 1980s saw race riots there, as well as in various other British cities, and a flourishing of reports on 'race-relations'.[20] In 1989, a copy of Salman Rushdie's *The Satanic Verses* (1988) was publicly burnt here, bringing Bradford forcibly to global attention as a site of cultural and religious passion and fundamentalism.

The decision to fund the building of a collection of South Asian art was made, then, against this backdrop of increasingly antagonistic racialised city politics; with the intention that it would help ameliorate the situation. Drawing on the museum's legitimacy-giving function, the inclusion of South Asian culture in this key civic institution was acknowledged as a means of demonstrating the city's acceptance of the inclusion of South Asians within its own patrimony and public spaces. It was also seen as a way of showing the non-South Asian population the richness of South Asian heritage and so, it was hoped, of fostering greater respect and, through accompanying educational information, of increasing understanding of cultural difference. At the same time, however, exhibiting South Asian material culture was also hoped to act as a magnet for bringing South Asians – who at that time rarely visited Cartwright Hall – into the museum, and, thus, more fully into the community of fellow citizens that museums help to instantiate.

There was clearly a risk, however, that the museal logic of culture would act to reify South-Asian culture as an exotic 'other' presence within the galleries. This can be seen as part of a broader dilemma of the politics of recognition and of social inclusion, which themselves typically work with a model of discrete 'cultures', often through the trope of 'community' (Çağlar 1997).[21] In a robust critique of the politics of social inclusion, Irit Rogoff argues that

> this infinitely expansive inclusiveness is actually grounded in an unrevised notion of the museum's untroubled ability simply to *add* others without losing a bit of the self ... [I]t assumes the possibility of change without loss, without alteration, without remapping the navigational principles

that allow us to make judgments about quality, appropriateness, inclusion and revision.

(2002: 66)

While she perhaps gives too little credit to the unsettlement that some of these projects can, nevertheless, create within museums and the extent that it can prompt questioning of what is included in the museum and on what criteria, her argument that 'social inclusion' often just leads to 'compensatory visibility' – making minorities visible in public space – rather than more ramifying change is an important challenge to such initiatives.[22]

The shift to a more transcultural approach was a significant attempt to move beyond mere 'inclusion' and to avoid the zoological representation of cultures. In devising this approach, Poovaya Smith drew on her reading of post-colonial critical discourse theorists such as Edward Said, Homi Bhabha and Gayatri Spivak (1998: 112).[23] At the same time, she sought to consult with South Asians in Bradford and to mount a series of temporary exhibitions on topics that she hoped would engage local, especially though not exclusively South Asian, interest. These included exhibitions on gold and silver, Islamic calligraphy and textiles (especially *saris* – garments worn by women in many areas of the Indo-Pakistan sub-continent and also in Bradford). Interestingly, these subjects, developed in consultation with people of South Asian descent in Bradford, used a variety of media and broached the usual distinction between fine art and craft.[24] Importantly for Poovaya-Smith's project, the temporary exhibitions succeeded in bringing considerably increased numbers of South Asian visitors to Cartwright Hall (Poovaya Smith 1991: 126).

Transcultural connections

It is worth looking more closely here at the strategies that Poovaya Smith used to try to express the transcultural. First, there are the areas of collection. These included the themes of some of the temporary exhibitions and were subject-matters which cut across territorial boundaries. Thus, gold and silver, for example, are not only the chosen media for many skilful artists across much of South Asia (rather than just certain countries) but also have symbolic and social significance across a wide area. Moreover, some of these skills and significances reach across to West Yorkshire and other sites beyond South Asia. Islamic calligraphy also provided an opportunity to explore a subject that, while of especial interest to Muslims in Bradford, also stretched across a wide geographical territory, drawing its examples not only from South Asia but also from the Middle-East. The collecting strategy was, however, even more encompassing than this, for Poovaya Smith also included works by some British artists not of South Asian origin but who have been influenced by South Asian styles. So, for example, jewellery by Clarissa Mitchell and Roger Barnes was included in the original exhibition on gold. This was, however, objected to by some members of the 'South Asian community' in Bradford on the grounds that these artists 'were exploiting the subcontinent for their own ends' (Poovaya Smith 1991: 126). Poovaya Smith's view, however, was that the work of these artists 'did not so much imitate Indian jewellery so much as let the influence of India itself impress itself upon their work, often in highly original ways' (1991: 126); and she chose, therefore, to ignore this criticism: 'The voices of the community are important voices but they do not necessarily always embody a God-like infallibility or collective wisdom' (ibid.). In doing so, she privileged her 'transcultural' vision over that which, from this perspective, 'indicated a certain narrowness of vision and prejudice' (ibid.). This was not the only area of potential dissent. In the exhibition on gold, Poovaya Smith hoped to include commentary on the 'pernicious' elements of dowry which sometimes result in 'dowry deaths' where a bride's family is unable to pay the sums, generally in the form of gold jewellery, demanded by a groom's family. She consulted a group of people from 'the community' who were all very much in favour of this idea, though they did not want this to be the only dimension of the subject discussed. However, these selected 'community representatives' were all under 35 years old and had grown up in Britain. An exhibition in Leicester on a similar theme received a very different response when older members of 'the South Asian community' were consulted. There 'the community' argued that anything which might caste a negative light on South Asian cultural practices should not be displayed in a museum (see Poovaya Smith 1991: 122–5). Evident here is that the trope of community can mask differences of perspective, including about how culture should be represented. Also clear are differing expectations about the role of the museum – as a representation of uncontested culture or as a possible prompt for debate.

In attempting to cut across geographical and traditional 'community' identities, the exhibitions in the Transcultural Galleries do nevertheless employ the idea of *locality* in relation to Bradford or West Yorkshire itself. Again, however, this is done not so much to 'museumise' a clear-cut identity as to highlight the plural nature of the locality and to explore the theme from multiple perspectives. (The slippage between referring to the locality as 'Bradford' and as 'West Yorkshire' is itself indicative of the fact that locality is not precisely demarcated.) Thus, while the exhibition contains a substantial proportion of work either from the Indo-Pakistan subcontinent or by artists who self-identify as at least partly from this region, many, though by no means all of these are also from Bradford. Moreover, the galleries also contain works by artists from West Yorkshire, such as David Hockney, who have no South Asian connections; and there are various other items, such a Japanese suit of armour, whose only 'Bradfordness' lies in the fact that it was originally purchased by a Bradford philanthropist. The theme of locality is also explored through various commissioned works where artists were asked to reflect on either the city of Bradford or Cartwright Hall and its collections themselves. Such works include Lubna Chowdhary's miniature mysticised sculptures of Bradford buildings; Fahmida Shah's cryptic and surprising depiction of a motorbike (which was part of a temporary exhibition at Cartwright Hall) as an artistic reflection on Cartwright Hall; and Mah Rana's contemporary jewellery, with titles such as 'I never promised you a rose garden', which provide elegant ironic commentaries on South Indian marriage pendants.

The ways in which both 'South Asia' and 'locality' are evoked, then, are multi-perspectival and plural. In the galleries there is no attempt to arrange artefacts in terms of separate cultures; and nor is there a historical narrative. This is not to say that it is all totally disorganised, however. Certainly, there is not the same strong sense of order – and the potential to survey a long gallery vista as you walk in – that you find in many traditional galleries, and elsewhere in Cartwright Hall. There is less sense here of an objectively positioned viewer. Instead, perspective depends on a specific and potentially different standpoint.

There is organisation, however. Rather than this working by a logic of distinction and taxonomic categories, the logic is one of *connection*. This is a word that Nima Poovaya Smith repeats many times as she explains the displays; and following a major redisplay of the galleries in 2008 they are now called *Connect* – and organised into three themes of Place, People Icons and Imagination. To some extent, connection has always been one of the logics employed in exhibitions, and Kevin Hetherington has written interestingly of what he calls 'the will to connect' in relation to museums and their analysis (1997). In the *Transcultural Galleries* and *Connect,* however, connection is not conceptualised as somehow 'bringing out' some underlying reality (a perspective which the historian John Pickstone (1994) refers to as 'diagnostic' or – taking his use from nineteenth-century museums – 'museological') but of connection as serendipitous, suggestive, and sometimes witty and ironic. Perhaps this is an instance of an increasingly common form, related to and maybe even partly modelled on the world-wide web, as Richard Terdiman suggests is the case for memory more generally (2003). The connections made are not supposed as in any way inevitable but it is hoped that they will spark reflection and a sense of the vigour of these kind of 'contacts' (Clifford 1997). 'Connection' is conceptualised as movement, process and creative agency. Moreover, the nature of the 'connections' varies in the galleries. For example, one set of exhibits are all on the theme of water: David Hockney's painting 'Le Plongeur (paper pool)' (1978); another painting, reflecting on the Hockney, Howard Hodgkin's 'David's Pool' (1985), and 'Water Weaver' (2000), by Indian artist, Arpana Caur. And in the *People Icons* gallery of *Connect,* curator Nilesh Misty, also includes reflexive thematic connections – such as a set of images focusing very variously on religion: Hughie O'Donoghue's 'Three studies for crucifixion' (1996), Bradford artist William Rothenstein's (1872–1945) 'Carrying the Law' (1907) with a depiction of Rabbis carrying the Torah, juxtaposed with Indian Kalighat paintings of Hindu Gods from the early 1900s. The iconic Indian Film star Rekha is seen in the Bollywood Film Poster, 'Umrao Jaan', which sits

FIGURE 7.2 Connect, Cartwright's Textile Story, Cartwright Hall Art Gallery. Foreground: 'Dr Edmund Cartwright', 1901 by Henry Fehr. Left: 'Tree of Life and Leaves', 2008, blockprinted silk and cotton hangings by Jaipur master printer Abdul Rashid. Right: Samuel Cunliffe Lister (1815–1906) by John Collier. Photograph reproduced courtesy of Bradford Museums and Galleries

alongside a Popart screen-print classic of the western equivalent, Hollywood icon 'Marilyn Monroe', 1967, by Andy Warhol.

Historical connections include Yinka Shonibare's *'The Wanderer'* (2006) – a model of an evocative slave ship, with sails in West African batik fabrics – positioned close to a portrait by John Collier (1850–1934) of industrialist, textile inventor and entrepreneur Samuel Cunliffe Lister (1815–1906) whose wealth from the production of woollen Worsted fabrics and silk velvets, and export across the territories of the British Empire and beyond, enabled the construction of Cartwright Hall Art Gallery on the site of his former residence, Lister Park.

In order to try to escape from geographical definitions and 'the trope of community', and the 'taken-for-granted isomorphism of culture, place and people' (Çağlar 1997: 174) that these tend to conjure up, Ayşe Çağlar suggests focusing on 'person-object relations as these exist in space and time' (1997: 180). Thus, rather than beginning with 'a community' or a geographical area, her methodological suggestion is to begin with objects and then, '[b]y plotting the networks of interconnected practices surrounding objects, and the sentiments, desires and images these practices evoke, we can avoid the need to define collectivities in advance' (ibid.).[25] The *Transcultural Galleries* and *Connect* at Cartwright Hall exemplify this, with objects, rather than any particular geographical or ethnic categories, as the beginning point and main content of the exhibition. Moreover, by having rather little text in the exhibition (for the most part there are only short labels giving the artist's name, the title of the work and its date), it is able to largely circumvent geographical or ethnic descriptions. In this respect, the exhibition medium has a clear advantage over, say, a written account in that it can privilege objects and do away with linguistic categorisation almost entirely. In doing so, however, it risks forgoing the second stage of Çağlar's methodological process: the plotting of the social and cultural networks in which the objects are more usually enmeshed, and, as such, an endorsement of 'globalism as a kind of super-sociality' that may also 'conceal' that which does not connect or problematic connections, as Marilyn Strathern cautions (2002: xv). While leaving objects 'to speak for themselves' may be an appropriate strategy for art works which can be seen (controversially) as a more calculated attempt to speak directly to the viewer, it means that the biographical contexts of much that is displayed – the lives, worlds and histories of which they were part, the contexts which give meaning to the objects – are given much less shrift than their formal, 'artistic' qualities. At least one commentator on the *Transcultural Galleries* found the labelling 'predictable' and remarked that the approach was 'not innovative' at this level (Lovelace 1997: 22). As this commentator also noted, however, this problem was one that was being well countered by the employment of a linked CD-ROM in the exhibition which includes quotes (e.g. by the artists involved), video footage of various artefacts being demonstrated in use, and – perhaps most innovatively – videos of visitor discussion groups making various thematic links between works on display (ibid.); and *Connect* extends this further, also into thoughtful labels, sometimes encouraging visitors to see global and historical links that are not necessarily legible to most on the surfaces of the objects themselves.

What this example from Bradford surely shows is that it is possible for museums to create connections across the differences that heritage more usually speaks. These are not necessarily comfortable links – as those of slavery show. How far this possibility to create such connections really disrupts either the expectation that heritage *does* still belong to particular *communities* – or peoples – or the identities with which such heritage is usually associated, however, remains unclear. Cartwright Hall provides evidence both ways: on the one hand, in a request from Sikhs for more of *their* heritage to be put on display, and, on the other, in the work of younger artists who purposefully play with different traditions and identities.[26] But, in the very process of doing so, it opens up new conversations.

It is worth noting here that while heritage forms such as the public museum were tightly bound up with the development of the nation-state in late eighteenth- and nineteenth-century Europe, their potential always, surely, exceeded this. Most museums formed in this period collected a wide array of

FIGURE 7.3   Video commentary in *Connect*, Cartwright Hall, Bradford. Photograph by Sharon Macdonald, reproduced courtesy of Bradford Museums and Galleries

objects – not only the direct heritage of their own location but also from further afield. This was often from the colonies – but not only. This excess, however, is also what allows heritage institutions such as museums to be used in new ways today – as when collections formed as part of the colonial endeavour are used to try to tell transnational stories that it is hoped will lead to greater understanding of the colonial relations themselves and even, perhaps, to more convivial transcultural relations (cf. Gilroy 2004).

Exhibiting migration

Since the opening of the *Transcultural Galleries* there have been numerous further exhibitions that attempt in various ways to recognise cultural diversity within Europe today and also to rethink how the nation is performed (Ostow 2008). That many of these are framed in terms of ambitions to 'increase social inclusion', 'bring communities together' or 'foster intercultural communication', speaks both to the fact that museums and exhibitions are widely conceptualised as social agencies, capable of initiating or channelling social change, as well as to a predominant working model of separate communities and cultures. While the latter is often part of the social reality within which cultural institutions operate – that is, they may be confronted by self-identifying 'communities' requesting that their 'own culture' is represented in the museum – their challenge is to make sure that they do not overlook more hybrid, transcultural forms or identities, and also that they do not contribute to further reifying pristine 'cultures' and so generating further 'exclusions'.[27]

Migration itself has become a frequent topic of exhibitions and of an expanding number of new museums in Europe. The most high profile, and so far only *national* museum of migration in Europe, is the Cité Nationale de l'Histoire de l'Immigration (the National Museum of the History of Immigration), which opened in Paris in 2007, partly in response to growing unrest in areas of high migrant populations in Paris.[28] Both Switzerland and the UK are currently considering the case for national museums on this topic.[29] More often, however, the topic is included in smaller museum developments and individual exhibitions, usually run by local museums and migrant organisations. In Germany, for example, the organisation DOMiD (*Dokumentationszentrum und Museum über die Migration in Deutschland*/ Documentation Centre and Museum of Migration in Germany) – originally established by Turkish migrants but since expanded to include many other migrants – has been especially instrumental in organising or co-organising exhibitions, such as *Projekt Migration,* which ran in various locations in 2005.[30] City Museums and ethnographic museums have frequently mounted exhibitions, or devoted sections of the museum, to immigration and communities with migrant backgrounds. In addition, there is also a growth in numbers of museums of emigration, for example, in Denmark, Ireland and Portugal. The cultural dynamic of these differs from the focus on immigration – and the increasing multi- and fusion-culture of Europe – but they act as a reminder nonetheless of global movement.[31]

A major question concerning these museums and exhibitions is how far they succeed in allowing for more fluid and possibly transcultural identity formations. Kirsten Poehls argues that exhibitions on migration 'challenge the relevance of the nation' (2011: 350–1), unsettling partly simply by the fact that they focus on movement rather than boundaries. She observes that maps are frequently used in such exhibitions. While maps have been part of the visual apparatus for assembling the nation-state, she suggests that maps in migration exhibitions may work differently, to '*undercut* the meaning of European geopolitical boundaries' (2011: 345, original emphasis) and even disrupt the taken-for-granted objectivity of the map, with their arrows showing movement across borders and perhaps more subjective, personalised mappings of routes taken by particular migrants. Another prevalent visual trope in migration exhibitions is the suitcase (Macdonald 2008: 56; Poehls 2011: 346). As Poehls notes, this is an apt metaphor for the 'cultural baggage' that migrants take with them (ibid.). The suitcase evokes culture as package-able, containable and transportable across borders; but perhaps also hints at a transitory status, as requiring unpacking. And in exhibitions such as the thoughtful *Destination X* in the Museum of World Cultures in Gothenburg, which addresses migration and forced movement alongside tourism and business travel, the multiplicity of suitcases exhibited

FIGURE 7.4 Exhibition of 'world' of suitcases in Destination X, Museum of World Cultures, Gothenburg, Sweden. Photograph by Sharon Macdonald, reproduced courtesy of the Museum of World Cultures

reminds further that it is not just migrants who carry 'cultural baggage' across borders (Poehls 2011: 347).

While exhibitions and museums addressing migration and cultural diversity are certainly capable of expanding the range of 'voices' included in the public sphere, and, in this way, of potentially unsettling existing identity formations, they do not necessarily do so, or not as extensively as they might. One strategy that has been much deployed is the object-biography.[32] In many ways this follows Çağlar's injunctions above to begin not with a community or population, but to make the object or collection the focus for highlighting different players and their connections. Sometimes this can be rather innocuous and even turn into heroic stories of collectors, but done well it can highlight unexpected connections and histories, and give real detail to colonial encounters or the politics by which objects may travel to museums. As such, it can be capable of injecting certain memories into a public sphere from which they were previously absent and at the same time of revealing processes of public memory-making and earlier forgetting. A related approach begins with individuals and their stories. As well as allowing for a traversing of cultures and categories, this can also have the effect of humanising an exhibition, allowing for identifications at more intimate, personal, levels. We are presented with the city, or nation, not through some overall account but through individual portraits – especially of migrants of various kinds. It is a recovery of individual variety; it avoids reducing the place to a single persona, to the long-time resident perhaps; and it signals the multiplicity of cultural heritage and memory. Too often, however, it is reduced to a rather insubstantial formula of the smiling face accompanied by a text which shows multiple cultural affiliations – a liking for chapatis and hip hop and Manchester United, thus reducing those displayed to a new motif: that of the 'happily hybrid citizen' (Macdonald 2008: 56). The real content of their difference, and perhaps the dilemmas that they face because of it, is submerged under the sea of smiling faces and the uncannily similar form that the depictions take. In her analysis of the Cité Nationale de l'Histoire de l'Immigration and Ellis Island Migration Museum in the US, Julie Thomas also points out how individual migration stories are presented as 'memory of the *process* of becoming, rather than any specific culturally defined memory'. She argues that this

> succeeds in normalizing and rationalizing the process of migration. The economic threat of migrant communities is defused by the narrative of *plus ça change,* and the cultural threat of transnational identities is removed as they are seen as subject contributors to the national heritage.
>
> (Thomas 2011: 220)

Another brake on the potential unsettlement of migration stories is the tendency for these to crystallise rather than dissolve a division between migrants and non-migrants. That is, migration, migrants and descendants of migrants are staged against a backdrop of an assumed stable, usually national, population. This may be accentuated by the geo-politics of location: migration being, perhaps, included only in temporary exhibitions or a museum's more marginal spaces. The Cité Nationale de l'Histoire de l'Immigration is located far from the centre of Paris, in an area rarely visited by tourists and, moreover, is in a former building of colonial administration that has subsequently served as a museum of the colonies and then of African and Oceanic art. Rather than making migrants central to French society, therefore, they remain – in museological topography – in its margins, part of a colonial inheritance requiring administration and perhaps too without yet quite having rid themselves of the taint of the colonial curio. According to Andrea Meza Torres' ethnographic observations (2011), based on fieldwork in the Cité Nationale de l'Histoire de l'Immigration, this plays out in other aspects of the museum's practice too. The well-intentioned deployment of ethnically diverse – and ethnically clad – front-of-house staff, for example, ends up, she argues, making the museum appear to be engaged in a continuation of colonial relations and empire. In some ways the problem is exacerbated by the relative inattention to colonialism itself in the museum. As Mary Stevens (2009) shows from her fascinating detailed analysis of the making of the museum, this was not always the case but a series of decisions about 'containment' of the topic of immigration and disciplinary specialisms contributed to its marginalisation in the finished exhibitions.

★ ★ ★

This chapter has considered the challenge posed to the existing memory-identity complex by migration, and the transculturalism that this potentially – though far from inevitably – unleashes. It has done so especially in relation to heritage, in some of its most widespread cultural forms: monuments and museums. Precisely because these have been so implicated in identity work – especially in the assemblage of stable, national identities – they constitute key sites in which to examine some of the claims of identity transformation. What we have seen in this chapter are transformations in museums and monuments, as part of a struggle to address and perhaps even shape the changing identity-constellations of Europe today. In particular, what we have seen is heritage being drawn upon in less declarative and more provocative modes. That is, we see heritage being actively deployed not in service of ontological and legitimacy claims but as part of a more tentative setting out of alternatives or even an explicit provocation to debate. This is not only a change of the operation of heritage but also a reconfiguring of the public sphere and of the role of material cultural forms – monuments/public sculpture and exhibitions and museums – within it. Rather than constituting authoritative 'definitive statements', exhibitions and public sculpture increasingly operate in more conversational modes to help encourage the making of a more fluid, plural and contested public sphere. This is not to say that this is the only direction, however. Existing forms persist and even proliferate alongside new, more plural, interventions; and those interventions, and even the transcultural itself, can be, and are, contested, as we have seen in examples in this chapter. In addition, and as we have also seen here, both the migrant and the transcultural can be pushed to the margins of what then becomes even more fully 'mainstream'; or they may even be appropriated – partially and perhaps with significant 'blanks' – within it. It is also salutary to note that it is probably still the case that for the most part new museums and monuments are being produced in the service of making and defending discrete 'cultures' rather than to help encourage the transcultural or conversational.

As cultural forms, this chapter makes evident that monuments – if understood broadly as memorial sculptural forms – and museums are capable of articulating more fluid and transcultural identity formations than they have previously done, though they may sometimes struggle with aspects of their existing form and the perhaps conservative expectations of publics. In the case of museum attempts to work beyond nation-statist models, it is worth noting that this can involve drawing on museums' existing collections. Museum objects already often hold the potential for telling new memory stories, and especially for making connections between continents and between times, thus allowing for objects to be re-presented into new, perhaps more connective, displays.

As we have seen, the transcultural is usually conceptualised as a set of connections across or between cultures. This is the limit – and at least partial reality – against which it may also struggle. Just as a network is typically conceptualised as a mesh of threads between nodes or junctions, each 'trans'-(cultural)-action easily ends up being thought of as a movement between two points.[33] But this may not be enough to transcend either the existing model of culture or the national with which it is so often entangled. Perhaps cosmopolitan heritage and memory forms offer more potential to do so? Or perhaps it is possible not to dispense altogether with the national or the models of culture with which it is associated but nevertheless to simultaneously allow for, and encourage, more open understandings? The next chapter explores this further.

8

COSMOPOLITAN MEMORY

Holocaust commemoration and national identity

If the past is not to bind us, where can duty lie?

George Eliot[1]

In an influential argument, Daniel Levy and Natan Sznaider maintain that increasingly we are seeing a 'transition from national to *cosmopolitan* memory cultures' (2002: 88, 87; 2001). By this they mean that there has been a growth of forms of collective memory that are no longer primarily framed by the nation-state, or seen predominantly as the property of a particular nation or ethnic group, but that are instead relatively 'deterritorialised'. The Holocaust, according to their account, is 'the paradigmatic case' of such cosmopolitan memory; and has increasingly been decontextualised from its historical time and space, and, through processes of cultural mediation, turned into a universal and continually relevant 'moral story of good against evil' (2002: 98) whose central message is 'never again'. It has been turned from 'a set of facts' to 'an idea'; and increasingly is commemorated by people who have no direct connection to it (2002: 88), as witnessed not least in the proliferation of Holocaust memorials and museums and the millions of people across the globe who make treks, sometimes of thousands of miles, to visit them. Mostly, their argument about cosmopolitan memory is framed in terms of 'the global' or 'humanity', as when, for example, they argue that the deterritorialised cosmopolitan memory of the Holocaust plays a significant role in the development of a cosmopolitan politics of human rights (Levy and Sznaider 2002: 100). At others, however, 'cosmopolitan' is equated with 'European', as when they claim that the developments that they chart 'contribute to the creation of a common European cultural memory' (Levy and Sznaider 2002: 87).[2]

In this chapter, I explore the argument that a cosmopolitan memory, which 'cracks the container' of the nation-state as 'memory-holder', is underway, and that we are witnessing a growing Europeanisation and/or cosmopolitanisation of memory. I do so by looking at specific cases of what Novicka and Rovisco call 'cosmopolitanism in practice' in Europe (2009). As we will see, detailed studies often reveal tensions involved in such practice and also show how cosmopolitan developments can be made part of other assemblages, and 're-territorialised' or 'co-opted' in terms of other interests, too. As Levy and Sznaider's arguments focus especially upon the Holocaust, this chapter also considers the considerable expansion of commemoration and heritagisation of the Holocaust that has occurred in Europe – and beyond it – especially since the 1980s. Part of a wider expansion of 'difficult heritage' (Macdonald 2009a), the increased public attention to the Holocaust – or what is sometimes provocatively dubbed a 'Holocaust cult', 'the Holocaust industry', 'Shoah Business' or even 'post-Holocaust necrophilia'[3] – raises questions about why it should be subject to so much new heritagisation and commemoration over 50 years since it occurred.

Cosmopolitan memory

Levy and Sznaider's argument about cosmopolitan memory is that we are witnessing a process in which 'national and ethnic memories continue to exist' but they

> are subjected to a common patterning. They begin to develop in accord with common rhythms and periodizations. But in each case, the common elements combine with pre-existing elements to form something new… the result is always distinctive.
>
> (2002: 89)

We might conceptualize this, they say, as 'a process of "internal globalisation" through which global concerns become part of local experiences of an increasing number of people' (2002: 87). They illustrate this through a detailed charting of changes in ways that the Holocaust has been 'remembered' in Germany, Israel and the US, showing commonalities in its patterning since 1945, all of which contribute to the Holocaust becoming less 'a terrible aspect of a particular era' and instead 'a timeless and deterritorialized measuring stick for good and evil' (2002: 95).

First, there is a shift from social memory – first-hand biographical memories of those who lived through it – to historical or cultural memory, transmitted primarily through mediated representations. The latter allows for a globalisation of memory, especially through film and television. Here, they note how the US mini-series *Holocaust* in the 1970s and then films such as *Schindler's List* (1993) were widely disseminated around the world and also how they themselves universalised specific historical events into narratives of good and evil. *Schindler's*

List in particular helped to decouple the usual 'ethnic'/'national' identification of perpetration and victimhood by having a hero who is German. In such a representation, national identity is no longer depicted as the key determinant of where an individual stands in relation to the Holocaust. This, Levy and Sznaider see as part of a wider common patterning in which there is – to varying extents in the three countries – a diffusion of 'the distinction between memories of victims and perpetrators', resulting instead in a more generalised 'memory of a shared past' (2002: 103). The other common patterning of Holocaust memory, linked to its increasing universalism, is its 'future-orientation' (2002: 102). Applicable as an abstract principle, recollection of the Holocaust becomes primarily framed in terms of safeguarding against future repetition: 'Never again!' becomes the mantra.

Identification of the cosmopolitanising processes that Levy and Sznaider discuss with reference to the Holocaust have not yet been made as forcefully with reference to other countries or other 'memories'. In more recent work, however, they (sometimes with other colleagues) have sought to extend their arguments in various ways. This has included expanding the Holocaust argument to other countries, such as Austria and Poland, and exploring this too through analyses of public discourse and group interviews (Levy *et al.* 2011). Their research, they argue, provides evidence of a growing 'shared European memory', though also of national variations that they call 'reflexive particularism' (ibid.). They have also extended their argument to claim that a human rights discourse, which has its origins in the Holocaust, is now the discursive frame for any atrocity. And – in what seems a tautology but they see as part of the self-sustaining network of these ideas – they argue that (sometimes competing) cultural memories of atrocities have become the global currency for articulating notions of human rights (Levy and Sznaider 2010).

In an overlapping argument, together with Ulrich Beck, they claim that the Holocaust has informed a wider mobilisation of notions of forgiveness, guilt and restitution in international political relations – witnessed, for example, in public apologies by politicians.[4] The 'self-critique' inherent in such apologies and any associated reparations is, they argue, part of how 'cosmopolitan Europe' is being constituted (2009: 120). Thus, '[t]he radically self-critical European memory of the Holocaust does not destroy the identity of Europe, it constitutes this very identity' (ibid.). Although national histories are often referenced within this self-critique, and as part of the 'reflexive particularism' of Holocaust discussion, what is involved here, they claim, is that '[t]he nation is being remembered in order to overcome it' (2009: 125).

While Levy and Sznaider's position is primarily descriptive of a process that they are attempting to document, they sometimes present their case in terms of a normative cosmo-optimism – the view that cosmopolitanism is a good thing – as argued for by Ulrich Beck and others, such as Kwame Anthony Appiah (2006). It should be noted here that what is meant by cosmopolitanism varies to an extent between theorists, though an 'openness to difference' is generally regarded as a key feature.[5] As Nina Glick-Schiller and colleagues point out, however, this is typically conceptualised in terms of a binary opposition between openness and closedness, with a concomitant understanding of openness as entailing some kind of celebration of difference (Glick-Schiller *et al.* 2011: 403). They suggest instead that we might focus on 'daily cosmopolitanism', understood in terms of 'relationalities of openness across differences', in which people are seen 'as capable of relationships of experiential commonalities despite differences' (ibid.: 410, 403). This potentially expands the field of what might be considered cosmopolitan as well as allowing for attention to some of the more subtle processes of making and experiencing commonality and difference that may be involved in everyday life, though it does not necessarily rule out the possibility that binary oppositions – including between openness and closedness – may be invoked in practice.

While politically I largely share a cosmo-optimistic viewpoint, my main concern below is investigative rather than normative. To this end, I examine the cosmopolitan memory thesis in relation to anthropological research in Europe in order to examine cosmopolitanism in various spheres of social life and cultural production. I do so primarily, though not exclusively, with reference to mobilisations of Holocaust memory. In what follows, then, I first provide a background to the rise of Holocaust commemoration and heritagisation in Europe, before examining arguments about cosmopolitanism through a range of ethnographic examples. As we will see, these pose various complications and problems for the cosmopolitan memory thesis in its current form and for a straightforward cosmo-optimistic outcome, though they also highlight some significant transformations underway within European memory cultures.

The rise of Holocaust commemoration and heritagisation

The timing that Levy and Sznaider see as marking a shift from social to cultural memory of the Holocaust can also be seen as that of the expansion of more widespread public Holocaust commemoration and heritagisation; as well as broadly coincident with the memory phenomenon. In various counties, such as Germany and the US, this 'Holocaust boom' began in the 1970s, with considerable further expansion in most of Europe, as well as in many countries beyond it, especially those in the New World, towards the end of the twentieth century and into the present one.[6] While the looming loss of first-hand social memory, resulting from the passing away of those who directly witnessed events, has certainly legitimated and fuelled the expansion of Holocaust commemoration, it does not fully explain it.

Other conflicts have been commemorated well before any dwindling of social memory, as Peter Novick (2000) writes of Vietnam, for example, and as can be seen for World War I and other aspects of World War II. Neither do psychological nor psychoanalytic accounts provide adequate explanation. According to these, the trauma of the Holocaust was so great that its full recognition was 'repressed' and could only be contemplated after time had passed and as direct memory was receding. As scholars such as Novick (2000) and Kansteiner (2002) have argued, however, such explanations ignore the fact that the Holocaust was usually not so much avoided as framed in different – historically and socially specific – terms. Immediately after the war, in many countries, as Novick writes of the US, 'the Holocaust was *historicised* – thought about and talked about as a terrible feature of the period that had ended with the defeat of Nazi Germany. The Holocaust had not, in the post-war years, attained transcendent status as the bearer of eternal truths or lessons that could be derived from contemplating it' (2000: 100). In Britain the historicisation of the Holocaust also fed in to a national redemptive allegory of Britain having overcome the Nazi evil. It was further allied with a Christianised discourse of forgiveness and a more general assumption that looking back at the horrors was psychologically unhealthy. In both West and East Germany too, there was a pervasive public discourse of 'moving on' as a healthy post-war response (Moeller 2003; Macdonald 2009). This is not to say that there was necessarily forgetting, however, for at the same time there were reminders in popular media, such as the 'flood of images' of concentration camps published in the press in the aftermath of war and local forms of commemoration (Moeller 2003; Gregor 2009), though this may not have been widely embedded in familial remembering (Kaschuba 2005; Welzer *et al.* 2002).

There was also war commemoration – of World Wars I and II – across most of Europe, in which commemoration of the Jewish Holocaust was subsumed under more general World War II commemoration. This, in turn, built upon World War I commemoration and in many European countries the two world wars were mostly commemorated together, with memorials often being adapted and extended (Rowlands 1999). In Germany, for example, the usual form of commemorative language was remembrance of 'the victims of Fascism', a category that also included others such as political objectors, as well as ordinary German soldiers who died in the war.[7] Even in Israel, the first official commemoration of the Holocaust did not begin until 14 years after the war (Levy and Sznaider 2002: 92) and it remained relatively marginal and ambivalent, regarded primarily as 'a reminder of helpless passivity typical of Jewish existence outside the sovereign space of the territorial state' (ibid.: 95) until the 1960s, when it was reshaped, in the relation to the Eichmann trial and Six-Day War to being regarded as 'the culmination of the history of anti-Semitism' (ibid.: 96).

While the broadcasting of the Eichmann trial around the world raised awareness of the Nazi genocide of Jews, it was not until the 1980s, and in some cases even later, that most European countries began any state-sponsored Holocaust commemoration. There were some more or less isolated efforts, primarily by Jewish groups, but these were generally small scale and sometimes foundered through lack of wider support. In the case of Britain, for example, in 1965 a group of Holocaust survivors was refused permission to take part in events at the Cenotaph to mark the twentieth anniversary of the end of the War –

a refusal which was endorsed by leading Jewish and Christian organisations; and in 1980 the erection of a Holocaust memorial next to the Cenotaph was also refused, though the placing of a small – and largely forgotten – memorial stone in Hyde Park was allowed (Kushner 1998: 230).

Language and the global-assemblage 'Holocaust'

It is worth noting here too that the term 'Holocaust' was little used prior to the late 1970s, when the US-produced mini-series *Holocaust* – which came to be broadcast in many European countries – popularised the term, it coming to be used by many who had not seen or even heard of the series, not only in English-speaking countries but also in most others (Levi and Rothberg 2003: 12). The French director, Claude Lanzmann's, extraordinary documentary, *Shoah,* first screened in 1985, also helped to disseminate the Hebrew term 'Shoah', which some regard as more appropriate than the Greek-rooted 'Holocaust', though it has not gained the same widespread currency.[8] Although both terms had historically been used for other atrocities, during the 1980s they became firmly preceded by the definite article to designate the organised murder of Jews during World War II. This had the effect too of marking out the Holocaust as a specific assemblage (see Chapter 1), with its own particular set of properties and momentum. This was, moreover, an increasingly 'global assemblage' (Collier and Ong 2005), constituted and reconstituted in different parts of the world with specific effects. It was materialised especially in a panoply of forms of museumisation, heritagisation and commemoration, as I discuss below.

Before turning to these, however, it is worth noting other linguistic terms and semantic shifts that have also become elements in the formation of the global Holocaust assemblage. Events that had previously been cast primarily in terms of conflict between nations, and of victory and defeat, were now characterised as being to do with the Holocaust, thus putting the overriding emphasis upon the victims of Nazi terror. This reframing, however, occurred alongside, as part of an interlinked set of mutually supporting elements, a change in what Novick describes as 'the attitude towards victimhood' (2000: 8). As he puts it, since the 1960s 'victimhood' has moved

> from a status all but universally despised to one often eagerly embraced. On the individual level, the cultural icon of the strong, silent hero is replaced by the vulnerable and verbose antihero. Stoicism is replaced as a prime value by sensitivity. Instead of enduring in silence, one lets it all hang out. The voicing of pain and outrage is alleged to be 'empowering' as well as therapeutic.
>
> (2000: 8)

This shift of victimhood from being a denigrated status of the powerless and abject to providing a potentially powerful platform for articulating grievance and seeking redress, is part of a broader identity politics and discourse of 'exclusion', as discussed in the previous chapter.

In the case of Holocaust, the reclaiming of agency that it represents has been further articulated through an increased usage of the term 'survivors' rather than 'victims', and equivalents in various other languages. Beginning in the US in the 1980s, the use of the term 'survivor' was intended to foreground the fact and achievement of endurance rather than perpetuate an emphasis on helplessness. But it caused discomfort for some of those so reclassified because it accorded agency where they felt they had none and seemed to downgrade the status of those who did not survive.[9] This is perhaps partly why its adoption has been patchy. In Germany, for example, while the term *Überlebende* – survivor – is sometimes used, it is not as widespread as *Opfer* – a term that means both 'victim' and 'sacrifice', and whose dual connotation plays into Christianised notions of sacrifice to some higher good that are deeply problematic in this context (Rowlands 1999: 142; Thomas 1999: 201).

On the one hand, then, there has been a widely shared global discourse of Holocaust that incorporates many of the same semantic elements in different languages and contexts. At the same time, however, there are particular linguistic inflections and connotations that contribute to how it plays out in specific, often national, situations. This is the case too for more material elements of the Holocaust assemblage.

Holocaust heritage

The most visible sign in Memoryland Europe of the proliferation of the Holocaust assemblage is the number of Jewish museums that have opened since the 1980s. Unlike the Holocaust Memorial Museum in Washington DC, which opened in 1981 and was followed by a continuing wave of Holocaust museums throughout the US, most of these prefer to characterise themselves as *Jewish* museums, giving a broader presentation of Jewish life in Europe prior, and in some cases subsequent, to its decimation in the mid-twentieth century. In Germany, Frankfurt's Jewish Museum opened in 1988, Berlin's in 2001 and that of Munich in 2007; and at least 10 further Jewish museums, as well as related sites such as synagogues showing exhibitions, have opened over this period.[10] Other new Jewish museums in Europe include the Jewish Museum of Lithuania, Vilnius (1989);[11] the Jewish Museum of Belgium, Brussels (1990);[12] the Slovak Museum of Jewish Culture, Bratislava (1991);[13] Greece's Jewish Museum, Athens (1998);[14] the Galicia Jewish Museum in Cracow, Poland (2004);[15] the Jewish Museum of Rome (2004);[16] the Danish Jewish Museum, Copenhagen, designed by Daniel Libeskind, opened in 2004; and the Jewish Museum in Oslo in 2008.[17] A Museum of the History of Polish Jews will open in Warsaw in 2013.[18]

It should be noted that some of Europe's Jewish Museums have a longer history, as does that of Vienna, originally founded in 1896; the Czech Jewish

FIGURE 8.1 Jewish Museum, Berlin. Photograph by Sharon Macdonald

Museum in Prague, founded in 1906; the Jewish Historical Museum, Amsterdam (1932)[19] and London's Jewish Museum, founded in 1932.[20] But these too have all been variously supplemented, renovated and expanded in the late twentieth and early twenty-first centuries. Vienna's Jewish Museum was closed by the Nazis in 1938, after the annexation of Austria; and some of its collections were shown for a while during the 1960s by the city's Jewish community but without any state support. Then, in the 1990s a Jewish Museum was founded and opened in 1993 in Dorotheergasse. This was refurbished in 1996 – introducing its controversial holograms exhibition (see below, and Bunzl 2003); and supplemented by a further new Jewish Museum in Judenplatz in 2000, which itself underwent considerable refurbishment in 2010.[21] Currently, the Dorotheergasse Jewish Museum is being refurbished again (its holograms exhibition having been dismantled).[22] The Czech Jewish Museum was closed to the public in 1938 but from 1942 the Nazis added items from around Europe to its collections with the sinister aim of creating what they planned would become a 'museum of an extinct race'.[23] Today, Prague's Jewish Museum consists of a set of sites around the city, several of which were opened in the 1990s.[24] The Amsterdam Jewish Historical Museum was thoroughly renewed and relocated in 1987.[25] London saw the opening of the new London Museum of Jewish Life in 1983, which amalgamated institutionally with the earlier Jewish Museum in 1995, and became part of a new, single building in 2010.[26]

FIGURE 8.2 Queues of visitors at one of the sites of Prague's Jewish Museum. Photograph by Sharon Macdonald

FIGURE 8.3 Holocaust memorial Vienna, by Rachel Whiteread. Photograph by Sharon Macdonald

As well as museums, Europe has seen a massive wave of Holocaust memorials. This includes well-known examples such as Rachel Whiteread's 'inverted library' memorial in Vienna, unveiled in 2000, and the Memorial to the Murdered Jews of Europe, Berlin, unveiled in 2005. It also includes numerous smaller memorials, such as plaques on houses of former Jewish citizens; and the thought-provoking 'counter-monuments', of artists such as Horst Hoheisel and Jochen Gerz and Esther Shalev-Gerz, that seek to resist the stasis of many memorials and thus to avoid the paradoxical forgetting that some suggest is a consequence of much memorialisation (Young 1993, 2000). This commemorative activity has been accompanied by the growth of touristic production of Jewish heritage, such as that in Poland – including *Schindler's List* tours in Krakow – since the late 1990s,[27] and a wave of signs of what Elisabeth Beck-Gernsheim (1999), in the German context, has described as a shift in the 'memory landscape' (*Erinnerungslandschaft*). These include the opening of Jewish restaurants and courses in Jewish Studies (the latter being, she notes, now more popular – overwhelmingly with non-Jewish Germans – at the University of Munich than is Gender Studies). As Ruth Ellen Gruber puts it in her lively documentation of what she calls 'the Jewish phenomenon' – a pan-European embracing of 'Things Jewish' is underway.

> From Milan to Munich, from Krakow to Cluj and well beyond, Jewish exhibitions, festivals and workshops of all types abound, as do conferences and academic study programmes on all aspects of Jewish history, culture, and tradition. Readings, lectures, seminars, talk shows and films spotlight Jewish issues; and articles and programs on Jewish subjects are being given frequent and prominent space in the print-media and on prime-time television. Private volunteers and civic organizations clean up abandoned Jewish cemeteries and place plaques on empty synagogues … Yiddish song, klezmer (traditional eastern European Jewish instrumental music), and other Jewish music – performed by Jewish and non-Jewish groups alike – draw enthusiastic (and overwhelmingly non-Jewish) audiences to concert halls, churches, clubs and outdoor arenas. Hundreds – even thousands – of new books on Jewish topics are published in local languages … Old Jewish quarters are under development as tourist attractions, where 'Jewish-style' restaurants with 'Jewish-sounding' names write their signs in Hebrew or Hebrew-style letters, use Jewish motifs in their décor, and name their dishes – sometimes even dishes made from pork or a nonkosher mix of meat and dairy products – after rabbis and Old Testament prophets.
>
> (Gruber 2002: 6)

Again, while this is frequently depicted as being about 'Jewish culture' rather than the Holocaust, the two cannot be disentangled in post-Holocaust Europe. This is made particularly and ironically evident by the fact that the embracing of Things Jewish is so frequently carried out by non-Jews in contexts in which, due to the Holocaust, only few and sometimes no Jews now live.

FIGURE 8.4 Jewish figurines for sale in Krakow. Photograph courtesy of Erica Lehrer

This is evident, for example, in Erica Lehrer's detailed account of a trade in carved wooden figurines of old-fashioned Jews – 'all men, traditionally coiffed and black-coated', with melancholic expressions (2003: 336; 2013). Produced for the expanded tourist market by non-Jewish Poles, they traffic in a stereotype that might be deemed anti-Semitic, not least in its depiction of Jews as part of a *past* that is incongruous with modernity. Yet, she argues, numerous different affects and identifications circulate around and through these souvenirs, resisting uni-dimensional explanations.[28] Some of their makers claim that they create them as a memorial duty, atoning for post-Holocaust Jewish absence; 'It is my aim not to let traces of this ancient culture sink into oblivion', said one carver (2003: 346). While this might seem disingenuous from somebody who produces them for sale en masse, others too – including Jews – may see it in similar ways. One Jewish woman from the US, owner of a substantial collection of the figurines, explained:

> 'The real significance for me, and why I was so drawn to them ... was that I felt they were a symbol, just sitting there, that Judaism would never die no matter what happened. That here in the midst of all this destruction that you saw, with few Jews left, that sitting in a market were these dolls ... That's really what it is for me. That no matter how many times you try to put the Jews down, they pop up somewhere'.

(2003: 321–2)

Lehrer's research is an important reminder of the multiple and also transnational motivations that may be entangled in the growth of Holocaust heritage – even in its most apparently kitschy forms.

Explaining the Holocaust phenomenon

To some extent, the new level of public marking of the Holocaust can be seen as part of a more general public preoccupation with the past that has taken off since the 1970s and that has been discussed in previous chapters. Yet many of the arguments typically used to try to explain this do not work for the case of Holocaust remembrance. This is clearly no nostalgic looking back to a time of tradition, community or greater stability. World War and Holocaust highlight precariousness and violence, even – or, as Bauman (1989) argues, especially – in the midst of modernity and rationalisation. While there is an element of recuperating the voices of those whose experiences have been left out of many historical accounts – in this case the victims/survivors – this is not all there is to it, and it does not explain the state-sponsorship of commemorative activity in most countries, nor the form that much Holocaust commemoration takes.

In his discussion of growing public discourse of Holocaust in the US, Peter Novick (2000) shows a detailed interweaving of activity by American Jews – including growing fears of losing their identity in the face of *reduced* evident anti-Semitism in the States – and wider events, including the Eichmann trials and the altered discourse of victimhood, which changed the frameworks within which the events of the 1930s and 1940s were talked about. What Novick dubs an increased 'Holocaust fixation' (2000: 10) in the US also had consequences for Europe, not least through the growth of American Holocaust-related tourism to Europe (e.g. Kugelmass 1992; Cole 2000). For the European case, Ruth Ellen Gruber also emphasises not simply generational change and concern over the disappearance of direct witnesses but also attention to questions of wartime activity and culpability raised by the '68er generation, especially in West Germany (2002: 15). In Eastern Europe, a 'waning of communism' also made filling what were perceived as the 'blanks' of history – dimensions ignored under communism – a moral project of self-definition, in which Jewish history became one such 'blank' to be recovered (2002: 18). In addition, she attributes the development of a more sympathetic Christian view of Jews to the 1965 *Nostra Aetate* Second Vatican declaration that withdrew the former attribution of Jewish collective responsibility for the murder of Jesus, and to Polish Pope John Paul II's attempts to build bridges with Judaism, stemming partly from his own wartime experiences (2002: 18). Furthermore, she suggests, Jews' own attempts to redefine their identities, partly in light of some of the events above, has also resulted in a turn to 'roots and heritage' (2002: 18).

As Gruber acknowledges, this turn is also part of a wider pan-European interest in heritage. And while there are significant differences from that wider heritage phenomenon, as noted above, there are also elements that are shared. In particular, both rest on and, in a feedback loop, help to sustain the increasingly widespread assumption that the past deserves attention in the present and that it can provide lessons for the future. Indeed, the Holocaust has become a key constitutive case in the widespread positioning of history as an educational resource for the present and future. Despite the fact that it has been subject to extensive debate (especially but not only in the famous Historians' Debate (*Historikerstreit*) in Germany in the 1980s (Maier 1987)) over whether or not it should be regarded as so singular as to be unable to provide analogies with other events, it has nevertheless become the basis for numerous educational programmes across Europe.[29] These attempt to operationalise the principle of *Never again!* – a phrase that became widespread in the wake of World War II (initially with reference to war) and later more specifically in relation to Holocaust. By providing awareness of the horror of the Holocaust, educational programmes aim to help prevent future atrocity. Involved here too is not just an idea that the past is capable of providing lessons for the present and future but that there is a moral duty to look to history for such lessons. This understanding of the past as a source for moral witnessing and debate is a key feature of the late twentieth- and twenty-first century heritage and memory phenomenon that this book explores. World War II and the Holocaust – events that ravaged Europe and beyond, destroying and disrupting millions of lives – surely played a central role in shaping this particular perspective on the past.

This 'take' on history is one that we could readily consider to be a form of 'cosmopolitan memory'. Rather than history being understood as about *specific* pasts, it is plumbed as a source for 'bigger' and 'broader' 'lessons'. It is 'lifted out' of its particular settings and put to work in others. Yet, as has also been evident from earlier chapters in this book, there is much else that may be entailed in past presencing in practice. In what follows, I discuss both the specific phenomenon of Holocaust commemoration and cosmopolitan memory arguments through a set of examples drawn primarily from anthropological research. This not only provides a more fine-grained examination of what is underway 'on the ground' in particular and differentiated contexts, it also highlights other considerations, limits and paradoxes that may be involved and that theorising needs to address.

Ritual commemoration of the Holocaust

Commemorative ceremonies and ritual deserve attention as distinctive memorial forms. While these frequently occur at monumental sites, they also have a specific character as collective activity of condensed symbolic significance (Turner 1967). Individuals come together to participate in more or less choreographed actions, that contain at least some shared movements, and that are recognised as being meaningful for collective identity. This does not require that individuals need to decode the particular meanings of actions or symbols employed – indeed elements of ritual are not necessarily de-codable in this way, though they often reference other ceremonies or rituals in an inter-rituality analogous to intertextuality. Especially important, however, are ritual's performative dimensions – in two senses of the term 'performative'. First, the classic Austinian sense, in analogy with speech acts that accomplish what they utter – e.g. 'I promise' (Austin 1962a; see also Butler 1997). A national ritual, for example, in this sense of performative would not be interpreted as merely *expressing* the nation but as bringing the nation into being. Second, a ritual is performative also in the sense of being a form of performance, analogous with that of theatre, in which matters such as staging, scripts, props, actors and audience all contribute to the making of a specific, affectively rich, event. This form of performance is partly what makes ritual performative in the first sense.

While rituals and ceremonies are generally held at designated monuments or sites, they do not operate the same temporality as do monuments and sites. Typically the temporality of ritual and ceremony is both punctuated (i.e. at designated time-limited moments) and repetitive, often along annual cycles in the case of national ceremonies. As Émile Durkheim (1912) argued, this may have an 'effervescent' effect, re-imbuing the social with affect and significance. Due to the non-material nature of ceremonies, however, changes are usually fairly easy to introduce, meaning that even while rituals may repeat, they can respond to context and contingency, resulting in variations over time. Likewise, despite collective action, the fact that much is left verbally unarticulated in ritual may allow for divergences of interpretation, as argued in Victor Turner's classic account (1967), as well as in more recent analyses of ritualised memorial practices (e.g. Sturken 1997; Handelman 1998; Michaels and Wulf 2011).

Below I turn to two examples of Holocaust commemorative ritual – the first a 'life-cycle' ritual by Israeli citizens to Holocaust death camps in Europe; and the second, the UK's first Holocaust Memorial Day in 2001. In both, I am concerned with how far ritualised public Holocaust commemoration 'cracks the container' of the nation state and offers cosmopolitan potential.

Nationalism in Israeli Holocaust commemoration in Poland

Trips by young Israelis to Polish death camps can be seen as 'a central rite … in Israel's civil religion' (Feldman 2002: 85), according to Jackie Feldman. Run since the 1980s, these organised trips have now taken hundreds of thousands of young Israelis on visits to Auschwitz-Birkenau and other camps. As Feldman describes, this practice is highly nationalistic, instilling strong and embodied, emotional senses of national identity through collective participation in ritualised activity (2002, 2008). As such, it clearly does not fit the cosmopolitan memory thesis. Because Levy and Sznaider put so much emphasis on mediated forms of memory, he argues, they 'underestimate the power of rituals and embodied practices to create coherent, totalistic local worlds of meaning' (Feldman 2008: 260). Moreover, far from disappearing or being displaced by mediated memory, such embodied ritual remains important. Nations in particular, maintains Feldman, continue to use ritual in this way, thus 'ground[ing] their ontology in

FIGURE 8.5 A ceremony at the Warsaw Ghetto (Rapaport) Memorial, Auschwitz. The Memorial, one of the very few depicting Jewish heroism, is framed as the transition and re-entry point from the Holocaust to Israel. The ceremony, generally performed immediately before boarding the bus for the airport and the voyage home, appropriates the site and the legacy of the Warsaw Ghetto Uprising for the State. Photograph and caption courtesy of Jackie Feldman

FIGURE 8.6 Students line up to photograph each other by the *Arbeit Macht Frei* gate at Auschwitz. As students' albums are one of the main means of transmission of their testimony to others, the snapshots form part of the bank of images that will shape future participants' understandings of the Shoah and their expectations of the voyage. Photograph and caption courtesy of Jackie Feldman

traditional religion-based paradigms and embodied practices' (ibid.); and they further support this through a 'deploy[ment of] cultural history in service of the State' (ibid.). 'In other words', he concludes, 'reports of nationalism's death – and the victory of secularization – have been premature' (2008: 260).

Not only does Feldman's research show how Holocaust commemoration can act in service of nationalistic sentiments, it also provides a basis for criticising some of Levy and Sznaider's other assumptions. In particular, he argues that the proliferation of mediated forms of memory and the increased international traffic of people can support rather than diminish nationalism. As he explains: 'The permeability of national boundaries, the ease and relative affordability of travel, and the ability to diffuse knowledge of the voyages through mass media all enable the State to promote voyages to the dead Diaspora as a source of stable roots in the state' (2008: 260). Videos and photographs of the events enable those who have been on such visits to Poland to tell others about it, and circulate this information – and their accompanying sentiments – more widely. Moreover, Feldman argues, cosmopolitan ideas make it difficult to oppose nationalistic activity. Even when Israel engages in highly nationalistic acts, such as raising the Israeli flag during the visits in 'rituals closely resembling those of the cult of fallen soldiers' (2008: 260), Poles are rendered unable to object because 'the very recognition of the cosmopolitan (or inter-European) significance of the Holocaust makes [them] loath to openly confront Israel over the extremely nationalist (and often anti-Polish) tenor of the voyages' (2008: 260).

The UK's first Holocaust Memorial Day

That the UK government created a major new national ceremony and sponsored thousands of smaller commemorative rituals and events across the country to mark its first Holocaust Memorial Day in 2001 can also be seen as evidence of the continued importance that nations may put on ritualised activity.[30] The capacities of technical mediation were put to use here too, the new ceremony being broadcast on prime-time television. This too, however, was in service of the nation, as indicated among other things by the fact that the ceremony was attended by numerous 'national figures', including the Prime Minister and Prince Charles. Nevertheless, as I argue in my detailed analysis of the context and structure of, and debate about, the new national commemoration, while the event was thoroughly *national,* it was also a performative bid to configure the nation in a new way (Macdonald 2005a). While not directly framed in terms of arguments about cosmopolitanism, my account of the UK's first Holocaust Memorial Day showed on the one hand that this was no 'breaking of the national container'. On the other, however, it showed an attempt to revise the nation itself *as* cosmopolitan.

In numerous ways throughout the planning and instantiation of the new UK Holocaust Memorial Day, the nation was referenced both directly and also indirectly through the more implicit ways that Michael Billig refers to as 'banal' (1995; and see below). At times, this drew directly on the imagery of Britain as 'war hero' that Kushner argues is 'central to post-1945 national identity' (Kushner 1997: 10; see also Cesarani 1997). For example, the national ceremony included a film about the Bergen-Belsen camp being liberated by British troops, and another about children being brought to Britain via the Czech Kindertransport; and throughout, there was emphasis on survivors of the Holocaust and other atrocities seeking, and gaining, refuge in Britain.[31] The 'national' character of the event even trumped its potential Jewishness. As Gaby Koppel, responsible for producing the inaugural national ceremony, put it: 'we were very clear about one thing. Holocaust Memorial Day wasn't to be an event just for Jews. It was a national occasion, relevant to all British citizens' (Koppel 2001: 7).

The Holocaust was, then, 'lifted out' of a specific Jewish reference – or, in terms used earlier in this book, given greater 'semantic reach'. This was not just with reference to the diverse population of Britain, however. In addition, other parts of the world were also reached out to through reference to other atrocities, including in Bosnia, Cambodia and Rwanda, all of which were included in the televised national ceremony. While this was a clear cosmopolitanising move in Levy and Sznaider's sense, the nation remained intact. Indeed, in some ways it was strengthened. It was so through the repeated referencing of the country as an actor (e.g. 'Britain's role in …') and use of the first-person plural pronoun (e.g. 'our country…'), thus taking the nation's existence, agency and a collective citizenly subscription to it for granted. The nation was also strengthened by being cast as hero; through modes such as reports from refugees in Britain, reference to Britain's military role in trying to resolve ongoing conflicts, and analogies implied with Britain's role in World War II.

The depiction of Britain as a haven for those escaping persecution also, however, served to support a portrait of Britain as multicultural. This was an explicit government aim, stated in the Government Proposal for a Holocaust Remembrance Day, published in October 1999. The proposal only mentions Jews in order to emphasise that the Holocaust should not be regarded as concerning them alone: 'Although it was a tragedy whose primary focus was the Jewish people, many other groups were persecuted and it has implications for us all' (Home Office 1999: 2). The proposal goes on to spell out those implications, and the kind of Britain that the Home Office hopes the new ceremony could help support:

> The Government has a clear vision of a multi-cultural Britain – one which values the contribution made by each of our many ethnic, cultural and faith communities. We are determined to see a truly dynamic society, in which people from different backgrounds can live and work together, whilst retaining their distinctive identities, in an atmosphere of mutual respect and understanding.
>
> (Home Office 1999: 1)

This 'vision' was also dramatised in the national ceremony in acts such as citizens of visibly different ethnicities and faiths coming together to light candles of remembrance. Depicting the nation itself as cosmopolitan – as open to different cultures and traditions – was, then, a central ambition of the new Holocaust commemoration.

It was not, however, without its contradictions and ironies. On the one hand, for example, the official rhetoric was of Britain working together with other European nations in commemorating the Holocaust. This was prompted in part by the Stockholm Forum on the Holocaust of 2000, which had spurred various other nations (including Sweden and Italy) to also begin new Holocaust Memorial Days; and that was part of a wider European concern over the Balkan wars and growing racism and anti-Semitism.[32] Yet, at the same time, the national ceremony contained representation of World War II in the form of what Kushner describes as the 'Britain alone myth' (1997: 10), in which Britain is depicted as separate from the rest of Europe and even as a solitary adversary of Germany. Some commentators also pointed out that the cosmopolitan rhetoric of openness to difference, and specifically the projection of Britain as a place of refuge, was contrary to aspects of the country's asylum and immigration legislation and practice (Yuval-Davis and Silverman 2002). Furthermore, the new commemoration was itself the basis for inter-cultural dispute, the Muslim Council of Britain refusing in 2002 to take part in the commemoration in protest at Israel's occupation of Palestine (Macdonald 2005a; Werbner 2009).[33]

What these ironies of practice showed was that while cosmopolitan aspirations worked well when safely removed from their specific context – i.e. when 'the Holocaust' operated as a generalisable case of the perpetration of evil – they could founder when reinserted into *Realpolitik*. More widely, the new ceremony showed the risk that the very premise of the Holocaust as 'offering lessons' could easily be transformed into a sacrificial trope of movement towards a higher end – as when Prime Minister, Tony Blair, commented: 'Let not one life sacrificed in the Holocaust be in vain'.[34] As Michael Rowlands points out, this trope is deeply inappropriate to the case of the Holocaust, in relation to which 'nobody can claim that the deaths served any purpose whatsoever' (1999: 142).

National identity dilemmas

Part of my argument in my analysis of the UK's first Holocaust Memorial Day was that some of the main ways in which national identities have been constructed historically have become increasingly problematic. As various theorists have argued, this typically involves processes of opposition – of defining 'us' in relation to 'them' (e.g. Jenkins 1997); with this then consolidated by identifying content that can be taken as marking 'Us-ness' and constructing differentiating symbols and what in German are called '*Gegenbilder*' (counterimages) (Beck-Gernsheim 1999). In the production of nation-states there seem to be two oppositional tendencies involved. One is externally-oriented: self-definition in relation to other nations, e.g. British versus French. War has always been one of the most fertile arenas for this kind of definitional activity, though it also goes on in more 'banal' ways, such as sport or media discussions of food (Billig 1995). The other means is internally-oriented: the identification of, say, the 'really Us/British', through contrast with the 'not-Us/not-British', within (e.g. Gilroy 1987). In the histories of all modern nation-states we can see the identification of 'out-groups' within, which serves to foster and maintain a majority identity in relation to the minority, and also processes such as the scapegoating of these minorities as sources of blame for the fact that the nation-state does not achieve the perfection to which it aspires. Nazi Germany is, of course, the most striking example of this, Jews being the principal 'Other' in this process. But the very overt and state-perpetrated way in which this process occurred in Germany should not obscure the fact that the same basic process has been at work in identity formation in other nation-states too.

In a world of increased international dependency, global communication, trade and supra-national organisations, self-definition contra other nations has become less politic – though it still goes on. Post-Holocaust and in contexts of greater ethnic and cultural mixing, and sometimes vociferous identity-politics, self-definition by majorities through opposition to minorities has also become less politic, not least because minorities may be crucial in electoral terms – though it too still goes on. What is more acceptable, however, is self-definition in relation to the past. This can take the form of seeking continuities, though today these are less likely to take the straightforward triumphalist form of earlier national narratives (Samuel 1998; Phillips 1998). They can also operate oppositionally, either through contrast with a past self (as in contemporary Germany; or as witnessed in apologies for past events); or through contrast with past adversaries (though this risks being conflated with the present). Holocaust commemoration in Britain, for example, makes a contrast between Britain and Nazi Germany, and also other countries that perpetrate atrocities; and also seeks to evoke a sense of continuity with a time that is popularly seen as one when Britain was strong, people 'pulled together', shared common values, and exhibited 'moral backbone'. This potential that the past offers for different – and usually safer – kinds of identity-formation is, I suggest, a significant element in the wider turn to public history and heritage.

A cosmopolitan battle in Denmark?

One context in which strong 'us' versus 'them' national oppositions are typically made is that of war. For this reason, battles have frequently had important roles in national history, especially those that marked victories of the nation over enemies that threatened its national sovereignty. In some circumstances, however, defeats can also become part of a nation's history by acting as moments from which the nation rallied and projected itself into the future – though here too oppositional national identity-construction as well as continuity-making is at work. The 1864 Battle of Dybbøl is just such an iconic 'noble defeat' in Danish national history, as Mads Daugbjerg (2009, 2011, 2013) describes. An event in which Denmark was defeated by Prussia and lost considerable land to what later became Germany, it nevertheless is often celebrated as the symbolic 'cradle of the "pure" Danish nation' (Daugbjerg 2011: 245), from which modern Denmark was born. Dybbøl, and especially the annual commemorative ceremonies that mark the battle, has also been the focus for considerable anti-German sentiment in Denmark.[35]

In his in-depth research at the battle site in 2006–7 however, Daugbjerg witnessed a series of interesting attempts to revise the commemorative ceremonies and the battlefield heritage centre to play down Danish nationalism and to try to be more conciliatory towards Germans and Germany. In 2001, German soldiers were invited for the first time to take part in the annual commemorative ceremony, marching and laying wreaths alongside the Danish military. The representations at the battlefield centre were also altered in order to emphasise stories of ordinary experience and shared human hardship rather than to focus on aggression between warring states. All this, writes Daugbjerg, was an explicit attempt to be 'non-national', 'post-heroic' (2011: 249) or 'cosmopolitan' (2009, 2011, 2012). The national was played down in favour of 'universal humanitarian ideals' (2011: 249).

Yet, as his detailed research shows, these attempts to 'not mention the nation' (2011) did not fully succeed. This was partly because, although the nation was mentioned less frequently in explicit terms, it was nevertheless subtly reasserted in 'banal' ways. Here, he draws on Billig's argument (1995) that nations are 'flagged' in everyday interactions through subtle means, such as *deixis* – a process in which the nation is implied (for example through linguistic reference, such as to 'our newspapers') without being explicitly named. A nice example of this in Daugbjerg's account is how in the Dybbøl heritage centre the verbal content of an audio-visual guide was altered to include more Prussian perspectives and to create what was regarded as 'a more balanced view on the war' (2011: 257). However, the audio-visual's background soundtrack, which consisted of a well-known nationalistic, martial song (whose lyrics and metaphors have been mobilised in recent years by the anti-immigrant Danish People's Party), remained unchanged. As Daugbjerg observes, visitors could sometimes be heard whistling this tune around the site after visiting the centre (2011: 257). Explicitly excised, the nation thus remained implicitly in place.

On the basis of this research, then, Daugbjerg cautions against readily accepting arguments about the nation being superseded by cosmopolitan reframing of memory. The nation is difficult to dislodge as it is subtly reasserted in banal interactions. Moreover, as I have argued for the UK case, there is also sometimes an attempt to recast the nation as cosmopolitan, witnessed in a 'conflation of cosmopolitan and national values' (2009: 443) and '"universal" values [being] celebrated as quintessentially Danish' (2009: 442).

FIGURE 8.7 Dybbøl ceremony 2006, including both Danish and (on the right-hand side) German soldiers. Photograph courtesy of Mads Daugbjerg

Incorporating Jews in the New Europe

The cases discussed above, then, variously show a persistence – and sometimes even a performance and strengthening – of the nation in what might potentially be cosmopolitan commemorative contexts. At the same time, however, some provide evidence for a reconfiguration of the nation itself as more 'multicultural' and cosmopolitan. Just how this plays out, however, is at least partly 'reflexively particular' within specific national contexts.

Matti Bunzl's discussion of the growth and form of Holocaust commemoration in Austria (2003, 2004) is also interesting in this regard, for he both shows Austria's distinctive position as well as offering a more general argument about changes underway in Europe. In relation to World War II, Austria has long regarded itself as victim of German aggression. From the 1980s, however, this self-image has increasingly been questioned, especially in light of President Kurt Waldheim's wartime activities in the Nazi *Wehrmacht* and his subsequent right-wing affiliations and the success of the Right Wing Freedom Party in Austria in the late 1990s. This, argues Bunzl (2003), played a part in a considerable expansion of public marking of Jewish heritage in the 1990s, which included the Jewish Museum developments noted above, with the contentious holograms exhibition that is the starting point for Bunzl's discussion.

Bunzl's argument is that while Jews historically 'were abjected as the nation's constitutive Other' (2003: 436), the expansion of Jewish heritage and a wider visibility of Jewishness in the public sphere in late 1990s Austria is evidence of their inclusion. He notes that even Jörg Haider's Freedom Party began to use more positive rhetoric towards Jews during the 1990s, going so far as to elect a member of Vienna's Jewish community to a leadership position in the Party (2003: 455). This inclusion, which operates across the political spectrum, is, according to Bunzl, a function of the nation-state's being superseded by 'Europe', and thus a performance of new, European rather than national, boundaries. Jews, he writes, 'have become useful in Austria and elsewhere for the postmodern constitution of a European Self effected through the violent exclusion of a new set of Others – Muslims and Africans foremost among them' (2003: 436; 2005; see also Bangstad and Bunzl 2010). The holograms exhibition in the Jewish Museum is, he suggests, a rare and brave attempt to de-reify the Jewishness that is generally essentialised in public life (2003: 457) – in the new incorporation of Jews as much as in their earlier exclusion. The widespread negative reactions to it, however, speak to the investments in what he calls the 'cultural normalization of Jews' (2003: 457). Whether the closure of the holograms exhibition in the Dorotheergasse Jewish Museum signals a final victory of 'cultural normalisation' will depend on what kind of exhibition comes to replace it.[36]

What Bunzl's argument suggests for the cosmopolitan memory thesis is that there does indeed seem to be Europeanisation underway and that a focus on Holocaust plays a constitutive part in this. However, rather than this being necessarily a positive cosmopolitan development, it is part of a new set of exclusions and the creation of Europe not as 'open to the world' but as 'Fortress Europe' (see also Gingrich and Banks 2006). It is also worth noting here, echoing arguments above, that actual practice may also diverge from public rhetoric. While there is a public performance of incorporation of Jews in the New Europe, this does not necessarily mean full or unequivocal incorporation in everyday life. Ruth Mandel's *Cosmopolitan Anxieties* (2008), for example, gives sensitive attention to numerous, often subtle, exclusions or demarcations of Jews as Other – including analogies drawn between Jews and Turks – even amidst the 'Jewish renaissance' underway in Berlin since the 1980s. Furthermore, there may be divergence from the moves towards incorporation when it comes to particular groups of Jews. In Germany, for example, there is often considerable ambivalence towards the Russian Jews who have significantly increased the country's Jewish population since 1990 (Peck 2006: 40), and who, as Jeffrey Peck notes, are 'widely regarded as merely using their real or supposed Jewishness to get out of the Soviet Union for a better life in the West' (2006: 44; see also Bodemann and Bagno 2008). In contrast to the Jewishness being recovered from the past and enshrined in heritage, actually existing Russian Jews – who often do not go to synagogue or follow kosher rules – may fail to live up to the kind of Jewishness that the 'renaissance' has been bringing into being (Beck-Gernsheim 1999: 153–6).

So far, this chapter has looked especially at the linked rise of Holocaust heritage and Jewish renaissance in Europe. In some cases at least, this rise appears to be linked to Europeanisation and a reconfiguration of the nation as more culturally diverse and open to difference. At the same time, however, in most of these cases the nation remains an active player, and in some seems to be strengthened rather than merely 'being remembered in order to overcome it' (Beck, Levy and Sznaider 2009: 125), as Levy and Sznaider suppose. In the next section, I explore the cosmopolitan memory thesis further through a different set of ethnographic examples that are all concerned in various ways with the Balkan wars and attempts at post-war memory reconstruction.

Overcoming national sentiments in the post-war Balkans?

The Balkan wars of the 1990s are widely regarded as a resurgence of the kind of dangerous ethnic and nationalistic sentiments that it had been hoped that greater cosmopolitanisation, Europeanisation and memory of the Holocaust would prevent. That some of the atrocities of the Balkan wars came to be framed in international media through language referencing the Holocaust – with accompanying images of 'concentration camps' – was a clear mobilisation of Holocaust memory (Levy and Sznaider 2004: 153). In turn, this helped to mobilise NATO intervention and for the first time Germany participated militarily to help end ethnic cleansing. The analogy – and 'never again' motif – has also been deployed since in various attempts to 'repair' the region through numerous Europeanisation projects of various kinds. These seek to promote some kind of cosmopolitan or European identity in order to reduce ethnic and national affiliations. More widely, discourses of cosmopolitanism and of being European have been and continue to be used in popular discourse by certain groups. This does not necessarily mean, however, that these result in all of the cosmopolitan characteristics that cosmo-optimistic normative accounts, such as those of Beck, Levy and Sznaider, might hope, as we will see in the following ethnographic studies from the post-war Balkans.

Cosmonostalgia and closures

In fieldwork in post-war Belgrade and Zagreb, Stef Jansen (2009) encountered an explicit discourse of cosmopolitanism, employed by 'antinationalists'. These were individuals, usually fairly well educated, who were very critical of the nationalism that had fuelled the war. The term *kozmopolit* (or synonyms of it) was used to describe life in the cities as they had been before the conflicts arose and that anti-nationalists hoped would be restored. A student banner of the late 1990s, *Beograd is the World,* for example, expressed 'at once the city's worldliness and the desire to end isolation from "the World"' (2009: 84). What was meant by 'the World' here was 'the liberal democracies of the West' (ibid.). On the one hand, then, a cosmopolitan outlook was deployed to articulate anti-nationalist sentiments. But as Jansen points out, it was neither as future-oriented nor as straightforwardly 'open' as cosmopolitan theorising tends to expect – or hope.

Rather, references to Belgrade and Zagreb as cosmopolitan were deeply nostalgic – harking back to a pre-war 'normality'. While on the one hand they entailed an opening to the West in order to end a sense of isolation from it, at the same time cosmopolitanism was frequently articulated as a quality of the *city* in contrast to the 'primitivism' of rural life. This could be seen, as Anna Di Lellio and Stephanie Schwander-Sievers argue of Albania in the aftermath of the Balkan conflict, as a form of 'internal "nesting Orientalism"' in which 'city dwellers … look … down on the "backward" peasants of the villages, transferring to them the stereotypical generalisations of "backwardness" ascribed to all Albanians in the dominating mental maps of the former Yugoslavia' (Di Lellio and Schwander-Sievers 2006: 522). As such, maintains Jansen for his Balkan subjects, what was produced in cosmopolitan discourse was not so much an 'openness' to the other, as 'alternative closures' – 'between cities and villages, between citizens and peasants, between open, nationally heterogeneous, modern, urban life and closed, nationally homogeneous, backward, rural life' (2009: 84). In effect, what this also did was to curtail the openness to cultural and national difference that is normally seen as part of a cosmopolitan outlook. The celebration of this particular kind of urban cosmopolitanism, he suggests, ironically produced a 'flattening [of] the cultural-national differences it was programmatically open to, through emphasising (in this case, urban) sameness across its boundaries' (2009: 90). In other words, the kind of cosmopolitanism in practice here operated on the one hand to create a hierarchical boundary between the city and the rural, in which the difference of the latter was denigrated; and on the other to downplay – or close itself off towards – other kinds of difference.

History and heritage in post-war reconciliation

In the aftermath of the Balkan wars, many international organisations have been involved in various forms of 'repair work', and these have often involved organised attempts at 'memory management' (Sorabji 2006). In some cases this has involved 'intervening in the process of transgenerational transmission of trauma' (Sorabji 2006: 2) in order to encourage people to 'put the past behind them' and to 'move forward'. This is often modelled on the psychoanalytically informed idea of 'working through' traumatic memories as a means of avoiding being 'haunted' by them in the future. In other cases, or other memory management programmes, however, there have been other strategies too. In Albania, Di Lellio and Schwander-Sievers (2006) argue that the international authorities have sought to foster a 'collective amnesia', by discouraging reference to the past or dismissing it as folklore, in the service of '"resetting" … to a timeless present of multi-ethnic tolerance' (2006: 526). As they show, however, this does not find compliance in a society in which historical recollection and narration are viewed as an integral part of life and, in effect, identity. The compulsion to tell 'stories' about the past is, they suggest, like a secular version of the Jewish *zakhor* – the religious prescription to transmit Jewish history to future generations (2006: 526; Yerushalmi 1982). Moreover, in such 'story-telling', 'the storyteller and historian are the same person' and 'history, legend and personal memories are mixed' (2006: 526).

Not only does this mean that organised efforts to encourage 'collective amnesia' are unlikely to succeed, it also helps maintain strong national and nationalist myth-making in the post-war period. The significance of this myth-making for local people is typically overlooked or underestimated by the international authorities who classify it as folklore. Di Lellio and Schwander-Sievers show this well through their account of how Adem Jashari, an Albanian rebel leader killed fighting against Serbian troops in 1998, has become a cult figure, memorialised at a memorial complex established at the bombed remains of houses where his family perished, and also on postcards and other memorabilia. Involved in this, producing it and also further generated by it in a feedback loop, are the kinds of national collective identity and sentiments – which sustain calls for Kosovo as an independent country – that the international authorities had hoped to avoid. Di Lellio and Schwander-Sievers argue, then, that the approach of the international authorities has in some respects, paradoxically, allowed and even encouraged such nationalism through its strategies of collective amnesia. It is further aggravated by the authorities' associated refusal to address the historical specificity of the Kosovan and Albanian case, and their stance of 'not taking sides' and trying to 'keep a distance'.

Elsewhere in the post-war Balkans, there have been attempts to expressly deploy heritage as a means of trying to transcend national identifications, as Claske Vos (2011, 2012) shows in her analysis of the 'Regional programme for Cultural and Natural Heritage in South-East Europe' begun by the Council of Europe and the European Commission in 2003. Like various other programmes before it, this aimed to produce 'integrated rehabilitation' (2011: 225) by implementing various forms of 'Europeanisation'. As she explains, 'European heritage was presented as equal to the notion of a "shared European memory" that should unite all Europeans in an attempt to "never again" have a war on European territory' (2012: 4). She looks in particular at how it operated in practice in Serbia, where it was promoted as creating the possibility to 'revisit the memories of Serbia's European past', as a tourist brochure that she quotes puts it (2011: 222). Heritage in this instance, she suggests, was promoted as 'inherently "good"' – 'a cause for celebration', as Barbara Kirshenblatt-Gimblett has also observed in relation to UNESCO world heritage (Kirshenblatt-Gimblett 2006: 190; Vos 2011: 234). The quest to find 'good' heritage that would help in 'integrative rehabilitation' resulted, however, in an 'avoidance of difficult heritage' (2011: 234) and a general 'distancing from ideological meaning' both in the selection of sites and their presentation (2011: 236–7). So, for example, Muslim sites were excluded as 'too problematic'. This was supported and legitimated by a bureaucratic preference for short-term success, itself promoted by what were referred to as 'European' management practices. This indicated particular technical procedures, such as using 'pilot projects' as

FIGURE 8.8 Adem Jashari monument in Tirana. Photograph by Antidiskriminator at Wikimedia Commons

'test-cases' from which 'emblematic monuments and sites' would be selected (2011: 228–9). As Vos shows, 'difficult heritage' would not only have been less assured of success according to the programme's model, it would also have proved more challenging and time-consuming to address within its time-frame and quest for the 'emblematic'. It was, therefore, excluded by these avowedly 'European' practices. Yet, it was just such problematic heritage that continued to matter to local people and that was more likely to disrupt wider Europeanising aims.

The ethnographic cases discussed in this section show that discourses of cosmopolitanism, attempts to reduce national affinities and to institutionalise Europeanisation, have been underway in the post-war Balkans, mobilised variously by international organisations and local people. What they also, show, however, is that these are more contested and complex in practice than the cosmo-optimistic arguments presume. In particular, what we have seen here is that what might superficially appear to be evidence of cosmopolitanism might entail paradoxical 'othering' or what Jansen calls 'closures'; and that international or Europeanising projects may risk evading, glossing over or even potentially aggravating the kinds of social divisions and sentiments that are viewed as problematic within the cosmopolitan position. In some instances they contribute to strengthening nationalistic sentiments and creating exclusions – such as Muslim heritage – that may threaten a cosmo-optimistic outcome in the future.

★ ★ ★

In highlighting some of the ways in which the cosmopolitan memory thesis does not operate in practice, my aim is neither to debunk the thesis nor to merely claim that practice is messy. The thesis is a powerful one that captures significant developments that are underway, especially, though not only, in relation to Holocaust commemoration. But there are other processes at work too, as the examples variously show. These include continuing processes of othering and of bounding, in which the nation remains an active agency. At the same time, however, 'the nation' is not a static entity but is itself being reconfigured – including within new forms of commemoration and heritage themselves.

Within Europe and to a large extent beyond it too, the Holocaust has become part of what we might call a 'cosmopolitan curriculum'. Knowing about it, and increasingly visiting some of its associated heritage – in Europe or outside it – has become a cosmopolitan credential. Levy and Sznaider have more recently expressed this in terms of the development of a *memory imperative,* especially in relation to human rights (2010). In research that I conducted in Nuremberg, with visitors to the former Nazi party rally grounds, many expressed their reasons for coming as a kind of moral duty – 'it's something we felt that we should do'.[37] I referred to this form of visiting as 'moral witnessing' and suggested that it entailed putting oneself in a place – a position – from which to be able to speak not only directly about the particular site and its history but wider historical matters too. My interviewees came from many countries – Australia, Britain, Canada, France, South Africa, Spain, Switzerland and the US as well as Germany – and most invoked their own country or nationality at some point during the interview, often to talk of how some aspect of uncomfortable history was dealt with (or not) there and sometimes to try to explain to me how I should understand their position. Talk of Germany and Germans was common to almost all interviews. Yet, although my interviewees often framed their comments in terms of nation-states and usually took for granted that these were the active agencies in creating public history, many also, simultaneously, engaged in trying to think in terms of the position of others – e.g. what must it be like to be German – and to more generally make comparisons between different ways of representing the difficult past. In other words, what different national – and also more localised – self-positioning offered was not a constraint to cosmopolitan thinking but a vantage point from which to think about others and their ways of seeing and being in the world. The outcome of this was not a form of cosmopolitanism that relied on an uncritical sense of sameness and sharing; rather, it was one that can be characterised in terms of 'relationalities of openness across differences' of the kind noted earlier in this chapter (Glick-Schiller *et al.* 2011: 410, 403). Visitors did make judgements of relatively good and bad approaches, and they sometimes judged their own countries or those of others unfavourably. Theirs was, then, a *critical cosmopolitanism* that in some ways relied upon national variation for its operation, while not being tied to it in its realisation.

Although nations were an accepted part of this discourse and although the ethnographic research discussed in this chapter clearly shows their continued significance both as frames of action and as affectively significant for their citizens, the chapter has also shown, like the previous one, that it has become more difficult to 'do nationness' in quite the ways in which it was formerly done. At the very least, gestures to alternative narratives and heritages, and to other kinds of moral legitimacy, need to be made – and perhaps harnessed to a reconfigured way of being national. This, I suggest, is something that Holocaust commemoration often – though not always, as Feldman's example shows so well – helps achieve. What we have mostly seen in the cases above, however, is not so much the nation being *displaced* or 'cracked' by cosmopolitan memory as the nation presenting itself as cosmopolitan through harnessing more widely shared pasts as part of its own. That cosmopolitanisation – of memory or society – does not necessarily require a breaking or superseding of the nation is also shown by examples such as the UK's inauguration of a Holocaust Memorial Day as part of a pan-European project. Even in the case of Austria, which Matti Bunzl presents as one in which the nation is being superseded by Europe, the fact that the ultra-nationalist and anti-European Freedom Party is making precisely the same accommodation of Jews that he sees as a New European development, suggests that it is also fully appropriable to service the nation and even nationalism.

What has emerged here, then, is a dynamic of potentially cosmopolitan developments that are sometimes appropriated to other ends or bump up against limits and other agendas in practice. Nevertheless, cutting across all of the many debates about the late twentieth-century heritage and history preoccupation – and indeed situating those debates themselves – is a casting of the past as a focus through which to debate moral and political concerns. In other words, it has become a moral forum, perhaps even the pre-eminent moral forum of our times. While the past may to some extent have long played something of this role, a more widespread public acknowledgement of differences among historians, historical revisionism, debates about school curricula, identity politics, public controversies over matters such as commemoration, and the spreading of a conception of history as potentially regressive rather than progressive (Wright 1985), have all contributed to history being publicly debatable, and to its centring as a site for political and ethical contemplation today.[38]

9

THE FUTURE OF MEMORY – AND FORGETTING – IN EUROPE

It is a poor sort of memory that only works backward.

Lewis Carroll[1]

Memory is never only about the past. As examples throughout this book have shown, what is remembered, how and by whom, is deeply entangled with both the present and the future. Sometimes this is instrumental – pasts are crafted to serve present interests and try to determine futures – but more often it is embedded in uncalculated and untidy, embodied as well as verbally articulated, ongoing practice. What is remembered is not always what people might wish to recall; forgetting can be difficult, not least when there are material prompts to recollection or others who want to ensure that certain pasts are kept in mind. Equally, some pasts can slip out of memory, unspoken and undocumented, though perhaps still retained in fragments and traces, available for later past presencing.

In this book, we have seen a wide array of forms of past presencing in Europe. These range from the active crafting of histories and traditions, often, though not only, by nation-states and institutions of the European Union, to involuntary, embodied triggers of memory. These do not necessarily exist separately from one another: hearing a national anthem may evoke earlier memories of hearing it and, perhaps, senses of belonging or exclusion; a taste from childhood might prompt reflection on what has been lost or rediscovered in processes of Europeanisation. By looking especially at some of the growing body of rich anthropological research on Europe, I have sought to highlight past presencing in practice, often occurring outside state recognition or relatively ignored within official process. This shows variations across Europe and within nation-states – sometimes even between neighbouring localities; and at the same time, it also reveals certain patterns – persistent concerns, themes and forms – within the European memory complex. Below I reflect further on the implications of these themes and this variety. One persistent pattern that has been a focus of this book is the memory phenomenon itself. A key question is whether this preoccupation with memory, history and heritage – especially with its materialisation and museumisation – will persist into the future. Will an emphasis on memory be an enduring feature of the European complex? Is gathering up so much past sustainable or might Europe sink under the sheer weight of its memorylands? As I discuss below, this question about the future of memory also reaches into further questions of what an emphasis on memory produces and what is at stake in remembering – and in forgetting. Here, the reconfigured forms of heritage and memory production – seeking to articulate new identity possibilities – discussed in the later chapters of the book also deserve attention. Perhaps they will simply add to the memory mountain, or perhaps they will allow for a supplanting and waning of earlier forms in a reconstitution of Europe's public spheres.

Europe's pasts

Some pasts loom especially large in both official and popular memory within Europe. That of World War II is perhaps the largest and loomiest, and, as we saw in the previous chapter, far from fading with the passage of time, its public marking is increasing, including in locations where there was little direct experience of war or Holocaust. While on the one hand it acts as a shared topic of remembrance and commemorative form across Europe, it is also a telling case for considerable variations in remembering. Even while there are developments that seem to 'forget' national differences, as Levy and Sznaider argue, there are also – especially if we look closely at what people say in everyday life, and at the detailed content of commemoration – still considerable variations both at national and sub-national level. Moreover, these differences are available for amplification at key moments of public debate, as we will see further below; and they also play a part in other differences, including positioning in relation to, or within, Europe as a political entity. As we saw in the previous chapter, for example, World War II and the Holocaust can be deployed in public commemoration in the UK in support of a 'Britain alone myth', in a way that would not be possible in other European countries; and that, arguably, contributes to the relatively Euro-sceptic position of the UK. By contrast, Germany's history of perpetration is a continued source for debate about questions of guilt and nationalism, and for some Germans' relative attraction to – and even 'flight into' – Europe, as discussed in Chapter 2. It has ramifications for forms of recollection by individuals and within families, as we saw in Chapter 3, though some of these, such as the hope for grandparents who behaved decently, are surely also more widespread. It also clearly plays a part in the constant vigilance for signs of growing neo-Nazism, in German intellectuals and artists playing leading international roles in reflecting on questions of social and cultural memory, witnessed, for example, in the

Historical Consciousness Project discussed in Chapter 2, and in the making of counter-monuments, noted in Chapter 8. Perhaps too, as some have argued, it has influenced the development of the compensation theories that seem to romanticise community and a non-industrial past, described in Chapter 6 (see Huyssen 1995). In addition, the enthusiastic embracing of at least some forms of multiculturalism in Germany, as discussed in Chapters 5 and 7, might be seen as part of a repudiation of the racism of its history.[2] In addition, there remains the constant possibility of Germany's past being drawn on by other nations to characterise contemporary developments, not least in relation to its role within Europe, as we will see in a further example below. Clearly, there is much more that might be said here and this brief account does injustice to the complexity of the situation, but it highlights the point that national variations in what counts as significant history – even in relation to a history that is taken as a central plank of modern Europe – remain part of Europe's memorylands.

It is possible to chart the main official positions on World War II and the Holocaust – as well as on other key global and European events, such as World War I and the end of the Cold War – of the various European countries, including to show changes in levels of acknowledging, say, collaboration rather than simply victimhood; and there is good research that has done so through, for example, looking at the content of school history texts or newspapers.[3] At the same time, however, it is important to note that how this plays out at a day-to-day level within particular localities can vary remarkably – as anthropological research is especially good at showing. Take, for example, Italian villages discussed in Chapter 3. In some, described by Francesca Cappelletto, there is a continued, 'emotionally dense', 'choral' remembering of the war; in another, described by Jaro Stacul, it is never mentioned. In the former, the surrounding woods summon up recollections of terror; in the latter they are seen by villagers as a sign of the stability of the past in contrast to the more volatile present. A key feature in this difference is the experience of the villages: those described by Cappelletto were devastated during the war, that by Stacul was untouched. But although actual experience clearly matters – and Cappelletto's villagers surely could not recount their trauma with such emotion and detailed reference to place had it not occurred – what a wide range of in-depth studies show is that it does not determine the extent or shape of recollection. As we also saw in Chapter 3, for example, Hungarian Roma – who were brutally treated by the Nazis – engage in none of the collective, 'choral' recounting that the Tuscan villagers do, neither in any other explicit forms of recollection or commemoration. Equally, more generalised accounts or those from the media can be appropriated as more localised – the experiences of others being made into one's own – as some of the World War II examples in Chapter 3 show.

None of this applies only to World War II and the Holocaust, of course, as evident from many examples – including, more recently, from the Balkan wars – which illustrates the selectivity of memory and processes such as indirection. Importantly too, the variations that we see concern not only historical content but also modes of remembering – what is sometimes called 'historical consciousness'. Historical depth – the length of memory – is partly a matter of content but extends beyond this in its present and future implications. Not only are those with 'longer memories' more likely to remind us of events from the more distant past, they are also likely to make it known that they will recall far into the future too. But while a long, known history can be a source for making analogies with the present or claiming historical precedent, it can also work to downplay the significance of particular historical events. In a presentation to the European Historical Consciousness project, for example, anthropologist of Japan, Joy Hendry, argued that it was Japan's sense of extensive time-depth that contributed to what the German organisers of the project saw as Japan's stubborn reluctance to address its World War II role. From the Japanese perspective, she suggested, this was just another event in a much bigger history, replete with even more nationally significant events. Perhaps this is also part of some of the apparent overlooking of certain historical events in the Greek cases discussed in Chapter 2. Longer memories are not necessarily more complete.

Temporalities

As well as variations within Europe in the 'length' and 'fullness' of memory, the ethnography of Europe provides numerous examples of variations in forms of temporal reckoning and understanding of the 'movement' or 'stability' of the past. Sometimes, as with the Italian villagers described by Stacul, the past is seen as steady and secure – in this case as rooted in natural rhythms; and this understanding of the past as more reliable and predictable than the present informs various nostalgic longings too. Nearly always, these involve a contrast with what is seen as a more fickle and untrustworthy present – perhaps the present as a fall from a state of grace, as part of a widespread Christianised conception, as Herzfeld suggests in his discussion of 'structural nostalgia' (Chapter 2). This is spoken most eloquently in this book, perhaps, by Jonathan Macdonald of the Skye Museum of Island Life (Chapter 6) in his evocation of 'old things'. It is evident in various ways too in the nostalgias discussed in Chapter 4. What such nostalgias implicitly and often explicitly challenge is an evolutionistic conception of temporality as progress. Treasured 'old things' show that it is not necessarily the case that 'things can only get better'. Perhaps some of the dismissive discourse that nostalgia attracts, especially from intellectuals, lies in its refusal to conform to progressivist narratives. Yet while nostalgias do not accept a logic of continuing improvement over time, the cases in this book also make clear that they are not straightforward wishes to return to the past, and neither – usually – do they regard *every* aspect of the past as better than the present. Rather, what nostalgia allows is an affective but also reflective selection – a mode for comparing and evaluating possible ways of living. Certainly, it does not typically do so in a rigorous and systematic mode – and usually it entails a skating over of uncomfortable or awkward dimensions of the past – but it may still operate with degrees of subtlety and awareness, evident, for example, in some of the ironic and witty post-Socialist reconstructions of the past, and that of the European 'Red Indians' described by Petra Tjitske Kalshoven (Chapter 5), which manages to be both playful and highly serious at the same time.

Nostalgia is in many respects a problematic term because it is applied to such a range of experiences. In some cases, it is little more than a wistful recollection of the past, whereas in others it acts as a force in contemporary life, perhaps shaping the activities of the state as well as criminals (as with the Greek 'structural nostalgia') or other individuals, and may entail some form of active recovery of certain aspects of the past – a bringing them into the present, perhaps through reconstruction of buildings or the collecting of old things. Sometimes this is experienced as the past forcing its way into the present – as a 'call' from old things themselves. Landscapes, buildings, monuments and other objects that endure over time can be especially compelling in this respect, their duration challenging an understanding of the past as passed. But even new things – a freshly-plucked peach perhaps – can make the past present, in this case its past referencing working through the repetition of natural cycles. Memory, thus, in some sense, doesn't need to 'only work backwards', as the White Queen points out to Alice in Lewis Carroll's *Alice through the Looking Glass*, because the past is ever being made present in numerous ways and because any memory is potentially projectable into the future. Yet still, how this is experienced – whether the past is something that is just part of the surroundings undistinguished from 'the present' or is something that unhelpfully intrudes into ongoing life or provides a welcome refuge from it – nevertheless varies widely, not only between different peoples but sometimes even between different spheres of experience.

This is so, too, for other dimensions of temporality, such as where significant 'breaks' or 'periods' are perceived to lie or the speed with which time is understood to pass. Certainly, disruptive events, such as war, are frequently used in before-after designations, and the idea of 'periods' imagined as thoroughly distinctive crystallises around this. In Germany, the notion of *Stunde Null* – Zero Hour – the year after the end of World War II thus transfigured as the clock beginning to tick again for the first time, represents this particularly well. The strong emphasis in Germany on 'generations' and 'phases' after the war is also part of a related parcelling up of time that serves to make the past more clearly passed (Chapter 2). Yet even such strong periodisation as this does not preclude the drawing of connections into longer histories, perhaps reaching to pasts predating the traumatic period. In Nuremberg, for example, where I conducted ethnographic research, many marketing accounts of the city emphasise its importance for both medieval trade and the industrial revolution – thus identifying what was hoped to be a precedent for the future.

Temporal co-presence

This co-presence of different temporalities – and switching between them – is characteristic of contemporary Europe. Understanding the contemporary world as one of rapid change and swift obsolescence may be commonplace but it can persist alongside perceptions of slower and longer temporalities, afforded by, say, stone monoliths or ancient buildings. Sometimes – as in the slow food movements discussed in Chapter 5 – creating these alternative temporalities, which are usually regarded as having their own roots in past times, is part of a wider moral and aesthetic commentary on rapidity; but it is likely to be only one part of life for most people. As I suggest further below, what 'heritage' offers is an alternative temporality to that of many other parts of life, not only in that it presents other times and perhaps other paces of life, but also in that it creates specific 'condensed' time for contemplation. Here, however, what I want to emphasise is that rather than understanding particular peoples or particular eras as characterised by a single temporal style – as in the 'hot' and 'cold' distinction discussed in Chapter 1 or the division between tradition and modernity discussed in Chapter 2 – alternative temporalities co-exist. They do not do so in isolation from one another, however. Rather, they are part of a semi-linked complex of ideas and practices, mostly fairly loosely assembled, though sometimes more tightly woven together. That is, they are part of what is here called the European Memory Complex – a set of more or less prevalent patterns and alternatives.

The point that co-present temporalities are neither random nor isolated deserves emphasis. There *are* widespread patterns and tendencies, and certain aspects of life are characterised by specific modes of apprehending time. Sometimes the contrast between temporalities is the source of moralising – as in valorisations of slow ways of life; and sometimes certain temporalities are experienced as 'wrong' for particular contexts – as reflected, for example, in some of the unease over the modernisation and commercialisation of tradition and heritage. The coming together of different temporalities can be a source of friction, as in the modern production of 'heritage' foods; or when the 'long' memory of one nation comes into conflict with what seems a shorter memory in another (as in certain points of conflict in the Balkan wars).

In addition, there can be leakage and transfer of certain modes of temporal reckoning into other domains. Science – and especially 'the sciences of memory' – is a major source of such processes. How collective memory is approached has, for example, been shaped by psychological and psychoanalytic theories, especially through notions of confronting difficult and traumatic pasts as often advocated by agencies of memory management, as noted in Chapters 3 and 8. Evolutionary ideas have fed into the formation of national historical narratives, shaping not only the content but also the physical layouts of many museums (Chapter 7); and they inform the idea, discussed especially in Chapter 6, that culture is the kind of thing that can vanish and that might need 'saving'. Their influence can also be seen in configurations of contests between different groups for public space for the performance of their memory as a 'zero-sum' battle for scarce resources in which only some will survive (Rothberg 2009). Transfer of metaphors is not only one-way, however, as Mary Bouquet shows in an analysis of the prevalence of tree depictions – which have a long history, certainly at least to the Old Testament – in evolutionary theory as well as in some European visual representations of kinship – especially those of the interlinked Royal families (1996; Pálsson 2009). Currently, genetic mapping is providing a new resource for thinking about heritage. In some cases, it seems to feed in to existing ideas about identity and heritage – as in Iceland, for example, which, as a supposedly 'homogeneous population' saw one of the first attempts to genetically map a human population, and where the mapping was interpreted in terms of cultural ideas about longstanding distinctiveness and even 'character' being inherited through 'substance' (Pálsson 2002: 338, 2009). Even here, however, as well as elsewhere and it seems increasingly, genetic mapping is providing a challenge to ideas of clear differentiation of peoples as it shows up unexpected links and ancestries.[4] How far it might thus contribute to a rethinking of popular notions of heritage and identity – through more mixed and multiple models – is an exciting area for the future of memory.

Memory and identity

This discussion of temporalities in this book, then, highlights both variation as well as pattern in how the past is related to ongoing identity; and it seeks to identify both prevalent patterns and some of the variations that help to highlight the cultural and historical specificity of what is prevalent as well as to encourage awareness of the kinds and extent of differences that may be encountered within Europe. It also includes discussion of ethnographic research in Europe that raises the further question of whether collective memory is even necessary for a sense of collective identity. Here, the Roma apparent lack of memory has been the focus of particular perplexity – and perhaps Stewart's attempt to identify traces of this in words used and a continual definition of Roma in opposition to those they call *gazé* speaks to a wider discomfort about those who seem not to care about the past, as much as does the psychoanalytically-driven idea of trying to get them to 'unrepress' their memory of trauma of which he is (rightly) so critical (Chapter 3). Part of the reason why it is so perplexing – and perhaps why research has thrown up so few examples – is surely, as Stewart acknowledges, how deeply it goes against the grain of more common and widespread understandings of memory and identity. In much of Europe – as a major element in the European memory complex – memory is taken for granted as a dimension and even prerequisite of identity. Individual distinctiveness only really 'counts' if it endures over time and if there is self-awareness of this. In analogy with individual identity – the mapping and mutual definition between individual and collective being another major element of the European memory complex – it is not just 'having a past' that matters but being in possession of memory of oneself over time. Like amnesiac individuals, cases of apparently amnesiac collectives cause concern, throwing into question ideas about what makes persons – and peoples.

Possessions and interiors

As we have also seen in previous chapters, these ideas are bound up, too, with notions of property and possession, and see a physical realisation especially in material heritage. As such, having a heritage is not only a marker of *having* an identity, but is in a sense another materialisation – an embodiment even – of one's (collective) self. This helps to at least partly explain why heritage often seems to matter so much and to be so affectively dense; and why either its desecration or aspersions cast upon its authenticity may generate such strong reactions. It also relates to some of the particular, prevalent, forms that heritage takes. Heritage that recollects persons – through figurative forms, domestic interiors, objects that have been personal possessions, as well as actual dead bodies – seems to be especially compelling. The creation of the 'alternative', traditionally figurative, 1956 monument in Budapest (discussed in the Prologue) was in part propelled by a sense that an abstract monument, even though it tried to literally incorporate those who visited, was not quite up to the task of becoming treasured heritage. In other cases, heritage objects are personified and made part of networks of social relations, as with some of the stone monuments discussed in Chapter 5. The emphasis upon 'home' that has surfaced in many chapters, and been discussed especially in relation to the trauma of dispossession (Chapter 4) and the spread of the musealisation of everyday life, often with reconstructions of domestic interiors (Chapter 6), is another linked element within this memory-identity assemblage. Imagined and often realised as a space of dense sociality and affect, the home is itself a manifestation of possessive individuation, and a home not only to persons but also to other possessions. Moreover, the home operates within the European memory complex as a lived metaphor of the interiorisation of identity itself – that is, of the idea that persons have inner depths that may not necessarily be read off from our surfaces. This is entangled, too, in widely mobilised dualisms between private and public, the authentic and the commercial, the traditional and the modern, and the local and the global. What numerous examples in this book have shown is that the idea that there are spaces and things that matter deeply – and that have enduring significance for identity and, as such, are and will remain ingrained, though perhaps unconscious, in *memory* – is prevalent throughout Europe. Often problematic, however, is defining just what these are and how they can be preserved. Heritage plays this out through innumerable disputes across the continent.

Not only is there a widespread idea in Europe that individuals possess 'inner depths' that exist substantially as personal memory – an idea that is not shared by all peoples either in the present or past – but also that there should be some kind of 'proper' relationship between inside and outside (Chapter 1). This idea about authentic *expression* extends also to collectives. And so too do problems caused by the possible failures of memory. If the 'interior' – the most personally meaningful – is to be authentically expressed, then the interior needs to be known or at least to be able to 'surface' without being corrupted. The sciences of memory that grew as part of this concern in relation to personal identity (Hacking 1995; see Chapter 1) – producing a spiralling of further concern in the process – have their correlate in the plethora of social memory initiatives that have been the backbone of the museum phenomenon, materialised especially in local history museums. Delving into the past thus provides potential resources for 'knowing who you are' – as so many genealogy sites, that are also part of this phenomenon, advertise – and thus potentially allowing for a more authentic expression of 'real' identity.

Authenticity and change

Here we see further what is at stake in the pervasive concern over authenticity in relation to heritage and memory. Certainly, claims about what is authentic and what is not can be made instrumentally and cynically. But it is also clear that concerns with authenticity – expressed in some form – matter too in contexts that do not involve disputes or potential economic gains. Davydd Greenwood's classic *Alarde* example, discussed in Chapter 5, can be re-interpreted in these terms. According to such a perspective, the crux of the problem was not so much the making of culture explicit, as he suggests, as a mismatch between what was understood as its 'interior' meaning to local people and its appearing as an expression of performance determined by others. Even though local people recalled its original significance and even though the ritual itself retained the same form, it could no longer straightforwardly represent the proud independence of the townspeople. In other contexts, however, as in the *Skye Story* example (also Chapter 5), local identity is defined as selectively absorbing the outside, thus more readily sidestepping the opposition between 'commerce' and 'authentic culture' that is so often raised in these debates.

Again, then, we see a prevalent complex of interrelated ideas that do not work out in identical ways everywhere. Sometimes – as to some extent in the *Skye Story* example – this is because of a conscious and well-articulated attempt to draw on the past to find other 'stories' (as the makers of the heritage centre themselves put it) and to overcome what are seen as cultural constraints that might otherwise restrict flourishing. (And we see aspects of the alternatives against which those at *Aros* position themselves in the following chapter, in the discussion of the museum of folk-life on the same island.) In others, it is how things have come to be, out of the untidy mix of past experience, models mobilised and daily life. Evident in this, too, is that people may well have senses of belonging and of the past that do not necessarily coalesce into a readily recognisable identity-heritage model. The example of the Argonne, provided by Paola Filippucci (in Chapter 3), shows this well. Here, the sense of repeated *disruption* over time, rather than continuity, provides a sense of the distinctiveness of place and the significance of the past within it. As with the *Skye Story* case, this also produces a model of identity that is more open to the incorporation of 'outsiders' and to change over time than are some other understandings and enactments of heritage. These models are better equipped than the more culturally fundamentalist ones for allowing for migration and the kinds of 'transcultural' heritage that are being developed in new initiatives (Chapter 7). Yet, they can come into conflict with more dominant expectations of heritage. This is evident in the Argonne villagers' cleaning up of historical artefacts in ways that shock the heritage agencies, and was perhaps part of the dilemma for *The Skye Story* – that it contained what some saw as too many reconstructions and things from elsewhere to make it worth visiting as 'heritage' – and that contributed to the closing of the exhibition.

If both the Argonne villagers and *The Skye Story* show – albeit in very different ways – certain alternatives to prevalent heritage-identity constructions, they also simultaneously show the very prevalence of the more typical models. We see this in the self-aware commentary of the makers of *The Skye Story* about other heritage sites and in the Argonne villagers' pointing out that, unlike in other areas, 'we don't even have a cheese'. As tourism and place-marketing spread – and as heritage potentially acts as a resource for drawing in visitors and income – so too does this model, in part at least. Perhaps it will not be long before these villages too have their own *fromage*?

To look at the spread of an 'identikit' of traditional products as just, or necessarily, a 'foreign imposition' upon the local is, however, too sweeping, though, of course, sometimes this is what happens. More often, however, there is a complex interplay between pre-existing and dynamic local conceptions and those that become familiar through the flourishing of so many examples elsewhere. Moreover, heritage models are likely to 'make sense' given other aspects of the memory complex which may already be familiar or even part of local life; and, furthermore, they may offer valuable economic and also expressive resources. The latter may be political – helping to legitimate identities in searches for recognition and the resources that may flow from this. They may also be aesthetic – providing sources of pleasure in the articulation of self. (And indeed both may be intertwined.) As Regina Bendix points out in a discussion that includes examples such as the reworking of traditional song, the aesthetic-expressive is too often overlooked in heritage research, as is its relationship with the economic (2008). At the same time, heritage has certain usual – if not inevitable – implications. Its 'visitability' has been noted in earlier chapters. What this typically produces is a panoply of accompanying visiting paraphernalia – not just the visitors themselves but guide books and signage, perhaps even gift shops, souvenirs and cafés; or, in the case of intangible heritage, the organised performances, CDs and DVDs. The effect is to make whatever culture is so designated 'available' for the consumption by others – and also to extend it beyond its locality through advertising, photographs and souvenirs. As heritage is also so intertwined with notions of property – with the idea of certain culture as 'ownable', exclusive and indicative of self – it is not surprising that this may feel uncomfortable or even lead to conflict. As we have seen in Chapter 5, however, while the ethnography of Europe provides examples of this it also shows that it is not inevitable. There are ways of 'keeping' even while engaged in exchange.

In this book I have emphasised the importance of in-depth anthropological research that pays attention to what is going on 'on the ground' in specific locales. This does not only mean what is done by villagers or farmers but also what is happening, say, in cities and particular institutions, such as museums; and the activities of official policy makers (what is sometimes called 'studying up') and memory workers, as well as tourists and people who like dressing up in the outfits of past times or using the internet to track down their ancestors. There is much more to be done – not just out of a documentary, collecting urge (though this is certainly worthwhile, perhaps especially in fast-changing contexts) – but also because so much policy and practice hinge on assumptions about matters such as that 'memory' will be materialised in certain ways, that 'communities' will typically have a discrete and distinctive body of heritage that they will want to maintain and present, that certain events will be recalled, perhaps even in similar ways, across Europe and that 'shared' heritage will necessarily bind people together. Understanding more about how this works – and doesn't – is an important prerequisite for further attempts to create any kind of common memory and identity for Europe (as we saw in Chapter 2). Not least, it will surely help highlight how people might relate to these and whether, say, avoiding mention of conflict or potential differences serves to reduce these – or just makes for less effective communication. It must also raise the question – which goes to the heart of what is widely taken for granted in the European memory complex – of whether shared memory really is needed for senses of connection, Europeanness and cosmopolitan conviviality.

Proliferation

For now, however, what is overwhelmingly evident is a proliferation of memory and heritage. Not only have there been more and more 'instances' of heritage and commemoration since the 1970s – that is, more and more buildings and traditions listed, more and more plaques put up, more and more old things collected in museums, more and more websites dedicated to 'must-see' heritage sites – there has also been an expansion of forms of heritage, that is, of what is deemed worthy of preserving and commemorating at all. While the musealisation of ordinary and everyday life pre-dates the 1970s, since then it has not only escalated but also come to include more recent, not necessarily folk, life; and, in particular, there has been a related growth of industrial heritage and of the heritage of migrants, sometimes configured through the topic of migration (Chapter 7). The heritage of trauma – witnessed for example in the Holocaust heritage discussed in Chapter 8 – has seen perhaps the most remarkable expansion, and increasingly it includes official remembering of crimes perpetrated as well as suffered by the nation.[5]

This proliferation raises the question, however, of whether it can be sustained. How much heritage and memory can Europe take? The question has been asked before. Back in 1984 Australian cultural critic Donald Horne raised it in his description of Europe as 'The Great Museum' (Horne 1984) and in the early 1990s Sir Neil Cossons worried that the whole landmass of the UK would soon be one big heritage site that one would enter on leaving Heathrow airport (1992). Some might say that this is pretty much now the case. But can the emphasis on the past continue? Or, as US historian Gavriel Rosenfeld puts it: 'Is there a looming memory crash?' (2009).

A looming crash?

It is worth looking at Rosenfeld's discussion of a possible demise of memory and heritage for he sets out a number of reasons why such a crash might be looming.[6] His concern is with both academic interest in memory – which he calls 'the memory industry' – and the wider public cultural phenomenon of interest in the past, especially in contested histories and subjective experiences, which he calls 'the memory boom'. The two are, of course, and as he acknowledges, linked.

The main reasons that he gives are, first, that there are simply cycles of fashion and that a boom cannot sustain itself indefinitely; second, that various factors that contributed to the memory boom are now less prevalent or significant; and third, that there are likely to be new concerns that will supplant an emphasis on the past. On the first point, which he makes especially in relation to academic study framed in terms of memory, he claims that most topics are only in fashion for about 20 years and that 'memory' has already lasted longer and so is likely to be nearing its end (2009: 154). In part, he employs a notion of 'natural rhythms' (ibid.), which from an anthropological perspective is, perhaps, more interesting as a specific form of historical consciousness than as an argument. It also, surely, relies upon what we count as a 'topic' – those such as particular periods or geographical regions, and many others that have become part of the internal classification of disciplines, last much longer. He does, however, partly supplement this claim with a suggestion that the field might be seeing 'academic overproduction' and 'exhaustion', scholars increasingly looking to more 'narrowly specialised topics' in the search for something new to say (2009: 157).

This relates too, to his second set of reasons – concerning factors propelling the memory boom. If the latter is itself dwindling, it will throw up fewer new topics for study. Here, he identifies dealing with difficult and contested pasts, especially those in the aftermath of war, and identity-politics as being major drivers of the memory boom. There has, however, he suggests, been significant progress dealing with awkward histories and conflicts, and while there is still further work to be done, there are now established models, including the spreading of that relatively novel form of the 'official apology' for past perpetrations (2009: 142). Identity politics, he believes, are becoming less compelling as part of a 'new world order post-9/11' and a linked 'waning of post-modernism' (2009: 149). Both postmodernism and identity politics fuelled the growth of interest in counter-memories and subjective experiences of the past that have been such a big part of the memory boom. Post 9/11, however, he claims that there is a growing backlash against this, witnessed in a return to 'objectivity' that will de-centre memory as a topic and approach. A concern that a politics of cultural recognition might contribute more to social problems than it resolves will similarly foster 'a growing desire for national unity' and 'integration' (2009: 148, 149); and searches for alternative models of affiliation rather than difference. Moreover, and this is his third point, with mounting world tensions – especially 'the global spread of radical Islamic terrorism' and the world financial crisis – 'the lure of the past will likely wane' (2009: 149) and memory will come to seem a luxury or even part of a 'neoconservative trend of political quietism' (2009: 154).

Before looking further at some of Rosenfeld's claims, it should be noted that he provides many counter-examples,[7] and concludes much more tentatively with a predicted 'soft landing' rather than a crash. His arguments are worth further attention, however, for they not only contribute to trying to guess whether memory has a future but also, if so, what forms it might take.

While identity politics and conflicts over the past have certainly helped fuel the memory phenomenon, as we have seen in this book, they are certainly not the only factors. Concerns over rapid and mass production, consumerism and social change, also contribute to a fascination with the past and practices such as collecting and preserving 'old things'. So too have opportunities for marking the distinctiveness of places and drawing on tradition as an aesthetic as well as economic resource. Perhaps most of all, however, the past has become something that just *is* made present, that is available to be visited and experienced and – especially importantly – that is available for ethical reflection and emotional encounter. As such, past presencing is not just a response to some temporary political problems or of concern just to a particular academic fashion but taps into more longstanding preoccupations in Europe that will surely continue to play out for many more decades. The phenomena that are so often referred to as cultural or social memory – and that I designate past-presencing and that are the basis of the memory phenomenon – are part of an interconnected complex of thinking and doing that concern so much that matters in contemporary Europe, especially, issues of who 'we' are, which have become unthinkable unless linked to the question of where we have come from. So many practices, interests and institutions are concerned with the memory phenomenon in some form – museums, heritage sites, vintage clothing and cars, collecting antiques and

FIGURE 9.1   'Don't destroy history!' Fragment of the Berlin wall, 2002. Photograph by Sharon Macdonald

retro furniture, traditional music and slow foods, to name but some – that, as assemblage theory would suggest, it has gained its own weight and inertia that will contribute to its durability into the future. Memory, as we have seen, has become deeply interwoven in much – if not all – of Europe in important matters such as how property, the home, nation and belonging are conceptualised and performed. Forgetting, moreover, has come to seem pathological – a failure not simply to recall particular details about the past but a kind of failure of self. That history and its artefacts should not be destroyed has become mostly taken-for-granted axiom – even if it sometimes needs to be proclaimed on walls (Figure 9.1). All of this, surely, makes it unlikely that memory and past presencing will become less preoccupying in any near or even medium term.

Demise of identity politics and conflict?

But what of the future of identity politics and contested history? It should be noted, first of all, that the concern with identity in the European memory complex is considerably broader and more ramifying than the developments that are usually designated by the term 'identity politics', which typically refers to calls for recognition from groups which consider themselves marginalised by the state. Nevertheless, with reference to the latter, it seems to me that there are fewer active new calls for recognition – demands by minorities to have their memories inserted into public space. This, however, is not so much a function of a waning of concern as of the fact that there are so many initiatives underway to recover and include marginal, forgotten or migrant memories into the public sphere (Chapter 7). While these may involve, or be begun by, activists – or 'memory entrepreneurs' or 'ethno-preneurs' – from what are now so often called 'communities', they frequently involve some form of official or state support, and in many cases it is memory workers from museums or other organisations who initiate the developments.[8] As we have seen, however, there have been concerns expressed by politicians about whether such approaches can help foster senses of collective citizenship and belonging to the nation or to Europe. Yet to create new national or European histories that exclude such memories would surely be a mistake – stimulating greater senses of exclusion and disenfranchisement as well as providing a basis for future memory contests. Like the UK's first Holocaust Memorial Day (Chapter 8) or its opening ceremony for the 2012 Olympics, acknowledging and including memories of the country's diverse population allows for cosmopolitan conviviality and inclusion even under the umbrella of the nation.

This might, however, imply that this incorporation could be completed and all memory work done, as Rosenfeld suggests may happen for contested histories, especially in the aftermath of war. But this seems unlikely. As we have seen, making nations and other entities, such as Europe, is not a 'once-and-for-all' matter but needs constantly re-making. Remembering has to happen anew and repeatedly. It works backwards and forwards. In doing so, remembering is unlikely to happen precisely as it did before; just as, say, nations are configured differently over time, not least in relation to new events, changing global circumstances, migration and the emergence of new memories. Moreover, each commemorative event is potentially a source of contest over the relative emphasis given to different memories – as was also the case with the UK's first Holocaust Memorial Day.

As a historian of German Nazism, it is the German case that informs much of Rosenfeld's optimism that the past may cease to be the source of conflict. Yet although Germany can be said to have led the way in facing up to its difficult past, with many impressive and thoughtful developments that do serve as models elsewhere, the situation seems to me much less settled than he implies. Creating museums and memorials, and making official apologies, have become widespread means of acknowledging perpetration and trauma. Yet, these do not necessarily always work in conciliatory ways, as we saw, for example, in the controversies over the 1956 Memorial in Budapest; and even in Germany some of the most high-profile developments, such as the Holocaust memorial and Jewish Museum, have generated controversy and accusations of creating 'alibis'.[9] The official apology – now widely globalised – does not always succeed in ending senses of disgruntlement and, as it is increasingly employed, seems to lose its moral currency, coming to be seen more and more as a cynical 'going through the motions' undertaken in place of more adequate addressing of wrongs perpetrated and their continuing consequences.[10]

Moreover, even in the case of Germany there is surely still much unfinished business, for example, in relation to the Socialist past that may in future erupt in forms other than the current *Ostalgie* (Chapter 4), as well as in relation to expulsions of Poles from Germany, and Germans from Poland, during and after World War II. The incorporation of memories of migration, especially from Turkey, has expanded with many reflective initiatives but still remains incomplete and marginal within the nation (Chapters 7 and 8). Even with reference to Nazism and Holocaust, although from many official points of view 'closure' has been achieved, there are others who would suggest otherwise. In Nuremberg, for example, the sense of having now faced up to the Nazi past in some landmark initiatives, such as a documentation centre (Macdonald 2009a), seems to inflect upon recent governmental reluctance to fund some of the major upkeep necessary for maintaining former Nazi buildings. The dedicated staff with whom I worked at the former Nazi party rally grounds are, however, emphatic that such upkeep is crucial to ensure that future generations will be able to encounter this history and they continue to see the need for new projects, not least in relation to changing demographic and political constellations in Germany.[11] Moreover, there has been no reduction in the number of visitors coming from around the world, as well as across Germany, to learn more about this past.

Memory as luxury

Let me turn, finally, to Rosenfeld's suggestion that we only look back when times are easy and we have the luxury to do so. While this might be partly applicable to the expansion of practices such as collecting and heritage tourism,[12] it overlooks how the past is invoked in the very unluxurious circumstances of war and conflict, as in the Balkan wars. More generally, it is unclear that difficult presents are less likely to encourage an interest in the past. As Dan Stone remarks in a discussion of the future of attention to the past in the 'new Europe', 'the more uncertain the present and future look, the more memory – precisely because it is future-oriented – will continue to be an arena of contestation' (2012: 730). Even in relation to the two 'crises' that Rosenfeld suggests will come to preoccupy us in future years more than will the past – namely, 'financial crisis' and 'radical Islamic terrorism' – it is hardly the case that questions of memory, history and heritage are absent. In relation to the financial crisis, memory and heritage have suffused how debates and actions in have been played out in Europe, with countries variously reaching into the past for precedents, reasons and excuses. This has been especially marked between Germany and Greece – two countries that, as we have seen, are both much concerned with history though keen to draw the lines rather differently. Take what might be called 'the battle of the

FIGURE 9.2 Heritage battles in Europe's financial crisis. Greek newspaper showing altered image of the Greek Goddess of Victory on Berlin's Victory Column (Siegessaüle), in which she holds a swastika. Photograph reproduced courtesy of the European Pressphoto Agency

classical statues'. In February 2010 a high-circulation German magazine carried a cover showing the Venus de Milo, goddess of love, giving the finger, with the caption: 'Cheats of Europe?'.[13] This followed the Greek government admitting that it had falsified accounts of its financial situation. The statue – known in Greece as Aphrodite of Milos – was found in Greece but is now in the Louvre. Accompanying a message of Greeks as cheats with a piece of heritage they considered looted looked like a bad memory lapse. Greece hit back – reminding Germany, as on the front-sheet of the Greek newspaper *Eleftheros*, of Germany's post-World War II gains and never having paid full reparations for their damage. The image (in Figure 9.2) showed the Greek Goddess of Victory, Nike, atop Berlin's Victory Column (Siegessaüle) – but holding a swastika – in what was also an effective reminder of the centrality of Greek heritage within Germany, and articulation of Greece's contention that Germany is acting the bully according to disturbing historical precedent.[14] Far from being just a battle of images, the case reached into still activable and highly potent historical memories, showing that even in relation to a highly preoccupying crisis, heritage and memory were far from mere luxuries.

Likewise in the case of radical Islamic terrorism, itself supported by certain memories and heritage. As well as the loss of life that this terrorism has caused, it has also contributed to, and gained further sustenance from, generating Islamophobia – a lumping together of everything Islamic and even vaguely Middle Eastern, and linking it with threats of various kinds (Chapter 7).

History gets entangled in this in various ways. On the one hand, loose historical allusions serve to compound it further, such as, in US President George Bush's use of the term 'crusade' in his post 9/11 'War on Terror', with its first campaign initially called 'Operation Infinite Justice': labelling that rendered the attack as a Holy War and his actions as against Islam *tout court*.[15] At the same time, however, there has been a blossoming of attempts to enrich understanding of Islamic culture in ways that do not restrict or reduce this to religion. This has included an expansion in the number of exhibitions concerned with Islam in various European countries, which variously seek to challenge stereotypes by, for example, illustrating Islam's civilising heritage, its long presence and role within Europe, or highlighting the differentiation of the specific histories and memories of groups dubbed Islamic. Given the way that Islam is often made to operate as a symbolic 'other' to Europe, as we have seen in Chapters 7 and 8, expanding this further is another pressing memory task for Europe's future. Not doing so is a luxury Europe cannot afford.

Reflective and affective past presencing

The fact that past presencing is entangled in such a wide range of experiences, themselves part of a wider complex of practices and ideas, as we have seen in this book and partially outlined above, is the most compelling reason for the likely continuation of the memory phenomenon. Particularly evident from the many various cases discussed is that making the past present affords opportunities for reflection, especially for making comparisons – drawing analogies or identifying differences – between ways of life. Because this is often done with a sense of connection to the particular past involved – it is often not just 'any' past but somehow 'ours' – it is often affectively charged and semantically dense. Research on popular genealogy, for example, has reported the very emotional ways in which people may respond to learning of the lives of their ancestors – perhaps crying at the thought of the hardship that they endured (Cannell 2011). Involved here seems to be a notion that the lives of previous generations contributed to the success of later ones – they in some sense suffered for us and we are thus indebted to them. This idea can be extended more widely too, perhaps, to help further explain the remarkable rise of the heritage of trauma and suffering, with its emphasis on ordinary lives. On a collective scale, those whose lives are usually shown in this heritage can be seen as collective ancestors – people we might have been and are metaphorically indebted to because we were not in their place. Witnessing their suffering by visiting such sites is a form of tribute, the small sacrificial act of giving up time to undertake such witnessing is an acknowledgement of the enormous sacrifice that they made. Increasingly, though unevenly, these heritage forms – which offer greater potential for connection through this logic of debt and sacrifice – seem to be replacing the lone hero, especially the aristocratic leader on his pedestal (and, usually, horse). As new forms of heritage emerge, various earlier ones may be forgotten or abandoned, though they or their ruins may still remain in the landscape, available for re-activation in the future. As such, the continued making of new heritage, and new forms of heritage, is accompanied too, though at a slower rate, by the demise of others, resulting in a greater overall diversification of heritage than at any point in the past.

The making of meaningful and affectively charged connections across time can also be seen in some aspects of changing forms of heritage display. While to some extent all such forms hold this potential, some do so more than others; and what is compelling in one period – the heroic monument or war memorial perhaps – may become less so in another. Currently, forms that Rosmarie Beier-de Haan describes as involved in *staging* rather than *representing* the past seem to be especially well designed to encourage senses of connection (2005, 2006; Macdonald 2009 139–40). In a consideration of changes in history museums, she suggests that the 1990s saw a shift from history to memory – by which she means less emphasis on presentation through either long chronologies or social categories (as in the 1970s tendency to use class or gender to frame exhibitions) and instead a use of strategies to elicit individual responses to topics. Sometimes this is effected through a personalisation of display – testimonies by eye-witnesses, perhaps, or being given an identity-card of a particular individual; and, at others, through art installations, which seem to allow more individualised and affective responses; or through strategies that involve the visitor becoming part of the exhibition, perhaps through having their responses beamed up onto screens within it. The very category of *memory* rather than history shifts the focus to the more subjective and experiential; and it allows for the acknowledgement of different perspectives and positions upon 'what happened'. Increasingly, it is the affective response that is most invited, as part, perhaps, of what Paul Virilio claims is a 'communism of public emotion that has recently, so discreetly, replaced the communism of public interest' (2007/2005: 86).

Even where strategies to encourage such affective response are not actively deployed, however, heritage offers opportunities for specific kinds of experiences. Material heritage, in forms such as museums or sites, as well as performances of intangible heritage, typically provides a temporally distinct experience, set apart from the everyday – even if the topic on display is everyday life. This is the 'condensed time' of heritage – time that is in effect marked as available for experience with some kind of depth or intensity; time that offers a different possible affect than the 'psychic numbing' that Jack Kugelmass suggests that many people fear is happening in the face of repeated exposure to events in the mass-media (1996). Typically, participating in heritage requires effort. Sometimes, this is extensive, as in the case of those involved in crafting historical reconstructions, as well as for those engaged in unraveling family connections over time. But even making a day trip to a former battlefield or a performance of traditional dance requires an effort of organisation and a full-body presence. This effort is part of what makes heritage. It is part of what gives it the capacity to 'sensualize history' (Kugelmass 1992: 401), making it different from engaging with the past through other media such as books, television or the internet. And it is part of what makes it 'ours', even if we have little previous connection with the past made present. The act of witnessing, via heritage, makes it part of our lived experience. So too does the sensory and bodily engagement of the heritage experience – the sounds and smells, and sometimes feel and tastes, as well as sights, involved. Certainly, social media and virtual technologies can enhance and to some extent mimic this – and how they do so and the implications this has for the wider memory complex is another area for further research in future. In doing so, this will need to be mindful, too, of the specific mix of the individualised and the collective that characterises particular forms of past presencing. Visiting heritage, for example, is usually undertaken with friends or relatives. But even if it is not, other people are still part of the experience – watching how they behave, what gets the loudest applause, what is written in the visitors' book. We are made aware with the very act of participation in certain forms of past presencing of what we may share with others, including the very fact that we participate in that particular cultural form. This includes those who we do not know directly. We may also find just how much we may differ. All of this work of comparison and reflection takes place not only during the condensed time of heritage itself but also after the event too, in discussion with others – and, as memory, available for comparison, that is carried from one heritage experience to another. As the White Queen further explains to Alice: 'That's the effect of living backwards … it always makes one a little giddy at first … But there's one great advantage in it, that one's memory works both ways'.

Memory, heritage and the broader field of what I have called past presencing are likely to make us giddy for some time to come, partly because they are not only about the past but also about so much else – including the future. As we have seen, there are new challenges for memory and heritage today, some of which involve at least partial disassembling of parts of the existing European memory complex. How to do memory and heritage in ways that allow for greater transnational and cosmopolitan connections, as is already being attempted in heritage forms discussed in Chapters 7 and 8, is one of those challenges. Will this supplant existing ways of doing and experiencing heritage? From what we have seen here, especially in Chapter 8, this seems unlikely, though it may alter existing modes, sometimes in subtle as well as more overtly evident ways. This suggests a continuation of the memory phenomenon. In addition, new challenges will no doubt also emerge in Europe's memorylands; and there will also be ongoing need for renewal and reminding about the past and existing memories. This shows no evident signs of coming to an end. Unless the future stands still, it is hard to see how memory can either.

NOTES

All online references were still active in October 2012 unless otherwise stated.

1   The European memory complex: introduction

1   Nora 1989: 14. Note: in this book the date that follows the first one is that of the original publication in whatever language a piece was first published in. In this case, the article by Nora was first published in English.

2   References for these terms include the following: 'memory fever' – Huyssen 2003; 'memory mania' and an 'obsession with memory' – Huyssen 1995; 'commemorative excess' – Eley 1997: viii; 'memory crisis' – Terdiman 1993; 'the memory industry' (talking especially of historians' emphasis on memory) – Klein 2000; 'the memory boom' – Berliner 2005 and Blight 2009; 'the memory craze' – Berliner 2005; a 'remembrance epidemic'– Bodemann 1996: 85; 'commemorative fever' – Mistzal 2003: 2; and a time of 'archive fever' – Nora 1989 and Derrida 1998 (though used somewhat differently by each). All also provide relevant discussion.

3   See Hewison 1987 for the first of these and Lowenthal 1998 for the second two.

4   Huyssen 1995, for example, refers especially to the 1980s and Lowenthal is specific in his claim that 'Modern preoccupation with heritage dates from about 1980, alike in Reagan's America, Thatcher's Britain, and Pompidou's France' (1998: 4). Both, however, also note some earlier developments and other authors, such as Samuel (1994), document an expansion of popular history developments in the 1960s with various earlier precursors. Historians' academic concern with memory is dated similarly. Blight, for example, writes that 'Before 1980, it was rare to see any citations with the word "memory" in the title' (2009: 241) but notes too that the general issue 'seems to have first crept into our discourse in the 1960s and 1970s' (ibid.).

5   Referred to in the online Encyclopaedia Britannica: www.britannica.com/EBchecked/topic/129940/complex.

6   Key theorists who are identified with what has come to be called assemblage theory are Gilles Deleuze e.g. Deleuze and Guattari 1987/1976, especially as expounded and expanded by Manuel DeLanda (especially 2006); and Bruno Latour, especially 2005. Bennett 2007, and Bennett and Healy 2009 and 2009a provide useful commentary and further extension. The French term used by Deleuze and Guattari is *agencement*,

which, as Margaret Wetherell points out, is more active than 'assemblage' might imply, especially as it is used in archaeology (2012: 15). For discussion of the notion of assemblage in relation to heritage, see Macdonald 2009 (which also informs my discussion here); and Harrison *et al.* 2013. Bennett's use of the term 'complex' in his important essay on the exhibitionary complex (in Bennett 1995) is especially influenced by Foucault and while it predates his explicit interest in 'assemblage' shares some of the same theoretical elements.

7   The subtitle of DeLanda's *A New Philosophy of Society,* for example, is *Assemblage Theory and Social Complexity.* For further discussion see also Byrne 1998; Hayles 1990; Law and Mol 2002; and Urry 2003.

8   See especially DeLanda's discussion of the 'linguisticality of experience' (2006: 45ff) and DeLanda 2011 (appendix). For an excellent critique of the tendency in some assemblage theory and non-representational theory to 'rubbish discourse' see Wetherell 2012.

9   *Ethnologie* has come into use in Germany post World War II, generally as a replacement for *Volkskunde* (Folklore); and the term *Empirische Kulturwissenschaft* (Empirical Cultural Studies) is also used – see also Chapter 2. The change in terminology was motivated largely by some regarding *Volkskunde* as tainted by Nazi associations, though concern to broaden the subject also played a part. For discussion see Dow and Lixfeld 1994; and Bendix 2012. Rogan's (2012) overview of the place of Folklore in European countries contains much of relevance on disciplinary formations of anthropology and ethnology in the various countries. See also Johler 2000 and 2001; Vermeulen and Roldán 1995; Hann *et al.* 2005; Boskovic 2008; Dietzsch *et al.* 2009; Kürti and Skalník 2009, and Kockel *et al.* 2012.

10 In Britain, Folklore is not established in the academy (and has no entry in a recent Blackwell Companion on the subject: Bendix and Hasan-Rokem 2012). In other European countries (and also in the US) it is usually stronger, though often generally fairly small in relation to other disciplines. See Rogan 2012 for an excellent overview. The place of Folklore is also related to questions about folk museums, discussed in Chapter 6.

11 For discussion of his use of this term see Dresch 1998; Gofman 1998; and Hart 2007. On the notion of ethnography as entailing particular commitments, see Miller's excellent ethnography of capitalism (1997).

12 In the UK the tradition, modelled on the agricultural year, is of at least a year's fieldwork, though shorter time periods and more episodic forms of fieldwork are increasingly common and used especially subsequent to the initiation rite of doctoral fieldwork. In most other European traditions the time period is shorter – with fieldwork of weeks or months being common – and episodic research, especially in the locality of the researcher's university, being widespread.

13 For discussion of this see Greverus *et al.* 2002, including Gisela Welz's thoughtful argument for why the village might nevertheless be a productive focus of study (2002), a discussion also continued in Welz *et al.*2011.

14 This point is one that is also made in assemblage perspectives, which attempt to eschew notions of scale in which the micro is seen as nestling inside the macro (Macdonald 2009). Instead, the emphasis, as here, is on examining how categories such as 'the global' are formed in concrete contexts and through specific materialisations and the like. In using the term 'worlds' here I do not intend to imply that these are discrete – the UNESCO meeting and the remote village are both intensely networked in their realisation of the global.

15 Numerous writers have commented upon this, including Klein 2000; Kansteiner 2002; Radstone 2000. For a discussion in relation to its uses in anthropology, see Berliner 2005.

16 See especially Carruthers 1992 and Yates 1966.

17 See Winter 2012; Bowker 2008; Locke 2000; and also, in relation to brain-scanning research, Dumit 2003.

18 See Kansteiner 2002: 185–7; see also Wertsch 2009: 118. Klein's lively discussion of the 'turn to memory' among historians also includes insightful commentary on the traffic between notions of individual memory – which he regards as often 'quasi-religious' – and social (2000). The concept of trauma has seen especially extensive use and discussion in recent years. For a robust critique see Kansteiner and Weilnböck 2008.

19 Locke 1836: 234. The essay was first published in 1690. For further discussion in relation to memory see Hacking 1995: 146–7 and in relation to material culture, Hides 1997.

20 Anderson 1983 is a key discussion. See also Handler 1988 for sensitive treatment, discussing MacPherson's ideas.

21 They also extend beyond Europe. Handler (1988), for example, writes of Quebecois nationalism.

22 There has been extensive discussion of this, especially amongst historians in relation to what they often refer to as 'the turn to memory'. For an overview see Cubitt 2007.

23 See also Kerwin Lee Klein's (2000) discussion of the rise of 'memory' in historical research.

24 See, for example, Klein 2000; Radstone 2000; Kansteiner 2002; Cubitt 2007. Michael Lambek's discussion, in which he draws on Mauss to question not only the history-memory distinction but also that between social and individual, is particularly insightful (2003).

25 J.L. Austin's discussion (posthumously published in *Sense and Sensibilia,* 1962) of notions of 'truth', 'evidence', 'real' and the like highlights the range of uses to which these may be put and difficulties of, for example, unverifiable statements or the fact that a general statement may be easier to corroborate than a more detailed report.

26 Olick and Robbins note that the term 'collective memory' was used earlier, in 1902, by Hugo von Hofmannsthal, Halbwachs first using it in his *The Social Frameworks of Memory* in 1925 (Olick and Robbins 1998; see also Klein 2000: 128). The term 'social memory' is sometimes said to have been first used by art historian Aby Warburg (1866–1929) (Assmann 2008: 110). There are numerous texts providing discussion and definitions of social memory, cultural memory and so forth. Particularly useful are Olick and Robbins 1998; Misztal 2003 and Erll and Nünning 2008.

27 For discussion see Misztal 2003: 54–5; Apfelbaum 2010.

28 For discussion see Rüsen 1990, 2001, 2005; and Seixas 2004. See also Chapter 2.

29 Although Gadamer's term *'wirkungsgeschichtliches Bewusstsein'* is sometimes translated as 'effective historical consciousness', translators J. Weinsheimer and D.G .Marshall prefer to translate it as 'historically effected consciousness' in order to indicate Gadamer's concern with a process in which the individual is 'affected *by* history… and conscious that it is so' (translators' preface in Gadamer 1989/1960, p.xv).

30 Hirsch and Stewart propose use of the term 'historicity' to describe 'a human situation in flow, where versions of the past and future… assume present form in relation to events, political needs, available cultural forms and emotional dispositions' (2005: 262). As I understand it, this would be one dimension of what I am referring to here as 'past presencing'.

31 See, for example, David Berliner's criticisms of the use of 'memory' and charge that its use in anthropology becomes indistinguishable from 'culture' (2005). Given that the term 'culture' is multiply fraught, collapsing discussion into this does not solve the problems. As Gable and Handler argue, '"culture" and "memory" are parallel concepts, sometimes useful and sometimes not' (2011: 23). What limits both is their entanglement with 'native use'. As they put it so well in relation to 'memory': 'In the study of Western societies … anthropologists will have to pay attention to the native discourse of memory. The trick is to include social scientists and historians among the natives' (2011: 43).

32 See Munn 1992 and Gell 1992 for discussions of the anthropology of time. Munn's essay includes delineation of an area similar to that which I here call 'past-presencing'.

33 Koselleck's terminology is closely linked with that of Heidegger and Gadamer, two important influences upon his thinking. See Zamitto 2004.

34 The literature is already vast. For some recent overviews and collections that indicate the newer directions see Peckham 2003; Anheier and Isar 2011; Anico and Peralta 2009; Hoelscher 2006; Butler 2006; Fairclough *et al.* 2007; Smith 2006, Heinich 2009, Harrison 2013. The *International Journal of Heritage Studies* is also a key venue for publishing in this field.

35 For discussion of the term 'intangible heritage' see Kirshenblatt-Gimblett 2006; and Hafstein 2009.

36 See also Dicks 2004 for a broad consideration of putting 'culture' on display and making it 'visitable'.

37 For discussion see Nic Craith 2008; Hemme *et al.* 2007a.

38 See Hoyau 1988 and Heinich 2009. In both cases they may be coupled with 'cultural' when referring to what would be called 'heritage' in English. Thanks also to Alejandra Jaramillo Vasquez for discussion. See also the interesting discussion of changing Czech terms – and heritage practices – from Socialism to post-Socialism in Aplenc 2004: 66.

39 Lévi-Strauss sets out these ideas over various publications but especially in *The Savage Mind* (1966/1962).

40 Gell 1992, Chapter 3, provides an excellent sympathetic as well as critical account, including an overview of criticisms made by others. See also Fabian 1983.

41 Strathern's *Gender of the Gift* (1988) was her first most significant work employing this approach, set out especially in the final chapter. See also Gingrich and Fox 2002 for discussion of the role of comparison – and different models of this – in anthropology.

42 Achebe 1984: ix, discussed in Clifford 1988: 207–9.

43 See, for example, a YouGov survey of 13 March 2012, which lists 62 per cent of the British population wanting either to leave the EU or to have a looser relationship with it, as opposed to 24 per cent of Germans wanting this (research.yougov.co.uk/news/2012/03/13/cross-country-attitudes-towards-europe).

44 See Trigger 1989; Díaz-Andreu 2007.

2   Making histories: Europe, traditions and other present pasts

1 Attributed to Marcel Proust by the character David Rossi (played by Joe Mantegna) in *Criminal Minds,* season 6, episode 3: *Remembrance of Things Past,* The Mark Gordon Company and CBS television, first broadcast October 2010.

2 See, for example, Dow and Lixfeld 1994; Jell-Bahlsen 1985; Hauschild 1997; and Bendix 2012.

3 Boissevain's 1992 volume *Revitalizing European Rituals* is a key text discussing this development and includes wide-ranging examples, such as the 'revitalization' of carnival (Cowan 1992; Poppi 1992), as well as practices such as pilgrimage (Crain 1992). See also Wilson and Smith 1993 for an early focus on cultural change and 'the new Europe'.

4 For overviews of the development of European social anthropology see Macdonald 1993; Herzfeld 1987; Borneman and Fowler 1997; Kockel, Nic Craith and Frykman 2012.

5 Critiques include Linnekin 1991; Kapferer 1988; Herzfeld 1991; Sahlins 1999; and Eriksen 2004. Boissevain's choice of the term 'revitalisation' (1992) is a search for an alternative that better expresses what he sees as more characteristic of developments underway.

6 See Dorson 1976, who coined the term. In German, the term *Folklorismus* similarly distinguished the properly authentic but in some uses gave consideration to different forms of 'folklorisation'. See Newall 1987 for general discussion; and Herzfeld 1982 for discussion of the place of folklore in Greece.

7 Ulrich Kockel has argued in favour of defining 'tradition' as part of ongoing change. He uses this in distinction from 'heritage', which he regards as 'culture that has (been) dropped out of the process of tradition' 2007: 20–21. While his attempt to make a distinction between that which is part of a more organic pattern of change and that which is static or frozen is potentially useful, it is not able to deal well with the multiple uses and dynamics of heritage that are also underway. See also Babadzan 2000 for a careful reading of Hobsbawm's arguments that seeks a recuperation of the notion of 'tradition'; Handler and Linnekin 1984 for a short but now classical insightful discussion; and Noyes 2009 for discussion of the term 'tradition' in folklore research.

8 Other studies of the instrumental use of tradition and ritual in Socialist systems include the ethnographies listed below; others, which include discussion of the post-Socialist context, include Creed 2011; Kürti 1990 and Mach 1992.

9 See, for example, Morgan 1983; Trevor-Roper 1983, 2008. For other excellent accounts looking at this constitutive disciplinary role see also Chapman 1978; Bendix 1997; Hodges 2011 and Noyes 2012.

10 Key English language texts making this argument were Boissevain 1975; Davis 1977 and Herzfeld 1987.

11 Ennew 1980; Parman 1990; Macdonald 1997.

12 Ringrose and Lerner 1993 make this point well and influence my own discussion (1997), in which I also use the term 're-imagining' in my title.

13 Research on European institutions includes Abélès 1992, 2000; Abélès, Bellier and McDonald 1993; Bellier 1997; Bellier and Wilson 2000; McDonald 1996; Shore 2000; Holmes 2000; Zabusky 1995. Wilken 2012 provides an excellent overview.

14 This is reported on in Berger *et al.* 2008.

15 As Berger discusses and see too, for example, Pók 2011.

16 For research on these in turn see Shore 2000: 56–60; van de Leeuw-Roord 2000; Sasatelli 2002; Papagaroufali 2005; for anthropological research on world fairs and/in Europe, Harvey 1996; Johler 2002; Maddox 2004 and Färber 2010; and on exhibitions see examples below and also in Chapter 7, and also Karaca 2009 for a discussion of the overall growth of exhibitions as part of a 'cultural turn' in Europeanisation.

17 See its website, see www.expo-europe.be/en/site/musee/musee-europe-bruxelles. html and also de Jong 2011, discussed below. See also Charléty 2004, Kaiser and Krankenhagen 2010, Krankenhagen 2011 and Kaiser *et al.* 2012.

18 See, for example, discussions in Mandel 1994 and 2008; Bunzl 2005; Gingrich and Banks 2006; and Chapters 7 and 8 below.

19 See www.koerber-stiftung.de.

20 See www.koerber-stiftung.de/bildung/eustory/gremien/eustory-charter.html; see also Woidelko 2011.

21 This is now available at the web-link above. In addition, the project ran conferences with history teachers and also academic conferences, and also produced publications, for which see Note 23 below.

22 At that time I was only just beginning research on Germany, though my ability to speak German – and ethnographic interest in Germany – probably contributed to my being invited to join the steering committee. The idea that I would also carry out ethnographic study of the project and group itself was quite often jokingly alluded to and I sometimes contributed 'ethnographic' observations to meetings. I have not, however, published on this before now.

23 Some of the debate is reflected in the publications from the project, especially the first: Macdonald and Fausser 2000; Pók *et al.* 2002; van der Leeuw-Roord 2001.

24 This is partly but not entirely expressed in his 2000 article in the first volume from the project: Boytsov 2000.

25 See, for example, Maier 1997; Assmann 2006.

26 Cf. also Forsythe 1989, who refers to 'refuge in the general category "European"' p.154. She also provides an interesting pre-unification discussion of the elusiveness

of German identity and the extent to which it is 'historisch belastet' – 'historically burdened' p.154.

27 This is a concern that I have also encountered in other contexts in Germany, as I discuss in relation to my research in Nuremberg: Macdonald 2009a: 23–4.

28 It is, for example, not mentioned in many ethnographies. The use of generational terminology is widespread in Germany, not only in relation to questions of Holocaust and World War II. I had personal experience of this when a journalist wrote an account of one of the European Historical Consciousness symposia and presented some disagreement among us as a generational dispute. I was positioned as a member of a 'young' generation against the older 'professor' generation. I had perceived the disagreement to concern disciplinary methodological difference. (The journalist, perhaps not incidentally, was about my age.)

29 For an interesting discussion of this see Schultheis 1997, which also includes reflection on how Germany's response to Nazism has shaped inattention to certain aspects of kinship study within anthropology.

30 The theme of indirection is a repeated theme in Michael Herzfeld's work. In his study of Rethemnos, Crete, for example, he makes the argument that because 'criticism of the national ideal is unthinkable, the alternative must suffice. They [i.e. local people] fight against the bureaucrats' (1991: xiv). Indirection is also a main theme of his *Cultural Intimacy* 1997. For studies of indirection in relation to history in other parts of Europe see, for example, Skultans 1998; Jansen 2002; Jerman 2006.

3   Telling the past: the multitemporal challenge

1 Fentress and Wickham 1992: 2.

2 The *Writing Culture* critique, named after the influential volume of that title edited by James Clifford and George Marcus (1986) was especially influential and several authors, including Clifford in his introduction, give attention to the question of the use of the ethnographic present. For a thoughtful further reflection on this see also Pina-Cabral 2000, and Davis 1992a.

3 The influence of the French *Annales* School, with which British anthropology in particular has had a long relationship, is significant here. For an account of the importance of the regional monograph in the French historical tradition see Burke 1989 and Rogers 2001. For more general discussion of the use of anthropology within history see Hunt 1989, Chapter 2; Rogers 1992; Jordanova 2000, Chapter 3; Burke 2008, Chapter 3. Also important to mention here are ethnological studies that look at change over time. Particularly notable here is Françoise Zonabend's *La Mémoire Longue* (1980; translated into English as *The Enduring Memory*), a study conducted by a team of researchers between 1965 and 1978 in the village of Minot in Burgundy. This included a considerable amount of oral history research and also attention to villagers' sense of time and of change itself.

4 See Silverman and Gulliver 1992: 16; and Comaroff and Comaroff 1992: 31.

5 Ardener 1989: 26 has a more sophisticated list of levels involved in the structuring of history.

6 Marcus 1998, original version 1995; see Greverus *et al.* 2002 for further discussion. A Google Scholar search in April 2012 for the term 'multi-sited fieldwork' produced 1,000 results.

7 See, for example, Thomas Hauschild's discussion of the difficulties he encountered exploring popular relationships to the saints in Southern Italy: the people of Ripacandidesi 'imitated the past while at the same time rewriting their history. They nostalgically lamented the decline of the old world while simultaneously renewing it' (1992: 38).

8 See, for example, E. Edwards 2010; Forty 1999; Hallam and Hockey 2001.

9 This has been subject to extensive discussion. See, for example, Tonkin 1995 and Radstone 2000, as well as the discussion below.

10 There is an extensive literature on this. See, for example, Clendinnen 2000; Hartman 1994; Lang 1999; Van Alphen 1997.

11 Van Alphen 1997: 30. Stephan Feuchtwang (2005), for example, describes how a Russian Jewish family in Germany story their flight from Minsk with reference to a documentary film that they felt encapsulated their experience.

12 See also Jonas Frykman's discussion of Croatia where, he writes, 'Second World War memories were not allowed to be history; instead they were used to explain present events' (2004: 107), though in the Istrian region – with its possibility of an alternative history shared with Italy – the opposite was largely the case: 'the past slowly passed into history, leaving the present open to a multitude of interpretations' (ibid.). See also Ballinger 2002; and Chapter 8 for further discussion of reference to World War II in the more recent Balkans; and Cappelletto's edited volume (2005a) for further examples and insightful discussion.

13 Feuchtwang 2011 illustrates this through his comparison of discussions of historical trauma by respondents in Germany with those in Taiwan and China, while also arguing that the German respondents, based in Berlin, often identify with the city rather than the nation as part of their way of avoiding the usual formats of victimhood and perpetration.

14 See Welzer *et al.* 2002; and Welzer 2010.

15 See Giddens 1991 and Campbell and Harbord 2002; Gullestad 1996 provides an insightful discussion and also ethnographic illustration through her study of Norway. Ethnographic studies elsewhere have sometimes illustrated the unfamiliarity of the notion. Hoskins, for example, writes of her Kodi interviewees in Indonesia: 'the notion of telling one's life directly to another person did not exist in Kodi' (1998: 2). Talking about objects, however, provided a route to the biographical information that she sought. See Chapter 6.

4   Feeling the past: embodiment, place and nostalgia

1 From the poem, *Old Furniture*, in *The Works of Thomas Hardy*, 1994 edition, Ware: Wordsworth Editions Ltd, p. 456

2 Some would argue that all memory is materialised in that it is a physiological process. My interest here, however, is in forms of externalising of memory beyond individuals.

3 The term 'affective' has come to be used more frequently than 'emotion' in most cultural research in that it puts more emphasis on 'relations practised between individuals, in contrast to emotion, which still bears the spectre of a psychological individualism' (Richard and Rudnyckyj 2009: 57). Moreover, 'Affect, which can be both a noun and a transitive verb simultaneously makes both its subject and object' (ibid.: 59).

4 Some of those drawing on and developing phenomenology in anthropology are Ingold (e.g. 2000), Csordas (e.g. 1994); Jackson (e.g. 2005); and Tilley 2004. Merleau-Ponty, especially 1962/1945 and Heidegger, especially the English language collection *Poetry, Language, and Thought* 1975, are the primary influences. Hsu 2008 is a clear review in relation to the senses.

5 See references above. For debate about this see also the dispute between Pink, Howes and Ingold in *Social Anthropology*: Pink 2010; Howes 2010, 2011; Ingold 2011.

6 Heidegger 1962/1927. For anthropological use of this see especially Ingold 2000.

7 For commentary on Heidegger see especially Dreyfus 1990.

8 See, for example, Latour 2005; Thrift 2008 and, on the new material culture studies, Hicks and Beaudry 2010, especially Hicks 2012, and Tilley *et al.* 2006. Assemblage theory is further discussed in Chapter 1.

9 I also develop their use in relation to the materiality of buildings (2009). Verdery (1999), Tilley 2004 and Connerton (2011) also draw, variously, on Hertz.

10 The exhumation and reburial of dead bodies, generally as skeletons, is a practice that in also infused by some of these same ideas, and that has been characteristic of various post-conflict situations in Europe. See, for example, Sant Cassia 2006 on Cyprus, and Ferrándiz 2006 on post-Civil War Spain

11 Verdery's description is on pp.41–7. For other accounts see Kligman 1988 and Sermetakis 1991. Paul Sant Cassia's research on exhumations and burials in post-partition Cyprus also effectively highlights local understandings, specific historical-political configurations and the significance of affect (2006).

12 Svetlana Boym's cultural historical study (2001) is a partial exception, though does not include much reference to anthropological study; Todorova and Gille (2010) brings together various post-communist cases; and Heady and Miller (2006) offer a comparative perspective on parts of rural Russia.

13 See also Sutton 2010. Holtzman 2006 provides a wide-ranging review of anthropological research on food and memory; and Welz 2012 discusses research on food primarily within the anthropology of Europe.

14 See Nash 2002 and Hirsch and Miller 2011 for discussion of the notion of 'roots'.

15 See also Tilley 2006 for a discussion of the multi-sensoriality of gardening. Based on interviews with gardeners in Sweden and the UK, Tilley argues that although they report that they are motivated primarily by the visual appearance of their gardens, other senses are also important.

16 Thousands of Maltese, along with various other Europeans, especially French, settled in Algeria from the early nineteenth century, many becoming French citizens under the country's colonial rule, and then moving to France as Algeria became independent in 1962. The nickname *pieds-noirs* – meaning 'black feet' – was given to those who came to France from Algeria at this time.

17 See also Dicks (2000) for an account of mining heritage in Wales, which argues that this can allow communities and individuals to reflect upon their social identities.

18 This is similar to Svetlana Boym's distinction between 'restorative' and 'reflective' nostalgia. The former 'attempts a transhistorical reconstruction of the lost home' (2001: xviii) and the latter is concerned with 'meditation on history and the passage of time' (2001: 49).

19 Elsewhere Papadakis *et al.* (2006) caution against drawing overly stark contrasts between Greek and Turkish Cypriots, a point that is also well made in their edited volume by Yael Navaro-Yashin (2006), who explores differences between Turkish Cypriots whose families lived in Cyprus before partition of the island and more recent Turkish settlers.

20 The term 'post-Socialist nostalgia', or 'post-Communist nostalgia' as Todorova and Gille (2010) prefer, has become the term to describe nostalgia for the Socialist past that has emerged in post-Socialist countries. I have chosen to use a capital S to indicate that this is a particular form of Socialism.

21 Even so-called 'intangible heritage' is closely associated with *some* place, usually via narratives of origin, ownership and ethnicity.

22 The notion of haunting and ghosts is often used in relation to memory, see, for example, Carsten 2007; and it has been used in social analysis, see, especially, Gordon 1997. Miller 2001 provides an interesting discussion in relation to the home and György 2008 in relation to places in Europe that have experienced traumatic history.

23 See Hareven 1993 for a discussion of the development of the idea of the home as a refuge from the public sphere in Europe; and Frykman and Löfgren (1987/1979) for an historical ethnography of this in Sweden. Anthropological accounts of 'home' in various contexts of diaspora, exile or displacement include Basu 2007; Bender and Winer 2001; Jerman 2006; Hautaniemi 2006; Jansen and Löfving 2007; Smith 2003a; Hirsch and Miller 2011a.

24 Anthropological discussions of the significance of the house include Ardener 1981; Carsten and Hugh-Jones 1995; Cieraad 1999; Birdwell-Pheasant and Lawrence-

Zúñiga 1999; and more specifically on the house in (mostly) European contexts see Chapman and Hockey 1999; Chevalier 1998; Miller 2001a and Macdonald 2007. On the sensory qualities of the home, and methodological implications, see also Pink 2004 and 2009.

25 The use of objects to elicit memories has been used in both academic practice and in contexts such as museums or old people's homes (e.g. E. Edwards 2010; Arigho 2008) – in this way, not only reflecting on questions of the past and memory but also contributing to their production and visibility.

26 For other examples of discussion of the emotional complexes of home repossession and restitution see Verdery 2004; Svašek 2007; Zerilli 2006; Capo Zmegac 2007; Diner and Wunberg 2007.

27 The name 'Haus der Geschichte' simply means House of History. In Germany, however, the name usually conjures up the major museum of German history opened in Bonn in 1994. The choice of name, therefore, also indicated the Wittenberg museum's deploying of validating strategies. It is produced to a very high standard, as can be seen too on its website: www.pflug-ev.de/. The museum opened in 2007.

28 Schwander-Sievers notes that there is in fact quite a lot spoken privately and through encoded means; see also Chapter 8; and the discussion in Chapter 3. *Contra* Creed's suggestion it is the disappointment of living standards *not* improving that is a prompt for some of this nostalgia.

29 These examples are variously drawn from Volčič 2007 and 2011, Burić 2010 and a BBC report 'Tourists offered rides on Tito's train' (news.bbc.co.uk/1/hi/4098823.stm).

30 For the Ostel see: www.ostel.eu.

31 This is argued in much psychology of memory, though requires further understanding, especially in relation to notions of 'repression' and the role of inter-subjectivity and narration in recall.

5 Selling the past: commodification, authenticity and heritage

1 In 2011: 24.

2 See, for example, Abram and Waldren 1997: 1; Coleman and Crang 2002: 4–5; Meethan 2001: Chapter 5; Martin 2010.

3 My use of the term 'spheres' here draws on classical anthropological analyses of economies in which certain things could only be exchanged with certain others, in differentiated 'spheres of exchange'. Usually this is regarded as a pre-money arrangement. For a discussion of this and extension to modern market economies see Hart 2005.

4 In the 1989 epilogue to his original article Greenwood concedes the possibility that 'under some conditions', which have 'not been formulated with any precision' (1989: 185) this might not always follow.

5 See also, for example, Abram 1997; Wright 1992; Edwards 2000.

6 The *Aros* centre remains open at the time of writing but 'The Skye Story' exhibition is now closed.

7 This development is thoroughly intertwined with the memory phenomenon – ethnic revival often seeking out legitimacy through history, and turning both to textual and oral sources. As noted in Chapter 3, it can also be seen as part of 'identity politics'. Smith 1981 is a classic review. Macdonald 1993 and Llobera 2004 provide discussion in relation to anthropology; see also Hsu 2010 for a recent overview and examples. I look at the specific case of Gaelic in Scotland in 1997; see also Oliver 2005.

8 I should note that there has been criticism of aspects of Weiner's theorizing. This includes for not recognizing the 'variable nature of alienable/inalienable categories' (Rowlands 2004: 208) and for importing 'Western' notions, such as the

boundedness of individuals, into her interpretation of Melanesian materials (see Mosko 2000) and more general questioning of whether in the Melanesian context the objects that she describes as 'inalienable' do function as she argues (Sillitoe 2005). None of these, however, make the concept less amenable to analytic work in the European context; on the contrary. Moreover, it is potentially of wider use for understanding identity debates as Harrison has argued (1999). There are nevertheless limitations in its use to replace notions of reciprocity – as was part of the original aim (ibid.; and see Brown 2004 in relation to its applicability in relation to debates about cultural property). Graeber's (2001: 34) criticism, that the emphasis on 'inalienability' leaves too little room for the building up of histories that occurs during the circulation of objects – and their transmission over time – is also apt, though perhaps overstated as she also leaves room for *relative* value, especially through the notion of 'symbolic density'. Nevertheless, it may be usefully coupled with the concept of 'biographical objects', as I do in the following chapter. The notion of 'inalienable possession' also remains analytically productive in relation to heritage which is often locally understood as 'inalienable' in the sense understood by Weiner.

9   There is much else also at issue in this dispute, of course, and much has been written about it. For an excellent account see Leahy 2011.

10   See also Aplenc (2004) for an interesting discussion of ideas about reconstruction and related notions in Socialist and early post-Socialist times in Czechoslovakia/Czech Republic.

11   This is evident from anthropological work on this topic, from Handler and Saxton's seminal discussion of 1988 and continued in more recent work on Europe including Filippucci 2002; McNeese-Mechan 2003; Daugbjerg 2009 and Kalshoven 2012. Decker (2009) discusses discourses of authenticity at the wonderfully named Society for Creative Anachronism (US) – a name which itself speaks to the reflexivity that re-enactors often exhibit.

12   Tzanelli (2012) provides an interesting parallel case in Thessaloniki, Greece, where 'Oriental' cafés are also opening, presenting themselves, and Thessaloniki more generally, as cosmopolitan, and, especially, as open to tourists from Turkey.

13   This can be related too to the late twentieth century 'ethnographic turn' in art, in which artists seek to engage in 'authentic' contact with people and situations – in modes they deem 'ethnographic' (Foster 1996). In some ways this development echoes the reliance on person-based assessments of truth that came to be superseded by 'objective' methods in modern science (Shapin 1994).

14   Jones draws on Weiner's notion of 'inalienable possessions', following my 2002 use of this, but not the specific notion of 'symbolic density'.

15   See discussion in Chapter 4; and also Tilley 2004; and Chalk 2012.

16   See www.international.icomos.org/naradoc_eng.htm.

17   For a detailed discussion of debates and positions involved in creating what came to be called the UNESCO Representative List of the Intangible Cultural Heritage of Humanity see Hafstein 2009; and for further discussion of the various UNESCO lists see also Kuutma 2007; Strasser 2007. A related key issue here is that of ownership and copyright. Because ownership is generally legally defined through notions of individual ownership, and because copyright typically is seen as a matter relating to individual creativity, traditional practices and cultural heritage often fall outside existing legislation, leading in some cases to the appropriation, and commodification, of the traditions of others. For discussion, see Brown 2004, 2005; Hafstein 2004; Noyes 2006; Skrydstrup 2012.

18   This theme was noted especially by Anthony P. Cohen in an edited volume entitled *Belonging* (1982), which was concerned with ethnographic studies in the UK. It also pervades anthropological studies of tourism, e.g. Boissevain 1996; Abram and Waldren 1997: 1; Coleman and Crang 2002 and community, e.g. Welz *et al.* 2011.

6 Musealisation: everyday life, temporality and old things

1 From a letter of 1857, in Hysop and Hysop 1957, p. 135; quoted in Benjamin 1999: 203.

2 He refers especially to a special issue of the journal *Ästhetik und Kommunikation* on the topic of *Kulturgesellschaft*, 67/7, 1987, especially the essay by Kamper *et al.*

3 See, for example, Karp and Lavine 1991; Karp *et al.* 1992; Simpson 1996; Littler and Naidoo 2005.

4 Some of the key texts were Hewison 1987; Wright 1985; though actively opposed by Samuel 1994. See also Walsh 1992; Dicks 2000; Hoelscher 2006; Smith *et al.* 2011, and Waterton 2010.

5 In German, the term *Alltagsmuseum* – everyday-life museum – has come to be used especially since the 1980s, sometimes being a re-naming of former museums of *Heimat* but especially in relation to museums of everyday life of the German Democratic Republic. See Schöne 1998. The introduction to the Museum für Alltagsgeschichte (Museum of Everyday History) in Brühl puts the matter of 'ordinary' objects well under its heading 'The small things of everyday life': 'Usually a museum shows the visitor the most unusual as possible. Not so the Museum of Everyday History in Brühl. The collected everyday items bring the simple life of ordinary people of past times before the eyes of the visitor' (www.nrw-stiftung.de/projekte/projekt. php?pid=100; my translations). Angela Janelli provides an excellent discussion of different kinds of what she calls 'wild' museums, and that include museums of amateurs and clubs, community museums and centres, provincial museums, and various other 'small' museums (2012: 21–2). Central to her definition is that these operate primarily through non-scientific forms of knowledge-making.

6 See, for example, Bennett 1995; Abt 2006; Duncan 1995.

7 Though Stephanie Gerson (2003) argues that there was in fact a 'cult of local memories' – witnessed in forms such as local archaeology and local museums in nineteenth-century France, and that this helped to 'buttress' the nation, rather than to oppose it, rather in the manner argued for *Heimat* museums. Acknowledging this at the political centre – in the form of a national museum – seemed, however, to be a step too far for a long time at least, and then only suitably tempered by the equation with 'savage culture'.

8 For examples from the UK see Dicks 2000; Bennett 1995: Chapter 4; Samuel 1994; and for a broader overview, Alfrey and Putnam 1992; Walsh 1992; and for an excellent account of Germany, Barndt 2010.

9 More recently still, this museum has changed its focus again: this time to documents that can be used in family-history research (Edwards 2012: 75–6). Edwards argues that what is central to this development is that it offers the opportunity for 'narrating and reflecting on both one's and other's classedness' (2012: 78). This museal refocusing from wider natural environment, to the town's own past to that of individual families could almost be seen as an increasingly fine resolution of reflection upon ongoing changes experienced by local people.

10 In museums in some parts of the world alternative models operate in which this is acceptable. Cristina Kreps, for example, writes of it in her work on indigenous museums (2006).

11 This is Hoskins' characterisation of Morin's relational fields/levels (1998: 8). Morin provides four rather than three, that which she calls the relationship 'with the owner or consumer' (ibid.) covers what Morin discusses as 'existence'/'personality' (which is concerned with how the object comes to identify the consumer through ownership and consumption), and 'essence'/'presence' (which alludes to authority, or what she calls 'the weight of certitude' (1969: 134). As my discussion already covers aspects of the stabilising authority of museums I use Hoskins' characterisation rather than Morin's.

12 See www.highlandfolk.com.

13   Karl Marx and Friedrich Engels *The Manifesto of the Communist Party,* first published in German in 1845. Samuel Moore's English translation is available at: www.marxistsfr.org/archive/marx/works/download/manifest.pdf. The quotation is on p.5. For discussion of what was meant by this – and his ambivalence about the developments involved – see Berman 1983, especially Chapter II.

14   See www.skyemuseum.co.uk/index.html.

15   See Macdonald 1997; Greverus *et al.* 2002; Welz *et al.* 2011; Macdonald 2011.

16   The affective density of home was discussed in Chapter 4. Didier Maleuvre provides insightful discussion of the relationship between the museum and the home: 1999, especially Chapter 2.

17   Indeed, the establishment of a museums registration scheme by the Museums and Galleries Commission in the 1980s was partly intended to try to deal with the potentially conflicting notions of 'ownership' involved in such donations in the face of the massive expansion of independent museums. In donating objects to museums, the Commission recognised, individuals did not regard these as becoming the property of the museum owners to do with whatever they wanted but conceptualised their donations as in a sense 'public' and assumed that objects would be kept in the museum and preserved for ever.

18   For example, Weber 1922 and 1923. See also Macdonald 2005 for discussion of museums and enchantment.

19   In his analysis of Scandinavian folk museums Mark Sandberg writes of how these techniques could be even more effective *without* mannequins – the visitor themselves then filling the space of the 'missing persons' (2005: 181). Scandinavian folk museum makers developed what they called 'the interior principle': 'the strategy of placing objects back in relation to bodies, and both back into domestic interiors by staging a scene imagined to be taking place before the viewer's eyes' (2005: 181–2).

20   In English, Lévi-Strauss's term *sauvage* is often translated as 'savage' rather than 'wild' but the latter better captures the unruly but nevertheless sophisticated nature of these museums. Janelli provides detailed discussion of her use of this term.

21   In Macdonald 2011 I discuss museum shops and attempt a typology of kinds of things sold by their form of relationship to the museum.

22   There is now an extensive literature on consumption as 'sacralising' objects or mass consumption or otherwise making them meaningful. In particular, it is a repeated theme in the work of Daniel Miller (e.g. 1998, 2008).

23   For these various forms of 'modernity' see, in order of mention: Harvey 1989; Giddens 1991; Bauman 2000; and the first two for these terms of time-space relations.

7   Transcultural heritage: reconfiguring identities and the public sphere

1   From his poem, *Ars Poetica?* The former lines refer to the 'purpose of poetry' being 'to remind us how difficult it is to remain just one person'. The poem is quoted in Lehrer 2010: 161.

2   For discussion of 'hybridity' see especially Werbner 1997; Çağlar 1997; Young 1995; Brah and Coombes 2000, and Wade 2005. On 'creolisation' see also Hannerz 1996 and Sheller 2003; on 'syncretism', Stewart and Shaw 1994; and for discussion of a range of terms and theorisations, Pieterse 2009. In museums, there has also been some use of the notion of hybridity in relation to mixing disciplines and categories of collection, such as those of natural history and art. This has probably been most actively developed in Kelvingrove Museum, Glasgow, where, interestingly, it is also linked to a thoughtful social inclusion agenda. See O'Neill 2006 and Morgan 2011.

3   In an earlier essay (Macdonald 2003) which covers some of the same territory as the present chapter, I elided the notions of 'transcultural' and 'postnational',

perhaps reflecting the more widely held assumption at that time that transcultural developments would threaten the future of the nation-state. Discussion in this chapter and the next shows that this is not necessarily so.

4 Some scholars make a distinction between the monument and the memorial – regarding the former as a relatively celebratory remembrance and the latter as a wish not to forget a more traumatic event, such as war; though both share a mnemonic motivation and in practice are often used interchangeably. See Sturken 1997, pp. 46–9, for helpful discussion.

5 Jordanova 1989: 32; Coombes 1994; Bennett 1998, 2004; Sherman 2008. These also variously discuss the point that follows in the text below. See also Bennett 2004: 95–6 for an insightful Deleuze-influenced discussion of the notion of mastery in relation to colonial relations.

6 Mitchell draws especially on Heidegger's essay 'The age of the world picture', in which Heidegger uses the term *Weltbild,* in Heidegger 1977/1949.

7 The following are some of the most influential theorisations: Bauman 1992, 2000, 2001; Beck 1992, 1998; Beck and Beck-Gernsheim 2002; Beck *et al.* 1994; Giddens 1990, 1991.

8 Samuel 1994 and 1998 provides an illuminating account. See also the discussion in the previous chapter.

9 For discussion of 'multiculturalism' see Werbner and Modood 1997, especially Werbner 1997, and Werbner 2012; Bauman 1999; Modood 2007; Vertovec 2010.

10 See references in the previous footnote and also Friedman 1997 and Hage 2000.

11 Welz 1996 is an important early example. Others studies include Werbner 2005, Karaca 2009, and Kosnick 2009. Werbner 2012 provides a range of examples, mainly from Britain, in her excellent analysis of 'multiculturalism'; and see also Vertovec 2010 for a range of anthropological examples.

12 See Gingrich and Banks 2006, and Vertovec and Wessendorf 2009, for anthropological examples of neo-nationalism and 'backlash' against multiculturalism; and also Holmes 2000. For reporting of Cameron and Merkel, see, for example, Wheeler 2011.

13 He references his argument to Hardt and Negri 2000: 161–204; and also Holmes 2000. In an analysis of the experiences of Dutch women converts to Islam, discussed below, Karin van Nieuwkerk argues even more strongly that Islam constitutes the 'Other' through which Dutch culture is constituted as 'a universal non-identity' (2004: 244). For an anthropological discussion of the reception of Islam in Europe – and possibility for a 'European Islam' – see Schwab 2009.

14 Information available at: www.kunsthallewien.at/cgi-bin/event/event.pl?id=2509; lang=en.

15 The argument that memorials serve not so much in service of remembrance as forgetting was famously made by Alois Riegl 1903. See also Forty 1999.

16 Göle references this theorising of public space – and the public sphere – to Arendt 1958; see also Fischer 2009. Beverly M. Weber, also discussing veiling, also discusses the challenge of difference to Habermas' original formulation of the public sphere, drawing on Mouffe for a theorisation that sees difference as fundamental to the effective operation of the public sphere (2012: 103–5).

17 The collective term *hijab* is often also used for all of these various forms and for the practice of veiling, though some only use it for veiling that is heavier than the *duppatta*. There is a wide variety of terms for different kinds of headscarves and veils in use by different populations, drawn from various languages.

18 For example, Werbner 2007: 173; Mandel 2008: 298–300; Weber 2012.

19 See Poovaya-Smith 1998, Phillips n.d. and Valentine n.d. (probably 2006).

20 Eighty per cent of textile jobs were lost in Bradford between 1961 and 1991 (Lewis 1997: 130). Race reports included the Scarman Report of 1981; see Holdaway 1981. For an overview of the Bradford context see Valentine n.d.

21 In the years following the opening of the Galleries, which coincided with the election of a 'New Labour' government, a good deal of social and cultural policy has been couched as 'social inclusion', with funding often available for such projects

(Sandell 1998, 2002; Waterton 2010). There have also been similar movements in other parts of Europe, such as France (ibid.). It has been the spur to a good deal of innovative work in UK museums dedicated to trying to give public space to those who had previously not seen representation of 'their culture' in national or civic museums; and to developments such as the new migration museum in Paris, the Cité Nationale de l'Histoire de l'Immigration.

22 This unsettlement may also be generated by the collaborative work that is sometimes involved in producing such exhibitions. For examples, see, Phillips 2003; Sandell 2002, 2007.

23 My account here also draws on an interview with Nima Poovaya Smith, and interviews with Nilesh Misty and Janet Simmonds, Cartwright Hall, for which I am very grateful.

24 The distinction between art and craft has often been mapped on to distinctions between 'European' and 'non-European', and 'male-produced' and 'female-produced'. Moreover, 'crafts' have been more likely to be displayed in museums of folklife and ethnography, where individual authorship is effaced, and 'art' in art galleries where the individual creativity is fetishised.

25 This is a 'following' approach partly influenced by work on object biographies: see Appadurai 1986 and Kopytoff 1986. It is also advocated for multisited fieldwork, as discussed in Chapter 3; and see Marcus 1998; and is shared by actor-network theory: see Latour 1987 for a classic account and Law and Hassard 1999 for commentary.

26 Nilesh Mistry and Janet Simmonds, personal communication. The work of dialogue effected by this exhibition is also through a lively programme of accompanying initiatives, such as the Young Ambassadors arts and heritage initiative, in which young people from various backgrounds in Bradford work together, including to create exhibitions such as *Precious Cargo,* 2012: www.bradfordmuseums.org/education/cargo.php. This is not a lone example. One of the major developments in museums over the last 20 years has been an expansion of work with different populations – see references in Note 21 above. Some, such as Manchester Museum's award-winning *Collective Conversations* (www.museum.manchester.ac.uk/community/collectiveconversations), are inspired by James Clifford's theorising of museums as 'contact zones' (1997).

27 For discussion of work with 'communities' see Karp and Lavine 1991; and for more recent work, framed in terms of 'source communities' see Peers and Brown 2003.

28 A report proposing such a museum was produced in 2001 and then given public support by Jacques Chirac in his presidential election campaign in 2002. Planning began in 2003. The project cost over 20 million Euros. See Toubon 2007, which is included in a special issue of *Museum International* (Vol. 59, nos 1–2, 2007) on the topic of migration museums with a particular focus on the Cité nationale de l'histoire de l'immigration; also discussed in Macdonald 2008. Glynn and Kleist 2012 provide a useful broader overview on migration as a focus for 'social inclusion' and history and memory work in a range of initiatives.

29 In both, plans have been drawn up, though neither has government approval yet. The following website is a useful portal of links to information about migration museums across the world: www.migrationmuseums.org/web; as is UNESCO's migration museum initiative website: www.unesco.org/new/en/social-and-human-sciences/themes/international-migration/projects/unesco-iom-migration-museums-initiative. Information that follows in this paragraph too is largely drawn from these sites and their links. As yet, the reception, or even detailed making, of these museums in Europe has not been much studied. The special issue of *Museum International* noted above provides a beginning; and the MeLa – *European Museums in an Age of Migration* – project will provide more: www.mela-project.eu.

30 www.domid.org/index-en.html.

31 An in-depth comparative analysis of museums that focus on emigration and on immigration would be a useful contribution to further understanding of

constructions of global movement and cultural diversity. It should also be noted that the first major museums of immigration were in new world countries: the US, Australia and Canada (see Baur 2009). Insights drawn from studies of these cannot, however, be simply transferred to the European context. In the new world cases, the immigrants have since become the dominant majorities; whereas in Europe this is not the case.

32 See Note 25 above.

33 Ingold 2007 is an interesting discussion of this, though his own notion of 'meshwork' and emphasis on lines does not solve the problem. See also Strathern 2004/1991 and 1996.

8 Cosmopolitan memory: Holocaust commemoration and national identity

1 *The Mill on the Floss*, 1860, Edinburgh and London: William Blackwood and Sons.

2 The equation of Europeanisation and cosmopolitanisation is more frequent in the writing of Ulrich Beck, e.g. Beck 2006/2004; Beck and Grande 2007: see also Rumford 2005. More specifically, the idea that Europe's twentieth-century history of atrocity and trauma, including the Holocaust, could act as a shared memory supporting a contemporary European identity has been suggested by Beck (2006/2004) and various commentators, particularly by a number of German intellectuals (e.g. Giesen 2004; see Heinbach 2009 for debates by intellectuals played out in German newspapers; and see also Delanty and Rumford 2005: 95–102 for relevant discussion; and Poole 2010 for a critique of the arguments). It informs developments such as the establishing of a European network of Holocaust memorial activities. As Schlesinger and Foret (2006: 69) point out, this is a problematic proposition, not least because of the differential positioning not just of individuals, but also of nations and groups, in relation to perpetration and victimhood. Sharing a memory of atrocity is very different depending upon such positioning.

3 For references to these see, in turn: Goldberg 1995, quoted in Flanzbaum 1999: 12; Finkelstein 2000; Cole 2000 and Gruber 2002: 8. See also Piper 2001.

4 Beck *et al.* 2009; see also Olick 2007.

5 Glick-Schiller 2010; Glick-Schiller *et al.* 2011: 400, 403; Vertovec and Cohen 2002. For an insightful discussion of cosmopolitanism in relation to heritage see Daugbjerg and Fibiger 2011.

6 See Kushner 1998: 228; Kushner 1994; Hartman 1994; Bodemann 2002.

7 The language of 'victims of fascism' was used in both Germanys. In the GDR, the framing in terms of fascism and the emphasis on political victims was especially strong and led to even greater reluctance to acknowledge the Jewish Holocaust (Herf 1997; Niven 2010). Indeed, since German reunification many concentration camps in the former GDR have been restored in order to give fuller acknowledgment of Jewish victimhood (Niven 2002; Niven and Paver 2010; Niven 2010).

8 My computer's Word-automated spell-check, for example, recognises the term 'holocaust' but not 'shoah'.

9 See Greenspan 1999 and Novick 2000 for discussion.

10 See: www.memorialmuseums.org/deutschland. Lackmann 2000 is an interesting participant-observation style account, with a terrible title, of the debates and events involved in the making of the Jewish Museum, Berlin. Bishop 2008 provides an overview of the German memorial landscape, and Bishop 2010 and 2011 provide accounts of visitor experience in the Jewish Museum Berlin – showing how clichés are sometimes reinforced in process or how certain exhibits may generate confusion – drawn from her ongoing ethnographic fieldwork.

11 Lithuania also has a long history of Jewish museums, the first having been established in 1913 but damaged and then almost destroyed first in World War I and

then World War II. It was re-established between 1944 and 1949. www.muziejai.lt/vilnius/zydu_muziejus.en.htm#History.

12 www.memorialmuseums.org/eng/denkmaeler/view/534/Jewish-Museum-of-Belgium.

13 www.memorialmuseums.org/denkmaeler/view/749/Museum-of-Jewish-Culture.

14 In 1998 the museum was established in a new building, though it had been running on a small scale since the late 1970s: www.jewishmuseum.gr/en/the_museum/history.html.

15 www.en.galiciajewishmuseum.org/museum-history.html.

16 This is the dating of a new building, some parts of the collection having been shown previously in two small rooms: www.jewishitaly.org/detail.asp?ID=165.

17 www.oslo.com/en/product/?TLp=16789.

18 www.jewishmuseum.org.pl/en/cms/home-page/.

19 www.jhm.nl/organisation/history.

20 www.jewishmuseum.org.uk/history-of-the-museum-new.

21 See www.jmw.at/history.

22 See, for example, museologien.blogspot.com/2011/02/recent-events-at-jewish-museum-vienna.html.

23 See www.jewishmuseum.cz/en/amuseum.htm; for a discussion of the Nazi Central Jewish museum project see Greenblatt 1991.

24 www.jewishmuseum.cz/en/amuseum.htm.

25 www.jhm.nl/organisation/history; Greenberg 2002.

26 www.jewishmuseum.org.uk/history-of-the-museum-new.

27 See Kugelmass and Orla-Bukowska 1998; Charlesworth 2004; Lehrer 2007, 2013. Mach (2007) provides a useful discussion of changing relationships with Jewishness in Polish post-war identities. Jan Lorenz's forthcoming PhD on the Jewish revival in Poland will provide an in-depth ethnographic analysis. I am indebted to him for discussion.

28 Jeffrey Shandler also provides a nuanced discussion of the wider embracing of Jewishness, making the interesting argument that we should recognise new – 'post-vernacular' – ways of being Jewish as legitimate ways of being Jewish. Jonathan Webber's in-depth investigations of Auschwitz also provide a multi-dimensional portrait, recognising complexities (2006, 2009).

29 It was part of what informed the European Historical Consciousness project, and the President's History Competition that this was linked to, discussed in Chapter 2.

30 Information from www.holocaustmemorialday.gov.uk/2002, which was active in February 2004 but is not so any longer. The date chosen for Holocaust Memorial Day, 27 January – the date of the liberation of Auschwitz-Birkenau, had already been adopted by Germany in 1996 for its Day of the Victims of National Socialism. Israel's national Holocaust Remembrance Day, on the anniversary of the 1943 Warsaw uprising (a date that usually falls in April) is the most longstanding of state Holocaust commemorations, having been first held in 1951. In the US, the Holocaust Memorial Museum took responsibility for the new Day for Remembrance of the Victims of Holocaust, the first of which was held in 1982, on the same date as Israel's. In 2005, the United Nations adopted 27 January for International Holocaust Memorial Day.

31 This entailed, of course, considerable 'forgetting' of indifference to the Jewish plight at that time and to other limitations on granting refuge since.

32 For primary documentation of the conference, on which this account draws, see: www.manskligarattigheter.gov.se/stockholmforum/2000/conference_2000.html.

33 The Muslim Council's non-participation in Holocaust Memorial Day remained in place until 2007; and then in 2008 it was re-introduced (Werbner 2009: 459).

34 www.pm.gov.uk/news.asp?NewsId=1754 (active in February 2004).

35 See also Andrew Buckser's (2002) discussion of the role of the rescue of the Jews of Copenhagen in the construction of Danish national identity.

36 In online reporting about the renovations, Peter Menasse explained in 2011 that the original plan had been to repair and re-use some of the holograms but they were too damaged for this to be possible; and only some were able to be preserved at all due to difficulties in removing them. See www.jmw.at/we-are-renovating.
37 This is discussed in Macdonald 2009a, especially Chapter 8.
38 The rise of 'public history' as a focus of academic interest in the US and more recently in Britain is itself indicative of this. See Jordanova (2000). Within this, the Holocaust has emerged as one of – or perhaps even the – pre-eminent foci of such political and moral activity: perhaps not the 'moral and ideological Rorschach test' that Novick dubs it (2000: 12) but a moral and ideological touchstone nonetheless (Thomas 1999).

9 The future of memory – and forgetting – in Europe

1 The White Queen to Alice in *Alice through the Looking Glass, and What Alice found There,* 1871.
2 This is part of Ruth Mandel's argument (2008), witnessed especially in philosemitism but also in certain versions of multiculturalism; though she argues that this goes alongside many forms of discrimination against Turkish Germans.
3 See, for example, van der Leeuw-Roord 2001; Berger *et al.* 2008.
4 This is a major theme in the popular BBC series *Who do you think you are?* Pálsson notes that this extension of connections may eventually make the idea meaningless as everybody feels connected to everybody else; and he also observes that some genetics research is highlighting links with other species, with bacteria acting as vectors – which may potentially lead to rethinking ideas of connection (2009: 106).
5 There has been a growing literature on this topic. Recent work includes my own on 'difficult heritage' (2009a); see also Logan and Reeves 2009; Smith *et al.* 2010; Carr 2012; and Lehrer *et al.* 2011; and some cast within the frame of 'dark tourism', e.g. Lehrer, Milton and Patterson 2000. Lehrer 2010a is a thoughtful exploration of the possibilities that this raises for what she calls 'conciliatory heritage'.
6 As he acknowledges, he is not alone among historians in making such a suggestion. See, for example, Stone, who writes 'it is no doubt the case, if only because of the cycles of fashion, that the memory boom has reached its zenith' (2012: 729). Rosenfeld does, however, develop the argument most extensively, also providing much counter-argument. Interestingly, and perhaps surprisingly, his article does not seem to have generated any rebuttals; on the contrary, it seems to be viewed as uncontentious, as, for example, by Stone. See also Eley 2011 for related discussion.
7 For example, in one of the few attempts to put some numerical substance to his claims he looks at the number of US history PhDs with the word 'memory' in the title. As he acknowledges, this does not really support his arguments for although he sees a slight dip in the numbers for theses begun soon after 9/11 this seems to have picked up again since then (2009: 152–3, fn.102).
8 'Memory entrepreneurs' is used by Jordan 2006; 'ethno-preneurs' by Comaroff and Comaroff 2009; and I use the term 'memory workers' in 2009a.
9 Lackmann 2000; Jeismann 1999 and Brumlik *et al.* 2004 are collections of some of the controversies about these.
10 There is now a considerable literature on the official apology. See, for example, Nobles 2008; Olick 2007. I especially like Bernhard Schlink's thoughtful discussion of distinctions between asking for forgiveness and reconciliation. He writes, 'Forgiveness is something too crucial, too existential to be made into a political ritual' or to be used in 'negotiations and contracts for restitution' (2010: 72, 74).
11 See, for example, in this interview in 2011 with the Centre's Director: www.berlinbiennale.de/blog/en/allgemein-en/the-city-of-toys-16530. Thanks to Erica Lehrer for bringing this to my attention.

12 Collecting may itself be conducted in circumstances of considerable hardship, as when people try to assemble fragments from their past lives following dispossession (Chapter 4); and even forms of heritage tourism, such as 'pilgrimages' to sites of Holocaust (Chapter 8), may be regarded as more part of an essential life-cycle ritual.

13 The cover and accompanying discussion are available at: www.focus.de/magazin/videos/focus-titel-betrueger-in-der-euro-familie_vid_15672.html.   Unfortunately, it was not possible to reproduce the image in this book.

14 Other Greek newspapers have also shown images of German Chancellor Angela Merkel with a swastika armband. See, for example, the image of a Greek newspaper cover reported in the *Washington Post* in February 2012: www.washingtonpost.com/blogs/blogpost/post/angela-merkel-depicted-as-nazi-in-greece-as-anti-german-sentiment-grows/2012/02/10/gIQASbZP4Q_blog.html.   In   May   2010, *Focus* magazine used the Venus de Milo on another cover, this time with her hand outstretched as if begging and the title: 'Greece – and our money!': www.focus.de/magazin/videos/focus-titel-griechenland-und-unser-geld_vid_17109.html.

15 The name 'Infinite Justice' was also deemed offensive by Muslims as only Allah can dispense infinite justice. In response to objections, the name was soon changed to 'Operation Enduring Freedom'. See the BBC news report of 25/09/2001 at: news.bbc.co.uk/1/hi/world/americas/1563722.stm.

REFERENCES

Abélès, Marc 1992 *La Vie Quoitidienne au Parlement Européen*. Paris: Hachette

Abélès, Marc 2000 'Virtual Europe'. In I. Bellier, I. and T.M. Wilson (eds) *An Anthropology of the European Union,* pp.31–52. Oxford: Berg

Abélès, Marc, Irène Bellier and Maryon McDonald 1993 *An Anthropological Approach to the European Commission.* Brussels: European Commission

Abram, David 1996 *The Spell of the Sensuous. Perception and Language in a More-than-Human World.* New York: Random House

Abram, Simone 1996 'Reactions to the tourist gaze: a view from the Deep Green Heart of France'. In J. Boissevain (ed.) *Coping with Tourists,* pp.174–203. Oxford: Berghahn

Abram, Simone 1997 'Performing for tourists in Rural France'. In S. Abram, J. Waldren and D.V.L. McLeod (eds) *Tourists and Tourism: Identifying with People and Places,* pp.29–50. Oxford: Berg

Abram, Simone and Jacqueline Waldren 1997 'Introduction: tourists and tourism – identifying with people and places'. In S. Abram, J. Waldren and D. V .L. McLeod (eds) *Tourists and Tourism: Identifying with People and Places,* pp.1–11. Oxford: Berg

Abt, Jeffrey 2006 'The origins of the public museum'. In S. Macdonald (ed.) *Companion to Museum Studies,* pp.113–34. Oxford: Blackwell

Achebe, Chinua 1984 'Foreword'. In H.M. Cole and C.C. Aniakor (eds) *Igbo Arts: Community and Cosmos,* pp.viii–xi. Los Angeles, CA: Museums of Cultural History, UCLA

Aciman, André 2000 *False Papers. Essays on Exile and Memory.* New York: Picador

Adam, Barbara 1995 *Timewatch. The Social Analysis of Time.* Cambridge: Polity

Adorno, Theodor 1986 'What does coming to terms with the past mean?' In G.H. Hartmann (ed.) *Bitburg in Moral and Political Perspective*, pp.114–30. Bloomington, IN: Indiana University Press

Adorno, Theodor and Max Horkheimer 1979 (1947) *Dialectic of Enlightenment*. London: Verso

Alexander, Jeffrey 2009 *Remembering the Holocaust.* Oxford: Oxford University Press

Alfrey, Judith and Putnam, Tim 1992 *The Industrial Heritage.* London: Routledge

Anderson, Benedict 1983 *Imagined Communities: Reflections on the Origin and Spread of Nationalism*. London: Verso

Anheier, Helmut and Yudhishtair Raj Isar (eds) 2011 *Heritage, Memory and Identity*. Thousand Oaks, CA: Sage

Anico, Marta 2009 'Representing identities at local municipal museums: cultural forums or identity bunkers?' In M. Anico and E. Peralta (eds) 2009 *Heritage and Identity. Engagement and Demission in the Contemporary World*, pp.63–75. London: Routledge

Anico, Marta and Elsa Peralta (eds) 2009 *Heritage and Identity. Engagement and Demission in the Contemporary World*. London: Routledge

Apfelbaum, Erika 2010 'Halbwachs and the social properties of memory'. In S. Radstone and B. Schwartz (eds) *Memory: Theories, Histories, Debates,* pp.77–92. New York: Fordham University Press

Aplenc, Veronica E. 2004 'Authentically socialist: Czech heritage management at the former Liechtenstein estate of Lednice-Valtice'. *Focaal – European Journal of Anthropology* 44: 61–71

Appadurai, Arjun 1986 'Introduction: commodities and the politics of value'. In A. Appadurai (ed.) *The Social Life of Things: Commodities in Cultural Perspective*, pp.3–63. Cambridge: Cambridge University Press

Appadurai, Arjun 1996 *Modernity at Large. Cultural Dimensions of Globalization*. Minneapolis, MN: University of Minnesota Press

Appadurai, Arjun and Carol Breckenridge 1992 'Museums are good to think: heritage on view in India'. In I. Karp, C. Kreamer and S.D. Lavine (eds) *Museums and Communities: The Politics of Public Culture*, pp. 34–55. Washington and London: Smithsonian Institution Press

Appiah, Kwame Anthony 2006 *Cosmopolitanism. Ethics in a World of Strangers*. Harmondsworth: Penguin

Ardener, Edwin 1975 'Belief and the problem of women'. In S. Ardener (ed.) *Perceiving Women,* pp.1–17. London: J.M. Dent and Sons

Ardener, Edwin 1975a 'The problem revisited'. In S. Ardener (ed.) *Perceiving Women,* London: J.M. Dent and Sons, pp.19–27

Ardener, Edwin 1989 'The construction of history: "vestiges of creation"'. In E. Tonkin, M. McDonald and M. Chapman (eds) *History and Ethnicity*, pp.22–33. London: Routledge

Ardener, Shirley 1975 'Introduction'. In S. Ardener (ed.) *Perceiving Women,* pp.vii–xxiii. London: J.M. Dent and Sons

Ardener, Shirley (ed.) 1981 *Women and Space. Ground Rules and Social Maps*. London: Taylor and Francis

Arendt, Hannah 1958 *The Human Condition*. Chicago, IL: Chicago University Press

Arigho, Bernie 2008 'Getting a handle on the past: the use of objects in reminiscence work'. In H.J. Chatterjee (ed.) *Touch in Museums,* pp.205–12. Oxford: Berg

Assmann, Aleida 2006 *Der lange Schatten der Vergangenheit. Erinnerungskultur und Geschichtspolitik*. Munich: C.H. Beck

Assmann, Jan 2008 'Communicative and cultural memory'. In A. Erll and A. Nünning (eds) *Cultural Memory Studies: An Interdisciplinary Reader,* pp.10–18. Berlin: de Gruyter

Austin, J.L. 1962 *Sense and Sensibilia*. Oxford: Oxford University Press

Austin, J.L. 1962a *How to Do Things with Words*. London: Routledge and Kegan Paul

Babadzan, Alain 2000 'Anthropology, nationalism and "the invention of tradition"'. *Anthropological Forum* 10(2): 131–55

Ballinger, Pamela 2002 *History in Exile. Memory and Identity at the Borders of the Balkans*. Princeton, NJ: Princeton University Press

Bangstad, Sindre and Matti Bunzl 2010 '"Anthropologists are talking" about Islamophobia and Anti-Semitism in the new Europe', *Ethnos* 75(2): 213–28

Barndt, Kerstin 2010 '"Memory traces of an abandoned set of futures": Industrial ruins in the post-industrial landscapes of East and West Germany'. In J. Hell and A. Schönle (eds) *Ruins of Modernity*, pp.270–93. Durham NC: Duke University Press

Barth, Fredrik 1969 'Introduction'. In F. Barth (ed.) *Ethnic Groups and Boundaries: The Social Organisation of Difference*, pp.9–38. London: George Allen and Unwin

Basu, Paul 2007 *Highland Homecomings. Genealogy and Heritage Tourism in the Scottish Diaspora*. London: Routledge

Baudrillard, Jean 1983 *Simulations*. New York: Semiotext(e)

Bauman, Gerd 1999 *The Multicultural Riddle: Rethinking National, Ethnic and Religious Identities*. London: Routledge

Bauman, Zygmunt 1989 *Modernity and the Holocaust*. Ithaca. NY: Cornell University Press

Bauman, Zygmunt 1992 *Intimations of Postmodernity*. London: Routledge

Bauman, Zygmunt 2000 *Liquid Modernity*. Cambridge: Polity

Bauman, Zygmunt 2001 *The Individualized Society*. Cambridge: Polity

Baur, Joachim 2009 *Die Musealisierung der Migration. Einwanderungsmuseen und die Inszenierung der multikulturellen Nation*. Bielefeld: Transcript

Bausinger, Hermann 1990 (1961) *Folk Culture in a World of Technology,* trans. E.Detmer. Bloomington, IN: Indiana University Press

Beck, Ulrich 1992 *Risk Society. Towards a new Modernity.* London: Sage

Beck, Ulrich 1998 *Was ist Globalisierung?* Frankfurt: Suhrkamp

Beck, Ulrich 2006 (2004) *The Cosmopolitan Vision.* Cambridge: Polity

Beck, Ulrich and Elisabeth Beck-Gernsheim 2002 *Individualization: Institutionalized Individualism and its Social and Political Consequences.* Cambridge: Polity

Beck, Ulrich and Edgar Grande 2007 *Cosmopolitan Europe.* Cambridge: Polity

Beck, Ulrich, Anthony Giddens and Scott Lash 1994 *Reflexive Modernization.* London: Sage

Beck, Ulrich, Daniel Levy and Natan Sznaider 2009 'Cosmopolitanization of memory. The politics of forgiveness and restitution'. In M. Nowicka and M. Rovisco (eds) *Cosmopolitanism in Practice*, pp.111–30. Aldershot: Ashgate,

Beck-Gernsheim, Elisabeth 1999 *Juden, Deutsche und andere Erinnerungslandschaften.* Frankfurt: Suhrkamp

Beier de-Haan, Rosmarie (ed.) 2000 *Geschichtskultur in der Zweiten Moderne.* Frankfurt: Campus

Beier de-Haan, Rosmarie 2005 *Erinnerte Geschichte – Inszenierte Geschichte: Museen und Ausstellungen in der Zweiten Moderne.* Frankfurt: Suhrkamp

Beier de-Haan, Rosmarie 2006 'Re-staging histories and identities'. In S. Macdonald (ed.) *Companion to Museum Studies*, pp.186–97. Oxford: Blackwell

Bellier, Irène 1997 'The Commission as an actor: an anthropologist's view'. In H. Wallace and A.R. Young (eds) *Participation and Policy-Making in the European Union*, pp. 91–115. Oxford: Oxford University Press

Bellier, Irène and Thomas M. Wilson (eds) 2000 *An Anthropology of the European Union.* Oxford: Berg

Bender, Barbara and Martin Winer (eds) 2001 *Contested Landscapes: Movement, Exile and Place.* Oxford: Berg

Bendix, Regina 1997 *In Search of Authenticity. The Formation of Folklore Studies.* Wisconsin, WI: University of Wisconsin Press

Bendix, Regina 2008 'Expressive resources: knowledge, agency and European ethnology', *Anthropological Journal of European Cultures* 17(2): 114–29

Bendix, Regina 2009 'Heritage between economy and politics. An assessment from the perspective of cultural anthropology'. In L. Smith and N. Akagawa (eds) *Intangible Heritage,* pp.253–69. London: Routledge

Bendix, Regina 2012 'Folklore studies in German-speaking Europe since 1945'. In R. Bendix and G. Hasan-Rokem (eds) *A Companion to Folklore,* pp.364–90. Oxford: Wiley-Blackwell

Bendix, Regina and Galit Hasan-Rokem 2012 (eds) *A Companion to Folklore.* Oxford: Wiley-Blackwell

Benjamin, Walter 1992 (1955) *Illuminations.* London: Fontana

Benjamin, Walter 1999 (1982) *The Arcades Project,* trans. H. Eiland and K. McLaughlin. Cambridge, MA: The Belknap Press of Harvard University Press

Bennett, Tony 1995 *The Birth of the Museum.* London: Routledge

Bennett, Tony 1998 'Speaking to the eyes: museums, legibility and the social order'. In S. Macdonald (ed.) *The Politics of Display*, pp.25–35. London: Routledge

Bennett, Tony 2004 *Pasts beyond Memory: Evolution, Museums, Colonialism.* London: Routledge

Bennett, Tony 2007 'The work of culture', *Cultural Sociology* 1(1): 33–47

Bennett, Tony and Diane Watson 2002 'Understanding everyday life: introduction'. In T. Bennett and D. Watson (eds) *Understanding Everyday Life,* pp.ix–xxiv. Oxford: Blackwell

Bennett, Tony and Chris Healy 2009 'Introduction: assembling culture', *Journal of Cultural Economy* 2 (1–2): 3–10

Bennett, Tony and Chris Healy (eds) 2009a *Assembling Culture*, special issue of *Journal of Cultural Economy* 2 (1–2)

Berdahl, Daphne 1999 *Where the World Ended. Re-Unification and Identity in the German Borderland.* Berkeley, CA: University of California Press

Berdahl, Daphne 2010 *On the Social Life of Postsocialism. Memory, Consumption, Germany.* Bloomington, IN: Indiana University Press

Berger, Stefan 2009 'History and forms of collective identity in Europe: why Europe cannot and should not be built on history'. In L. Rorato and A. Saunders (eds) *The Essence and the Margin: National Identities and Collective Memories in Contemporary European Culture,* pp.21–36. Oxford: Berghahn

Berger, Stefan, Linus Eriksonas and Andrew Mycock (eds) 2008 *Narrating the Nation: Representations in History, Media and the Arts.* Oxford: Berghahn

Berliner, David 2005 'The abuse of memory: reflections on the memory boom in anthropology', *Anthropological Quarterly* 78(1): 197–211

Berman, Marshall 1983 (1982) *All that is Solid Melts into Air. The Experience of Modernity.* London: Verso

Berman, Marshall 2009 (1970) *The Politics of Authenticity. Radical Individualism and the Emergence of Modern Society.* London: Verso

Billig, Michael 1995 *Banal Nationalism.* London: Sage

Binder, Beate 2009 *Streitfall Stadtmitte: Der Berliner Schlossplatz.* Cologne: Böhlau

Birdwell-Pheasant, Donna and Denise Lawrence-Zúñiga (eds) 1999 *HouseLife. Space, Place and Family in Europe.* Oxford: Berg

Bishop, Victoria Kendzia 2008 'Holocaust memorialisation in Germany: a paradoxical landscape', *Feldnotizen* 3: 86–98

Bishop, Victoria Kendzia 2010 'Clichés reinforced, clichés challenged? Visitors' perceptions of the Jewish Museum Berlin'. In M. Waligórska and S. Wagenhofer (eds) *Cultural Representations of Jewishness at the Turn of the 21st Century.* Florence: European University Institute

Bishop, Victoria Kendzia 2011 'Site affects: a room as object. Reflections on some "confusion" in the Holocaust tower in the Jewish Museum Berlin'. In F. von Bose, K. Poehls, F. Schneider and A. Schulze (eds) *Museum^X Zur Neuvermessung eines mehrdimensionalen Raumes,* pp.67–76. Berlin: Panama

Bithell, Caroline 2003 'On the playing fields of the world (and Corsica): politics, power, passion and polyphony', *British Journal of Musicology* 12(1): 67–95

Blair, Tony 2001 'Holocaust Memorial Day: reflection', *Perspectives,* Summer, pp.4–5

Blight, David W. 2009 'The memory boom: why and why now?' In P. Boyer and J.V. Wertsch (eds) *Memory in Mind and Culture,* pp.238–51. Cambridge: Cambridge University Press

Bodemann, Y. Michal 1996 *Gedächtnistheater. Die jüdische Gemeinschaft und ihre deutsche Erfindung.* Hamburg: Rotbuch Verlag

Bodemann, Y. Michal 2002 *In den Wogen der Erinnerung. Jüdische Existenz in Deutschland.* Munich: dtv

Bodemann, Y. Michal and Olena Bagno 2008 'In the ethnic twilight: the paths of Russian Jews in Germany'. In Y.M. Bodemann (ed.) *The New Germany, Jewry and the European Context: The Return of the European Jewish Diaspora,* pp. 158–77. New York: Palgrave Macmillan

Boissevain, Jeremy 1975 'Introduction: towards a social anthropology of Europe'. In J. Boissevain and J. Friedl (eds) *Beyond the Community: Social Process in Europe,* pp. 9–17. The Hague: Department of Eductional Science of the Netherlands

Boissevain, Jeremy (ed.) 1992 *Revitalizing European Rituals.* London: Routledge

Boissevain, Jeremy (ed.) 1996 *Coping with Tourists. European Reactions to Mass Tourism.* Oxford: Berghahn

Borneman, John 1992 *Belonging in the Two Berlins.* Cambridge: Cambridge University Press

Borneman, John and Fowler, Nick 1997 'Europeanization', *Annual Review of Anthropology* 26: 487–514

Boskovic, Aleksandar (ed.) 2008 *Other People's Anthropologies.* Oxford: Berghahn

Bossak, Barbara 2006 'Monuments and social memory in Gdansk'. In H. Jerman, P. Hautaniemi and S. Macdonald (eds) *Anthropological Perspectives on Social Memory,* special issue of *Anthropological Yearbook of European Cultures* 15: 63–76

Bouquet, Mary 1996 'Family trees and their visual affinities: the visual imperative of the genealogical diagram', *Journal of the Royal Anthropological Institute* 2(1): 43–66

Bowker, Geoff 2008 *Memory Practices in the Sciences.* Cambridge, MA: MIT Press

Boyer, Dominic 2006 'Ostalgie and the politics of the future in Eastern Germany', *Public Culture* 18(2): 361–81

Boyes, Georgina 1993 *The Imagined Village: Culture, Ideology and the English Folk Revival.* Manchester: Manchester University Press

Boym, Svetlana 2001 *The Future of Nostalgia.* New York: Basic Books

Boytsov, Michail 2000 '"No community without history, no history without community"'. In S. Macdonald with K. Fausser (eds) *Approaches to European Historical Consciousness. Reflections and Provocations,* pp.68–74. Hamburg: Körber

Brah, Avtar and Annie E. Coombes (eds) 2000 *Hybridity and its Discontents.* London: Routledge

Brown, Michael F. 2004 'Heritage as property'. In K. Verdery and C. Humphrey (eds) *Property in Question: Value Transformation in the Global Economy,* pp.49–68. Oxford: Berg

Brown, Michael F. 2005 'Heritage trouble: recent work on the protection of intangible cultural property', *International Journal of Cultural Property* 12: 40–61

Brumlik, Micha, Hajo Funke and Lars Rensmann (eds) 2004 *Unkämpftes Vergessen. Walser-Debatte, Holocaust Mahnmal und neurere deutsche Geschichtspolitik.* Berlin: Verlag Hans Schiller

Buckser, Andrew 2002 *After the Rescue: Jewish Identity and Community in Contemporary Denmark.* Basingstoke: Palgrave Macmillan

Bunzl, Matti 2003 'Of holograms and storage areas: modernity and postmodernity at Vienna's Jewish Museum', *Cultural Anthropology* 18(4): 435–68

Bunzl, Matti 2004 *Symptoms of Modernity. Jews and Queers in Late-Twentieth-Century Vienna,* Berkeley, CA: University of California Press

Bunzl, Matti 2005 'Between anti-Semitism and Islamophobia: some thoughts on the New Europe', *American Ethnologist* 32(4): 499–508

Burić, Fedja 2010 'Dwelling on the ruins of post-socialist Yugoslavia: being Bosnian by remembering Tito'. In M. Todorova and Z. Gille (eds) *Post-Communist Nostalgia,* pp.227–43. Oxford: Berghahn

Burke, Peter 1989 'French historians and their cultural identities'. In E. Tonkin, M. McDonald and M.Chapman (eds) *History and Ethnicity*, pp.157–67. London: Routledge

Burke, Peter 2008 (2004) *What is Cultural History?* Cambridge: Polity

Butler, Beverley 2006 'Heritage and the present past'. In C.Y. Tilley (ed.) *Handbook of Material Culture*, pp.463–79. Thousand Oaks, CA: Sage

Butler, Judith 1997 *Excitable Speech: A Politics of the Performative.* London: Routledge

Butterfield, Andrew 2003 'Monuments and memories', *The New Republic,* February 3: 27–32

Byrne, David 1998 *Complexity Theory and the Social Sciences.* London: Routledge

Byron, Reginald and Ulrich Kockel (eds) 2006 *Negotiating Culture: Moving, Mixing and Memory in Contemporary Europe.* Münster: LIT

Çağlar, Ayşe S. 1995 'McDöner: Döner Kebap and the social positioning struggle of German Turks'. In J.A. Costa and G.J. Bamossy (eds) *Marketing in a Multicultural World: Ethnicity, Nationalism and Cultural Identity*, pp.209–30. London: Sage

Çağlar, Ayşe S. 1997 'Hyphenated identities and the limits of "culture"'. In T. Modood and P. Werbner (eds) *The Politics of Multiculturalism in the New Europe. Racism, Identity and Community*, pp.169–85. London: Zed Books

Campbell, Jan and Harbord, Janet (eds) 2002 *Temporalities, Autobiography and Everyday Life.* Manchester: Manchester University Press

Cannell, Fenella 2011 'English ancestors: the moral possibilities of popular genealogy', *Journal of the Royal Anthropological Institute* 17(3): 462–80

Capo Zmegac, Jana (ed.) 2007 *Strangers Either Way: The Lives of Croatian Refugees in Their New Home.* Oxford: Berghahn

Cappelletto, Francesca 2003 'Long-term memory of extreme events: from autobiography to history', *Journal of the Royal Anthropological Institute* 9: 241–60

Cappelletto, Francesca 2005 'Public memories and personal stories: recalling the Nazi-fascist massacres'. In F. Cappelletto (ed.) *Memory and World War II: An Ethnographic Approach,* pp.101–30. Oxford: Berg

Cappelletto, Francesca (ed.) 2005a *Memory and World War II: An Ethnographic Approach.* Oxford: Berg

Carr, Gilly 2012 'Occupation heritage, commemoration and memory in Guernsey and Jersey', *History and Memory* 24(1): 87–117

Carrier, James G. 1994 *Gifts and Commodities: Exchange and Western Capitalism since 1700.* London: Routledge

Carruthers, Mary J. 1992 *The Book of Memory: A Study of Memory in Mediaeval Culture.* Cambridge: Cambridge University Press

Carsten, Janet 2007 'Introduction: ghosts of memory'. In J. Carsten (ed.) *Ghosts of Memory. Essays on Remembrance and Relatedness,* pp. 1–35. Oxford: Wiley-Blackwell

Carsten, Janet and Stephen Hugh-Jones (eds) 1995 *About the House. Lévi-Strauss and Beyond.* Cambridge: Cambridge University Press

Casey, Edward 1996 'How to get from space to place in a fairly short stretch of time: phenomenological prolegomena'. In S. Feld and K. Basso (eds) *Senses of Place*, pp.13–52. Santa Fe: School of American Research Press

Castells, Manuel 1997 *The Power of Identity*. Oxford: Blackwell

Cesarani, David 1997 'Lacking in convictions: British war crimes policy and national memory of the Second World War'. In M. Evans and K. Lunn (eds) *War and Memory in the Twentieth Century*, pp.27–42. Oxford: Berg

Ceuppens, Bambi 2011 'From "the Europe of the regions" to "the European Champion League": the electoral appeal of populist autochthony discourses in Flanders', *Social Anthropology* 19(2): 159–74

Chalk, Hannah-Lee 2012 'Romancing the stones: earth science objects as material culture'. In: S. Dudley, A.J. Barnes, J. Binnie, J. Petrov and J. Walklate (eds) *The Thing about Museums: Objects and Experience, Representation and Contestation*, pp.18–30. London: Routledge

Chapman, Malcolm 1978 *The Gaelic Vision in Scottish Culture*. London: Croom Helm

Chapman, Tony and Jenny Hockey (eds) 1999 *Ideal Homes?* London: Routledge

Charlesworth, Andrew 2004 'A corner of a foreign field that is forever Spielberg's: understanding the moral landscape of the site of the former K.L. Płaszow, Kraków, Poland', *Cultural Geographies* 11(3): 291–312

Charléty, Véronique 2004 'The Invention of the Museum of Europe', *HEIRS Working Papers*, 63–73, URL: http://www.heirs-eu.org/documents/heirscolloquium2004.pdf

Chevalier, Sophie 1998 'From woollen carpet to grass carpet: bridging house and garden in an English suburb'. In D. Miller (ed.) *Material Culture: Why Some Things Matter*, pp.47–71. London: UCL Press

Cieraad, Irène (ed.) 2006 (1999) *At Home: An Anthropology of Domestic Space*. New York: Syracuse University Press

Clendinnen, Inga 1999 *Reading the Holocaust*. Cambridge: Cambridge University Press

Clifford, James 1988 *The Predicament of Culture. Twentieth-Century Ethnography, Literature and Art*. Cambridge, MA: Harvard University Press

Clifford, James 1997 *Routes. Travel and Translation in the late Twentieth Century*. Cambridge, MA: Harvard University Press

Clifford, James and Marcus, George (eds) 1986 *Writing Culture. The Poetics and Politics of Ethnography*. Berkeley, CA: University of California Press

Cohen, Anthony P. (ed.) 1982 *Belonging: Identity and Social Organisation in British Rural Cultures*. Manchester: Manchester University Press

Cohen, Anthony P. 1985 *The Symbolic Construction of Community*. London: Routledge

Cohn, Bernard 1990 (1987) *An Anthropologist among the Historians and Other Essays*. Oxford: Oxford University Press

Cole, Tim 2000 *Selling the Holocaust: From Auschwitz to Schindler. How History is Bought, Packaged and Sold*. London: Routledge

Coleman, Simon and Crang, Mike (eds) 2002 *Tourism. Between Place and Performance*. Oxford: Berghahn

Collard, Anna 1989 'Investigating "social memory" in a Greek context'. In E. Tonkin, M. McDonald and M. Chapman (eds) *History and Ethnicity*, pp.89–103. London: Routledge

Collier, S.J. and A. Ong 2005 'Global assemblages, anthropological problems'. In A. Ong and S.J. Collier (eds) *Global Assemblages. Technology, Politics, and Ethics as Anthropological Problems*, pp.3–21. Oxford: Blackwell

Collingwood, R.G. 1939 *An Autobiography*. Oxford: Clarendon

Comaroff, John L. and Comaroff, Jean 1992 *Ethnography and the Historical Imagination*. Boulder, CO: Westview Press

Comaroff, John L. and Comaroff, Jean 2009 *Ethnicity, Inc.* Chicago, IL: Chicago University Press

Confino, Alon 1997 *The Nation as Local Metaphor. Württemberg, Imperial Germany and National Memory, 1871–1918*. Chapel Hill, NC: University of North Carolina Press

Connerton, Paul 1989 *How Societies Remember*. Cambridge: Cambridge University Press

Connerton, Paul 2009 *How Modernity Forgets*. Cambridge: Cambridge University Press

Connerton, Paul 2011 *The Spirit of Mourning*. Cambridge: Cambridge University Press

Coombes, Annie E. 1994 *Reinventing Africa. Museums, Material Culture and the Popular Imagination in Late Victorian and Edwardian England*. New Haven, CT: Yale University Press

Corner, John and Sylvia Harvey (eds) 1991 *Enterprise and Heritage: Cross-currents in National Culture.* London: Taylor and Francis

Cossons, Neil 1992 'Rambling reflections of a museum man'. In P. Boylan (ed.), *Museums 2000: Politics, People, Professionals and Profit*, pp.123–33. London: Routledge

Counihan, Carole M. 2004 *Around the Tuscan Table: Food, Family and Gender in Twentieth-Century Florence.* New York: Routledge

Cowan, Jane 1992 'Japanese ladies and Mexican hats: contested symbols and the politics of tradition in a northern Greek carnival celebration'. In J. Boissevain (ed.) *Revitalizing European Rituals,* pp.173–97. London: Routledge

Cowan, Jane and K.S. Brown 2000 'Introduction: Macedonian inflections'. In J. Cowan (ed.) *Macedonia: The Politics of Identity and Difference,* pp.1–27. London: Pluto

Cox, Rupert and Christoph Brumann 2010 'Introduction'. In C. Brumann and R. Cox (eds) *Making Japanese Heritage*, pp. 1–17. London: Routledge

Crain, Mary 1992 'Pilgrims, "yuppies", and media: the transformation of an Andalusian pilgrimage'. In J. Boissevain (ed.) *Revitalizing European Rituals,* pp.95–112. London: Routledge

Creed, Gerald W. 2010 'Strange bedfellows. Socialist nostalgia and neoliberalism in Bulgaria'. In M. Todorova and Z. Gille (eds) *Post-Communist Nostalgia*, pp.29–45. Oxford: Berghahn

Creed, Gerald W. 2011 *Masquerade and Postsocialism: Ritual and Cultural Dispossession in Bulgaria.* Bloomington, IN: Indiana University Press

Csordas, Thomas (ed.) 1994 *Embodiment and Experience. The Existential Ground of Culture and Self*. Cambridge: Cambridge University Press

Cubitt, Geoffrey 2007 *History and Memory*. Manchester: Manchester University Press

Darieva, Tsypylma 2011 'Rethinking homecoming: diasporic cosmopolitanism in post-Soviet Armenia', *Ethnic and Racial Studies* 34(3): 490–508

Daugbjerg, Mads 2009 'Pacifying war heritage. Patterns of cosmopolitan nationalism at a Danish battlefield site', *International Journal of Heritage Studies* 15(5): 431–46

Daugbjerg, Mads 2011 'Not mentioning the nation: banalities and boundaries at a Danish war heritage site', *History and Anthropology* 22(2): 243–59

Daugbjerg, Mads 2013 *Borders of Belonging. Experiencing History, War and Nation at a Danish Heritage Site*. Oxford: Berghahn

Daugbjerg, Mads and Thomas Fibiger 2011 'Introduction: heritage gone global. Investigating the production and problematics of globalized pasts', *History and Anthropology* 22(2): 135–47

Davis, John 1977 *People of the Mediterranean: A Comparative Essay in Social Anthropology*. London: Routledge

Davis, John 1992 'History and the people without Europe'. In K. Hastrup (ed.) *Other Histories*, pp.14–28. London: Routledge

Davis, John 1992a 'Tense in ethnography: some practical considerations'. In J. Okely and H. Callaway (eds) *Anthropology and Autobiography*, pp.205–20. London: Routledge

Decker, Stephanie K. 2009 'Being period: an examination of bridging discourse in a historical reenactment group', *Journal of Contemporary Ethnography* 39(1): 273–96

Degnen, Cathrine 2005 'Relationality, place and absence: a three-dimensional perspective on social memory', *Sociological Review* 53(4): 729–44

De Jong, Steffi 2011 'Is this us? The construction of the European man/woman in the exhibition *It's our History!*', *Culture Unbound* 11: 369–83

DeLanda, Manuel 2006 *A New Philosophy of Society*. London: Continuum

DeLanda, Manuel 2011 *Philosophy and Simulation. The Emergence of Synthetic Reason*. London: Continuum

Delanty, Gerard and Rumford, Chris 2005 *Rethinking Europe. Social Theory and the Implications of Europeanization*. London: Routledge

Deleuze, Gilles and Guattari, Félix 1987 (1976) *A Thousand Plateaus*. Minneapolis, MN: University of Minnesota Press

Delpha, Isabelle 2007 'In the midst of injustice: the ICTY from the perspective of some victim associations'. In X. Bougarel, E. Holmes and G. Duijzings (eds) *The New Bosnian Mosaic: Identities, Memories and Moral Claims in a Post-War Society*. Farnham: Ashgate

Demoissier, Marion 2011 'Beyond *terroir*: territorial construction, hegemonic discourses and French wine culture', *Journal of the Royal Anthropological Institute* 17(4): 685–705

Derrida, Jacques 1998 (1995) *Archive Fever: A Freudian Impression*, trans. E. Prenowitz. Chicago, IL: Chicago University Press

Des Chene, Mary 1997 'Locating the past'. In A. Gupta and J. Ferguson (eds) *Anthropological Locations: Boundaries and Grounds of a Field Science*, pp.66–87. Berkeley, CA: University of California Press

Díaz-Andreu, Margarita 2007 *A World History of Nineteenth-Century Archaeology. Nationalism. Colonialism and the Past*. Oxford: Oxford University Press

Dicks, Bella 2000 *Heritage, Place and Community*. Cardiff: University of Wales Press

Dicks, Bella 2004 *Cultures on Display: The Production of Contemporary Visitability*. Milton Keynes: Open University Press

Dietzsch, I., Wolgang Kashuba and Leonore Scholze-Irrlitz (eds) 2009 *Horizonte etnografischen Wissens*. Cologne: Böhlau

Di Lellio, Anna and Stephanie Schwander-Sievers 2006 'The legendary commander: the construction of an Albanian master narrative in post-war Kosovo', *Nations and Nationalism* 12 (3): 513–29

Diner, Dan and Gotthart Wunberg (eds) 2007 *Restitution and Memory: Historical Remembrance and Material Restitution in Europe*. Oxford: Berghahn

Dorson, Richard M. 1976 *Folklore and Fakelore: Essays Toward a Discipline of Folk Studies*. Cambridge, MA: Harvard University Press

Dorst, John D. 1989 *The Written Suburb. An American Site, an Ethnographic Dilemma*. Philadelphia, PA: University of Pennsylvania Press

Dow, James R. and Hannjost Lixfield (eds) 1994 *The Nazification of an Academic Discipline: Folklore in the Third Reich*. Bloomington, IN: Indiana University Press

Dresch, Paul 1998 'Mutual deception: totality, exchange, and Islam in the Middle East'. In W. James and N.J. Allen (eds) *Marcel Mauss: A Centenary Tribute*, pp.111–33. Oxford: Berghahn

Driessen, Henk 1992 'Celebration at daybreak in southern Spain'. In J. Boissevain (ed.) *Revitalizing European Rituals*, pp.80–94. London: Routledge

Dreyfus, Herbert L. 1990 *Being-in-the-World: A Commentary on Heidegger's Being and Time, Division 1*. Cambridge, MM: MIT Press

Dumit, Joseph 2003 *Picturing Personhood: Brain Scans and Biomedical Identity (In-formation)*. Princeton, NJ: Princeton University Press

Duncan, Carol 1995 *Civilizing Rituals. Inside Public Art Museums*. London: Routledge

Durkheim, Émile 1912 *Les Formes Élementaires de la Vie Religieuse*. Paris: Alcan

Dwelly, Edward 1977 (1911) *Faclair Gàidhlig gu Beurla le Dealbhan (Dwelly's Illustrated Gaelic to English Dictionary)*. Glasgow: Gairm

Eder, Karl 2001 'Integration through culture? The paradox of the search for a European identity'. In K. Eder and B. Giesen (eds), *European Citizenship between National Legacies and Postnational Projects*, pp.222–44. Oxford: Oxford University Press

Edwards, Elizabeth 2010 'Photographs and history: emotion and materiality'. In S. Dudley (ed.) *Museum Materialities. Objects, Engagements, Interpretations*, pp.21–38. London: Routledge

Edwards, Jeanette 1998 'The need for a "bit of history": place and past in English identity'. In N. Lovell (ed.) *Locality and Belonging*, pp.147–67. London: Routledge

Edwards, Jeanette 2000 *Born and Bred. Idioms of Kinship and New Reproductive Technologies in England*. Oxford: Oxford University Press

Edwards, Jeanette 2010 'Genealogical ancestors'. In V. Fons, A. Piella and M. Valdés (eds) *Procreacíon, crianza y género*, pp.43–60. Barcelona: PPU

Edwards, Jeanette 2012 'Ancestors, class and contingency', *Focaal – European Journal of Anthropology*, 62: 70–80

Eley, Geoff 1997 'Foreword'. In M. Evans and K. Lunn (eds) *War and Memory in the Twentieth Century*, pp.vii–xiii. Oxford: Berg

Eley, Geoff 2011 'The past under erasure? History, memory, and the contemporary', *Journal of Contemporary History* 46(3): 555–73

Ennew, Judith 1980 *The Western Isles Today*. Cambridge: Cambridge University Press

Eriksen, Thomas Hylland 2004 'Keeping the recipe: Norwegian folk costumes and cultural property', *Focaal – European Journal of Anthropology*, 44: 20–34

Erll, Astrid and Anskar Nünning (eds) 2008 *Cultural Memory Studies. An International Interdisciplinary Handbook*. Berlin: Walter de Gruyter

Fabian, Johannes 1983 *Time and the Other. How Anthropology Makes its Object*. New York: Columbia University Press

Fairclough, Graham, Rodney Harrison, John H. Jameson Jnr and John Schofield (eds) 2010 *The Heritage Reader*. London: Routledge

Färber, Alexa 2010 'The making of geographies of knowledge at world's fairs: Morocco at Expo 2000 in Hanover'. In Meusberger, Peter, David N. Livingstone and Heike Jöns (eds) *Geographies of Science*, pp.165–81. Berlin: Springer

Färber, Alexa 2012 'Urban ethnicity, world city and the hookah: the potential of thick-thin descriptions in urban anthropology'. In D. Brant, S. Disko, G. Wagner-Kyora (eds) *Thick Space. Approaches to Metropolitanism*, pp.333–55. Bielefeld: Transcript

Feldman, Allen 1991 *Formations of Violence. The Narrative of the Body and Political Terror in Northern Ireland*. Chicago, IL: Chicago University Press

Feldman, Jackie 2002 'Marking the boundaries of the enclave: defining the Israeli collective through the Poland "experience"', *Israel Studies* 7(2): 84–114

Feldman, Jackie 2008 *Above the Death Pits, Beneath the Flag. Youth Voyages to Poland and the Performance of Israeli Nation*. Oxford: Berghahn

Fentress, James and C.J. Wickham 1982 *Social Memory*. Oxford: Blackwell

Ferrándiz, Francisco 2006 'The return of Civil War ghosts: the ethnography of exhumations in contemporary Spain', *Anthropology Today*, 22(3): 7–12

Feuchtwang, Stephan 2005 'Mythical moments in national and other family histories', *History Workshop Journal* 59: 179–93

Feuchtwang, Stephan 2011 *After the Event. The Transmission of Grievous Loss in Germany, China and Taiwan*. Oxford: Berghahn

Filippucci, Paola 2002 'Acting local: two performances in Northern Italy'. In S. Coleman and M. Crang (eds) *Tourism between Place and Performance*. Oxford: Berghahn

Filippucci, Paola 2004 'A French place without a cheese: problems with heritage and identity in Northeastern France', *Focaal – European Journal of Anthropology*, 44: 72–86

Filippucci, Paola 2004a 'Memory and marginality: Remembrance of war in Argonne (France)'. In D. Kaneff, F. Pine and H. Haukanes (eds) *Politics, Religion and Remembering the Past*, pp.35–57. Münster: LIT

Filippucci, Paola 2009 'Heritage and methodology: a view from social anthropology'. In M.S. Sorensen and J. Carman (eds) *Heritage Studies: Methods and Approaches*, pp.319–25. London: Routledge

Filippucci, Paola 2010 'In a ruined country: place and the memory of war destruction in Argonne (France)'. In N. Argenti and K. Schramm (eds) *Remembering Violence*, pp.165–89. Oxford: Berghahn

Finkelstein, Norman 2000 *The Holocaust Industry: Reflections on the Exploitation of Jewish Suffering*. London and New York: Verso

Fischer, Michael M.J. 2009 'Iran and the boomeranging cartoon wars: can public spheres at risk ally with public spheres yet to be achieved?', *Cultural Politics* 5(1): 27–62

Flanzbaum, Hilene 1999 'Introduction'. In H. Flanzbaum (ed.) *The Americanization of the Holocaust*, pp.1–32. Baltimore and London: The Johns Hopkins University Press

Fonseca, Isobel 1995 *Bury Me Standing*. London: Chatto and Windus

Forsythe, Diana 1989 'German identity and the problem of history'. In E. Tonkin, M. McDonald and M. Chapman (eds) *History and Ethnicity*, pp.137–56. London: Routledge

Fortier, Anne-Marie 2000 *Migrant Belongings: Memory, Space and Identity*. Oxford: Berg

Forty, Adrian 1999 'Introduction'. In A. Forty and S. Küchler (eds) *The Art of Forgetting*, pp.1–18. Oxford: Berg

Foster, Hal 1996 *The Return of the Real. The Avant-Garde at the End of the Century*. Cambridge, MA: MIT Press

Frank, Sybille 2007 'Grenzwerte – Zur Formation der "Heritage Industry" am Berliner Checkpoint Charlie'. In D. Hemme, M. Tauschek and R. Bendix (eds) *Prädikat "Heritage". Wertschöpfungen aus kulturellen Ressourcen*, pp.297–322. Münster: Lit

Freud, Sigmund 1990 (1901) *The Psychopathology of Everyday Life*, trans. A. Tyson. New York: Norton

Friedman, Jonathan 1997 'Global crises, the struggle for cultural identity and intellectual porkbarrelling: cosmopolitans versus locals, ethnics and nationals in an era of de-hegemonisation'. In P. Werbner and T. Modood (eds) *Debating Cultural Hybridity. Multi-cultural Identities and the Politics of Anti-racism*, pp.70–89. London: Zed Books

Frykman, Jonas 2004 'Making sense of memory: monuments and landscapes in Croatian Istria'. In R. Bendix and J. Bendix (eds) *Sleepers, Moles and Martyrs: Secret Identifications, Societal Integration and the Differing Meanings of Freedom*, pp.107–19. Copenhagen: Museum Tusculanum Press

Frykman, Jonas and Löfgren, Orvar 1987 (1979) *The Culture Builders: A Historical Anthropology of Middle-Class Life*. New York: Rutgers

Gable, Eric and Handler, Richard 2011 'Forget culture, remember memory?'. In M.W. Huber (ed.) *Museums and Memory*, pp.23–44. Knoxville, TN: Newfound Press

Gadamer, Hans Georg 1989 (1960) *Truth and Method*, trans. J. Weinsberger and D.G. Marshall. London: Continuum

Gal, Susan 1991 'Bartók's funeral: representations of Europe in Hungarian political rhetoric', *American Ethnologist* 18: 440–58

Gallinat, Anselma 2006 'Difficult histories: public discourse and narrative identity in Eastern Germany', *Ethnos* 71(3): 343–66

Gallinat, Anselma 2009 'Intense paradoxes of memory: researching moral questions about remembering the socialist past', *History and Memory* 20(2): 183–99

Geertz, Clifford 1989 *Works and Lives. The Anthropologist as Author.* Stanford, CA: Stanford University Press

Gell, Alfred 1992 *The Anthropology of Time.* Oxford: Berg

Gell, Alfred 1998 *Art and Agency.* Oxford: Clarendon

Gerson, Stephanie 2003 *Pride of Place Local Memories and Political Culture in Nineteenth-Century France.* Ithaca, NY: Cornell University Press

Ghodsee, Kirsten 2008 'The miniskirt and the veil: Islam, secularism, and women's fashion in the New Europe', *Historical Reflections,* 34(3): 105–25

Ghodsee, Kirsten 2010 *Muslim Lives in Eastern Europe: Gender, Ethnicity and the Transformation of Islam in Postsocialist Bulgaria.* Princeton, NJ: Princeton University Press

Gibson, James J. 1979 *The Ecological Approach to Visual Perception.* Boston, MA: Houghton

Giddens, Anthony 1990 *The Consequences of Modernity.* Cambridge: Polity

Giddens, Anthony 1991 *Modernity and Self-Identity: Self and Society in the Late Modern Age.* Cambridge: Polity

Giesen, Bernhard 2004 *Triumph and Trauma.* Boulder, CO: Paradigm

Gille, Zsuzsa 2010 'Postscript'. In M. Todorova and Z. Gille (eds) *Post-Communist Nostalgia*, pp.278–89. Oxford: Berghahn

Gilmore, James H. and Pine, Joseph 2007 *Authenticity: What Consumers Really Want.* Cambridge, MA: Harvard University Press

Gilroy, Paul 1987 *There Ain't No Black in the Union Jack.* London: Hutchinson

Gilroy, Paul 2004 *After Empire. Melancholia or Convivial Culture?* London: Routledge

Gingrich, André and Richard Fox (eds) 2002 *Anthropology by Comparison.* London: Routledge

Gingrich, André and Marcus Banks (eds) 2006 *Neo-nationalism in Europe and Beyond. Perspectives from Social Anthropology.* Oxford: Berghahn

Ginzburg, Carlo 1980 'Morelli, Freud and Sherlock Holmes: clues and the scientific method', *History Workshop* 9: 5–36

Glick-Schiller, Nina 2010 'Old baggage and unpacking luggage: a commentary on Beck and Sznaider's "Unpacking cosmopolitanism for the social science"', *British Journal of Sociology* 61(1): 414–20

Glick-Schiller, Nina, Tsympylma Darieva and Sandra Gruner-Domic 2011 'Defining cosmopolitan sociability in a transnational age. An introduction', *Ethnic and Racial Studies* (special issue) 34(3): 399–418

Glynn, Irial and Kleist, J. Olaf (eds) 2012 *History, Memory and Migration. Perceptions of the Past and the Politics of Incorporation.* London: Palgrave Macmillan

Godard, Victoria A., Josep R. Llobera, and Cris Shore (eds) 1994 *The Anthropology of Europe. Identities and Boundaries in Conflict.* Oxford: Berg

Gofman, Alexander 1998 'A vague but suggestive concept: the "total social fact"'. In W. James and N.J. Allen (eds) *Marcel Mauss: A Centenary Tribute,* pp.63–70. Oxford: Berghahn

Goldberg, Michael 1995 *Why should Jews survive? Looking Past the Holocaust Toward a Jewish Future.* New York: Oxford University Press

Göle, Nilüfer 2009 'Turkish delight in Vienna: art, Islam and European public culture', *Cultural Politics* 5(3): 277–98

Gordon, Avery F. 1997 *Ghostly Matters: Haunting and the Sociological Imagination.* Minneapolis, MN: University of Minnesota Press

Graeber, David 2001 *Toward an Anthropological Theory of Value: The False Coin of Our Own Dreams*. New York: Palgrave Macmillan

Grasseni, Cristina 2005 'Slow food, fast genes: timescapes of authenticity and innovation in the anthropology of food', *Cambridge Anthropology*, special issue: *Creativity or Temporality?* 25(2): 79–94

Green, Sarah 2005 *Notes from the Balkans: Locating Marginality and Ambiguity on the Greek-Albanian Border*. Princeton, NJ: Princeton University Press

Greenberg, Reesa 2002 'Jews, museums and national identities' *Ethnologies* 24(2): 125–37

Greenblatt, Stephen 1991 'Resonance and wonder'. In I. Karp and S.D. Lavine (eds) *Exhibiting Cultures: The Poetics and Politics of Museum Display*, pp.42–56. Washington, DC: Smithsonian

Greenspan, Henry 1999 'Imagining survivors. Testimony and the rise of Holocaust consciousness'. In H. Flanzbaum (ed.) *The Americanization of the Holocaust*, pp.45–67. Baltimore, MD: Johns Hopkins University Press

Greenwood, Davydd J. 1989 (1972) 'Culture by the pound: an anthropological perspective on tourism as cultural commoditization'. In V.L. Smith (ed.) *Hosts and Guests. The Anthropology of Tourism*, pp.171–85. Philadelphia: University of Pennsylvania Press

Gregor, Neil 2009 *Haunted City. Nuremberg and the Nazi Past*. New Haven, CT: Yale University Press

Gregson, Nicky and Crewe, Louise 2003 *Second-Hand Cultures*. Oxford: Berg

Greverus, Ina-Maria 2002 *Anthropologisch Reisen*. Münster: LIT

Greverus, Ina Maria, Sharon Macdonald, Regina Römhild, Gisela Welz and Helena Wulff (eds) 2002 *Shifting Grounds. Experiments in Doing Ethnography,* special issue of *Anthropological Journal on European Cultures*. Berlin: LIT

Grossman, Alyssa 2010 'Chorographies of memory: everyday practices of remembrance work in post-socialist EU-accession-era Bucharest'. PhD thesis, University of Manchester

Gruber, Ruth Ellen 2002 *Virtually Jewish: Reinventing Jewish Culture in Europe*. Berkeley, CA: University of California Press

Gullestad, Marianne 1991 'The transformation of the Norwegian notion of everyday life', *American Anthropologist* 18(3): 480–99

Gullestad, Marianne 1996 *Everyday Life Philosophers: Modernity, Morality and Autobiography in Norway*. Oslo: Scandinavia University Press

György, Peter 2008 *Spirit of the Place*. Budapest: Central European University Press

Hacking, Ian 1995 *Rewriting the Soul. Multiple Personality and the Sciences of Memory*. Princeton, NJ: Princeton University Press

Hafstein, Valdimar T. 2004 'The politics of origins. Collective creation revisited', *The Journal of American Folklore* 117(465): 300–15

Hafstein, Valdimar T. 2009 'Intangible heritage as a list. From masterpieces to representation'. In L. Smith and N. Akagawa (eds) *Intangible Heritage*, pp.93–111. London: Routledge

Hage, Ghassan 2000 (1998) *White Nation. Fantasies of White Supremicism in a Multicultural Society*. New York: Routledge

Halbwachs, Maurice 1950 *La Mémoire Collective*. Paris: Les Presses Universitaires de France

Hallam, Elizabeth and Jenny Hockey 2001 *Death, Memory and Material Culture*. Oxford: Berg

Handelman, Don 1998 *Models and Mirrors. Towards an Anthropology of Public Events*. Oxford: Berghahn

Handler, Richard 1988 *Nationalism and the Politics of Culture in Quebec*. Madison, WI: Wisconsin University Press

Handler, Richard and Jocelyn Linnekin 1984 'Tradition, genuine or spurious', *The Journal of American Folklore* 97(385): 273–90

Handler, Richard and William Saxton 1988 'Dyssimulation: reflexivity, narrative and the quest for authenticity in "living history"', *Cultural Anthropology* 3(3): 242–60

Hann, Chris 1985 *A Village Without Solidarity: Polish Peasants in the Years of Crisis.* New Haven, CT: Yale University Press

Hann, Chris 2012 'Europe in Eurasia'. In U. Kockel, M. Nic Craith and J. Frykman (eds) 2012 *A Companion to the Anthropology of Europe,* pp.88–102. Oxford: Wiley-Blackwell

Hann, Chris, Mihály Sárkáby and Peter Skalník (eds) 2005 *Studying Peoples in People's Democracies: Socialist Era Anthropology in East-Central Europe.* Münster: LIT

Hannerz, Ulf 1996 *Transnational Connections. Culture, People, Places.* London: Routledge

Harbottle, Lynn 2004 *Food for Health, Food for Wealth: The Performance of Ethnic and Gender Identities by Iranian Settlers in Britain.* Oxford: Berghahn

Hardt, Michael and Antonio Negri 2000 *Empire.* Cambridge, MA: Harvard University Press

Hareven, Tamara K. 1993 'The home and the family in historical perspective'. In A. Mack (ed.) *Home: A Place in the World.* New York: New York University Press

Harrison, Rodney 2013 *Heritage: Critical Approaches.* London: Routledge

Harrison, Rodney, Sarah Byrne and Anne Clarke (eds) 2013 *Reassembling the Collection: Ethnographic Museums and Indigenous Agency.* Santa Fe: School for Advanced Research Press

Harrison, Simon 1999 'Identity as a scarce resource', *Social Anthropology* 7(3): 239–51

Hart, Keith 2005 'Money: one anthropologist's view'. In J.G. Carrier (ed.) *A Handbook of Economic Anthropology,* pp.160–75. Cheltenham: Edward Elgar

Hart, Keith 2007 'Marcel Mauss: in pursuit of the whole', *Comparative Studies in Society and History* 49(2): 1–13

Hartman, Geoffrey (ed.) 1994 *Holocaust Remembrance. The Shapes of Memory.* Oxford: Blackwell

Harvey, David 1989 *The Condition of Postmodernity.* Oxford: Blackwell

Harvey, Penny 1996 *Hybrids of Modernity. Anthropology, the Nation-State and the Universal Exhibition.* London: Routledge

Hastrup, Kirsten 1985 *Culture and History in Mediaeval Iceland: An Anthropological Analysis of Structure and Change.* Oxford: Oxford University Press

Hastrup, Kirsten 1990 *Nature and Policy in Iceland, 1400–1800. An Anthropology of History and Mentality.* Oxford: Oxford University Press

Hastrup, Kirsten 1992 'Introduction'. In K. Hastrup (ed.) *Other Histories,* pp.1–13. London: Routledge

Hauschild, Thomas 1992 'Making history in southern Italy'. In K. Hastrup (ed.) *Other Histories,* pp.29–44. London: Routledge

Hauschild, Thomas 1997 'Christians, Jews and the Other in German anthropology', *American Anthropologist* 99(4): 746–53

Hautaniemi, Petri 2006 'Fugitive memories. How young Somali men recall displacements and emplacements of their childhood'. In H. Jerman, P. Hautaniemi and S. Macdonald (eds) *Anthropological Perspectives on Social Memory,* special issue of *Anthropological Yearbook of European Cultures* 15: 77–92

Hayles, N. Kathleen 1990 *Chaos Bound: Orderly Disorder in Contemporary Literature and Science.* Ithaca, NY: Cornell University Press

Heady, Patrick and Liesl L. Gambold Miller 2006 'Nostalgia and the emotional economy: a comparative look at rural Russia'. In M. Svašek (ed.) *Postsocialism. Politics and Emotions in Eastern Europe,* pp.34–52. Oxford: Berghahn

Hecht, Anat 2001 'Home sweet home: tangible memories of an uprooted childhood'. In D. Miller (ed.) *Home Possessions*, pp.123–45. Oxford: Berg

Hecht, Anat 2013 *Pasts, Places and People: Contemporary Museum Consumption and Cultural Change*. Clevedon: Channel View

Heidegger, Martin 1962 (1927) *Being and Time*, trans. J. MacQuarrie and E. Robinson. Oxford: Blackwell

Heidegger, Martin 1975 *Poetry, Language, and Thought*, trans. A. Hofstader. New York: Harper and Row

Heidegger, Martin 1977 (1949) *The Question Concerning Technology and Other Essays*, trans. W. Lovitt. New York: Garland Publishing Inc.

Heinbach, Gesa 2009 'Die Europäisierung des Kosmopolitismus Begriff'. In G. Welz and A. Lottermann (eds) *Projekte der Europäisierung: Kulturanthropologische Forschungsperspektiven*, pp.233–44. Frankfurt: Institute für Kulturanthropologie und Europäische Ethnologie of the University of Frankurt am Main

Heinich, Nathalie 2009 *La Fabrique du Patrimoine. De la Cathedrale à la Petite Cuillière*. Paris: Maison des Sciences de l'Homme

Held, David, Anthony McGrew, David Goldblatt and Jonathan Perraton 1999 *Global Transformations. Politics, Economics, Culture*. Cambridge: Polity

Hemme, Dorothee, Makus Tauschek and Regina Bendix (eds) 2007 *Prädikat, 'Heritage'. Wertschöpfung aus kulturellen Ressourcen*. Münster: LIT

Herf, Jeffrey 1997 *Divided Memory. The Nazi Past in the Two Germanys*. Cambridge, MA: Harvard University Press

Hertz, Robert 1960 (1910) *Death and the Right Hand*, trans. R. and C. Needham. London: Routledge

Herzfeld, Michael 1982 *Ours Once More: Folklore, Ideology, and the Making of Modern Greece*. Austin, TX: University of Texas Press

Herzfeld, Michael 1987 *Anthropology Through the Looking-Glass. Critical Ethnography in the Margins of Europe*. Cambridge: Cambridge University Press

Herzfeld, Michael 1991 *A Place in History. Social and Monumental Time in a Cretan Town*, Princeton, NJ: Princeton University Press

Herzfeld, Michael 1992 'Segmentation and policy in the European nation-state: making sense of political events'. In K. Hastrup (ed.) *Other Histories*, pp.62–81. London: Routledge

Herzfeld, Michael 1997 *Cultural Intimacy. Social Poetics in the Nation-State*. London: Routledge

Herzfeld, Michael 2009 *Evicted from Eternity. The Restructuring of Modern Rome*. Chicago, IL: Chicago University Press

Hetherington, Kevin 1997 'Museum topology and the will to connect', *Journal of Material Culture* 2(2): 199–218

Hewison, Robert 1987 *The Heritage Industry. Britain in a Climate of Decline*. London: Methuen

Hicks, Dan 2010 'The material-cultural turn: event and effect'. In D. Hicks and M.C. Beaudry (eds) *The Oxford Handbook of Material Culture*, pp.25–98. Oxford: Oxford University Press

Hicks, Dan and Mary C. Beaudry (eds) 2010 *The Oxford Handbook of Material Culture*. Oxford: Oxford University Press

Hides, Sean 1997 'The genealogy of material culture and cultural identity'. In S. Pearce (ed.) *Experiencing Material Culture in the Western World*, pp.11–35. London: Leicester University Press

Hirsch, Eric and Charles Stewart 2005 'Introduction: ethnographies of historicity', *History and Anthropology*, 16(3): 261–74

Hirsch, Marianne and Nancy K. Miller 2011 'Introduction'. In M. Hirsch and N.K. Miller (eds) *Rites of Return. Diaspora Poetics and the Politics of Memory*, pp.1–20. New York: Columbia University Press

Hirsch, Marianne and Nancy K. Miller (eds) 2011a *Rites of Return. Diaspora Poetics and the Politics of Memory.* New York: Columbia University Press

Hobsbawm, Eric 1983 'Introduction: inventing traditions'. In E. Hobsbawm and T. Ranger (eds) *The Invention of Tradition,* pp.1–14. Cambridge: Cambridge University Press

Hobsbawm, Eric and Terence Ranger (eds) 1983 *The Invention of Tradition.* Cambridge: Cambridge University Press

Hodges, Matt 2009 'Disciplining memory: heritage tourism and the temporalisation of the built environment in rural France', *International Journal of Heritage Studies* 15(1): 71–99

Hodges, Matt 2010 'The time of the interval: historicity, modernity and epoch in rural France', *American Ethnologist* 37(1): 115–31

Hodges, Matt 2011 'Disciplinary anthropology? Amateur ethnography and the production of "heritage" in rural France', *Ethnos* 76(3): 348–74

Hoelscher, Steven 2006 'Heritage'. In S. Macdonald (ed.) *Companion to Museum Studies*, pp.198–218. Oxford: Blackwell

Holdaway, Simon 1981 'The Scarman report: some sociological aspects', *Journal of Ethnic and Migration Studies,* 9(3): 366–70

Holmes, Douglas R. 2000 *Integral Europe. Fast-capitalism, Multiculturalism and Neofascism.* Princeton, NJ: Princeton University Press

Holtzman, John 2006 'Food and memory', *Annual Review of Anthropology,* 35: 361–78

Holy, Ladislav 1998 'The metaphor of "home" in Czech nationalist discourse'. In N. Rapport and A. Dawson (eds) *Migrants of Identity. Perceptions of Home in a World of Movement*, pp.111–37. Oxford: Berg

Home Office 1999 *Government Proposal for a Holocaust Remembrance Day.* London: Home Office Communications Directorate

Horne, Donald 1984 *The Great Museum: The Re-Presentation of History.* Ann Arbor, MI: University of Michigan Press

Hoskins, Janet 1998 *Biographical Objects. How Things Tell the Stories of People's Lives.* London: Routledge

Howes, David 2010 'Response to Pink', *Social Anthropology* 18(3): 333–6

Howes, David 2011 'Reply to Ingold', *Social Anthropology* 19(3): 318–22

Hoyau, Philippe 1988 'Heritage and "the conserver society": the French case'. In R. Lumley (ed.) *The Museum Time-Machine,* pp.25–34. London: Routledge

Hsu, Elisabeth 2008 'The senses and the social: an introduction', *Ethnos* 73(4): 433–43

Hsu, Roland (ed.) 2010 *Ethnic Europe: Mobility, Identity, and Conflict in a Globalized World.* Stanford, CA: Stanford University Press

Hunt, Lynn (ed.) 1989 *The New Cultural History.* Berkeley, CA: University of California Press

Huyssen, Andreas 1995 *Twilight Memories. Marking Time in a Culture of Amnesia.* New York: Routledge

Huyssen, Andreas 2003 *Present Pasts. Urban Palimpsests and the Politics of Memory.* Stanford, CA: Stanford University Press

Hysop, Lois Boe and Frances E. Hysop (eds and trans.) 1957 *Baudelaire: A Self-Portrait.* London: Oxford University Press

Ingold, Tim 2000 *The Perception of the Environment. Essays on Livelihood, Dwelling and the Self.* London: Routledge

Ingold, Tim 2007 *Lines: A Brief History.* London: Routledge

Ingold, Tim 2011 'Worlds of sense and sensing the world: a response to Sarah Pink and David Howes', and 'Reply to David Howes' *Social Anthropology* 19(3): 313–17 and 323–7

Irving, Andrew 2006 'The skin of the city'. In H. Jerman, P. Hautaniemi and S. Macdonald (eds) *Anthropological Perspectives on Social Memory,* special issue of *Anthropological Yearbook of European Cultures* 15: 9–36

Jackson, Michael 2005 *Existential Anthropology: Events, Exigencies and Effects.* Oxford: Berghahn

James, Wendy 1970 *'Kwanim Pa: The Making of the Uduk People.* Oxford: Clarendon

Janelli, Angela 2012 *Das wilde Museum – Eine eigenständige Museumsform.* Berlin: Transcript

Jansen, Stef 1998 'Homeless at home: narrations of post-Yugoslav identities'. In N. Rapport and A. Dawson (eds) *Migrants of Identity. Perceptions of Home in a World of Movement,* pp. 85–109. Oxford: Berg

Jansen, Stef 2002 'The violence of memories: local narratives of the past after ethnic cleansing in Croatia', *Rethinking History* 6(1): 77–94

Jansen, Stef 2007 'Remembering with a difference: clashing memories of Bosnian conflict in everyday life'. In X. Bougarel, E. Helms and G. Duijzings (eds) *The New Bosnian Mosaic: Identities, Memories and Moral Claims in a Post-War Society,* pp.193–208. Oxford: Berghahn

Jansen, Stef 2009 'Cosmopolitan openings and closures in Post-Yugoslav anti-nationalism'. In M. Novicka and M. Rovisco (eds) *Cosmopolitanism in Practice,* pp.75–93. Farnham: Ashgate

Jansen, Stef and Staffan Löfving (eds) 2007 *Movement, Violence and the Making of Home,* special issue of *Focaal – European Journal of Anthropology,* 49

Jay, Martin 1988 'The scopic regimes of modernity'. In H. Foster (ed.) *Vision and Visuality,* pp.3–7. Seattle, WA: Bay Press

Jeismann, Karl-Ernst 1985 *Geschichte als Horizont der Gegenwart. Ueber den Zusammenhang von Vergangenheitsdeutung, Gegenwartsverständnis und Zukunftsperspektive.* Paderborn: Schoenagh Ferdinand

Jeismann, Michael (ed.) 1999 *Mahnmal Mitte. Eine Kontroverse.* Cologne: DuMont

Jell-Bahlsen, Sabine 1985 'Ethnology and fascism in Germany', *Dialectical Anthropology* 9: 313–35

Jenkins, Richard 1997 *Rethinking Ethnicity.* London: Sage

Jepson, Anne 2006 'Gardens and the nature of rootedness in Cyprus'. In Y. Papadakis, N. Peristianis and G. Welz (eds) *Divided Cyprus. Modernity, History, and an Island in Conflict,* pp.158–75. Bloomington, IN: Indiana University Press

Jerman, Helena 2006 'Memory crossing borders: a transition in space and time among second and third generation Russians in Finland'. In H. Jerman, P. Hautaniemi and S. Macdonald (eds) *Anthropological Perspectives on Social Memory,* special issue of *Anthropological Yearbook of European Cultures* 15: 117–41

Johler, Reinhard 2000 'Ethnological aspects of "rooting" Europe in a "de-ritualised" European Union'. In R. Bendix and H. Roodenburg (eds) *Managing Ethnicity: Perspectives from Folklore Studies, History and Anthropology,* pp.171–84. Amsterdam: Het Spinius

Johler, Reinhard 2001 'Telling a national story with Europe: Europe and European Ethnology'. In P. Niedermüller and B. Stoklund (eds) *Europe: Cultural Construction and Reality,* pp.67–74. Copenhagen: Museum Tusculanum Press

Johler, Reinhard 2002 'Local Europe: the production of cultural heritage and the Europeanisation of places'. In P. Niedermueller and B. Stoklund special issue of *Ethnologia Europea: Journal of European Ethnology,* pp.7–18. Copenhagen: Museum Tuscalanum Press

Jones, Siân 2010 'Negotiating authentic objects and authentic selves. Beyond the deconstruction of authenticity', *Journal of Material Culture* 15(2): 181–203

Jones, Siân 2011 '"Sorting the stones": monuments, memory and resistance in the Scottish Highlands'. In M.C. Beaudry and J. Symonds (eds) *Interpeting the Early Modern Worlds. Transatlantic Perspectives*, pp.113–39. Berlin: Springer

Jordan, Jennifer A. 2006 *Structures of Memory.* Stanford, CA: Stanford University Press

Jordanova, Ludmilla 1989 'Objects of knowledge: a historical perspective on museums'. In P. Vergo (ed.) *The New Museology,* pp.22–40. London: Reaktion

Jordanova, Ludmilla 2000 *History in Practice.* London: Arnold

Jung, Carl G. 1971 (1921) *Psychological Types* (Vol. 6 of *Collected Works*). Princeton, NJ: Princeton University Press

Kaiser, Wolfram and Stefan Krankenhagen 2010 'Europa ausstellen: Zur Konstruktion europäischer Integration und Identität im geplanten Musée de l'Europe in Brüssel'. In M. Gehler and S. Vietta (eds) *Europa – Europäisierung – Europäistik. Neue wissenschaftliche Ansätze, Methoden und Inhalte*, pp.181–96. Vienna: Böhlau

Kaiser, Wolfram, Stefan Krankenhagen and Kerstin Poehls 2012 *Europa Ausstellen: Das Museum als Praxisfeld der Europäisierung.* Vienna: Böhlau

Kalshoven, Petra Tjitske 2010 'Things in the making. Playing with imitation', *Etnofoor* 22(1): 59–74

Kalshoven, Petra Tjitske 2012 *Crafting 'the Indian'. Knowledge, Desire and Play in Indianist Reenactment.* Oxford: Berghahn

Kamper, Dietmar, Eberhard Knödler-Bunte, Marie-Louise Plessen and Christoph Wulf 1987 'Tendenzen der Kulturgesellschaft: eine Diskussion', *Ästhetik und Kommunikation* 67/68: 55–74

Kaneff, Deema 2004 *Who Owns the Past? The Politics of Time in a "Model" Bulgarian Village.* Oxford: Berghahn

Kansteiner, Wulf 2002 'Finding meaning in memory: a methodological critique of collective memory studies', *History and Theory,* 41(May): 179–97

Kansteiner, Wulf and Harald Weilnböck 2008 'Against the concept of cultural trauma (or "How I learned to love the suffering of others without the help of psychotherapy")'. In A. Erll and A. Nünning (eds) *Cultural Memory Studies: An Interdisciplinary Reader,* pp.229–40. Berlin: de Gruyter

Kapferer, Bruce 1988 *Legends of People, Myths of State.* Washington, DC: Smithsonian Institution

Kaprow, Miriam L. 1982 'Resisting respectability: gypsies in Saragossa', *Urban Anthropology* 11: 399–431

Karaca, Banu 2009 'Governance *of* or *through* culture? Cultural policy and the politics of culture in Europe', *Focaal – European Journal of Anthropology,* 55: 27–40

Karakasidou, Anastasia N. 1997 *Fields of Wheat, Hills of Blood. Passages to Greek Nationhood in Greek Macedonia 1870–1990.* Chicago, IL: Chicago University Press

Karp, Ivan and Stephen D. Lavine (eds) 1991 *Exhibiting Cultures. The Poetics and Politics of Museum Display*. Washington, DC: Smithsonian Institution Press

Karp, Ivan, Christine Kreamer and Stephen D. Lavine (eds) 1992 *Museums and Communities. The Politics of Public Culture.* Washington. DC: Smithsonian Institution Press

Kaschuba, Wolfgang 2005 'Gedächtnis und Generationen'. In P. Fank and S. Hördler (eds) *Der nationalsozialismus im Spiegel des öffentliches Gedächtnisses: Formen der Aufarbeitung des Gedenkens,* pp.183–96. Berlin: Metropol

Kaschuba, Wolfgang 2008 'Cultural heritage in Europe. Ethnologists' uses of the authentic', *Anthropological Journal of European Cultures* 17(2): 34–46

Kavanagh, Gaynor 1990 *History Curatorship.* London: Leicester University Press

Kirshenblatt-Gimblett, Barbara 2006 'World heritage and cultural economics'. In I. Karp, C.A. Kratz, L. Szwaja, T. Ybarra-Frausto, G. Buntinx and B. Kirshenblatt-Gimblett (eds) *Museum Frictions: Public Cultures/Global Transformations*, pp.161–202. Durham, NC: Duke University Press

Klein, Kerwin Lee 2000 'On the emergence of memory in historical discourse', *Representations* 69: 127–50

Kligman, Gail 1988 *The Wedding of the Dead. Ritual, Poetics and Popular Culture in Transylvania*. Berkeley, CA: University of California Press

Klumbyte, Neringa 2010 'The Soviet sausage renaissance', *American Anthropologist* 112(1): 22–37

Knaller, Susanne 2007 *Ein Wort aus der Fremde. Geschichte und Theorie der Begriffs Authentizität*. Heidelberg: Universitätsverlag Winter

Kockel, Ilrich 2007 'Reflexive traditions and heritage production'. In U. Kockel and M. Nic Craith (eds) *Cultural Heritages as Reflexive Traditions*, pp.19–33. Basingstoke: Palgrave Macmillan

Kockel, Ulrich, Máiréad Nic Craith and Jonas Frykman (eds) 2012 *A Companion to the Anthropology of Europe*. Oxford: Wiley-Blackwell

Koppel, Gaby 2001 'To stage a nation's remembrance', *Perspectives*, Summer, pp.6–8

Kopytoff, Igor 1986 'The cultural biography of things'. In A. Appadurai (ed.) *The Social Life of Things: Commodities in Cultural Perspective*, pp.64–91. Cambridge: Cambridge University Press

Koselleck, Reinhart 2002 *The Practice of Conceptual History: Timing History, Spacing Concepts*. Stanford, CA: Stanford University Press

Koselleck, Reinhart 2004 (1979) *Futures Past: On the Semantics of Historical Time*, trans. Keith Tribe. New York: Columbia University Press

Kosnick, Kira 2009 'Cosmopolitan capital or multicultural community? Reflections on the production and management of differential mobilities in Germany's capital city'. In M. Novicka and M. Rovisco (eds) *Cosmopolitanism in Practice*, pp.161–80. Farnham: Ashgate

Krankenhagen, Stefan (ed.) 2011 *Exhibiting Europe*, special issue of *Culture Unbound. Journal of Current Cultural Research* 3

Kreps, Christina 2006 'Non-Western models of museums and curation in cross-cultural perspective'. In S. Macdonald (ed.) *Companion to Museum Studies*, pp.457–72. New York: Blackwell

Kugelmass, Jack 1992 'The rites of the tribe: American Jewish tourism in Poland'. In I. Karp, C. Kreamer and S.D. Lavine *Museums and Communities*, pp.382–427. Washington, DC: Smithsonian

Kugelmass, Jack 1996 'Missions to the past: Poland in contemporary Jewish thought and deed. In P. Antze and M. Lambek (eds) *Tense Past. Cultural Essays in Trauma and Memory*, pp.199–214. London: Routledge

Kugelmass, Jack and Annamaria Orla-Bukowska 1998 '"If you built it they will come": recreating an historic Jewish district in post-communist Krakow', *City and Society* 10(1): 315–53

Kürti, László 1990 '"People vs the state": political rituals in contemporary Hungary', *Anthropology Today* 6(2): 5–8

Kürti, László and Peter Skalník (eds) 2009 *Postsocialist Europe. Anthropological Perspectives from Home*. Oxford: Berghahn

Kushner, Tony 1994 *The Holocaust and the Liberal Imagination: A Social and Cultural History*. Oxford: Blackwell

Kushner, Tony 1997 '"I want to go on living after my death": the memory of Anne Frank'. In M. Evans and K. Lunn (eds) *War and Memory in the Twentieth Century*, pp.3–26. Oxford: Berg,

Kushner, Tony 1998 'Remembering to forget: racism and anti-racism in post-war Britain'. In B. Cheyette and L. Marcus (eds) *Modernity, Culture and 'the Jew'*, pp.226–4. Cambridge: Polity

Kushner, Tony 2006 'Holocaust ethics, testimony and the problem of representation', *Poetics Today* 27(2): 275–95

Kuutma, Kristen 2007 'The politics of contested representation. UNESCO and the masterpieces of intangible cultural heritage'. In D. Hemme, M. Tauschek and R. Bendix (eds) *Prädikat "Heritage". Wertschöpfungen aus kulturellen Ressourcen,* pp.117–96. Münster: LIT

Lackmann, Thomas 2000 *Jewrassic Park. Wie baut man (k)ein Jüdisches Museum in Berlin.* Berlin/Vienna: Philo

Lambek, Michael 1996 'The past imperfect. Remembering as a moral practice'. In P. Antze and M. Lambek (eds) *Tense Past. Cutural Essays in Trauma and Memory,* pp.235–54. London: Routledge

Lambek, Michael 2003 'Memory in a Maussian universe'. In K. Hodgkin and S. Radstone (eds) *Regimes of Memory,* pp.202–16. London: Routledge

Lampland, Martha 1988 *Working through History: Ideologies of Work and Agricultural Production in a Hungarian Village, 1918–1983.* Chicago, IL: Chicago University Press

Lampland, Martha 1995 *The Object of Labor: Commodification in Socialist Hungary.* Chicago: University of Chicago Press

Lang, Berel 1999 *The Future of the Holocaust. Between History and Memory.* Ithaca, NY: Cornell University Press

Latour, Bruno 1987 *Science in Action: How to Follow Scientists and Engineers through Society.* Milton Keynes: Open University Press

Latour, Bruno 2005 *Reassembling the Social.* Oxford: Oxford University Press

Law, John and John Hassard (eds) 1999 *Actor Network Theory and After.* Oxford: Blackwell

Law, John and Anne-Marie Mol (eds) 2002 *Complexities: Social Studies of Knowledge.* Durham, NC: Duke University Press

Leahy, Helen Rees 2011 '"Fix'd statue on the pedestal of Scorn": the politics and poetics of displaying the Parthenon marbles in Athens and London'. In P. Bonaventura and A. Jones (eds) *Sculpture and Archaeology,* pp.179–196. Farnham: Ashgate

Lehrer, Erica 2003 'Re-populating Jewish Poland – in wood'. In M. Steinlauf and A. Polonsky (eds) *Focusing on Jewish Popular Culture in Poland and its Afterlife*, pp.335–55. Oxford: The Littman Library of Jewish Civilization

Lehrer, Erica 2007 'Bearing false witness? Vicarious Jewish identity and the politics of affinity'. In D. Glowacka and J. Zylinska (eds) *Imaginary Neighbors: Mediating Polish-Jewish Neighbours after the Holocaust*, pp.84–109. Lincoln, NE: University of Nebraska Press

Lehrer, Erica 2010 '"Jewish like an adjective": Confronting Jewish identities in contemporary Poland'. In S.H. Glenn and N.B. Sokoloff (eds) *Boundaries of Jewish Identity*, pp.161–87. Washington DC: University of Washington Press

Lehrer, Erica 2010a 'Can there be a conciliatory heritage?', *International Journal of Heritage Studies* 16(4–5): 269–88

Lehrer, Erica 2013 *Re-visiting Jewish Poland: Tourism, Heritage, Reconciliation.* Bloomington, IN: Indiana University Press

Lehrer, Erica, Cynthia E. Miller and Monica E. Patterson (eds) 2011 *Curating Difficult Knowledge. Violent Pasts in Public Places.* London: Palgrave Macmillan

Leitch, Alison 2003 'Slow food and the politics of pork fat: Italian food and European identity', *Ethnos* 64(4): 437–62

Lennon, J.John and Malcolm Foley 2000 *Dark Tourism. The Attraction of Death and Disaster*, London: Thomson

Le Roy Ladurie 1979 (1975) *Montaillou: The Promised Land of Error*, trans. B. Bray. London: Vintage

Leutloff-Grandits, Carolin 2006 'Claiming ownership in Postwar Croatia: the emotional dynamics of possession and repossession in Knin'. In M. Svašek (ed.) *Postsocialism. Politics and Emotions in Eastern Europe*, pp.115–37. Oxford: Berghahn

Levi, Neil and Michael Rothberg 2003 'General introduction: theory and the Holocaust', In N. Levi and M. Rothberg (eds) *The Holocaust. Theoretical Readings*, pp.1–22. Edinburgh: Edinburgh University Press

Lévi-Strauss, Claude 1963 (1962) *Totemism*, trans. R. Needham. Boston, MA: Beacon Press

Lévi-Strauss, Claude 1966 (1962) *The Savage Mind*, trans. J. Weightman and S. Weightman. Chicago, IL: University of Chicago Press

Levy, Daniel and Natan Sznaider 2001 *Erinnerung im globalen Zeitalter: der Holocaust*. Munich: Suhrkamp

Levy, Daniel and Natan Sznaider 2002 'Memory unbound: the Holocaust and the formation of cosmopolitan memory', *European Journal of Social Theory* 5(1): 87–106

Levy, Daniel and Natan Sznaider 2004 'The institution of cosmopolitan morality: the Holocaust and human rights', *Journal of Human Rights* 3(2): 143–57

Levy, Daniel and Natan Sznaider 2010 *Human Rights and Memory*. Pennyslvania, PA: Pennsylvania University Press

Levy, Daniel, Michael Heinlein and Lars Breuer 2011 'Reflexive particularism and cosmopolitanization: the reconfiguration of the national', *Global Networks* 11(2): 139–59

Lewis, Philip 1997 'Arenas of ethnic negotiation: cooperation and conflict in Bradford'. In T. Modood and P. Werbner (eds) *The Politics of Multiculturalism in the New Europe. Racism, Identity and Community*, pp. 126–146. London: Zed Books

Linnekin, Jocely 1991 'Cultural invention and the dilemma of authenticity', *American Anthropologist* 93(2): 446–9

Littler, Jo and Roshi Naidoo (eds) 2005 *The Politics of Heritage. Legacies of 'Race'*. London: Routledge

Llobera, Josep P. 2004 *The Foundations of National Identity: From Catalonia to Europe*. Oxford: Berghahn

Locke, Chris 2000 'Digital memory and the problem of forgetting'. In S. Radstone (ed.) *Memory and Methodology*, pp.25–36. Oxford: Berg

Locke, John 1836 (1690) *An Essay Concerning Human Understanding*. London: T. Tegg and Son

Logan, William and Keir Reeves (eds) 2009 *Places of Pain and Shame: Dealing with 'Difficult Heritage'*. London: Routledge

Lottermann, Annina 2009 'Von der Mitte an den Rand: Die locale Unsetzung der Bewerbung von Görlitz/Zgorzelec zur "Kulturhauptstadt Europas 2010" und ihre Folgen'. In G. Welz and A. Lottermann (eds) *Projekte der Europäisierung: Kulturanthropologische Forschungsperspektiven*, pp.19–34. Frankfurt: Institute für Kulturanthropologie und Europäische Ethnologie of the University of Frankurt am Main

Lovelace, Antonia 1997 'The hidden costs of looking good', *Museums Journal*, July, 22

Lowenthal, David 1985 *The Past is a Foreign Country*. Cambridge: Cambridge University Press

Lowenthal, David 1998 *The Heritage Crusade and the Spoils of History*. Cambridge: Cambridge University Press

Lübbe, Hermann 1982 *Der Fortschritt und das Museum. Über den Grund unseres Vergnügens an historischen Gegenständen*. London: Institute of Germanic Studies

Lübbe, Hermann 1983 *Zeit-Verhältnisse: Zur Kulturphilosophie des Fortschritts*. Graz: Verlag Styria

MacCannell, Dean 1992 *Empty Meeting Grounds. The Tourist Papers*. New York: Routledge

Macdonald, Sharon 1993 'Identity complexes in Western Europe: social anthropological perspectives'. In S. Macdonald (ed.) *Inside European Identities: Ethnography in Western Europe*, pp.1–26. Oxford and Providence, RI: Berg

Macdonald, Sharon 1995 'Consuming science: public knowledge and the dispersed politics of reception among museum visitors', *Media, Culture and Society* 17(1): pp.13–29

Macdonald, Sharon 1997 *Reimagining Culture: Histories, Identities and the Gaelic Renaissance*. Oxford: Berg

Macdonald, Sharon 1997a 'A people's story? Heritage, identity and authenticity'. In C. Rojek and J. Urry (eds) *Touring Cultures. Transformations of Travel and Theory*, pp.155–75. London: Routledge

Macdonald, Sharon 2002 'Trafficking in history: multitemporal practices', *Anthropological Journal on European Cultures* 11: 93–116

Macdonald, Sharon 2002a 'On "old things": the fetishization of past everyday life'. In N. Rapport (ed.) *British Subjects. An Anthropology of Britain*, pp.89–106. Oxford: Berg

Macdonald, Sharon 2003 Museums, national, postnational and transcultural identities', *Museum and Society* 1(1): pp.1–16

Macdonald, Sharon 2005 'Enchantment and its dilemmas: the museum as a ritual site'. In M. Bouquet and N. Porto, (eds) *Science, Magic and Religion: The Ritual Processes of Museum Magic*, pp.209–27. Oxford: Berghahn

Macdonald, Sharon 2005a 'Commemorating the Holocaust: the ethics of national identity in the twenty-first century'. In J. Littler and R. Naidoo, (eds) *The Politics of Heritage: The Legacies of Race,* pp.49–68. London: Routledge

Macdonald, Sharon 2007, 'Changing cultures, changing rooms: fashioning identities and anthropological research'. In D.F. Bryceson, J. Okely and J. Webber (eds), *Fashioning Identities and Weaving Networks: Gender and Ethnicity in a Cross-Cultural Context*, pp.21–37. Oxford: Berghahn

Macdonald, Sharon 2008 'Museum Europe. Negotiating heritage', *Anthropological Journal of European Cultures* 17: 47–65

Macdonald, Sharon 2009 'Reassembling Nuremberg, reassembling heritage', *Journal of Cultural Economy* 2(1–2): 117–34

Macdonald, Sharon 2009a *Difficult Heritage: Negotiating the Nazi Past in Nuremberg and Beyond*. London: Routledge

Macdonald, Sharon 2011 'Ex-siting and insighting: ethnographic engagements with place and community'. In G. Welz, A. Davidovic-Walther and A. Weber (eds) *Epistemische Orte. Gemeinde und Region als Forschungsformate,* pp.29–43. Frankfurt: Institut für Kulturanthropologie und Europäische Ethnologie

Macdonald, Sharon 2011a 'The shop: multiple economies of things in museums'. In F. Von Bose, K. Poehls, F. Schneider and A. Schulze (eds) *Museum^X Zur Neuvermessung eines mehrdimensionalen Raumes,* Berliner Blätter 57: 37–48

Macdonald, Sharon 2012 'Presencing Europe's pasts'. In U. Kockel, M. Nic Craith and J. Frykman (eds) 2012 *A Companion to the Anthropology of Europe,* pp.233–52. Oxford: Wiley-Blackwell

Macdonald, Sharon with Fausser, Katja (eds) 2000 *Approaches to European Historical Consciousness,* Hamburg: Koerber

Mach , Zdzisław 1992 'Continuity and change in political ritual: May Day in Poland'. In J. Boissevain (ed.) *Revitalizing European Rituals,* pp.43–61. London: Routledge

Mach, Zdzisław 2007 'Constructing identities in a post-Communist society: ethnic, national and European'. In D.F. Bryceson, J. Okely and J. Webber (eds) *Fashioning Identities and Weaving Networks: Gender and Ethnicity in a Cross-Cultural Context*, pp.54–72. Oxford: Berghahn

MacPherson, C.B. 1962 *The Political Theory of Possessive Individualism.* Oxford: Oxford University Press

Maddox, Richard 2004 *The Best of all Possible Islands: Seville's Universal Exposition, the New Spain and the New Europe.* New York: State University of New York Press

Maier, Charles S. 1997 (1988) *The Unmasterable Past. History, Holocaust, and German National Identity.* Cambridge, MA: Harvard University Press

Maleuvre, Didier 1999 *Museum Memories. History, Technology, Art.* Stanford, CA: Stanford University Press

Malinowski, Bronislaw 1922 *Argonauts of the Western Pacific.* London: Routledge

Mandel, Ruth 1994 '"Fortress Europe" and the foreigners within: Germany's Turks'. In V.A. Godard, J.R. Llobera, and C. Shore (eds) *The Anthropology of Europe. Identities and Boundaries in Conflict*, pp.113–24. Oxford: Berg

Mandel, Ruth 2008 *Cosmopolitan Anxieties. Turkish Challenges to Citizenship and Belonging in Europe.* Durham, NC: Duke University Press

Marcus, George 1998 *Ethnography through Thick and Thin.* Princeton, NJ: Princeton University Press

Marcus, George and Michael Fischer 1986 *Anthropology as Cultural Critique: An Experimental Moment in the Human Sciences.* Chicago, IL: Chicago University Press

Martin, Keir 2010 'Living pasts: contested tourism authenticities', *Annals of Tourism Research* 37(2): 537–54

Marx, Karl 1976 (1876) *Capital: A Critique of Political Economy*, vol.1, trans B. Fowkes. New York: Vintage

Mathisen, Stein R. 2010 'Narrated Sámi Siedis: Heritage and ownership in ambiguous border zones', *Ethnologia Europea* 39(2): 11–25

Mauss, Marcel 1967 (1925) *The Gift: Forms and Functions of Exchange in Archaic Societies*, trans. I. Cunnison. London: Routledge

Mazarella, William 2003 *Shovelling Smoke: Advertising and Smoke in Contemporary India.* Durham, NC: Duke University Press

McCrone, David, Angela Morris and Richard Kiely 1995 *Scotland the Brand: The Making of Scottish Heritage.* Edinburgh: Edinburgh University Press

McDonald, Maryon 1993 'The construction of difference: an anthropological approach to stereotypes'. In S. Macdonald (ed.) *Inside European Identities*, pp.219–36. Oxford: Berg

McDonald, Maryon 1996 '"Unity in diversity!": some tensions in the construction of Europe', *Social Anthropology* 4(1) 47–60

McNeese-Mechan, Amy 2003 'Playing the past: historical re-enactment societies and the performance of identity in Scotland'. PhD thesis, University of Edinburgh

Meethan, Kevin 2001 *Tourism in a Global Society.* Basingstoke: Palgrave Macmillan

Merleau-Ponty, Maurice 1962 (1945) *Phenomenology of Perception,* trans. C. Smith. London: Routledge

Meyer-Rath, Anne 2007 'Zeit-nah, Welt-fern? Paradoxen in der Prädikatisierung von immateriellem Kulturerbe'. In D.Hemme, M.Tauschek and R.Bendix (eds) *Prädikat "Heritage". Wertschöpfungen aus kulturellen Ressourcen*, pp.147–76. Münster: LIT

Michaels, Axel and Christoph Wulf (eds) 2011 *Emotions in Rituals and Performance.* London: Routledge

Michman, Dan (ed.) 2002 *Remembering the Holocaust in Germany, 1945–2000. German Strategies and Jewish Responses*. New York: Peter Lang

Miller, Daniel 1997 *Capitalism: An Ethnographic Approach*. Oxford: Berg

Miller, Daniel 1998 *A Theory of Shopping*. Cambridge: Polity

Miller, Daniel 2001 'Possessions'. In D. Miller (ed.) *Home Possessions. Material Culture Behind Closed Doors,* pp.107–21. Oxford: Berg

Miller, Daniel (ed.) 2001a *Home Possessions. Material Culture Behind Closed Doors*. Oxford: Berg

Miller, Daniel 2008 *The Comfort of Things*. Cambridge: Polity

Misztal, Barbara A. 2003 *Theories of Social Remembering*. Maidenhead: Open University Press

Mitchell, Timothy 1988 *Colonizing Egypt*. Cambridge: Cambridge University Press

Modood, Tariq 2007 *Multiculturalism*. Cambridge: Polity

Moeller, Robert G. 2003 *War Stories. The Search for a Usable Past in the Federal Republic of Germany*. Berkeley, CA: California University Press

Morgan, Jennifer 2011 'Change and everyday practice at the museum: an ethnographic study'. PhD thesis, University of Manchester

Morgan, Prys 1983 'From a death to a view: the hunt for the Welsh past in the romantic period'. In E. Hobsbawm and T. Ranger (eds) *The Invention of Tradition,* pp.43–100. Cambridge: Cambridge University Press

Morin, Violette 1969 'L'objet biographique', *Communications* 13: 131–9

Mosko, Mark S. 2000 'Inalienable ethnography: keeping-while-giving and the Trobriand case', *Journal of the Royal Anthropological Institute* 6: 377–96

Munn, Nancy 1992 'The cultural anthropology of time: a critical essay', *Annual Reviews of Anthropology* 21: 93–123

Nadel-Klein, Jane 2003 *Fishing for Heritage. Modernity and Loss along the Scottish Coast*. Oxford: Berg

Nadkarni, Maya 2010 '"But it's ours". Nostalgia and the politics of authenticity in Post-Socialist Hungary'. In M. Todorova and Z. Gille (eds) *Post-Communist Nostalgia*, pp.190–214. Oxford: Berghahn

Nash, Catherine 2002 'Genealogical identities', *Environment and Planning D*, 20: 27–52

Navaro-Yashin, Yael 2002 'The market for identities: secularism, Islamism, commodities'. In D. Kandiyoti and A. Saktanber (eds) *Fragments of Culture*, pp.221–53. London: I.B. Tauris

Navaro-Yashin, Yael 2006 'De-ethnicizing the ethnography of Cyprus: political and social conflict between Turkish Cypriots and settlers from Turkey'. In Y. Papadakis, N. Peristianis and G. Welz (eds) *Divided Cyprus. Modernity, History, and an Island in Conflict,* pp.84–99. Bloomington, IN: Indiana University Press

Navaro-Yashin, Yael 2009 'Affective spaces, melancholic objects: ruination and the production of anthropological knowledge', *Journal of the Royal Anthropological Institute* 15(1): 1–18

Neumann, Klaus 2000 *Shifting Memories. The Nazi Past in the New Germany*. Ann Arbor, MI: Michigan University Press

Newall, Venetia J. 1987 'The adaptation of folklore and tradition (Folklorismus)', *Folklore* 98(2): 131–51

Nic Craith, Máiréad 2008 'Intangible cultural heritages: the challenge for Europe', *Anthropological Journal of European Cultures* 17(1): 54–73

Nic Craith, Máiréad, Ulrich Kockel and Reinhard Johler (eds) 2008 *Everyday Culture in Europe: Approaches and Methodologies*. Farnham: Ashgate

Niven, Bill 2002 *Facing the Nazi Past. United Germany and the Legacy of the Third Reich*. London: Routledge

Niven, Bill 2010 'Remembering Nazi anti-Semitism in the GDR'. In B. Niven and C. Paver (eds) *Memorialization in Germany since 1945,* pp.205–13. Basingstoke: Macmillan

Niven, Bill and Chloe Paver(eds) 2010 *Memorialization in Germany since 1945.* Basingstoke: Macmillan

Nobles, Melissa 2008 *The Politics of Official Apologies.* Cambridge: Cambridge University Press

Nora, Pierre 1989 'Between memory and history: les lieux de mémoire', *Representations* 26 (Spring): 7–25

Novick, Peter 2000 (1999) *The Holocaust and Collective Memory. The American Experience.* London: Bloomsbury

Novicka, Magdalena and Maria Rovisco (eds) 2009 *Cosmopolitanism in Practice.* Farnham: Ashgate

Noyes, Dorothy 2006 'The judgement of Solomon: global protection for tradition and the problem of community ownership', *Cultural Analysis* 5: 27–56

Noyes, Dorothy 2009 'Tradition: three traditions', *Journal of Folklore Research* 46(3): 233–68

Noyes, Dorothy 2012 'The social base of folklore'. In R. Bendix and G. Hasan-Rokem (eds) *A Companion to Folklore,* pp.13–39. Oxford: Wiley-Blackwell

Okely, Judith 2001 'Visualism and landscape: looking and seeing in Normandy', *Ethnos* 66(1): 99–120

Olick, Jeffrey K. 2003 'Introduction'. In J.K. Olick (ed.) *States of Memory. Continuities, Conflicts, and Transformations in National Retrospection,* pp.1–16. Durham, NC: Duke University Press

Olick, Jeffrey K. 2007 *Politics of Regret.* London: Routledge

Olick, Jeffrey K. and Robbins, Joyce 1998 'Social memory studies: from "collective memory" to historical sociology of mnemonic practices', *Annual Review of Sociology* 22: 105–40

Oliver, James 2005 'Scottish Gaelic identities: contexts and contingencies', *Scottish Affairs* 51

O'Neill, Mark 2006 'Essentialism, adaptation and justice: towards a new epistemology of museums', *Museum Management and Curatorship* 21(1): 95–116

Ostow, Robin (ed.) 2008 *(Re)visualizing National History. Museums and National Histories in Europe in the New Millennium.* Toronto: University of Toronto Press

Pálsson, Gísli 2002 'The life of family trees and the Book of Icelanders', *Medical Anthropology* 21(3/4): 337–67

Pálsson, Gísli 2009 'The web of kin: an online genealogical machine'. In S. Bamford and J. Leach (eds) *Kinship and Beyond. The Genealogical Model Reconsidered,* pp.84–110. Oxford: Berghahn

Papadakis, Yiannis, Nicos Peristianis and Gisela Welz 2006 'Modernity, history, and conflict in divided Cyprus. An overview'. In Y. Papadakis, N. Peristianis and G. Welz (eds) *Divided Cyprus. Modernity, History, and an Island in Conflict,* pp.1–29. Bloomington, IN: Indiana University Press.

Papagaroufali, Eleni 2005 'Town-twinning in Greece: reconstructing local histories through translocal sensory-affective performances', *History and Anthropology* 16(3): 335–47

Parla, Ayse 2009 'Remembering across the border: postsocialist nostalgia among Turkish immigrants from Bulgaria', *American Ethnologist* 36(4): 750–67

Parman, Susan 1990 *Scottish Crofters. A Historical Ethnography of a Celtic Village.* New York: Holt, Rinehart and Winston

Patel, Kieran (ed.) 2012 *The Cultural Politics of Europe: European Capitals of Culture and the EU since 1980.* London: Routledge

Peck, Jeffrey M. 2006 *Being Jewish in the New Germany.* New Brunswick, NJ: Rutgers University Press

Peckham, Robert (ed.) 2003 *Rethinking Heritage: Cultures and Politics in Europe.* London: Taurus

Peel, J.D.Y 1989 'The cultural work of Yoruba ethnogenesis'. In E. Tonkin, M. McDonald and M. Chapman (eds) *History and Ethnicity,* pp.198–215. London: Routledge

Peers, Laura and Brown, Alison (eds) 2003 *Museums and Source Communities.* London: Routledge

Peralta, Elsa 2009 'Public silences, private voices: memory games in a maritime heritage complex'. In M. Anico and E. Peralta (eds) *Heritage and Identity. Engagement and Demission in the Contemporary World,* pp.105–16. London: Routledge

Petridou, Elia 2001 'The taste of home'. In D. Miller *Home Possessions,* pp.87–104. Oxford: Berg

Phillips, Deborah n.d. 'The changing geography of South Asians in Bradford'. Available online at www.bradford2020.com/pride/docs/Section5.doc

Phillips, Rob 1998 *History Teaching, Nationhood and State: A Study in Educational Politics.* London: Cassell

Phillips, Ruth 2003 'Community collaboration in exhibitions: towards a dialogic paradigm: introduction'. In L. Peers and A. Brown (eds) *Museums and Source Communities*, pp.153–70. London: Routledge

Pickstone, John 1994 'Museological science? The place of the analytical/comparative in nineteenth century science, technology and medicine', *History of Science* 32(2): 111–38

Pieterse, Jan 2009 *Globalization and Culture. The Global Mélange.* Lanham, MD: Rowan and Littlefield

Pietz, William 1985 'The problem of the fetish, I', *Res* 9: 5–17

Pina-Cabral, João, 2000 'The ethnographic present revisited', *Social Anthropology* 8(3): 341–8

Pink, Sarah 2004 *Home Truths. Gender, Domestic Objects and Everyday Lives.* Oxford: Berg

Pink, Sarah 2009 *Doing Sensory Ethnography.* Thousand Oaks, CA: Sage

Pink, Sarah 2010 'The future of sensory anthropology/anthropology of the senses', *Social Anthropology* 18(3): 331–3

Piper, Ernst (ed.) 2001 *Gibt es wirklich eine Holocaust-Industrie?* Zürich: Pendo

Poehls, Kerstin 2011 'Europe blurred: migration, margins and the museum', *Culture Unbound* 11: 337–53

Pók, Attila 2011 'European history – still a challenge'. In O. Rathkolb (ed.) *How to (Re-) Write European History,* Innsbruck: Studien Verlag

Pók, Attila, Jörn Rüsen and Jutta Scherrer (eds) 2002 *European History: Challenge for a Common Future.* Hamburg: Koerber

Poole, Ross 2010 'Misremembering the Holocaust: universal symbol, nationalist icon or moral kitsch?'. In Y. Gutman, A.D. Brown and A. Sodaro (eds) *Memory and the Future. Transnational Politics, Ethics and Society,* pp.31–49. Basingstoke: Palgrave Macmillan

Poovaya Smith, Nima 1991 'Exhibitions and audiences: catering for a pluralistic public'. In G. Kavanagh (ed.) *Museum Languages: Objects and Texts*, pp.121–33. Leicester: Leicester University Press

Poovaya Smith, Nima 1998 'Keys to the Magic Kingdom. The new transcultural collections of Bradford art galleries and museums'. In T. Barringer and T. Flynn (eds) *Colonialism and the Object. Empire, Material Culture and the Museum*, pp.111–29. London: Routledge

Poppi, Cesare 1992 'Building difference: the political economy of tradition in the Ladin Carnival of the Val di Fassa'. In J. Boissevain (ed.) *Revitalizing European Rituals,* pp.113–36. London: Routledge

Poulot, Dominique 1994 'Identity as self-discovery: the ecomuseum in France'. In D. Sherman and I. Rogoff (eds) *Museum Culture: Histories, Discourse, Spectacles,* pp.66–84. London: Routledge

Rabikowska, Marta 2010 'The ritualization of food, home and national identity among Polish migrants in London', *Social Identities* 16(3): 377–98

Radstone, Susannah 2000 'Working with memory: an introduction'. In S. Radstone (ed.) *Memory and Methodology*, pp.1–22. Oxford: Berg

Rakowski, Tomasz 2006 'Body and fate: the pension as a practice of social remembering'. In H. Jerman, P. Hautaniemi and S. Macdonald (eds) *Anthropological Perspectives on Social Memory*, special issue of *Anthropological Yearbook of European Cultures* 15: 37–48

Rapport, Nigel and Andrew Dawson 1998 'The topic and the book'. In N. Rapport and A. Dawson (eds) *Migrants of Identity. Perceptions of Home in a World of Movement*, pp.3–17, Oxford: Berg

Richard, Annelise and Daromir Rudnyckyj 2009 'Economies of affect', *Journal of the Royal Anthropological Institute* 15: 57–77

Riegl, Alois 1982 (1903) 'The modern cult of monuments: its character and origin', trans. K. Forster and D. Ghirado, *Oppositions* 25: 21–50

Ringrose, Marjorie and Adam J. Lerner (eds) 1993 *Reimagining the Nation*. Buckingham: Open University Press

Ritter, Joachim 1974 (1963) 'Die Aufgabe der Geisteswissenschaften in der modernen Gesellschaft'. In J. Ritter *Subjektivität: Sechs Aufsätze*, pp.105–40. Frankfurt: Suhrkamp

Robertson, Roland 1992 *Globalization. Social Theory and Global Culture*, London: Sage

Rogan, Bjarne 2012 'The institutionalization of folklore'. In R. Bendix and G. Hasan–Rokem (eds) *A Companion to Folklore*, pp.598–629. Oxford: Wiley-Blackwell

Rogers, Nicholas 1992 'The anthropological turn in social history'. In M. Silverman and P. Gulliver (eds) *Approaching the Past*, pp.325–70. New York: Columbia University Press

Rogers, Susan Carol 1991 *Shaping Modern Times in Rural France: The Transformation and Reproduction of an Aveyronnais Community*. Princeton, NJ: Princeton University Press

Rogers, Susan Carol 2001 'Anthropology in France', *Annual Reviews of Anthropology*, 481–504

Rogoff, Irit 2002 'Hit and run – museums and cultural difference', *Art Journal* 61(3): 63–73

Römhild, Regina 2002 'Practised imagination. Tracing transnational networks in Crete and beyond' In I-M. Greverus, S. Macdonald, R. Römhild, G. Welz and H. Wulff, *Anthropological Journal on European Cultures,* special issue *Shifting Grounds. Experiments in Doing Ethnography* 11: 159–90

Roseman, Mark 2000 *A Past in Hiding. Memory and Survival in Nazi Germany.* Harmondsworth: Penguin

Rosenfeld, Gavriel D. 2009 'A looming crash or a soft landing? Forecasting the future of the memory "industry"', *Journal of Modern History* 81: 12–58

Rothberg, Michael 2009 *Multidirectional Memory: Remembering the Holocaust in the Age of Decolonization.* Stanford, CA: Stanford University Press

Rowlands, Michael 1999 'Remembering to forget: sublimation as sacrifice in war memorials'. In A. Forty and S. Küchler (eds) *The Art of Forgetting*, pp.129–45. Oxford: Berg

Rowlands, Michael 2004 'Cultural rights and wrongs: uses of the concept of property'. In K. Verdery and C. Humphrey (eds) *Property in Question: Value Transformation in the Global Economy*, pp.207–26. Oxford: Berg

Rumford, Chris (ed.) 2005 *Cosmopolitanism and Europe,* special issue of *Innovation* 18(1)

Rüsen, Jörn 1990 *Zeit und Sinn. Strategien historischen Denkens*. Frankfurt: Fischer

Rüsen, Jörn 2001 *Geschichtsbewusstseins*. Vienna: Böhlau

Rüsen, Jörn 2005 *History. Narration, Interpretation, Orientation*. Oxford: Berghahn

Sahlins, Marshall 1999 'One or two things I know about culture', *Journal of the Royal Anthropological Institute* 5(3): 399–421

Samuel, Raphael 1994 *Theatres of Memory*. London: Verso

Samuel, Raphael 1998 *Island Stories: Unravelling Britain*. London: Verso

Sandberg, Mark B. 2005 *Living Pictures, Missing Persons. Mannequins, Museums, and Modernity*. Princeton, NJ: Princeton University Press

Sandell, Richard 1998 'Museums as agents of social inclusion', *Museum Management and Curatorship* 17(4): 401–18

Sandell, Richard 2002 (ed.) *Museums, Society, Inequality*. London: Routledge

Sandell, Richard 2007 *Museums and the Re-framing of Difference*. London: Routledge

Sant Cassia, Paul 2006 'Recognition and emotion. Exhumation of missing persons in Cyprus'. In Y. Papadakis, N. Peristianis and G. Welz (eds) *Divided Cyprus. Modernity, History, and an Island in Conflict,* pp.194–213. Bloomington, IN: Indiana University Press

Sassatelli, Monica 2002 'Imagined Europe. The shaping of European cultural identity through EU cultural policy', *European Journal of Cultural Policy* 5(4): 435–51

Schlesinger, Philip and François Foret 2006 'Political roof and sacred canopy? Religion and the EU constitution', *European Journal of Social Theory* 9(1):59–81

Schlink, Bernhard 2010 *Guilt about the Past*. London: Beautiful Books

Schöne, Anja 1998 *Alltagskultur im Museum. Zwischen Anspruch und Realität*. Münster: Waxmann

Schultheis, Franz 1997 'The missing link: family memory and identity in Germany'. In M. Gullestad and M. Segalen (eds) *Family and Kinship in Europe*, pp.49–60. London: Cassell

Schulze, Gerhard 1992 *Die Erlebnisgesellschaft: Kultursoziologie der Gegenwart*. Frankfurt: Campus

Schwab, Katharina 2009 'Islam und seine Rezeption in Europa'. In G. Welz and A. Lottermann (eds) *Projekte der Europäisierung: Kulturanthropologische Forschungsperspektiven,* pp.197–212. Frankfurt: Institute für Kulturanthropologie und Europäische Ethnologie of the University of Frankurt am Main

Schwander-Sievers, Stephanie 2010 'Invisible – inaudible: Albanian memories of socialism after the war in Kosovo'. In M. Todorova and Z. Gille (eds) *Post-Communist Nostalgia,* pp.96–112. Oxford: Berghahn

Segalen, Martine 2001 'Anthropology at home and in the museum: the case of the Musée des Arts et Traditions Populaires in Paris'. In M. Bouquet (ed.) *Academic Anthropology and the Museum. Back to the Future,* pp.76–91. Oxford: Berghahn

Seixas, Peter (ed.) 2004 *Theorizing Historical Consciousness*. Toronto: Toronto University Press

Seixas, Peter 2004a 'Introduction'. In P. Seixas (ed.) *Theorizing Historical Consciousness,* pp.3–20. Toronto: Toronto University Press

Seremetakis, C. Nadia 1991 *The Last Word: Women, Death and Divination in Inner Mani*. Chicago, IL: Chicago University Press

Seremetakis, C. Nadia 1994 'The memory of the senses, Part I: marks of the transitory'. In C.N. Seremetakis (ed.) *The Senses Still. Perception and Memory as Material Culture in Modernity,* pp.1–18. Chicago, IL: University of Chicago Press

Shandler, Jeffrey 2006 *Adventures in Yiddishland. Postvernacular Culture and Language*. Berkeley, CA: California University Press

Shanklin, Eugenia 1985 *Donegal's Changing Traditions. An Ethnographic Study*. New York: Gordon and Breach

Shapin, Steven 1994 *A Social History of Truth. Civility and Science in Seventeenth-Century England*. Chicago, IL: University of Chicago Press

Sheller, Mimi 2003 'Creolization in discourses of global culture'. In S. Ahmed, C. Castañeda, A-M. Fortier and M. Sheller (eds) *Uprootings/Regroundings. Questions of Home and Migration,* pp.273–89. Oxford: Berghahn

Sherman, Daniel J. (ed.) 2008 *Museums and Difference*, Bloomington, IN: Indiana University Press

Shore, Cris 2000 *Building Europe. The Cultural Politics of European Integration.* Oxford: Routledge

Shoshan, Nitzan 2012 'Time at a standstill. Loss, accumulation, and the past conditional in an East Berlin neighbourhood', *Ethnos* 77(1): 24–49

Sillitoe, Paul 2006 'Why spheres of exchange?', *Ethnology* 45(1): 1–23

Silverman, Marilyn and P.H. Gulliver 1992 'Historical anthropology and the ethnographic tradition: a personal, historical, and intellectual account'. In M. Silverman and P.H. Gulliver (eds) *Approaching the Past. Historical Anthropology through Irish Case Studies,* pp.3–72. New York: Columbia University Press

Simič, Marina 2009 '"Exit to Europe": travel, popular music and "normal life" in a Serbian town'. PhD thesis, University of Manchester

Simpson, Moira 1996 *Making Representations: Museums in the Post-Colonial Era.* London: Routledge

Skrydstrup, Martin 2012 'Cultural property'. In R. Bendix and G. Hasan-Rokem (eds) *A Companion to Folklore,* pp.520–36. Oxford: Wiley-Blackwell

Skultans, Vieda 1998 *The Testimony of Lives. Narrative and Memory in Post-Soviet Latvia.* London: Routledge

Smith, Andrea L. 2003 'Place replaced: colonial nostalgia and *pieds-noir* pilgrimages to Malta', *Cultural Anthropology* 18(3): 329–64

Smith, Andrea, L. (ed.) 2003a *Europe's Invisible Migrants.* Amsterdam: Amsterdam University Press

Smith, Anthony D. 1981 *The Ethnic Revival.* Cambridge: Cambridge University Press

Smith, Laurajane 2006 *Uses of Heritage.* London: Routledge

Smith, Laurajane and Natsuko Akagawa (eds) 2009 *Intangible Heritage.* London: Routledge

Smith, Laurajane, Geoffrey Cubitt and Emma Waterton (eds) 2010 *Museums and the Bicentenary of the British Slave Trade,* special issue of *Museum and Society* 8(3)

Smith, Laurajane, Paul A. Shackel and Gary Campbell (eds) 2011 *Heritage, Labour and the Working Classes.* London: Routledge

Sorabji, Cornelia 2006 'Managing memories in post-war Sarajevo: individuals, bad memories and new wars', *Journal of the Royal Anthropological Institute* 12: 1–18

Spyer, Patricia 1998 'Introduction'. In P. Spyer (ed.) *Border Fetishisms: Material Objects in Unstable Places,* pp.1–12. London: Routledge

Stacul, Jaro 2005 'Natural time, political time: contested histories in Northern Italy', *Journal of the Anthropological Institute* 11(4): 819–36

Stallybrass, Peter 1998 'Marx's coat'. In P. Spyer (ed.) *Border Fetishisms: Material Objects in Unstable Places,* pp.183–207. London: Routledge

Steedman, Caroline 2001 *Dust. The Archive and Cultural History.* New York: Rutgers University Press

Stevens, Mary 2009 'Still the family secret? The representation of colonialism in the Cité de l'Histoire de l'Immigration', *African and Black Diaspora* 2(2): 245–55

Stewart, Charles and Rosalind Shaw (eds) 1994 *Syncretism/Anti-syncretism. The Politics of Religious Synthesis.* London: Routledge

Stewart, Kathleen 2005 'Trauma time: a still life'. In D. Rosenberg and S. Harding (eds) *Histories of the Future,* pp.322–39. Durham, NC: Duke University Press

Stewart, Michael 2004 'Remembering without commemoration: the mnemonics and politics of Holocaust memories among European Roma', *Journal of the Royal Anthropological Institute* 10(3): 561–82

Stolcke, Verena 1995 'Talking culture: new boundaries, new rhetorics of exclusion in Europe, *Current Anthropology* 36(1): 1–24

Stone, Dan 2012 'Memory wars in the "New Europe"'. In D. Stone (ed.) *The Oxford Handbook of Postwar European History*, pp.714–31. Oxford: Oxford University Press

Strasser, Peter 2007 'Welt-Erbe? These über das "Flaggschiffprogramm" der UNESCO immateriallem Kulturerbe'. In D. Hemme, M. Tauschek and R. Bendix (eds) *Prädikat "Heritage". Wertschöpfungen aus kulturellen Ressourcen*, pp.101–28. Münster: LIT

Strathern, Marilyn 1988 *The Gender of the Gift. Problems with Women and Problems with Society in Melanesia.* Berkeley, CA: University of California Press

Strathern, Marilyn 1996 'Cutting the network', *Journal of the Royal Anthropological Institute* 2: 517–35

Strathern, Marilyn 2002 'Foreword: not giving the game away'. In A. Gingrich and R. Fox (eds) *Anthropology by Comparison*, pp.xiii–xvii. London: Routledge

Strathern, Marilyn 2004 (1991) *Partial Connections.* Walnut Creek, CA: AltaMira

Sturken, Marita 1997 *Tangled Memories. The Vietnam War, the Aids Epidemic, and the Politics of Remembering.* Berkeley, CA: University of California Press

Sturm, Eva 1990 'Museifizierung und Realitätsverlust'. In W. Zacharias (ed.) *Zeitphänomen Musealisierung*, pp.99–113. Essen: Klartext

Sutton, David E. 1998 *Memories Cast in Stone. The Relevance of the Past in Everyday Life.* London: Routledge

Sutton, David E. 2001 *Remembrance of Repasts. An Anthropology of Food and Memory.* Oxford: Berg

Sutton, David E. 2010 'Food and the senses', *Annual Review of Anthropology* 39: 209–23

Svašek, Maruška 2007 'Postsocialist ownership: emotions, power and morality in a Czech village'. In M. Svašek (ed.) *Postsocialism. Politics and Emotions in Eastern Europe*, pp.95–114. Oxford: Berghahn

Tauschek, Markus 2007 '"Plus oultre" – Welterbe und kein Ende? Zum Beispiel Binche'. In D. Hemme, M. Tauschek and R. Bendix (eds) *Prädikat "Heritage". Wertschöpfungen aus kulturellen Ressourcen*, pp.197–224. Münster: LIT

Tauschek, Markus 2010 'Cultural property as strategy. The carnival of Binche, the creation of cultural heritage and cultural property', *Ethnologica Europea* 39(2): 67–80

Tauschek, Markus 2010a *Wertschöpfung als Tradition. Der Karneval von Binche und die Konstituierung kulturellen Erbes.* Münster: LIT

Taylor, Charles 1989 *Sources of the Self. The Making of the Modern Identity.* Cambridge: Cambridge University Press

Taylor, Charles 1992 *Multiculturalism and 'the Politics of Recognition'.* Princeton, NJ: Princeton University Press

Taylor, Mary N. 2009 'Intangible heritage governance, cultural diversity, ethno-nationalism', *Focaal – European Journal of Anthropology* 55: 41–58

Terdiman, Richard 1993 *Present Past: Modernity and the Memory Crisis.* Ithaca, NY: Cornell University Press

Terdiman, Richard 2003 'Given memory: coercion, reproduction and invention'. In S. Radstone and K. Hodgkin (eds) *Regimes of Memory.* London: Routledge

Terrio, Susan J. 1996 'Crafting *Grand Cru* chocolates in contemporary France', *American Anthropologist* 98(1): 67–79

Thomas, Julie 2011 'The manipulation of memory and heritage in museums of migration'. In H. Anheier and Y.R. Isar (eds) *Heritage, Memory and Identity*, pp.213–21. London: Sage

Thomas, Keith 1973 (1971) *Religion and the Decline of Magic: Studies in Popular Beliefs in Sixteenth and Seventeenth Century England.* Harmondsworth: Penguin

Thomas, Laurence Mordekhai 1999 'Suffering as a moral beacon: Blacks and Jews'. In H. Flanzbaum (ed.) *The Americanization of the Holocaust,* pp.198–210. Baltimore, MD: Johns Hopkins University Press

Thrift, Nigel 2008 *Non-representational Theory. Space, Politics, Affect.* London: Routledge

Tilley, Chris 2004 *The Materiality of Stone. Explorations in Landscape Phenomenology.* Oxford: Berg

Tilley, Chris 2006 'The sensory dimensions of gardening', *Senses and Society* 1(3): 311–30

Tilley, Chris, Webb Keane, Susanne Kuechler, Mike Rowlands and Patricia Spyer (eds) 2006 *Handbook of Material Culture.* London: Sage

Todorova, Maria and Zsuzsa Gille (eds) 2010 *Post-Communist Nostalgia.* Oxford: Berghahn

Tonkin, Elizabeth 1995 *Narrating our Pasts: the Social Construction of Oral History.* Cambridge: Cambridge University Press

Torres, Andrea Meza 2011 '"Colonial/racial subjects of empire" im Eingangsbereich der Cité nationale de l'histoire de l'immigration'. In F. von Bose, K. Poehls, F. Schneider and A. Schulze (eds) *Museum^X Zur Neuvermessung eines mehrdimensionalen Raumes,* pp.28–36. Berlin: Panama

Toubon, Jacques 2007 'The political genesis of the Cité nationale de l'histoire et de l'immigration', *Museum International* 59(1-2): 8–12

Trevor-Roper, Hugh 1983 'The invention of tradition: the Highland tradition of Scotland'. In E. Hobsbawm and T. Ranger (eds) *The Invention of Tradition,* pp.15–41. Cambridge: Cambridge University Press

Trevor-Roper, Hugh 2008 *The Invention of Scotland: Myth and History.* New Haven, CT: Yale University Press

Trigger, Bruce 1989 *A History of Archaeological Thought.* Cambridge: Cambridge University Press

Trilling, Lionel 1971 *Sincerity and Authenticity.* Cambridge, MA: Harvard University Press

Tschofen, Bernhard 2007 'Antreten, ablehnen, verwalten? Was der Heritage-Boom den Kulturwissenschaft aufträgt'. In D. Hemme, M. Tauschek and R. Bendix (eds) *Prädikat "Heritage". Wertschöpfungen aus kulturellen Ressourcen,* pp.19–32. Münster: LIT

Tschofen, Bernhard 2008 'On the taste of the regions: culinary praxis, European politics and spatial culture – a research outline', *Anthropological Journal of European Cultures* 17(1): 24–53

Turner, Victor 1967 *The Forest of Symbols,* Ithaca, NY: Cornell University Press

Tzanelli, Rodanthi 2012 'Domesticating the tourist gaze in Thessaloniki's Pripigos', *Ethnography* 13(3): 278–305

Ulin, Robert C. 1995 'Invention and representation as cultural capital: Southwest French winegrowing history', *American Anthropologist* 97(3): 519–27

Urry, John 1990 *The Tourist Gaze.* Thousand Oaks, CA: Sage

Urry, John 2003 *Global Complexity.* Cambridge: Polity

Valentine, Simon Ross n.d. *Muslims in Bradford, UK,* available online at: www.compas.ox.ac.uk/fileadmin/files/Publications/Research_projects/Urban_change_settlement/Muslims_community_cohesion/Bradford%20Background%20Paper%200506b.pdf

Valk, Ülo 2006 'Ghostly possession and real estate: the dead in contemporary Estonian folklore', *Journal of Folklore Research* 43(1): 31–51

van Alphen, Ernst 1997 *Caught by History. Holocaust Effects in Contemporary Art, Literature and Theory.* Stanford, CA: Stanford University Press

van der Leeuw-Roord, Joke 2000 'Working with history – developing European historical consciousness'. In S. Macdonald and K. Fausser (eds) *Approaches to European Historical Consciousness,* pp.114–23. Hamburg: Körber van de Leeuw-Roord, Joke (ed.) 2001 *History for Today and Tomorrow. What Does Europe Mean for School History?* Hamburg: Körber

van Nieuwkerk, Karin 2004 '"Veils and wooden clogs don't go together', *Ethnos* 69(2): 229–46

Vardaki, Elia A. 2006 'Cultural memory, social fame. The role of memory in the social construction of a local community'. In H. Jerman, P. Hautaniemi and S. Macdonald (eds) *Anthropological Perspectives on Social Memory,* special issue of *Anthropological Yearbook of European Cultures* 15: 49–62

Verdery, Katherine 1983 *Transylvanian Villagers: Three Centuries of Political, Economic and Ethnic Change.* Berkeley, CA: University of California Press

Verdery, Katherine 1991 *National Ideology under Socialism: Identity and Cultural Politics in Ceausescu's Romania.* Berkeley, CA: University of California Press

Verdery, Katherine 1999 *The Political Lives of Dead Bodies. Reburial and Postsocialist Change.* New York: Colombia University Press

Verdery, Katherine 2004 'The obligations of ownership: restoring rights to land in postsocialist Transylvania'. In K. Verdery and C. Humphrey (eds) *Property in Question. Value Transformation in the Global Economy,* pp.139–60. Oxford: Berg

Verkaik, Oskar 2010 'The cachet dilemma: ritual and agency in new Dutch nationalism', *American Anthropologist* 37(1): 69–82

Vermeulen, Hans F. and Arturo A. Roldán (eds) 1995 *Fieldwork and Footnotes: Studies in the History of European Anthropology.* London: Routledge

Vertovec, Steven 2010 *Anthropology of Migration and Multiculturalism: New Directions.* London: Routledge

Vertovec, Steven and Robin Cohen 2002 'Introduction'. In S. Vertovec and R. Cohen (eds) *Conceiving Cosmopolitanism: Theory, Context and Practice,* pp.165–79. Oxford: Oxford University Press

Vertovec, Steven and Susanne Wessendorf (eds) 2009 *The Multiculturalism Backlash. European Discourse, Policies and Practices.* London: Routledge

Virilio, Paul 2007 (2005), *Art as far as the Eye Can See,* trans. J. Rose. Oxford: Berghahn

Volčič, Zala 2007 'Yugo-nostalgia: cultural memory and media in the former Yugoslavia', *Critical Studies in Media Communication* 24(1): 21–38

Volčič, Zala 2011 'Post-socialist recollections: identity and memory in former Yugoslavia'. In R. Isar and H.K. Anheier (eds) *Culture and Globalization: Heritage, Memory and Identity,* pp.187–97. Thousand Oaks, CA: Sage

Vos, Claske 2011 'Negotiating Serbia's Europeanness: On the formation and appropriation of European heritage policy in Serbia', *History and Anthropology* 22(2): 221–42

Vos, Claske 2012 'The ideals and pragmatics of European heritage: the policy and practice of the regional heritage program in Serbia'. In K. Patel (ed.) *The Cultural Politics of Europe: Capital of Culture and the European European Union since the 1980s,* pp. xxx. London: Routledge

Wade, Peter 2005 'Hybridity theory and kinship thinking', *Cultural Theory* 19(5): 602–21

Walsh, Kevin 1992 *The Representation of the Past. Museums and Heritage in the Post-Modern World.* London: Routledge

Waterton, Emma 2010 *Politics, Policy and the Discourse of Heritage in Britain.* London: Routledge

Webber, Jonathan 2006 'Memory, religion and conflict at Auschwitz: a manifesto'. In O.B. Stier and J.S. Landres (eds) *Religion, Violence, Memory, and Place,* pp.51–70. Bloomington, IN: Indiana University Press

Webber, Jonathan (ed.) 2009 *Rediscovering Traces of Memory: The Jewish Heritage of Polish Galicia.* Bloomington, IN: Indiana University Press

Weber, Beverly M. 2012 '*Hijab* martyrdom, headscarf debates: rethinking violence, secularism and Islam in Germany', *Comparative Studies of South Asia, Africa and the Middle East* 32(1): 102–16

Weber, Max 1922 *Gesammelte Aufsätze zur Religionssoziologie I.* Tübingen: J.C.B. Mohr

Weber, Max 1923 *Gesammelte Aufsätze zur Religionssoziologie II.* Tübingen: J.C.B. Mohr

Weiner, Annette 1992 *Inalienable Possessions. The Paradox of Keeping-while-Giving.* Berkeley, CA: University of California Press

Weiner, Annette 1993 'Cultural difference and the density of objects', *American Ethnologist* 21(1): 391–403

Welsh, Peter H. 1997 'The power of possessions: the case against property', *Museum Anthropology* 21(3): 12–18

Welz, Gisela 1996 *Inszenierungen kulturelle Vielfalt: Frankfurt am Main und New York City.* Berlin: Academie Verlag

Welz, Gisela 2002 'Siting ethnography: some observations on a Cypriot highland village'. In I.M. Greverus, S. Macdonald, R. Römhild, G. Welz, and H. Wulff (eds) 2002 *Shifting Grounds. Experiments in Doing Ethnography,* special issue of *Anthropological Journal on European Cultures,* pp.137–57

Welz, Gisela 2007 'Europäische Produkte: Nahrungskulturelles Erbe und EU-Politik. Am Beispiel der Republik Zypern'. In D. Hemme, M. Tauschek and R. Bendix (eds) *Prädikat "Heritage". Wertschöpfungen aus kulturellen Ressourcen,* pp.323–36. Münster: LIT

Welz, Gisela 2012 'The diversity of Europe's food cultures'. In U. Kockel, M. Nic Craith and J. Frykman (eds) *A Companion to the Anthropology of Europe,* pp.355–72. Oxford: Wiley-Blackwell

Welz, Gisela and Andilios, Nicholas 2004 'Modern methods for producing the traditional: the case of the making of Halloumi cheese in Cyprus'. In P. Lysaght and C. Burckhardt-Seebass (eds) *Changing Tastes: Food Culture and the Process of Industrialization,* pp.217–30. Basel: Schweizerische Gesellschaft für Volkskunde

Welz, Gisela, Antonia Davidovic-Walther and Anke Weber (eds) 2011 *Epistemische Orte. Gemeinde und Region als Forschungsformate.* Frankfurt: Institut für Kulturanthropologie and Europäische Ethnologie

Welzer, Harald 2010 'Re-narrations: how pasts change in conversational remembering', *Memory Studies* 3(1): 5–17

Welzer, Harald, Sabine Moller and Karoline Tschugnall 2002 '*Opa war kein Nazi*' *Nationalsozialismus und Holocaust im Familiengedächtnis.* Frankfurt: Fischer

Werbner, Pnina 1997 'Introduction: the dialectics of cultural hybridity'. In P. Werbner and T. Modood (eds) *Debating Cultural Hybridity. Multi-cultural Identities and the Politics of Anti-Racism,* pp.1–26. London: Zed Books

Werbner, Pnina 2002 *Imagined Diasporas among Manchester Muslims: The Public Performance of Pakistani Transnational Identity.* London: James Currey

Werbner, Pnina 2007 'Veiled interventions in pure space: honour, shame, and embodied struggles among Muslims in Britain and France', *Theory, Culture and Society* 24(2): 161–86

Werbner, Pnina 2009 'Displaced enemies, displaced memories: diaspora memorial politics of Partition and the Holocaust', *Ethnos* 74(4): 441–64

Werbner, Pnina 2012 'Multiculturalism from below: analyzing a political discourse', *Journal of Intercultural Studies* 33(2): 197–209

Werbner, Pnina and Tariq Modood (eds) 1997 *Debating Cultural Hybridity. Multi-Cultural Identities and the Politics of Anti-Racism.* London: Zed Books

Wertsch, James V. 2009 'Collective memory'. In P. Boyer and J.V. Wertsch (eds) *Memory in Mind and Culture,* pp.117–37. Cambridge: Cambridge University Press

Wessendorf, Susanne 2007 '"Roots migrants": Transnationalism and "return" among second-generation Italians in Switzerland', *Journal of Ethnic and Racial Studies* 33(7): 1083–102

Wetherell, Margaret (ed.) 2009 *Identity in the 21st Century: New Trends in Changing Times.* Basingstoke: Macmillan

Wetherell, Margaret 2012 *Affect and Emotion. A New Social Science Understanding.* Thousand Oaks, CA: Sage

Wheeler, Brian 2011 'Global debate on Cameron's multiculturalism speech', BBC News 11 February 2011, available at: http://www.bbc.co.uk/news/uk-politics-12415597

Wilken, Lisanne 2012 'Anthropological studies of European identity construction'. In U. Kockel, M. Nic Craith and J. Frykman (eds) *A Companion to the Anthropology of Europe,* pp.125–44. Oxford: Wiley-Blackwell

Wilson, Thomas M. and M. Estellie Smith (eds) 1993 *Cultural Change and the New Europe. Perspectives on the European Community.* Boulder, CO: Westview

Winter, Alison 2012 *Memory: Fragments of a Modern History.* Chicago, IL: Chicago University Press

Winter, Jay 1995 *Sites of Memory, Sites of Mourning. The Great War in European Cultural History.* Cambridge: Cambridge University Press

Winter, Jay 2009 'Historians and sites of memory'. In P. Boyer and J.W. Wertsch (eds) *Memory in Mind and Culture,* pp.252–68. Cambridge: Cambridge University Press

Winter, Jay and Emmanuel Sivan 1999 'Setting the framework'. In J. Winter and E. Sivan (eds) *War and Remembrance in the Twentieth Century*, pp.6–39. Cambridge: Cambridge University Press

Woidelko, Gabriele 2011 'EUSTORY – the history network for young Europeans'. In H. Anheier and Y.R. Isar (eds) *Heritage, Memory and Identity,* pp.6–8. Thousand Oaks, CA: Sage

Wolf, Eric 1992 *Europe and the People without History.* Berkeley, CA: University of California Press

Wright, Patrick 1985 *On Living in an Old Country: The National Past in Contemporary Britain.* London: Verso

Wright, Susan 1992 '"Heritage" and critical history in the reinvention of mining festivals in North-east England'. In J. Boissevain (ed.) *Revitalizing European Rituals*, pp.20–42. London: Routledge

Yates, Bridget 2011 'Volunteer-run museums in English market towns and villages'. PhD thesis, University of Gloucestershire

Yates, Frances A. 1966 *The Art of Memory.* London: Routledge

Yerushalmi, Yosef Hayin 1982 *Zakhor: Jewish History and Jewish Memory.* Seattle, WA: Washington University Press

Young, James E. 1993 *The Texture of Memory: Holocaust Memorials and Meanings.* New Haven, CT: Yale University Press

Young, James E. 2000 *At Memory's Edge. After-Images of the Holocaust in Contemporary Art and Literature.* New Haven, CT and London: Yale University Press

Young, Robert C. 1995 *Colonial Desire. Hybridity in Theory, Culture and Race.* London: Routledge

Yuval-Davis, Nira 1997 *Gender and Citizenship.* London: Sage

Yuval-Davis, Nira and Max Silverman 2002 'Memorializing the Holocaust in Britain: a reply to David Cesarani', *Ethnicities* 2: 131–3

Zabusky, Stella 1995 *Launching Europe: An Ethnography of European Cooperation in Space Science.* Princeton: Princeton University Press

Zamitto, John 2004 'Koselleck's philosophy of historical time(s) and the practice of history', *History and Theory* 43(1): 124–35

Zerilli, Filippo M. 2006 'Sentiments and/as property rights: restitution and conflict in postsocialist Romania'. In M. Svašek (ed.) *Postsocialism. Politics and Emotions in Central and Eastern Europe,* pp.74–94. Oxford: Berghahn

Zonabend, 1980 *La Mémoire Longue: Temps et Histoire au Village.* Paris: Presses Universitaires de France

Zonabend, Françoise 1989 *La Presqu'île au nucléaire.* Paris: Éditions Odile Jacob

INDEX